Canoeing Ontario's Rivers

Percival and Ernest Grand on the road to Beaumaris (Circa 1925).

Grand family photo

Canoeing Ontario's Rivers

By

Ron Reid and
Janet Grand

Produced and Designed by
William Fox

Douglas & McIntyre
VANCOUVER/TORONTO

91 92 93 94 95 5 4 3 2

Douglas and McIntyre Ltd.
1615 Venables Street
Vancouver, British Columbia
V5L 2H1

Canadian Cataloguing in Publication Data
Reid, Ron.
Canoeing Ontario's rivers

Includes index.
Bibliography: p.
ISBN 0-88894-489-6

1. Canoes and canoeing – Ontario – Guide-books.
2. Rivers – Ontario. 3. Ontario – Description and travel – Guide-books. I. Grand, Janet. II. Title.
GV776.15.057R44 1986 917.13 C85-091284-9

DESIGN: William Fox/Associates
ILLUSTRATIONS: Hap Wilson
MAPS: Janet Grand
COVER PHOTOGRAPH: Irene Apps/Canoe Sport B.C.
TYPESETTING: Attic Typesetting Inc.

Printed and bound in Hong Kong

The excerpt from the poem "Rivers" by Conrad Hilberry is reprinted with the permission of the Ohio University Press, Athens.

Knowing rivers, you know the slope and bias
Of the earth's body. You know how the land lies.

From "Rivers" *by Conrad Hilberry.*

Contents

SECTION I
The Lay of the Land/*11*
(i) Meeting the Ontario Wilderness/*12*
(ii) The Land Along the River/*21*
(iii) The Flash of Distant Paddles/*27*

SECTION II
Pioneers and Pastures/*35*
(i) The Credit/*37*
(ii) The Saugeen/*52*
(iii) The Rankin/*69*
(iv) The Skootamatta-Moira/*78*
(v) Other Rivers in Farm Country/*98*

SECTION III
Big Pine Country/*101*
(i) The Magnetawan/*103*
(ii) The Black/*121*
(iii) The Lady Evelyn/*131*
(iv) Other Rivers of Pine Country/*145*

Maps for each river are included at the end of each chapter.

SECTION IV
Land of Grey Owl/*147*
(i) The Spanish/*149*
(ii) The Mississagi/*161*
(iii) The Temagami/*174*
(iv) Other Rivers in the Land of Grey Owl/*186*

SECTION V
Trails of Early Traders/*189*
(i) The French/*191*
(ii) The Mattawa/*206*
(iii) The Missinaibi/*221*
(iv) Other Fur Trade Routes/*245*

SECTION VI
Northward to the Coast/*247*
(i) The Chapleau-Nemegosenda/*249*
(ii) The Misehkow/*264*
(iii) The Kesagami/*282*
(iv) Other Arctic Watershed Rivers/*301*

BIBLIOGRAPHY/*303*

INDEX/*313*

Foreword

Fly over northern Ontario, and at times there seems to be more water than land spread beneath you. Small wonder that several thousand years ago this was the birthplace of the canoe, a versatile craft that transformed water barriers into highways and was light enough to be carried over the land links in this endless aquatic chain.

Today, in an age when watercourses are everywhere threatened by dams, pollution and abuse, Ontario still boasts hundreds of canoe routes in their natural state. Their preservation demands an informed and sympathetic public. Without question, the best way to create such support is to encourage people to experience the wilderness themselves. From that desire came the genesis of this book, in its early stages a project of the Sierra Club of Ontario. By providing reliable and detailed information, *Canoeing Ontario's Rivers* fills a gap in the canoeing literature of the province.

Ontario is blessed with many fine parks, encompassing a host of excellent canoe routes. Some of those are described in this book, but the authors have also looked beyond the popular parks to describe often-overlooked routes across the Crown lands of the north and the farm country of the south. In seeking to broaden your canoeing horizons, Ron and Janet have carried their crusade one step further, by providing the information to help you understand the natural and cultural history along your route as well.

This volume covers only 16 rivers in detail, but its intent is not simply to focus increased use on those routes. The sketches of history and ecology presented here can be applied to many other rivers, and we encourage you to select your own route, and using this book as a guide, to discover its own unique attractions as well. And having discovered, please join in the battles to keep Ontario's river heritage forever wild.

Ron Burchell, Chairman,
Sierra Club of Ontario

Acknowledgements

This book would not have been possible without the help and encouragement of many friends, old and new. Special thanks to our frequent canoeing companions, the indomitable Ric and Sandy Symmes. To David Kennedy, Bill Fox and Ron Burchell goes the credit for sparking the concept of this book to life. George Luste, Judith Kennedy, Frank Longstaff and Jill Malins kindly provided trip notes and personal recollections. Thor Conway has been especially generous in providing a wealth of interesting information from his archaeological research.

The Ministry of Natural Resources has provided encouragement and assistance in many ways, especially Norm Richards, Bob Davidson, Tom Beechey, Bill Ringham and Bill Lannin. As well, the Moira, Credit and Sauble Conservation Authorities have been of help. The staff of the Ministry of Citizenship and Culture have also been helpful in providing information and comments. The Public Archives of Canada, the Ontario Archives and the Hudson's Bay Company Archives have also been of assistance in providing photographic and historical materials.

Thanks also to those who reviewed chapters, including Martin Parker and Hap Wilson as well as many of those listed above. Our continuing association with our editor, Robin Brass, designer, Bill Fox, and illustrator, Hap Wilson, have been sources of particular pleasure, and their work has added greatly to the utility of the text.

Finally, a special dedication to all the Good Samaritans (including our long-suffering parents) who let us park our car while we canoed, picked us up in the rain on our hitchhike shuttles, fed us tea and cookies, and generally confirmed our high regard for the people along Ontario's rivers.

R.R.
J.G.

section 1

the lay of the land

Meeting the Ontario Wilderness

For tens of thousands of Canadians, and thousands more American visitors, it is the crowning rite of summer—digging out the familiar faded old clothes, packing up the stained and battered gear, and heading out into the wilderness by canoe. There with the black flies and the sweaty portages, far from the sidelong glances and low mutterings of relatives who think us slightly mad, we become part of a canoeing tradition stretching back thousands of years. Like the Indians before us who invented this versatile craft, we take to the canoe to seek the harmony of the wilderness music that renews the spirit as well as the body.

But in recent years too many of those thousands have flocked to the well-known, and often over-used, lakes of Algonquin, Killarney and Quetico. A vast northern landscape patterned with other routes lies just beyond our reach, simply because most canoeists don't know enough about this tremendous diversity of alternatives. Even in southern Ontario, many canoeists are surprised to discover the quality of routes available if we broaden our definition of the traditional canoe experience a little.

Worse yet, most of us fail to look beyond the lakes and rivers even when we reach our destination. It is easy to return home from our wilderness experience with little appreciation of the ecological and historical significance of the landscape we have traversed. How much greater our rewards might have been if the tales of voyageur and trapper were woven into every twist of the river, and if the granitic splinters underfoot were understood as something more than simply rock. Again, the limitations are usually lack of knowledge, and the prohibitive time and effort required to seek it out.

It was these frustrations that prompted us to begin this book, in the hope that the power of knowledge, assembled in an accessible form, would encourage our fellow canoeists to broaden their horizons. We hope that some snowy evening in February, when you are dreaming of next summer's adventure, our "snapshots" of various rivers will prompt you to try something different, beyond the well trodden paths of the canoeing masses. And if you choose one of our routes, we hope that our notes on its history and ecology will bring a new sense of understanding to your trip.

In the short space of this book, we are able to present only a few of the hundreds of canoeing rivers encompassed by Ontario's vast expanse. So in the 16 rivers described, we have tried to be as representative as possible. Some of our rivers are easy enough for beginners; others involve difficult portages and advanced white-water. Some meander through the farm country of southern Ontario; others penetrate the remote recesses of the boreal forest. On some of our rivers we emphasize historical features; on others we feature birds or wildflowers or landforms. But always we try to include enough of interest to whet your appetite, to encourage you to delve more deeply into the fascinating natural world around you.

Inevitably we have not been able to include all that we might have liked. We have not done justice to the fine canoeing rivers of northwestern Ontario, for example, simply because of our own unfamiliarity with them. Hopefully some other authors will fill that gap. On many northern rivers, natural features are so poorly understood and history so poorly documented that we have in all likelihood missed some features. We have personally paddled the great majority of the routes covered and drawn from the trip notes of others for the few sections we missed, but even then the possibility of overlooking some of the special areas is present.

We have also put the emphasis on river routes in this book, rather than the chains of lakes that often attract novice canoeists. In part, this stems from our personal preference for the sheltered intimacy of river canoeing, combined with the excitement of whitewater paddling. But in large part our approach reflects the ecological truism that a river acts as a system. Its natural life, and often its history, can be logically examined as a whole.

When using this book, please keep in mind that many rivers are similar in birds, wildlife, vegetation and even patterns of historical use. By browsing through other chapters, you are likely to learn a good deal about the life and times of your selected route as well.

To help this process, we have grouped similar rivers together. At the end of each section, we have also suggested other routes of a similar nature which we hope you will consider.

Our Points of Departure

In compiling this book, we have made several assumptions about you, the reader. First, we have assumed that you have already learned at least the basic canoe and safety skills. If the route involves whitewater, we expect that you will have learned this specialized set of skills as well, and that you can judge the level of whitewater that is safe for you to attempt. Canoeing is a highly individual activity, and a safe and happy trip depends entirely on your own judgement—that's part of its attraction.

We have tried to give some guidance on which rapids can be run, but that decision in each case must be made by you and your partner, based on your own skills and the water conditions at the time. There were many rapids which we carried around in researching this book because we were alone, without a back-up canoe for support, or because it was late or early in the season, when cold water would have compounded any error.

If you do not feel confident of your canoeing skills, don't feel compelled to stay home. Instead, join one of the guided canoe trips or outfitters that specialize in the Ontario wilderness. Canadian Nature Tours, a non-profit agency operated by the Federation of Ontario Naturalists (355 Lesmill Road, Don Mills, M3B 2W8) is one of the best, because it combines an interest in natural history with teaching wilderness skills. However, there are a number of others, with the most convenient source of information about them contained in *Lamont's Annual Ontario Canoe Guide*, published by Lamont Press, 5 Caithness Ave., Toronto.

We have also assumed that you will act responsibly in the wilderness. That involves not only packing out your garbage and properly disposing of human wastes, but also such basic wilderness courtesies as respecting private property and protecting archaeological sites. In the backwoods, you are your own policeman; please ensure that the next canoeist can enjoy the route as much as you did.

Archaeological sites deserve special mention, since they often occur on the same campsites and portages used today. Researchers are understandably nervous about releasing details on their work, for enthusiastic but misguided amateurs have often destroyed the integrity of sites in their casual search for artifacts. In a few cases pictographs have been vandalized or even stolen. For these reasons we have often been deliberately vague about the location of sensitive sites, and we would certainly ask that you take care not to disturb such areas. Burying cans and other garbage is particularly destructive—pack it out instead.

If you picked up this book, we presume that you must also be interested in learning more about the world around you. For canoeists that means two things. The first is that you must learn to slow down, to travel at a pace where you have the time and energy to experience the feel of nature around you, to poke into the rich backwaters along your way, or to alter your schedule on a whim to take advantage of "unadvertised specials." Twice now, for example, we have spotted marten on the portage trail, turning a 20-minute carry into a two-hour one! Flexibility gives you freedom, and to keep yourself flexible we recommend no more than 15–20 km per day as an average pace.

Secondly, your interest in nature means that you probably already know at least a little about birds or wildflowers. We have tried to cover many of the common species that you might expect to find along the river, and some of the more uncommon ones as well. We have not described their identification in detail, but rather assumed that you will carry one or two field guides. Modern field guides, such as the consistently excellent Peterson series, are designed to be easy to use, and one of their many advantages, by the way, is that they fit snugly into an empty milk bag, secured with several elastic bands, for waterproofing.

A Note about Maps

The maps in this book are designed not to be used alone, but rather in conjunction with more detailed topographic maps, which are referenced at the end of each chapter. As well, we recommend that you obtain a Ministry of Natural Resources brochure on your route if one is available. These brochures provide further information on location of campsites, for example, since we have noted camping spots only if they are particularly scarce. It is a good idea to contact the local Ministry office as well before you leave for your trip, both to check water levels and to ensure that a dry summer has not resulted in fire restrictions.

Lining a canoe along the edge of a rapid often requires both caution and ingenuity to use the current to your advantage. **Hap Wilson**

National Topographic System maps at scales of 1:250,000 and 1:50,000 are available from the federal and provincial governments. From the Canada Map Office (615 Booth St., Ottawa, K1A 0E9) you can obtain an excellent brochure called "Maps and Wilderness Canoeing," which includes a basic map index. The provincial map office (c/o Ministry of Natural Resources, Whitney Block, Queen's Park, Toronto, M7A 1W3) has a convenient drop-in service centre for maps and aerial photos.

Many canoeists use the detailed 1:50,000 topo maps, except in more remote northern areas where only 1:250,000 coverage is available. We prefer a middle alternative for much of central Ontario—Ministry of Natural Resources maps at a scale of either 1:100,000 or 1 inch to 2 miles. These maps do not include contour lines, but their depiction of rivers and rapids is usually accurate, and they reduce the bulk considerably on long trips. An index to these maps is available from the MNR map office.

Before you leave home, we suggest that you take a close look at your maps to lay out your general rate of progress, and that you transfer information on portages, rapids and points of interest onto your field maps. Throughout this book, we have used several terms to describe specific operations:

- Portage: used in the usual sense of carrying around unnavigable stretches. Marked on maps as P, left (L) or right (R), with the portage length in metres.
- Lift-over: a mini-portage, usually less than 20 m along the edge of the river. Marked on maps as L-O.
- Tracking and lining: variations of the same operation, manoeuvring the canoe up or down a rapids by walking alongside. (In lining, you use bow and stern ropes and walk along the shore to keep your feet dry.) Marked on maps as T.
- Check before running: a notation to indicate that a rapid may be runnable, but that you must check before starting to assess its difficulty and plot your route. Marked on maps as CBR.
- Small rapids, marked on the maps as a cross bar without any notation, are normally runnable but should be approached with caution.

When to Plan Your Trip

Some of the rivers included in this guide are best canoed in a particular season. A few, such as the Credit, are canoeable in springtime only, when water levels are high. More northerly rivers are subject to early frost and are warm enough to be pleasant only in high summer. In many areas insects can be a problem, especially in June and early July. And in others encounters with motorboats can impair your experience in the busy summer months.

If timing is crucial, we have made special mention of that in our route descriptions. However, we would encourage you to think beyond summer on all routes. One of the great joys of our research was discovering just how different a familiar river can be in a different season. In general you don't need special equipment to paddle spring and fall—perhaps a warmer sleeping bag, a special "inner sanctum" of triple-wrapped dry clothes for emergencies, waterproof footwear and gloves to keep your extremities warm, and a gritty disposition on frosty mornings to force yourself out of the sleeping bag.

Each season has its attractions. No one need tell you how wonderful spring can be when the wildflowers are at their brightest and spring migrants are singing fit to bust! You might discover all sorts of life that you had missed before—painted trilliums blanketing the valley side, flowering dogwood or juneberry in its early bloom, buffleheads or Nashville warblers on their way north. As you paddle through the flooded stands of silver maple along the Rankin or Moira, you can experience the vital role of wetlands in action, soaking up water to lessen flooding downstream.

Early summer is nesting season, with brightly clad birds dashing among the cloud of soft green leaves to establish territories. It's no coincidence that baby birds begin life at this season, for the clouds of insects provide a high-protein diet with a minimum of effort. Of course, the natural order of things decrees that the insects will regard you as their source of a high-protein diet, so prepare accordingly!

By August the bloom of summer is on the wane and a sense of mellowness comes stealing across the land. River levels are at their lowest, but the cool August nights eliminate most of the biting insects. As August leads into September, the fullness of nature's bounty becomes apparent in the feast of berries along the portage path.

September brings new challenges. Uncertain winds and cool nights often alternate with gorgeous sunny days. Often you will be sole possessor of a normally busy lake. Masses of orange berries might suddenly make you realize that all those undistinguished shrubs along the water's edge are winterberry. Before the coming of heavy frosts and hunting season closes off canoeing in October, the hardwoods of the southern half of the province provide a fitting climax in the warmth of their colours.

Watching for Wildlife

Wherever they go, most canoeists would love to see more wildlife. It is often the moose or the beaver that stays in your mind as the highlight of a trip. For that reason we have included a few hints, based on our own experience, on how to improve your chances of spotting the birds and animals that share our environment.

First of all, it helps to realize that season can make a difference. Most of our birds are migratory and are particularly visible in the spring when their colours and songs are at their brightest. By early July most birds stop singing and become secretive to protect their young, and the woods may seem quiet even though the number of birds is at its peak.

Seasons affect your chances of seeing mammals as well. Musk-rats are especially visible working away in the spring marshes, for example, while beavers are most active in the fall, laying away a store of branches for the winter. Moose come into a seasonal breeding rut in the fall and are less cautious then, but caution on your part is necessary to stay well back from the cantankerous bulls at this time of year. Your chances of seeing moose also increase at the height of fly season, when the animals take to the water to escape the annoying insects.

Time of day also makes a difference. Most animals are active at dusk and dawn, so a pre-breakfast or evening paddle into quiet waters may yield wildlife sightings. And if you are serious about seeing wildlife, you must be quiet, for talking or other noise soon puts wildlife into hiding.

One of the most rewarding ways to become more aware of the wildlife around you is to watch for their signs. Portage trails are especially good for this, since you are usually tramping along head-down anyway. Shredded pine cones on a stump, for example, are sure signs of a red squirrel. While owls are largely nocturnal, they leave their calling card in the form of thumb-sized hairy pellets and "whitewash" under an exposed limb. During the day most owls roost in the middle of thick trees, but a mob of noisy crows can often lead you to their hiding place.

Of course, tracks in soft mud or sand are direct indicators of wildlife, and if you watch carefully along the shore, with the help of a field guide, your list can grow quickly to include moose, deer, bear, raccoon, otter, mink and many others.

Feeding habits can identify animals as well. A pile of clam shells along the shore? Likely an otter. Poplar sticks gnawed clean and white, or floating branches with green leaves? Food source of the beaver. Bare patches gnawed on the limbs of standing live trees? Watch for a porcupine. Twigs of small bushes gnawed off? Take a closer look—if the twig is severed cleanly, it was probably taken by a rabbit, but if the break looks torn and irregular, the culprit is a deer.

And of course you can employ the wilderness science of "scatology" to identify who walked this way. Small round pellets mean rabbits; slightly larger oval pellets identify deer. Moose pellets are similar but larger, each about 2 cm long. Otter turds, usually seen on rocks along the shore, are often full of broken crayfish shells. If you find a large dark pancake, often full of berry seeds, along your path, you are in all likelihood following a bear.

You can also expand your horizons to see more wildlife. As you paddle, keep an eye skywards to catch high-flying birds such as

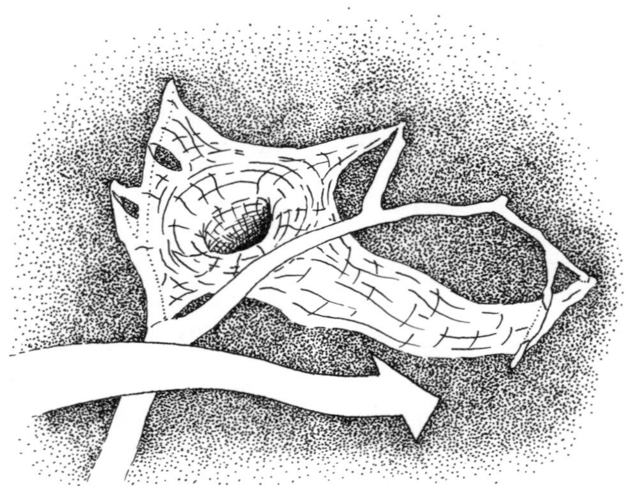

Adult caddisflies are nondescript moth-like insects, but the larval stages of some species build these silky nets in flowing water to collect food. **Hap Wilson**

hawks and finches. And in a quiet stretch of the river, relax for a few moments and watch beneath the surface. A bit of poking around with a small dip net can reveal a whole new world of colourful divers and swimmers. In faster water, you might see the ragged cone-shaped nets of caddisfly larvae, or discover that the furry coat of black algae is actually thousands of black fly larvae.

Finally, you can sometimes lure out some of the local wildlife right in camp. If you scraped a pot at the edge of the lake, take a look after dark with a flashlight and you will likely see all sorts of crayfish and leeches there for the feast. Or leave a small pat of margarine or lard a few feet from your tent door, so you can lie in wait for white-footed mice. But don't forget to clean it up before you go to sleep, or you may have an unwelcome visit from wildlife larger than you planned on!

The Land along the River

Diversity is the catchword in describing Ontario's ecology, a diversity that encompasses habitats from southern hardwood forests to Arctic tundra. As a canoeist, you are in an ideal position to see and experience that diversity, for your craft brings you into intimate contact with the rocks, forests and wildlife around you.

For many canoeists, that experience begins in the lake country of Algonquin or Quetico, where the irregular patches of blue scattered across the map like splashes of paint thrown by some frenzied divine artist create canoe routes limited only by the imagination. This is the landscape of the Canadian Shield, part of the great arc of ancient rocks that sweeps southwards below Hudson Bay to form the backbone of our country. A quarter as old as the Earth's crust, some 2–4 billion years since their fiery creation, these durable rocks lie exposed across much of central and northern Ontario.

But it is not simply rock that warms your behind as you choose a sunny spot for your lunch. Based on their texture and structure, rocks can be classified in ways that tell much about their origins and their character. And those characters are distinctive. Granite, for example, forms the middle-aged core of our society of stone, massive and reassuringly solid, flushed a healthy pink as the molten lava cooled slowly underground. In patches and bands across the north, you can also see the senior citizens of the family—ancient volcanic rocks known as greenstones, often wrinkled into smooth overlapping pillows.

In a band from the north shore of Lake Huron to Lake Timiskaming, younger rocks come crowding to the surface, cradling the far-flung arms of Temagami and Lady Evelyn in their folds. These are sedimentary rocks, the mud and sands of yesterday cemented

Geology of Ontario

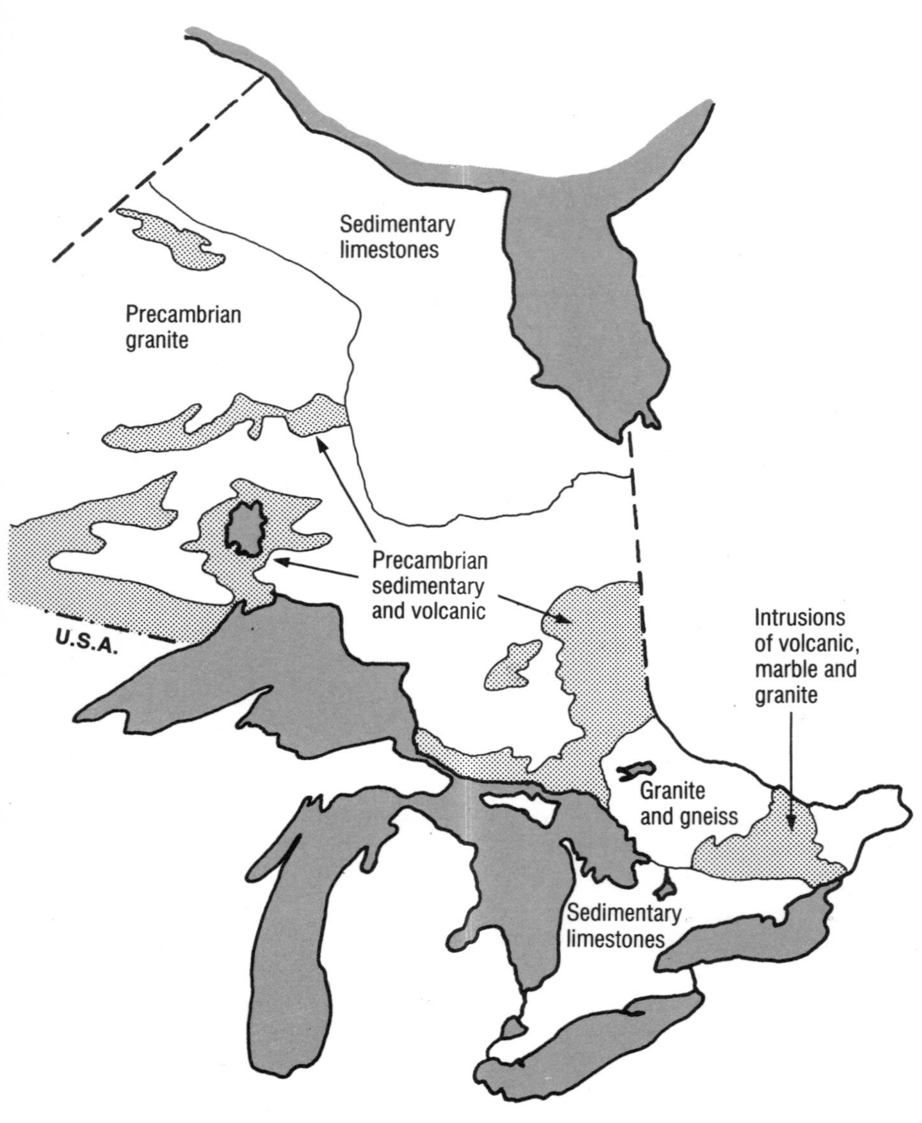

Generalized from: Geological Map of Canada, Dept. of Energy, Mines and Resources, 1969

together by the inexorable forces of pressure and time. Dramatic evidence of their origins can be found in greywacke, a common sedimentary stone that contains nuggets of granite and other earlier rocks buried within its structure.

East of Georgian Bay, the Shield rocks probe southwards, forming a great dome under Algonquin Park that serves as a source for rivers such as the Magnetawan to the west and the Black to the south. Much of the bedrock in this area has been strongly metamorphosed, subjected to great heat and pressure that has recrystallized limestone into marble, for example. The banded rocks known as gneiss which make up much of cottage country are not showing the original beds from their sedimentary origins; rather the bands have been created in the metamorphic process. The location of rivers across this irregular landscape is more than a matter of chance, for often the rivers follow fault lines where the ancient rocks have been cracked and dropped downwards to create a trough.

South of the Shield, and to the north in the Hudson Bay lowlands, the rocks are mere youngsters, mostly sedimentary limestones only 400–500 million years old. From a canoeist's point of view, however, these areas reflect more the legacy of recent glacial times than the history of their rocks.

Glaciation has been called a process of give and take, though the kind of take involved with a 2-km-thick mattress of ice is close to irresistible. Indeed, over much of the Shield, the glaciers have left little but their scratches in the five times they have descended over the last 100,000 years. On rivers such as the French, the scouring and plucking action of the glaciers is clearly pictured. On some of the short rivers flowing south from the height of land, such as the Spanish and Mississagi, layered gravels were left by the waters rushing from the glacial face. And above the divide, near the headwaters of the rivers flowing north to the Bay, a broad belt of clay was laid down at the bottom of a large glacial lake.

But it was the south that benefitted most from the gifts of the glaciers. Rich layers of soil and fragmented rock known as till formed the plains and low hills that now support Ontario's agricultural heartland. Great rounded smears called drumlins and gravelly kame hills added variety to the new-born land. Even the glacial

◀ *A simplified map of Ontario's geology shows the mosaic of older Precambrian rocks, with younger sedimentary layers in the extreme north and south.*

Vegetation Regions of Ontario

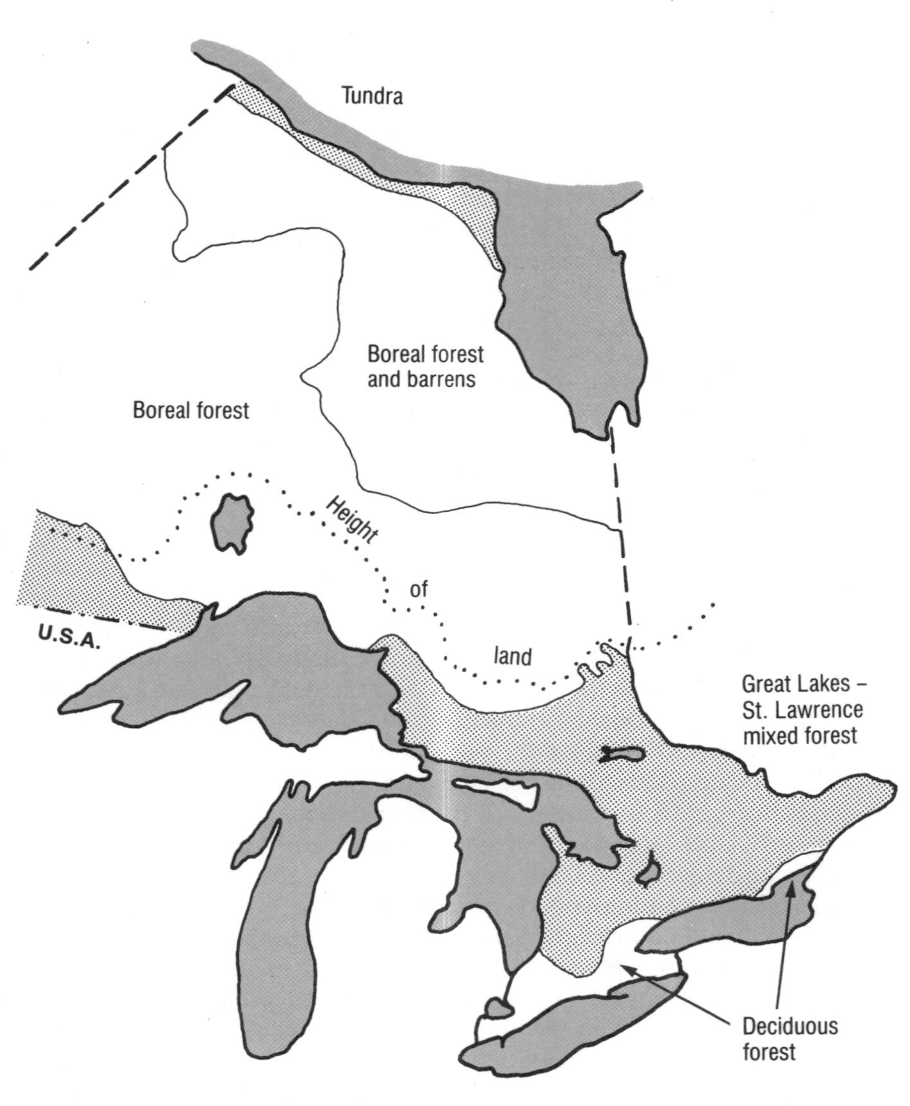

From: Rowe, J.S., Forest Regions of Canada, *Cdn. For. Serv., 1972*

lakes left a rich heritage in the level plains of clay and sand. Rivers flow more gently here, for these loose deposits of glacial debris are far more easily moulded by running water than the resistant rocks of the Shield.

On these deep fertile soils, enriched by the calcareous limestone that lay below, spectacular hardwood forests developed, so dense that it is said a squirrel could travel from Windsor to Montreal and never touch the ground. Along the southern lakes, north as far as the Credit and Moira rivers, the oaks and hickories of the Carolinean forest are able to survive. This deciduous forest has been particularly hard-hit by agriculture, so that many of its most interesting species are rare. Many of the woodlots that remain are in river valleys, where you might spot such southern specialties as pawpaw, tulip tree, running strawberry-bush and spicebush. A mild climate and varied vegetation encourage a diversity of wildlife as well, especially in the amphibian and reptile departments. Bird life is rich, with such southern species as Carolina wren, blue-gray gnatcatcher and yellow-breasted chat reaching their northern limit here.

From here almost to the height of land, a mixed forest known as the Great Lakes–St. Lawrence region holds sway over the heart of canoe country. This is the pine belt, whose great stands of red and white pine attracted the greed of the early loggers. It is also the land of maples and associated hardwoods such as yellow and white birch, whose leaves paint the woods a thousand colours in the fall. This is a transitional forest, incorporating vegetation and wildlife from both north and south, with few species occurring only here. Southern birds such as wood duck, scarlet tanager and rose-breasted grosbeak reach the limit of their summer range here, and typical northern wildlife such as snowshoe hare, woodland jumping mouse and porcupine find their southerly extent.

With the coming of European man, great patches of this mixed forest have been cleared, bringing new opportunities for wildlife of the grasslands. Prairie birds such as bobolink and upland plover now liven the fields of southern Ontario. Other birds that once occurred here in small numbers, such as savannah sparrows, now are abundant in this grassy habitat.

The north-flowing rivers of the Arctic watershed pass through the boreal forest, a very different assemblage dominated by coni-

◀ *The vegetation of Ontario is divided into bands by the effects of climate.*

fers and scattered stands of poplar and white birch. This is the home of the spruce, white and black, that form the base for Ontario's present forest industry. The ground is often carpeted with mosses and lichens, and the portage trail may be adorned with shrubs such as blueberry, squashberry and Labrador tea. In the more northerly reaches, the coniferous forests become more scattered and stunted on the vast peatlands of the lowlands, until only ribbons of trees along the rivers remain. Along the coast of Hudson Bay, a thin strip of treeless tundra marks the final transition to an Arctic climate.

The wildlife of this boreal region must cope with the twin forces of cold and deep snow which mark the long winters. Most of the familiar summer birds simply flee southwards, with only the seed-eaters and a few predators remaining. Most of the winter finches have heavy-duty bills for cracking the hulls of nutritious seeds, but none are so specialized as the crossbills, whose overlapping mandibles look like a bizarre birth defect—just the thing for extracting seed from the pine cones that form their diet. Some winter birds, such as the ruffed grouse, use the insulating quality of fresh snow to conserve energy when resting, and chickadees are known to be able to drop their body temperature and go into a kind of torpor to ride out cold spells.

Throughout much of Ontario, yellow pickerel and northern pike are the major game fish. In the south, bass and introduced salmonids from the Great Lakes add to the angler's catch. The native speckled and lake trout are both spotty in distribution, requiring cool, unpolluted water for survival.

Efforts to preserve the best of Ontario's natural heritage face a mounting barrage of threats from urban, agricultural and forestry expansion. However, the recent decision to double the provincial parks system, including many fine new wilderness and wild river parks, will go a long way to create a truly representative system of protected areas.

The Flash of Distant Paddles

The flow of Ontario history, like the flow of a good canoe river, is seldom smooth. Quiet stretches and backwaters contrast with turbulent surges forward, and the hidden undercurrents, obscured by the froth and busyness of the surface, act unseen to influence the flow of events large and small.

In many ways the early history of our province is the history of its rivers, for these corridors of transport, food and energy played a central role. Just as the geography of the landscape affects the human uses found there, the geography of various rivers has influenced the historical forces that shaped our past.

The people and events that came before us can be likened to a series of waves, sweeping up the St. Lawrence Valley and rolling over the rocky landscape of Ontario. First came the wave of native peoples, trickling in to hunt and fish in the wake of the glaciers. Then the first wave of Europeans arrived with fur trade, initially from Montreal and New York, later in a competing wave spreading out from Hudson Bay.

It was the lakes and river systems that provided access for these early peoples, and it was the rivers still that guided the third wave, that of the loggers in search of white pine. About the same time, the forests of the south fell back before a veritable tidal wave of agricultural settlers, and the rivers there became the beasts of burden for grinding grain or sawing boards. Only with the final wave has the importance of the rivers declined—the wave of urbanization and industrialization that has transformed the face of Ontario in the last half-century.

Large birchbark canoes, like this one under repair about 1896, were the traditional means of transport for northern Ontario Indians, and for the fur trade.

Public Archives Canada/C-73185

Native Peoples and Early Traders

From the numerous stone and copper tools found at various sites, archaeologists believe that most of Ontario was settled by Indians 4,000–7,000 years ago. By the time of Christ, at least some of the tribes were making extensive use of canoes. These early peoples used rivers for hunting and trapping, and seasonal sites, such as the mouth of the Saugeen, were regularly visited to capture spawning fish.

Well before the coming of the earliest explorers, the native cultures had divided in response to their environment. In the Shield country of the north, the Ojibway, Cree and Algonquins lived a nomadic life of hunting and fishing within carefully defined territories, and perfected the wilderness travel tools of birchbark canoe, snowshoe and toboggan. In the more fertile south, agricultural communities developed among the Hurons, the Petuns (or Tobacco) and the Neutrals.

There is no question that these pre-European natives knew well the pattern of rivers that served as their highways. Trade flourished. Copper from the east shore of Lake Superior and red ochre from the Mattawa and elsewhere could be found across the north. Tobacco, corn, pottery and pipes from the southern communities found their way north as well.

So it was that the early French explorers, men like Champlain and Brulé, were ushered into the unknown wilderness by Indian guides who knew it well. The coming of the French fur traders and missionaries had a profound effect on the natives. They brought diseases, such as smallpox and typhoid, which would kill thousands of natives. They brought steel guns and traps, which allowed the Indians to draw much more heavily from their environment. And they brought a ready market for furs, transforming the lifestyle of many Indians and escalating the rivalry between traditionally fractious tribes.

This rivalry boiled over in 1648–49 when the Six Nations Iroquois from south of Lake Ontario could no longer contain their jealousy of the Hurons' increasingly successful trade with the French. Approaching up the Trent River, the Iroquois fell upon the Huron villages of the Midland area, massacring both the Indians and the French priests there. Within a year the Iroquois had swept across all of southern Ontario, killing or driving out the agricultural tribes and reverting the land to a seldom-visited hunting ground.

In later years the Iroquois also harassed the northern Ojibway as

Cree

Hudson's Bay Company

to Cdn. Northwest

Ojibway

Algonquin

North West Company

Iroquois Invasion

Huron

Petun

Neutral

Early Ontario – Indians and the Fur Trade

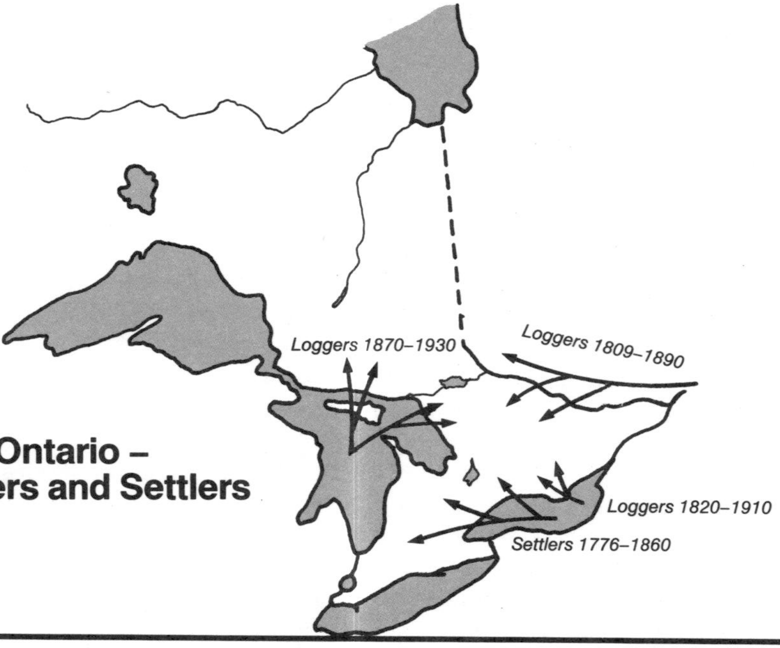

Loggers 1870–1930

Loggers 1809–1890

Loggers 1820–1910

Settlers 1776–1860

Early Ontario – Loggers and Settlers

they paddled down the French and Ottawa to trade their furs at Montreal. Finally the Ojibway and their allies responded, beginning a series of battles that would gradually push the Iroquois back towards their home ground. In those final years before the coming of the whites changed things forever, the familiar rivers must have been places of fear, stained by the blood of many battles, troubled by the cries of war and suffering.

But while the Indians fought, the fur trade carried on. Hardy independent traders from Montreal, known as *coureurs de bois*, pushed up the Ottawa and the French corridor to trade across central Ontario for furs. Not to be outdone, the British established their first post on James Bay at Moose Fort in the 1760s, drawing furs from the rich northern watersheds. Almost inevitably competition between the Hudson's Bay Company and the Montreal traders, now organized as the North West Company, intensified as the rich supply of beaver began to dwindle.

Both companies were reaching farther afield. HBC began its push into the interior, initially with posts on the Missinaibi and Albany rivers, and with several other unsuccessful attempts such as a short-lived outpost on the Kesagami. The North West Company responded with outposts of their own, often within sight of the Bay's. More significantly, the Canadiens, as the Montreal traders were known, established regular canoe links with the rich fur grounds of northwestern Canada, and for 40 years the annual passage of the voyageurs along the French and Mattawa on their way westward became a ritual of spring.

Fur trapping continues on a small scale in northern Ontario, but even by the time of the union of the two great companies in 1821 the peak of the trade was past. Soon the HBC was urging its northern trappers to adopt conservation policies for the beleaguered beaver, while at the same time using a policy of extermination along the southern frontier to discourage competition from independent traders. A century later the beaver was indeed near extinction, and only the strong conservation policies prompted by Grey Owl and other critics have restored this fur-bearer to its former abundance.

◀ *The initial traders came into Indian territories up the Ottawa valley and the rivers flowing to James Bay; later settlers spread from the Great Lakes.*

Sawmills and Settlers

In the early stages of the 19th century, the rivers of southern Ontario first began to feel the onslaught of the next wave, the loggers. Britain's supplies of Baltic pine had been cut off by the Napoleonic wars, and suddenly the towering pines of the Ottawa Valley became a thriving export. Squared into timbers and rafted together for the journey down the river, thousands of these pine made their way to the timber coves of Quebec, where they were loaded on sailing ships for the trip to distant markets.

By the 1850s the market for pine and quality hardwoods had extended to include the growing cities of the United States, and sawmills were springing up along the rivers of southeastern Ontario. Southeastern Georgian Bay also saw logging flourish in this era, but much of the Georgian Bay timber was towed in booms to the mills of Michigan without being sawed in Canada. After a provincial regulation outlawed this practice in 1898, mills sprang up at the mouth of every major river around the Bay.

Thus began the age of the river drives down the Magnetawan, the Spanish, the Mississagi and many other central Ontario rivers. With each spring freshet, the winter's accumulation of logs would tumble down to the mill, herded along by spike-booted drivers and their pointer boats, or towed across quiet stretches by tugs known as alligators. The remains of the timber camps of this era, as well as dykes and cable booms along the river, can often be seen today.

Further back from the shore in the northern bush, logging did not begin until the coming of the railways provided ready access to markets. Still, the rivers provided transport for logs to the mill, and early centres such as Elsas on the Chapleau depended totally on water transport. The same technique ushered in the switch to pulp production, as mills on the Spanish and Sturgeon, among others, drew their feedstock of spruce and pine from the rivers.

In the southern Shield country and along the Ottawa Valley, the timber trade stimulated agriculture as well, as farmers moved in to supply local camps with fresh meat and produce. But in much of southern Ontario, the lumbermen and the farmers were at odds, competing for a limited land base. Where the land was good, usually the settlers won, and much of the fine hardwood was simply burned in the rush to clear the fields.

Occasionally rivers such as the Saugeen helped transport settlers to their new land, but generally the rivers were seen as sources of power rather than transport. Grist mills, sawmills and small manufacturing plants of all types sprang up along the rivers, wherever there was enough fall to support a wheel or turbine. This had a profound influence on the geography of southern Ontario. Take a look at a map—virtually every rural town and village is centred around a mill site, the original reason for its existence.

With the coming of modern technology, the role of rivers in the economy of the province has dwindled. Even in the far north, the canoe has largely been replaced by the float plane as an efficient means of transport. Hydroelectric power still supplies about a third of the electricity in the province, but the price for that power has been high, in terms of rivers destroyed by dams and peaking operations that produce wide variations in flow.

Sadly, the history of Ontario's development has left us with more than just museum artifacts and romantic tales. Our legacy also includes too many rivers dammed and polluted, too many historic sites flooded or built upon, too few rivers of outstanding natural beauty protected from the cultural pollution of roads and recreational developments. Through the wild river category of the provincial parks system and the development of a national system of heritage rivers, efforts are being made at last to set aside the best of what remains.

section 2

pioneers and pastures

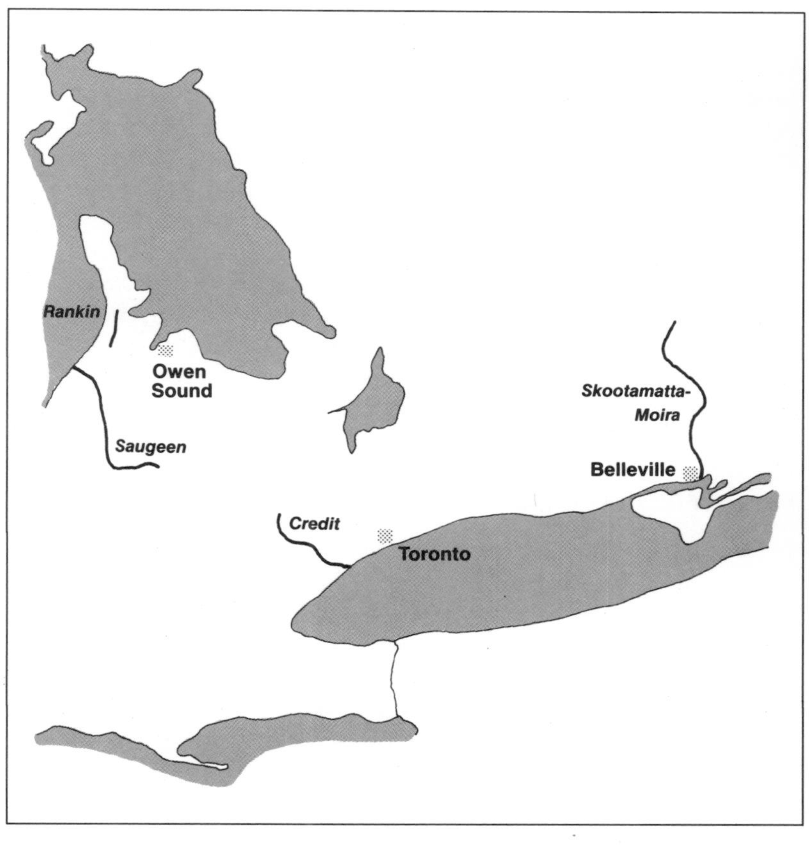

Often overlooked, often underestimated, the rivers of southern Ontario have much to offer the canoeist. Sometimes gentle, sometimes exuberant, these rivers of farm country have a flavour found only in the deciduous forests of the south. Over the hill the corn fields may roll on for mile after monotonous mile, but the sheltered valleys often seem little changed from the way the early settlers knew them.

The wooded valleys and wetlands of southern Ontario support an amazing array of wildlife and flowers. The limestone-based soils are rich, the climate is gentle and the great variety of habitats creates an abundance of "edge"—all conditions that encourage large numbers of birds and other wild creatures.

Paddle these rivers in the spring, when the run-off swells the flow and all nature comes alive. As you go, watch for the signs of those who have come before you—the settlers on their rafts, the loggers driving their winter harvest on the spring freshet, the early industrialists harnessing the rivers for their mills. They are part of the wilderness no longer, but the rivers of farm country may well impress you nonetheless with a charm all their own.

The Credit: Canoeing in Suburbia

In 1806 Charles Askins crossed a river newly known as the Credit on his way from Detroit to York. He described it as "a most beautiful, rapid river, with a stony bottom . . . where we forded it, and a small island in it; the banks very high indeed, but not very near the river."

This fine little river had appeared on early maps as the Ononront, but by 1757 the map showed Rivière au Credit, meaning a trading place between the French and the Indians. In 1776 the surveyor Augustus Jones used the Indian name Messinnike, translated as "trusting river"—again in reference to its trading function. But the earlier name stuck, perhaps appropriately, for the Mississauga Indians would find little trust in their future there.

Today things have changed. The Credit is probably the only river in Canada where you can start from rocky highlands and spongy cedar swamps near the source, paddle under three expressways, and see apartment towers and boatyards at the mouth. Though it slices through one of Ontario's fastest growing urban areas, the Credit is still "a most beautiful river." In the 54 km that are easily canoeable, the river's immediate surroundings are predominantly natural. And while you will spend some of your travels passing by the landscaped yards of urban refugees and the mills of modern industry, you will also be travelling down a river of history, crucial to the development of the surrounding area.

In many ways you are also travelling along a success story. In April 1963 Robert Turnbull wrote a three-part series in the *Globe and Mail* aptly titled "Crisis on the Credit." His description of the history of the river and its growing pollution helped stir a reawakening of interest in its management. Twenty years later the river's waters still are not safe to drink, but water quality has improved dramatically. Now the Credit's waters run clear, except after rainstorms when suspended clay can temporarily turn it brick-red.

For canoeists the Credit is a springtime river. In the first flush of meltwater, its rapids and swifts can put up standing waves that will quicken the pulse of even an experienced whitewater paddler. In late March, whitewater kayak enthusiasts flock to the river at Streetsville for competition. A more unconventional event takes place at Glen Williams, when a motley assortment of rafts and canoes take part in the annual Crazy Boat races.

By mid-April the Credit has settled down to a more leisurely pace, with enough riffles to provide good training for beginning river canoeists. The most serious danger is the chilling effect of icy spring water. By mid-May, as the waters warm, the Credit is reduced to bouldery shallows and the canoeing season is virtually over. Summer trips are possible on parts of the river but be prepared to wade occasionally. In places, farmers have fences across the river in summer months to control their cattle. Be very cautious approaching these fences if there is current, and do not damage them as you pass.

In the Shadow of the Escarpment

The Credit is a river whose genesis is linked closely to the Niagara Escarpment. Today only its headwaters lie among the rocky bluffs of the Escarpment, but at one time the entire Credit watershed was covered by the sedimentary rocks of this imposing landscape feature.

About 500 million years ago, give or take a few millennia, a giant bowl-shaped basin centred in Michigan became a bay of a vast tropical sea that covered much of central North America. As tributaries poured into this bay from the surrounding Precambrian uplands, layer upon layer of sediments were laid down, eventually to be formed into rock.

Near the shores of this ancient sea, rapid deposition of clay resulted in the red and grey shales now seen along the Credit. Above the shale, layers of limestone were created from sediments that were rich in marine life, and therefore rich in fossils. These harder layers form the distinctive cap of today's Escarpment, clearly seen in the cliffs to the west of the Credit.

As the ancient seas were drained away by a gradual uplifting of the land, the edge of this great bowl was chipped away by the combined forces of weather, erosion and glaciation, eventually retreating about 80 km. When the glaciers finally withdrew, about 10,000 years ago, the modern valley of the Credit was formed.

The glaciers left their own legacy, of course. The upper parts of the river follow the course of an old glacial spillway, leading down onto the Halton till plain, a thick layer of glacial debris that occupies most of the central part of the watershed. In the vicinity of Erindale, where the river cuts a notch through layers of rock and till, you can see the remnants of the Lake Iroquois shoreline, from a larger glacial lake that was the forerunner of Lake Ontario.

While the natural vegetation along a river is related to the soils and landforms occurring there, the Credit also demonstrates the effects of climate. Warmed by the moderating effects of Lake Ontario, the shelter provided by the Escarpment and the sheltered nature of the valley itself, the Credit lies right on the northerly edge of the deciduous forest zone.

This zone, also known as the Carolinean because it is more typical of the eastern U.S., contains a number of trees and shrubs unique in Canada. Forests here are dominated by maple, beech and red oak, which also occur further north, but a bit of exploration along the Credit will yield such southern species as shagbark hickory, black walnut, sycamore, black oak and witch-hazel. As you wind your way downstream, note that these southern specialties usually occur on sunny south-facing slopes. On the cooler north slopes, hemlock and white cedar, both with a northern flavour, are more likely to be present.

The diversity of wildlife in the watershed reflects the Credit's position at the edge of two major forest zones. Even a near-urban area such as the Upper Canada College property can boast a mammal list including mink, river otter, long-tailed weasel, southern flying squirrel, red fox, coyote and white-tailed deer, not to mention 161 species of birds. Eight species of bats are known to frequent the watershed, and 30 different kinds of reptiles and amphibians.

With the removal of many dams and the improvement of water quality, the aquatic fauna of the Credit is also rich. Both speckled and brown trout occur in the cool headwaters along the Escarpment. In the canoeable sections of the river, the most common sport fish in spring are rainbow trout, which run upstream from their Lake Ontario feeding grounds to spawn. At times you may find yourself dealing with an unusual kind of canoeing obstacle, as you pick your way down rapids amongst dozens of wading anglers. During the autumn months the lower Credit is also host to hundreds of spawning coho and chinook salmon, species introduced to Lake Ontario from the Pacific coast.

A River of Mills

As little as 300 years ago, when the great civilizations of Europe were vying to establish their empires, the Credit valley was a true wilderness, uninhabited even by Indians. The first white man to see it was likely the French explorer Etienne Brulé, who was employed by Samuel de Champlain. When Brulé reported the presence of the river in 1615, he made no mention of any inhabitants. Perhaps this deserted watershed was a sort of no-man's-land between the war-like Iroquois to the southwest and the agricultural Hurons to the north. In any case Champlain's map of 1632 shows a river in the position of the Credit but no villages are marked.

By the end of that century the Mississauga tribe had moved into the valley, creating a village near the river mouth. By the time the first survey of the lower Credit Valley was carried out in 1806, the Indians were so established that a strip of land a mile wide on either side of the river was reserved for their use. White settlers couldn't even fish the river without their consent. Such exclusive use could not withstand the tide of advancing settlers. By 1818 the Mississaugas had sold their river rights and mostly moved away to more remote areas.

The crossing of the Credit was an important landmark for the growing number of people travelling between the fledgling centre of York (now Toronto) and the then-capital at Niagara. In 1798 the government of Upper Canada recognized the needs of these travellers by building a "post house" or inn near the mouth of the river. This inn also became a gathering place for the local Indians to trade their furs and salmon.

Before the short-lived Indian occupation of the Credit Valley was squeezed out altogether, one final attempt to find them a place was made. On the present site of the Mississauga Golf and Country Club on the west bank of the river, a group of Methodist missionaries, one of whom was Egerton Ryerson, established an Indian community in 1826. By the end of 1837 the village had grown to 50 cabins, with 500 acres under cultivation and its own sawmill.

But ten years later the pressure of local white settlement had forced an end to this settlement as well. Forced to move, and angered by the government's offer of a tract of rocky wasteland near Owen Sound, the tribe was eventually rescued by the Six Nations Iroquois near Brantford, who gave them a piece of good land to found the village of New Credit. Sadly, all that remains of the Mississauga Indians on the Credit is the name they gave to the suburbia that has sprawled across their lands.

The main thrust of settlement in the Credit watershed began after new land surveys were undertaken in 1819. Entrepreneurs were quick to realize the value of the fast-flowing and reliable waters of the Credit, and a golden age of mill-building soon began. The new settlers provided a ready market for flour and lumber, so sawmills and grist mills were usually the first established. Demand for whiskey and beer was only a short way behind on the pioneer's agenda, and breweries and distilleries often formed important sidelines to these basic industries. And as the fledgling communities grew, the uses of Credit water power grew also, expanding into woollen and paper mills, and eventually the production of electricity.

By 1825 a trip down the Credit would have looked very different to the free-flowing river that we see now. As you eased your canoe into the current, your progress in the upper stretches would be speedy. But at Norval, a new dam to drive James McNab's grist mill would be in the process of construction. Under a succession of operators, including the distillers Gooderham and Worts, the Norval mill continued to produce flour until 1939 and feed grains to 1954.

A few kilometres downstream, below present-day Huttonville, Walker's mill interrupted the flow of the river. Then you would arrive at Densmore's dam near Churchville, Mr. Beattie's at Meadowvale, and Row's, just to the northeast of Streetsville. A little further down, just below Main Street, yet another dam supported a thriving enterprise, complete with sawmill, gristmill, distillery and tannery. This belonged to the enterprising Timothy Street, who subsequently gave his name to the town he founded.

While Street was expanding his business into the manufacture of such diverse necessities as brooms, tubs and pails, his neighbour John Barnhart was shipping lumber and furs, and Israel Ransom's store was doing a booming business in potash made from the great trees felled by the settlers. At the time of our imaginary trip down the Credit in 1825, Timothy Street would have been busy building the first brick house in the township.

Continuing downstream, our historic canoeists would have to portage yet another dam before leaving Streetsville, this one the Comforts' establishment. And before reaching the Credit's final quiet stretch, Mr. Racy's dam at Erindale would also be passed.

This was only the beginning. By mid-century, no fewer than 37 mills depended on water power from the Credit south of Cheltenham. Now only two of the dams still function, and you have to look hard to find evidence of many of the others in the tangled growth of silted mill ponds. But a more modern development would make a dramatic entrance before the age of water power on the Credit came to a close. In 1837, the year of the Mackenzie Rebellions, a pair of brothers named Barber walked up the length of the Credit looking for a suitable mill site. They settled in a tiny three-family community known as Hungry Hollow. The village prospered and grew to become Georgetown, and the Barber family became the propietors of a woollen mill, foundry and paper mill.

It was the descendants of these Barbers who in 1888 installed a 100-horsepower electric generator on the Credit about 2 km downstream from their mill. The Barber mill, which still stands just below the Paper Mill Dam in Georgetown, was the first on this continent to use electric power. This pioneering venture also involved the first long-distance transmission of electric power anywhere in the world.

By the beginning of the First World War, with the establishment of a provincial power utility, efficient rail and road tranport, and new manufacturing methods, the commercial heyday of the Credit was over. Over the years since, the dams that once provided such a focus for the surrounding countryside have fallen prey to ice and flood, or have been blasted away to free the river again for spawning fish. Only the Norval dam remains active, brought to life again by Julian Reed to generate electric power on a small scale.

Exploring the River

In theory a trip down the canoeable stretches of the Credit should take two or three days. However, due to a lack of suitable camping spots and difficulties with continuous access to the river, most canoeists tackle the Credit on one-day outings. Access points along the river can only be described as abundant, with cross roads every few kilometres and municipal parks at regular intervals. We will describe the most easily used access points for one-day trips; keep in mind that many other combinations are possible.

The first possible place to float a canoe downriver is at the Forks of the Credit, nestled in a notch on the Niagara Escarpment. We once spent a very long Sunday afternoon sweating our way downstream from there over innumerable log jams and through willow swales where the river simply disappears. Based on this personal assessment, we recommend the Credit as a canoeing river only from Cheltenham southwards, no matter how appealing the upper reaches look at first glance.

One unresolved dispute prevents a clear run down the entire river. The owner of the Norval dam prohibits access to the canoeists wishing to portage past his dam because of his concerns about irresponsible behaviour. Canoe Ontario, a nonprofit recreational group, established in the courts that the Credit is a "navigable water," but the courts ruled against granting a right to portage over private land. For now, we can only advise canoeists to avoid this stretch of water through several alternative means.

Unfortunately this also means that you will likely miss one of the prettiest parts of the Credit Valley, since the next feasible access is 5 km upstream. We have included information on this section of the river in the hope that the No Trespassing signs at Norval will soon come down, and that canoeists will be permitted to make full use of the river once again.

TERRA COTTA TO NORVAL

The easiest place to begin your Credit sojourn is at the north edge of Terra Cotta, about 13 km north of Hwy. 401 off Mississauga Road. An abandoned roadway at the corner of Heritage Road provides an ideal spot to leave your vehicle and take to your canoe for the 16 km to Norval.

The first few kilometres are suburban canoeing, with the grassy lawns of modern houses reaching down to the river. The convenient grounds of the Terra Cotta Inn lure you shorewards for an early tea and scones. But this area was not always so manicured. The village was known through the mid-1800s as Salmonville, with good reason, according to Mary Zatyko's local history, for "it was said that salmon in the Credit River there were so plentiful that they could easily be speared with a pitch fork."

That bounty soon passed. With the blocking of traditional spawning routes by dams on this river and others, the Lake

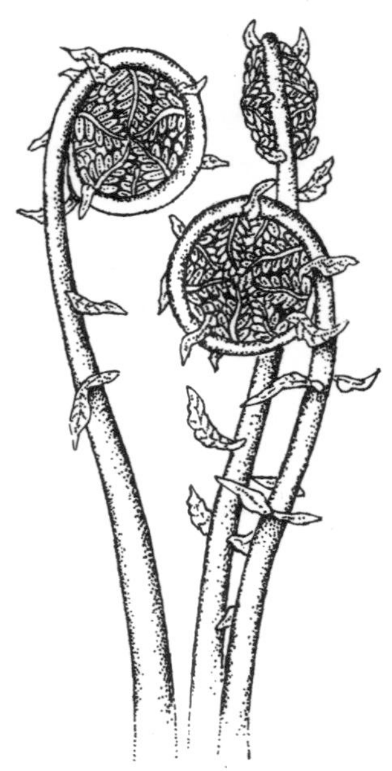

The spring crop of fiddleheads, common along the floodplains of the Credit, is actually the early growth of ostrich ferns. **Hap Wilson**

Ontario race of Atlantic salmon dwindled throughout the century and by 1890 was completely extinct. Now only the introduced Pacific salmon climb the clear waters of the Credit to spawn. As the salmon passed, so did the name. The present name, Terra Cotta, arose from the red clay pits that since 1903 have supported several brick factories in the area.

Just downstream from the village, stop and look at the bank of red Queenston shales undercut by the river. This stretch of the Credit lies along an old glacial spillway, where the meltwaters from an ancient glacier laid down a carpet of sand and gravel. Over the centuries the Credit has cut its way down through this glacial debris and notched into the soft shale bedrock as well.

On this north-facing valley wall, the harsher effects of Canada's climate are reflected in "colder" vegetation—hemlock and white cedar, with a dense shrub layer of Canada yew. But in the remnant maple woods that are more typical of this relatively natural section of the valley, spring wildflowers are abundant. Watch especially for the spring ephemerals, like the trilliums, trout lily, bloodroot and hepatica that take advantage of the early sunshine to bloom and set seed before the trees spread their shady leaves.

The river continues at a rapid pace, babbling over rounded rocks and a few small shelves, through the village of Glen Williams. Once again houses crowd the shore, but there is space here on the floodplain for luxuriant growths of ostrich fern. In April, as the first green shoots begin to unfurl, the gathering of these "fiddleheads" for a delicious meal has become a local tradition.

About a kilometre later, a straight run between banks of mill-pond silt brings you to the Paper Mill Dam, which is topped by not one, but two bridges. This is a convenient take-out point onto River Road in Georgetown, a pleasant three-hour paddle from Terra Cotta. Or, if the Norval dispute is resolved to allow more flexible access to the stretch downriver, the chute on the left can often be run straight through, after a careful reconnoitre.

Just downstream on the right is the Barber mill, now called Deltacraft. To see the remains of the historic Barber dynamo that supplied electricity to this mill, you must travel about 2 km downstream, past the railway bridge, and watch carefully for old stoneworks among the trees on the left.

The deeply incised valley leading down into Norval is also of interest for its natural history. The steep valley sides are densely forested, and once again the climatological effects—hemlock looking north, oaks facing south—are apparent. With a diversity of habitats ranging from old fields and fence rows to conifer plantations, this is an excellent place to watch for wildlife.

Much of this ravine is owned by Upper Canada College, perhaps the most prestigious of Canada's private schools. In the midst of their property, a footbridge across the river is known as the Bruce Litteljohn Bridge, in tribute to the well-known Ontario canoeist, photographer and wilderness writer who was headmaster at this nature school for many years. After plans to move the College to this location had been repeatedly frustrated by two wars and a stock market crash, UCC decided to retain its Toronto campus.

Canoeists who travel downriver this far are faced with several difficult choices when arriving at the No Trespassing signs near the entrance to the Norval mill pond. On the left the Credit Valley Footpath, marked by blue blazes, leads up over rugged terrain about .5 km to Winston Churchill Road, where another .8-km downhill carry will bring you back to the river. Faced with that rather daunting portage, some canoeists have risked the wrath of the landowner with a quick carry-over to the right of the dam.

Others have paddled a few hundred metres downstream of the signs to Willow Creek Trailer Park at the entrance of the Silver

Creek tributary on the right. Overnight camping is available for a fee here, and just across the creek a shortcut through Norval Community Park brings you onto Draper Street. A .6-km urban portage is possible here, going left down Guelph Street through the heart of the village (past the Shell Station, past the antique shop; don't forget to wait for the traffic light to turn green, watch for rough spots in the sidewalk, and don't be distracted passing by the Hollywood Hotel...). It's almost worth doing just to experience a portage with traffic lights! We suggest that if you are considering this section of the Credit, you contact Canoe Ontario (416-495-4180) for current information.

NORVAL TO MEADOWVALE

This central section of the Credit is a leisurely day's paddle through farmland and villages, a pleasant rural relief to the cities so close by. Access to the river is available on the north side of Hwy. 7 in Norval, and the 13 km to Meadowvale can easily be paddled in a day.

In a valley that gradually loses its steep wooded banks and broadens into rolling farmland, the river winds its way eastwards. In the first 5 km down to Huttonville, the valley cuts into a sandy plain left as a delta by the mouth of an ancient glacial river, creating light soils now used for orchards and market gardens. Past the ruins of the Huttonville dam, a dense floodplain forest is worth a look for southern birds during spring migration. Blue-gray gnatcatchers and golden-winged warblers have been reported here, both relatively rare species for Ontario.

Just downstream, you pass through Eldorado Park, a grass-and-picnic-table style municipal park now operated by the City of Brampton. When this park was developed in 1925, it was owned by the Toronto Suburban Railway. Another good idea that came too soon, the TSR operated electric trains on the "radial" line from Toronto to Guelph, beginning in 1917. Timetables from 1927 urge Torontonians to "travel the electric way" on hourly trains to Eldorado Park, Georgetown, Acton and Guelph. Many people did so and this little park must have bristled with picnic hampers on a sunny Sunday afternoon. But in spite of their parks, the TSR lost money, and the last electric train rolled across the Credit on August 15, 1931.

Three km later, a more modern railway bridge heralds your entrance into Meadowvale Conservation Area, which provides a good access point though no camping is allowed. The grassy flats

The pattern of slots and pillars at the exit of this former tributary is intended to dissipate the energy of swirling stormwaters. **Ron Reid**

here feature giant Canada geese. This largest race of the familiar honker was for many years thought to be extinct, but a few were rediscovered in Alberta and captive breeding has improved their status. They have adapted so well to modern parks and farmland that they are now abundant.

If you end your day's paddle here, stop for a quick look at the village of Meadowvale. In 1836, when the village was founded, the Credit provided power for two sawmills and a grist mill. The old mill channels can still be seen just north of Derry Road. By 1860 the hamlet had more people and businesses than Brampton, but the railway bypassed Meadowvale in the 1880s and spelled the end of its prominence. A century later, in 1980, the village was the first heritage conservation distict declared under the Ontario Heritage Act. It boasts several fine old houses typical of small-town Ontario, one of which contains the offices of the Credit Valley Conservation Authority.

MEADOWVALE TO PORT CREDIT

This final section of the Credit, 25 km long, offers more challenging rapids in some parts. For the first few kilometres south of Meadowvale the river maintains a leisurely pace. But as the village of Streetsville approaches, the waters flow more swiftly and a good deal of care is needed around the three dam sites there.

The first site is Row's, where the river bends through the old mill-pond bed into a scramble of fast water that should be scouted before running. Before the next dam is reached, you are confronted with an apparition of modernity on the right-hand bank. A former small tributary has been urbanized into a storm sewer, and where this feeds into the Credit, a huge concrete "energy dissipator" has been constructed to calm its flow. This surrealistic storm sewer, full of posts and bars and slots of sterile concrete, raises a disturbing thought—is this the river of the future?

Less than a kilometre later, you can step back into history again. Pull out your canoe on the right bank just below Main Street, and the red brick house you see nearest the river is Timothy Street's former residence, complete with historical plaque. A little way downstream the Streetsville town park makes another access point for those interested in a shorter trip.

The second Streetsville dam is known as the Reid Milling Co. dam and requires a short portage. A fish ladder has been installed here to allow the rainbow trout to pass upstream, while a lamprey barrier prevents access of these unwelcome parasites to the spawning grounds. A short way downstream, the McCarthy dam has been breached, but scout it first before deciding whether water conditions and your river experience allow it to be run.

As you pass beneath Eglinton Avenue, you descend into a wilder stretch of the valley, steep-sided and forested increasingly with Carolinean forest types—oaks, sycamores and walnuts. You have passed through the red shale layer, and here you see the older Georgian Bay formation—grey shale with limestone interbeds. Usually shales have very few fossils because they are derived from sediments laid down quickly near river mouths, but fossils are relatively common here, making this an important area for scientists. It is home to several uncommon plants as well, such as poke milkweed, soapberry and hay-scented fern.

Beyond the high river banks, the suburban sprawl of Mississauga is closing in. Despite several high-level bridges, this part of the valley has kept much of its natural character and the city seems far away. As the river loops its way around the Erindale Campus of the University of Toronto, keep a close watch for ring-necked snakes, small blueish-grey snakes with a bright yellow or orange neck band. A colony of these reptiles is known to live in this vicinity.

In the Erindale area as well, you should watch for the old Lake Iroquois shoreline, where the river has exposed layers of sand and clay over the shale bedrock. Below Dundas Street, the river swings to the east to pass through an ancient beach ridge also associated with that shoreline.

It is possible to end your trip at Dundas Street (Hwy.5), where Erindale Park provides access to the east side of the river. However, there are still a few kilometres of good swift-water canoeing remaining, as the river passes through the Mississauga Golf and Country Club, past the site of the Methodists' Indian village.

Just north of the Queen Elizabeth Way, the east bank of the valley supports a fine Carolinean forest known as the Stavebank Woods, including the largest known stand of black oak this far north. On its north edge, where the Hydro right-of-way maintains an open area, several prairie grasses grow, including turkey-foot, little blue-stem and Indian grass. Such prairie communities are of course rare in Ontario, but botanists have concluded that small patches of prairie were a feature of southern Ontario's vegetation mosaic even before settlement.

From the QEW southwards, the river flows through a series of small remnant marshes, often a productive area for birdlife. Before the railway bridge, the urban nature of the lower Credit watershed finally asserts itself, and the roar of traffic is likely to drown out any birdsong. The river mouth area is host to the Mississauga Canoe Club and the Port Credit Yacht Club, as well as several town parks where take-out points are readily available. This is also the site of the 1798 government post house, but all that remains is a plaque to remind us of its history.

National Topographic System Maps
1:50,000 scale: 30M/12

Ministry of Natural Resources Office
Box 2186, Cambridge, N3C 2W1

Credit River–Map 1

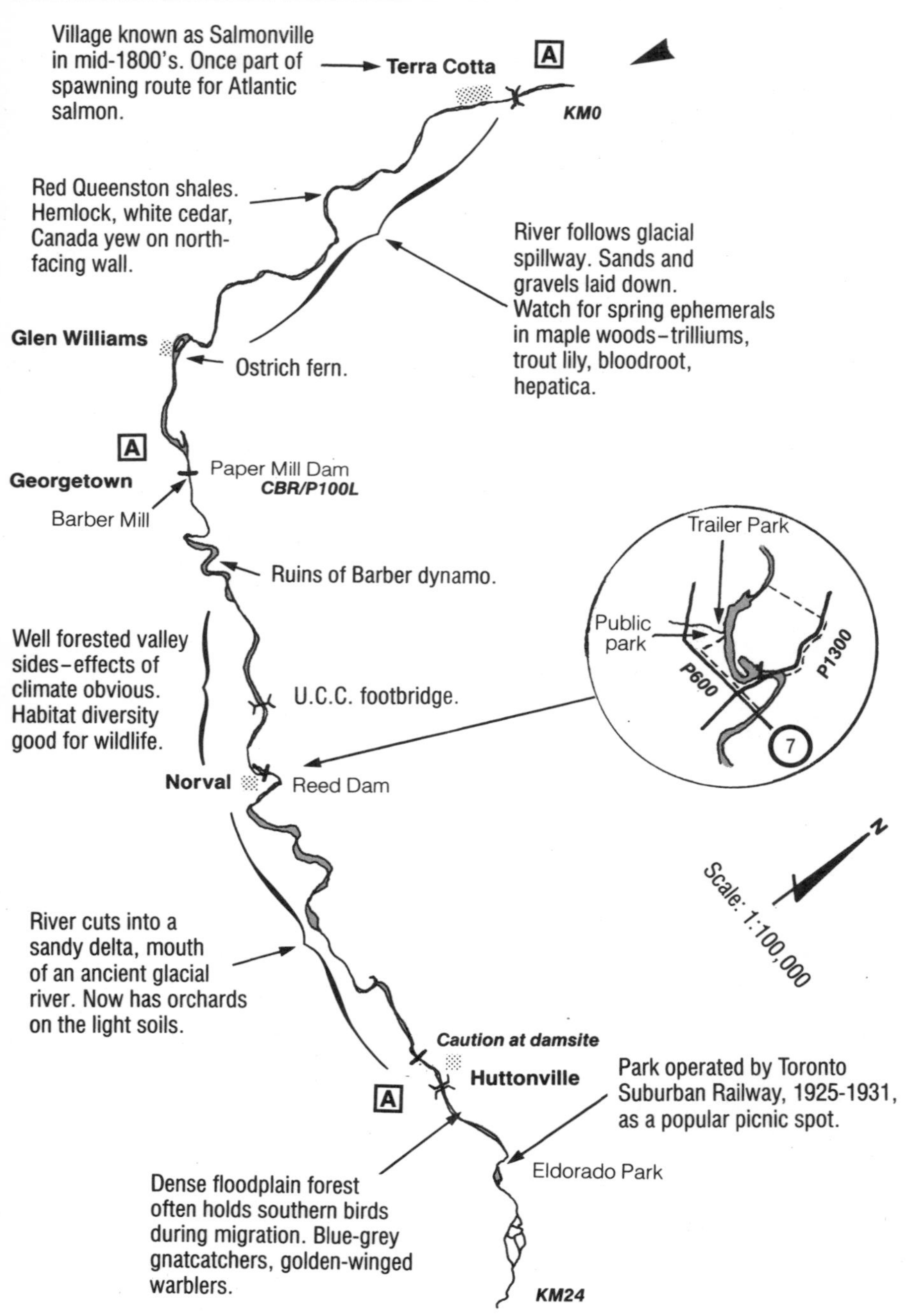

Ref: N.T.S. Map 30M/12, 1:50,000

Credit River–Map 2

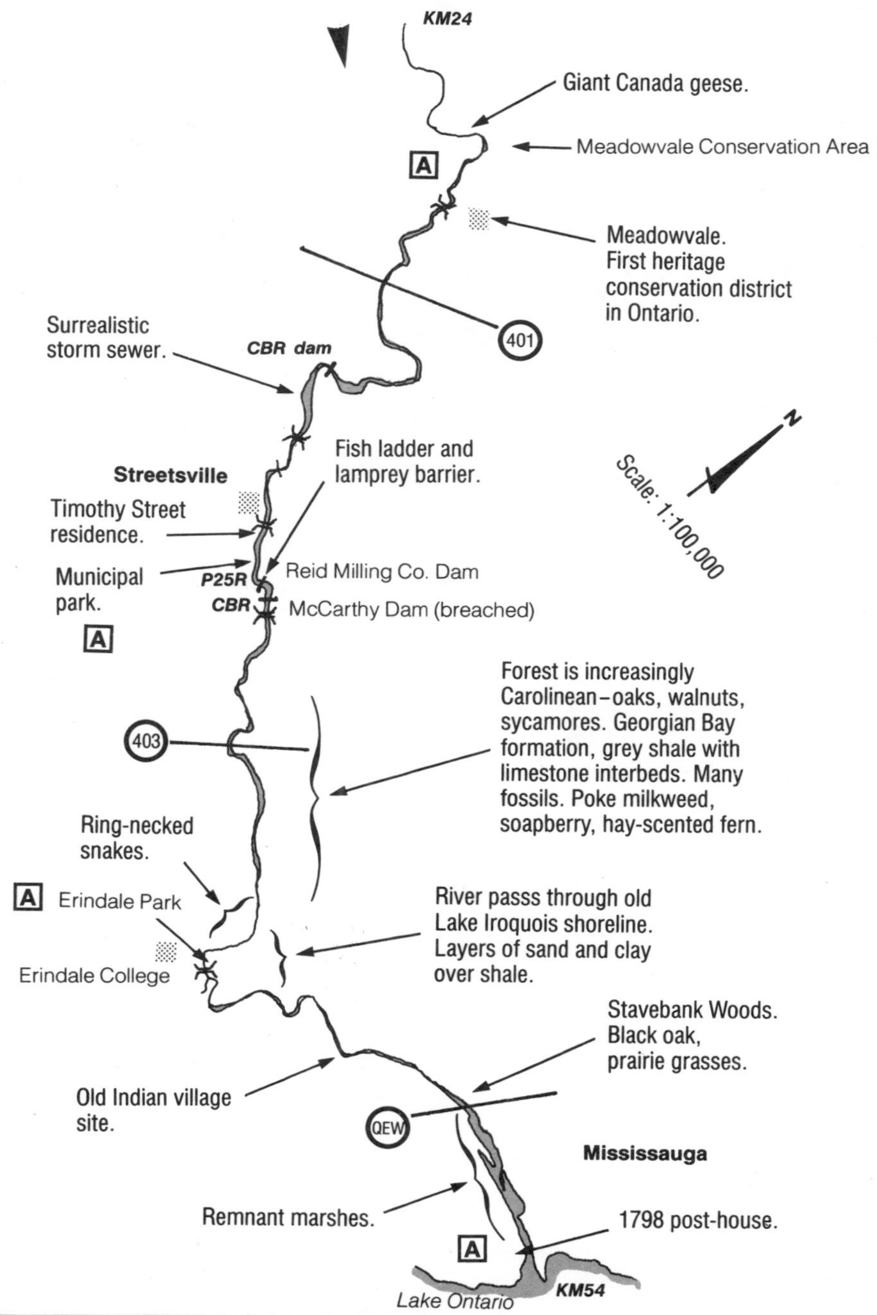

Ref. N.T.S. Map 30M/12, 1:50,000

The Saugeen: Paddling the Queen's Bush

By the 1840s the rush of settlers into the accessible parts of southern Ontario had already begun to diminish the supply of good farmland. Speculators such as the Canada Company, the German Company and others had obtained large tracts from the Crown to transform, at a profit, into thriving settlements. But in the wilds of Bruce and northern Huron counties, the map showed one area as untouched as it was unknown, the Queen's Bush. Over the next 30 years the Queen's Bush would be transformed, tamed into the geometric patterns of concession roads, farms and village plots that remain today. Central to that transformation was a river that could not be tamed, the Saugeen.

The people who invaded the Queen's Bush were overwhelmingly Scottish and Irish, poor crofters who left their countries in a desperate search for land. They proudly brought their heritage with them. Just as the concessions were peopled by MacDonalds and McAllisters and McNabbs, so too the place names developed a familiar ring—Port Elgin and Paisley, Arran and Elderslie, Dunkeld and Dunblane.

But the river would not be tamed like some docile English canal, and its Indian name remained. The first surveyor into the Queen's Bush, Charles Rankin, called this the "Rapid River." But it was a modified version of the Indian name Sahging which stuck, translated to mean "the outlet" or "mouth of river."

Because of spectacular floods, which often drown the towns of Walkerton and Paisley, the Saugeen is a dangerous river in the early spring, too powerful for all but the most experienced canoeists. Like most southern Ontario rivers, the Saugeen's regular flow has been altered by the loss of forest cover, intensifying spring floods and reducing summer flows. While these annual floods have caused much damage, they have also helped to keep a corridor of undeveloped green along the Saugeen Valley. Enough water remains in May to give an enjoyable ride, and by early summer the Saugeen becomes a family river, easy enough in most parts for novices. You should not plan extended trips in late summer unless there have been good rains, for shallow water in some areas will cause needless frustration.

In the three or four days going downriver the 104 km from Hanover, you pass a scattering of public parks and conservation areas where camping is encouraged. Most of the river banks are private property and must be treated with respect. Even though the Saugeen's waters are fairly clean, despite their load of silt, they should be boiled or treated before drinking. Supplies of fresh water and food can be obtained along the route at Walkerton and Paisley.

Unravelling the Clues of the Glaciers

The Saugeen River is underlain by dolomitic limestone but you will see little of that on your canoe trip. Instead many of the rounded rocks of the river bed will be the granites of the north country. The same colourful rocks, split open to show their sparkle of red or black or mauve, form the foundation walls of many of the barns of southern Bruce County. Those boulders, known as "hardheads" to the local farmers and "erratics" to the geologist, arrived here with the glaciers, tumbled and ground and smoothed along the way.

Most of the landforms we now see were created by the glaciers as they withdrew about 10,000 years ago. West of Paisley a carpet of rock fragments and soil from beneath the crust of ice forms gently rolling till plains. Where the melting of the glacier was temporarily stalled, long ridges of this till built up along its front. A quick look at southern Bruce County shows a series of these parallel till moraines, the most prominent just north of Walkerton.

In some areas the glacier left the till formed into smears—elongated, smooth-backed hills all pointing in the same direction. Most of these "whalebacks" or drumlins are concentrated in Arran Township east of the river mouth, but an isolated pair affects the course of the river south of Walkerton.

Associated with a melting glacier, of course, are vast quantities of water. Where this meltwater has carried away a cascade of rocks

Glacial Features along the Saugeen River

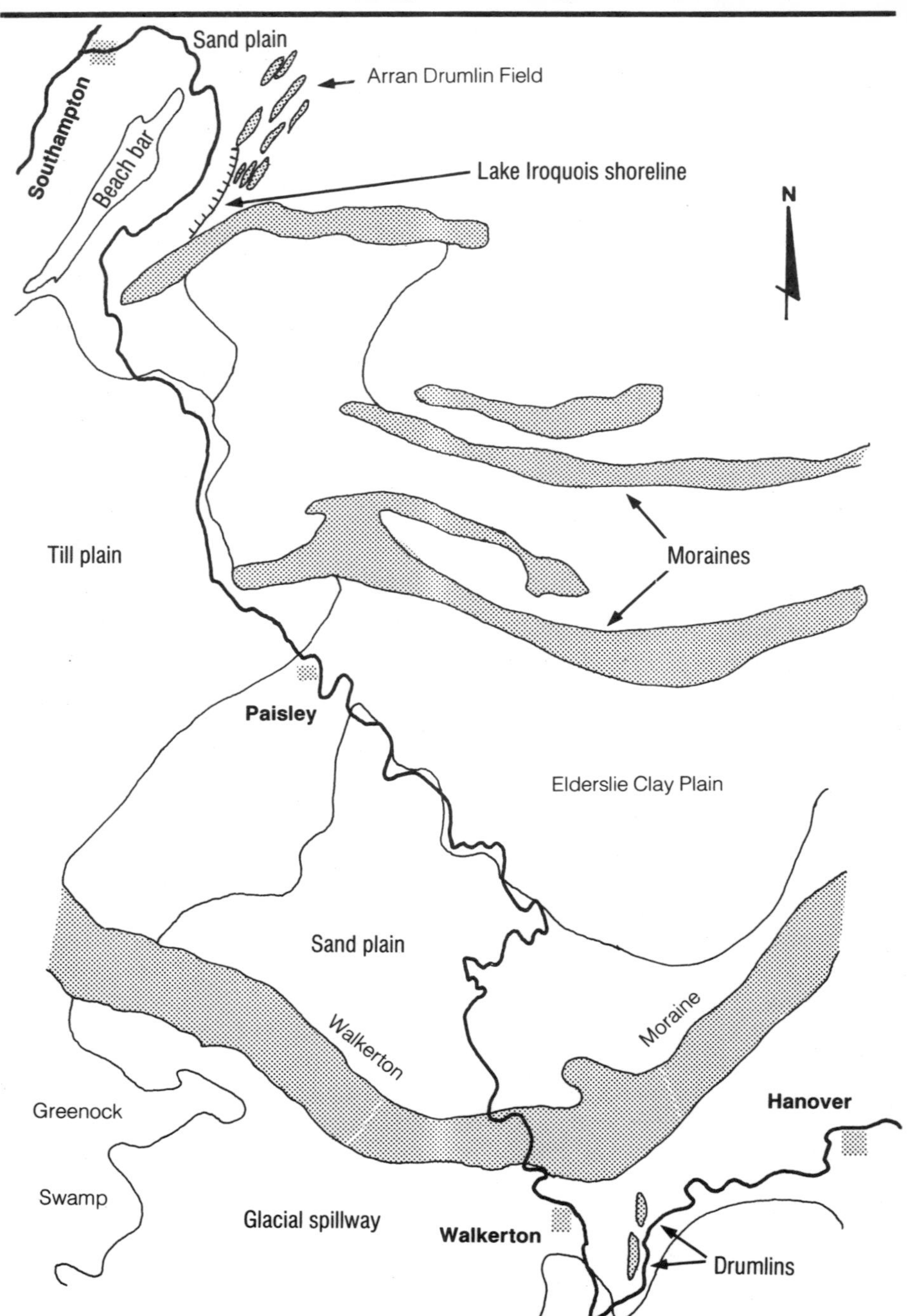

Ref: Southern Ontario Physiography Maps, 1 inch: 4 miles, Ontario Dept. of Mines and Northern Affairs, 1972

and gravel, a carpet of these coarse materials was laid down, as in the glacial spillway between Hanover and Walkerton. But where the torrents entered a lake, a delta of finer, more uniform sand was created.

At one stage a bay off glacial Lake Warren stretched from the foot of the glacier, then near Paisley, to the edge of the Walkerton moraine. This bay left its mark in the thick layer of silts that became the rich clay farmlands of Elderslie Township, and an extensive sand delta in the river valley just north of the Walkerton moraine, where the Saugeen and Teeswater rivers emptied into the bay.

In a later glacial lake known as Algonquin, a massive barrier beach formed along the shore from Port Elgin northwards, blocking the mouth of the Saugeen Valley. In the lagoon formed behind this gravel bar, the river dropped a level bed of silt and fine sand. The present course of the river is deflected 8 km northwards before it breaks through this old beach bar.

The fine stands of hard maple which developed on these varied landscapes provided the basis for local furniture manufacture. Hanover, Chesley and Southampton have all featured large furniture factories as an important part of their economy. Until the 1960s local elm was also much in demand for furniture, but the spread of Dutch elm disease wiped out almost all of these spreading "umbrella" trees. The skeletons of many fine elms can be seen along the course of the Saugeen.

The Saugeen pioneers were quick to make use of the forest around them to build their communities. Long straight sticks of white ash or rock elm formed the framing of many a barn, with smooth poles of tamarack or balsam fir for rafters. Broad weather-resistant boards of hemlock, of little value for other uses, often formed the barnboard cladding. Cedar shingles covered the roof. The versatile cedar also provided the materials for split-rail fences, many of which endure to this day, and cedar posts for modern wire fences.

One of the most striking features of the early surveyors' notes of forest cover along the Saugeen is the almost complete absence of white pine. Often a mainstay of pioneer life in other areas, pine must have been sorely missed by those early settlers. Even today there are very few natural white pines in the watershed.

Wildlife in the Saugeen basin has probably always been abun-

◀ *The physiography of the Saugeen basin shows landforms created by the glaciers, such as the parallel moraines, and water-lain deposits of clay and sand.*

dant, although some of the species have changed. For example, prehistoric records from archaeological sites at Inverhuron and Kincardine along the Lake Huron shore include bones from marten, fisher and woodland caribou, all species now restricted to the more remote reaches of northern Ontario. The last recorded bounty paid on a timber wolf scalp was in 1862. Only four years earlier a Mrs. Sullivan was paid a grant on account of her husband having "lost his life from the effects of a desperate encounter with a wolf."

For some species of wildlife the opening of the farmland brought new opportunities. The Saugeen is one of the few rivers where you can listen to the calls of field birds as you float by—meadowlarks, bobolinks and savannah sparrows. All of these species would have been uncommon or absent in the unbroken bush of pre-colonial times.

In the Footsteps of the Pioneers

As you travel past the corn fields and beef farms that now spread across the Saugeen watershed, you are seeing only the latest manifestations of a land that has been inhabited for centuries. The mouth of the Saugeen has long been an important gathering place for native peoples, especially in the spring when the fish enter the river to spawn. After the fierce Iroquois swept across southern Ontario in 1648–49, the river mouth was host to one of the invader's villages.

The Iroquois were soon to learn a lesson in humility. After angering the northern Ojibway by raiding their trading parties en route to Montreal, the Iroquois achieved a temporary peace at a 1652 meeting at the mouth of the Saugeen. Soon the Iroquois broke the truce once again. This time the Ojibway gathered their allies from far and wide to settle the score, assembling a flotilla of 700 war canoes. In the spring of 1656 the first major battle took place at the mouth of the Saugeen. The Ojibway were to chase the Iroquois across southern Ontario for the next 40 years. In 1845 visitors reported seeing bones sticking out from a great pile of human remains on the north bank of the river, which were said to be remnants of these battles, but which archaeologists now believe date from the burial mounds of much earlier cultures.

When the first white explorers arrived in 1818, they found a village of Indian traders on the north side of the Saugeen near its mouth. These were mostly Chippewa, of Ojibway descent, although a few of the Mississauga tribe pushed out of more settled areas near the Credit River were here as well. The descendants of these Indians still people the Saugeen Reserve on the banks of the river.

Historically access to the watershed had been almost exclusively from the lake, but with the ceding of Indian lands to the Crown in 1836 and the opening of a settlement road to Durham in 1842, that was soon to change. From this roadhead the first prospective settlers trudged westward in 1848. At first the river was merely an obstacle to their travels, often crossed at a jam of driftwood known as Buck's Crossing, now the town of Hanover. But the ingenious pioneers soon adapted to the arts of navigation and for the next 20 years the Saugeen became one of the most important pathways of access for the invading settlers.

Typically the newly arrived pioneer would build a cedar-log raft or flat-bottomed scow when he arrived in Hanover, load on his family and possessions, and head downriver. The craft were often 10 m long and 2 or 3 m wide, and consequently so cumbersome that nudging them down through the shallows and rapids must have been a difficult task. A few of the scows were pulled and poled back upriver, but most were dismantled to provide wood for the settler's shanty.

Arriving at the point nearest his intended settlement, the pioneer must have been faced with a daunting task. Heading along a survey line until a likely looking spot was reached, he would have to work unaided to build a small log shanty roofed with elm bark and with a simple bed of hemlock boughs. Here he would lodge his family until the returns from his first crop of peas or wheat could finance a better house.

Despite such primitive conditions, the settlers poured in. In 1850 the first bridges spanned the river at Hanover and Walkerton. By 1851 the first dam was being thrown across the mouth of the Teeswater in Paisley as the first settlers arrived in the heart of the Saugeen Valley. By the following year Joseph Walker was hard at work on his dam at Walkerton. The demand for land was strong, culminating in the big sale of unopened lots held in Southampton on September 27, 1854. The town was flooded with two or three thousand prospective purchasers, and money flowed so quickly into the Land Agent's office that it had to be carried away in laundry baskets.

Over the next 25 years, as the county was transformed from unbroken forest to farmland, the Saugeen continued to serve as a vital means of transport. Not only settlers' rafts descended the river: the *Paisley Advocate* of April 28, 1876, describes how a steam boiler for a sawmill had been floated down the river some 25 years previously, passing Paisley with a flag flying and the heads of the great rivets on the iron boiler "like the scales of some huge sea monster."

In the summer of 1879 navigation took a more modern turn when D. Hanna of Paisley built a flat-bottomed steamer. The *Waterwitch* spent the next few summers plying the river between Walkerton and Paisley. With a 6-hp engine, the boat took 13 hours to make the trip upstream but could return in four.

As the wave of farmers moved into the basin, to form a population of 65,000 in Bruce County only 30 years after first settlement, the accompanying roads and railways made the river less important. And with the opening of the Canadian West in the 1870s, the population of this part of Ontario began to dwindle. By 1901 the county's population had dropped to 59,000, and by the mid-1960s to only 41,000. As the footsteps of the pioneers faded into memory, so did the importance of the Saugeen.

Exploring the River

In the 104 km from Hanover to its mouth, the Saugeen passes through four towns and past dozens of other access points at concession roads and parks. Under normal water conditions you can paddle the length of the river in three days, although a fourth day would give you more time for exploring. With an easy gradient of about 1 metre per km, the Saugeen presents few difficult stretches except when it is in flood, when a great deal of caution is required.

HANOVER TO WALKERTON

This 22-km section of river begins at the Hanover town park, just north of the town centre on Bruce County Road 10. The old log jam just upstream that provided such an easy bridge for settlers is long gone, replaced by dams that first interrupted the river in 1854. As you swing your canoe easily down the bank, think how different it must have been for the pioneer, sweating away at a pit saw to construct a scow for his goods and family.

As you twist among the swampy flats and river debris west of Hanover, the earthy smells of wild forest include the pungent odour of balsam poplar, accounting for its local name of Balm of

Gilead. Grackles, red-winged blackbirds, blue jays and flickers add their spring songs to the woodland setting, introducing you quickly to the rich bird life of the Saugeen Valley.

Just under the Hwy. 4 bridge, the valley opens out into a grassy island, marking the junction of the South and Beatty branches of the watershed. Along the shrubby banks of this gentle stretch, yellow warblers call from their hidden perches and a green heron may be flushed from the cover of a fallen tree. A few kilometres downstream, past a quiet stretch lined with cedar banks, a new concrete bridge stands just above a 3-m dam. A short portage on the left is necessary.

Two km later, just as the river begins its swing southwards, a small sign on the right announces a private park where camping is available. The river is swifter now, chattering among the bouldery banks of the old glacial spillway as it detours around a lonely pair of drumlins. On you travel, past modern farmsteads and split rail fences and hillside woodlots, until the first of the Walkerton dams is reached.

Although this first dam can sometimes be run through the chute on the right, a safer course leads to a short portage on the left. Similarly the old Walkerton dam about 2 km further on is easily portaged on the left. This is the successor to the original sawmill dam erected there in 1852 by Joseph Walker, which was constructed from each side of the river to take advantage of a wooded island in the middle.

Passing between the flood-control dykes of Walkerton now, it is difficult to visualize what a picture of sylvan loveliness must have confronted the early settlers here. Norman Robertson reports that a normally dour Scot, Kenneth Kemp, was so moved by his first view of the Walkerton valley that he exclaimed, "Eh mon, if Eden was anything like this, what a fool Adam was to eat the apple."

Just past the second Walkerton bridge, the Walkerton town park on the right provides camping facilities, as well as a convenient access point.

WALKERTON TO PAISLEY

The 42 km from Walkerton to Paisley, route of the *Waterwitch*, can be paddled in a single long day, but you will likely want to break its length by a stop-over part way.

Almost immediately on leaving Walkerton, the nature of the river valley becomes wilder, with the steep valley sides covered with maple and ash. A quick look at the physiography maps shows

Where the Saugeen sliced across the Walkerton moraine, a high bank exposes layers of sand, clay and till that reflect the glacial history of the area.
Janet Grand

that the river here is cutting across the large Walkerton moraine after following its south edge for quite some distance. As the sediments of the glacial spillways show, at one time the river continued west, emptying into the vast basin of Greenock Swamp. At some point, thousands of years ago, the river turned north across a low spot in the moraine, helping to create the sandy delta on the other side.

Before it reaches that sandy plain, however, the river has carved into the side of a morainic hill, exposing the layers of sand, clay and boulder till. The result is a dramatic cross-section over 30 m high with some of the best rapids of the river at the base. Across the river a hardwood forest also shows the best of the spring wild-flowers—the fancy heart-shaped leaves of wild ginger, the dan-

At first glance, the brownish backs and light underparts of bank and roughwing swallows appear identical, but a brown neck band identifies the bank. **Hap Wilson**

gling yellow flowers and wilted leaves of bellwort, and an abundance of red and white trilliums.

Now the Saugeen twists northwards through gravelly banks and the air above is thick with swallows. All four common species can be seen here, sometimes all at once. The blue backs and chestnut breasts of barn swallows flash by, and then the blue-green backs and white breasts of tree swallows. In the sandy banks the nest-holes of two similar species are obvious—the bank swallow with a brownish neck-band, the rough-wing without. Another bank-nester is frequently seen around these sand banks—the belted kingfisher whose rattling scold is a familiar sound along this river.

For the next 5 km, as the river winds across the sand plain, its historical course has often been erratic. In several places the river has looped back on itself so much that a new channel has cut across the hairpin, and the abandoned "oxbow" is left as quiet water to form into swampland. These backwaters are excellent places for wildlife, ideal for mink and muskrat, and even for beaver. Even though the "bank" beaver here are the same species as those further north, these river beaver don't build dams and lodges in the same way. When you see lots of fresh beaver cuttings, watch for a small stick lodge set back into the bank, or even just a hole which marks the bank beaver's residence.

These oxbows are also an excellent area for waterfowl such as blue-wing teal, mallards and colourful wood ducks. As well, the Saugeen Field Naturalists have listed a number of uncommon plants here. Some species, such as the shrub shaggy ninebark, are normally found only along the lakeshore. In the easterly oxbow where the the Hydro lines cross the river, several southern trees, bitternut hickory and hackberry, make an appearance. Similarly, an upland woodlot just downstream near Ellengowan supports the southerly species of black walnut and white oak.

In this part of the river, where the river cuts down into the soft clays of the old Lake Warren bed, you can see a peculiar form of erosion known as slumping. As the river cuts away at the toe of the clay banks, the saturated soils eventually lose their strength and begin to flow, like liquid plastic. As the hillside slides downwards into the river, even fully grown trees are pushed into weird angles by the wrinkling of the slide's surface.

After a long slow paddle, you will finally reach McBeath Conservation Area, 1 km past the Elderslie-Brant township line bridge. A good campsite is available here, about 32 km downstream from Walkerton.

The remaining 10 km to Paisley lies through increasingly open farmland, with beef cattle the most common industry. About halfway, you will see the buildings of Paisley Brick and Tile atop the right bank. Thriving by 1900, this yard originally cured its bricks by burning huge tunnels of wood. It now makes tiles only, converting the red Elderslie clay into hard tiles used for underground drainage of local farmland.

As you approach Paisley, the fairground on the left provides both a convenient access point and overnight camping. But as you float downriver in your canoe, you might want to recall the *Paisley Advocate*'s description of an earlier craft, circa 1850: "On one occasion, early in the morning, a commodious raft passed where this village now is. On one end was a cow with her calf; on the other, along with considerable baggage, was a cooking stove, in which was a good fire, and while the enterprising settler was attending to the navigation of his vessel, the good wife was busy at the stove getting breakfast ready. The smoke, which streamed from the elevated pipe, gave the moving raft the appearance of a rustic steamer in motion."

One of the most historically minded towns in Ontario, Paisley has much to remember. Gone are the days of the Tidings Tree, a large white elm at the junction of the rivers where settlers left messages and notices. Gone too are the days when pioneers sent messages across the river strapped to a dog named Danger, or when a young widow ferried passengers across on a raft.

But the 1876 town hall, right at the junction of the Saugeen and Teeswater rivers, has recently been restored. Near it the green fire

Paisley's historic town hall stands on the very edge of the river, with a distinctive tower for drying fire hoses in the foreground.

Ron Reid

station hose tower, built around the turn of the century, still stands. So do several old mills near the mouth of the Teeswater, where commercial ventures date back to the first 1851 dam of cedar and pine held together by rock elm pegs. For more information about these structures and others, drop into the Paisley Town Hall for an informative brochure describing a historical walking tour of the village.

PAISLEY TO SOUTHAMPTON

As you set off on the last 40-km stretch to Southampton, you will soon see why Paisley represents the very heart of the Saugeen watershed. The river we have been following carries waters all the way from Dundalk, near the highest point in southern Ontario. From the south the dark waters of the Teeswater are added, stained by the organic soils of Greenock Swamp. A few hundred metres downstream, Willow Creek appears from between its massive flood-control shoulders, bringing contributions from half-way to Lake Huron. And just downstream, the North Branch pours in, carrying waters from the gravelly highlands of Grey County.

Swelled by the gathering of these far-flung tributaries, the

Saugeen continues to roll lakeward through a broad and often winding valley. Seven km downstream from Paisley the river passes through a heavily wooded section containing the Saugeen Bluffs Conservation Area, where excellent camping facilities are available.

For the next 25 km, the river continues to pass through a variety of rural scenery—high clay bluffs where the river is still actively eroding, pleasant riffles past islands wooded with cedar and ash, and quiet stretches where the farms reach down almost to touch you. In the woodlots and along the shore, occasional rarities can be found—Turk's cap lily, marsh pennywort and Goldie's fern. In places the river loosens the strands of its watery braid to form islands, some with unusual forest communities such as butternut.

Several county roads cross the river in this stretch, leading to Port Elgin and Southampton. It is possible to end your trip here but the prettiest and most challenging section of the lower Saugeen lies in its last 9 km to the lake, so include it if you can. As the river swings northward, it snuggles between the old shore cliff on one side and the Lake Algonquin beach bar on the other, creating a deep, heavily forested valley.

On these well drained soils sugar maple and ash are the most common species, but downriver the forest turns increasingly to birch. Why should that be? Perhaps the cold-tolerant birch can adjust better to the cool winds coming up the valley from Lake Huron, or perhaps the sandy soils don't provide enough nutrients for maple. In any case their silvery trunks give the ravine a more northerly feel.

About 3 km down from the last bridge, Sang's Creek enters from the east. Though little evidence remains of it today, this was the site of the first mill on the lower Saugeen, built in 1844 and operated by the local Indians for less than a year. Now the river is left undisturbed, home only to snapping turtles, mergansers and other wild creatures.

A final stretch of quiet water brings you to Denny's dam, which can be portaged easily on either side. On the left a fish-tagging station makes a convenient take-out point. As well, you can see the operation of a fish ladder which allows passage of spawning rainbow trout upstream in spring and fall.

When John Denny first put his grist mill into operation here in 1857, the dam did not extend right across the river. Instead a head-gate dam ascended the river about midstream, extending far enough to capture the required head of water. Around the turn of the century, hydro-electric power from the full dam lit the houses and streets of neighbouring towns. In 1970 the dam was rebuilt by federal and provincial fishery departments to block off the Saugeen from the destructive sea lamprey. After rasping through the outer scales of a fish with its sucker-like mouth, the lamprey draws blood from its host, wreaking havoc with Lake Huron's lake trout and whitefish. Denny's dam has a special overhanging steel lip across the face of the dam, to prevent the lamprey from clinging their way past.

Just downstream on the right, past the old bridge abutments, another conservation area provides camping facilities. This is also the site of archaeological investigations of a prehistoric Indian village. Evidence shows that the Indians would gather here in the spring to capture fish, including the lake sturgeon, which is now rare.

Fast water continues down to the lake level; some of the rapids are deceptively powerful, so be cautious in your maneouvres. On the hill to your right, the Saugeen Indian Reserve still is home to the descendants of the victorious Ojibway. Soon the grey waters of Lake Huron are in sight. You can most easily end your trip at the boat launch on the north side of the river, about 500 m before the Hwy. 21 bridge.

From the piers at the mouth of the river, you can see Chantry Island, about 2 km offshore. As well as providing a base for a historic lighthouse, this island contains a large colony of nesting ring-bill and herring gulls, along with great blue herons and the smaller black-crowned night herons. Chantry Island is protected as a federal wildlife sanctuary and should not be disturbed. Its colonies are the source of many of the herons and gulls that you see along the Saugeen River.

National Topographic System Maps
1:50,000 scale: 41A/3, A/6, A/11

Ministry of Natural Resources Office
611 Ninth Ave. E., Owen Sound, N4K 3E4

Saugeen River–Map 1

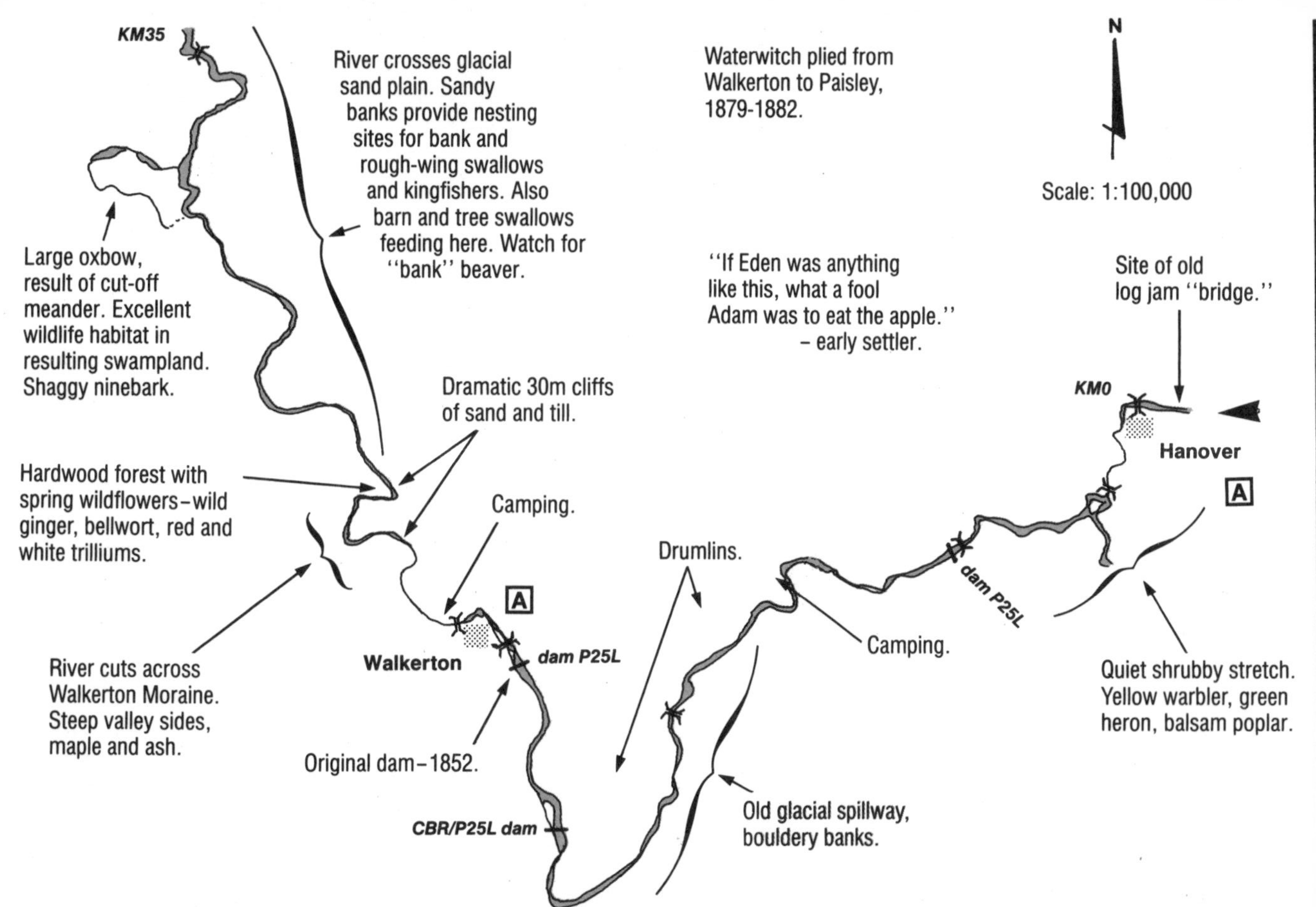

Ref: N.T.S. Map 41A/3, 1:50,000

Saugeen River – Map 2

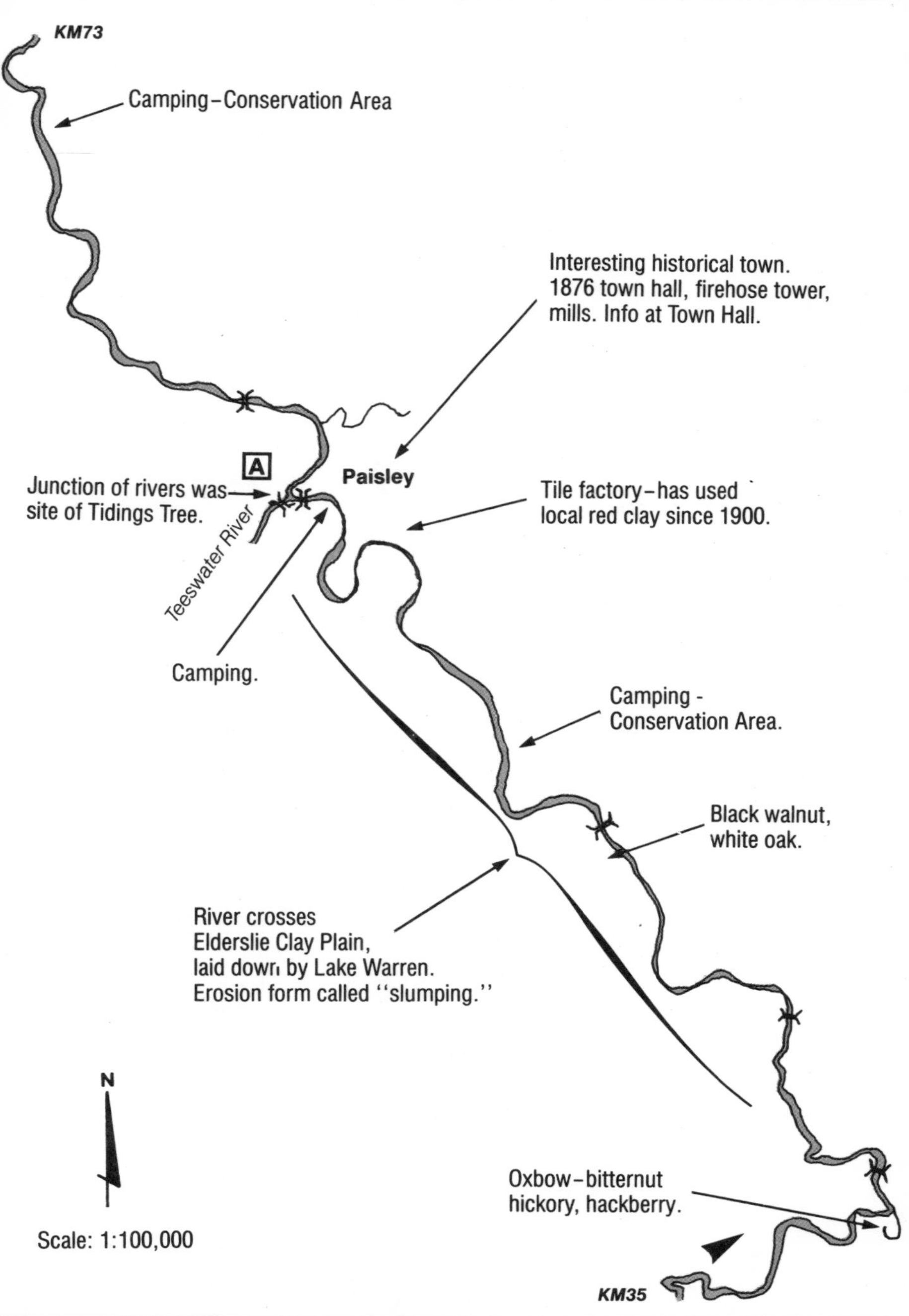

Ref: N.T.S. Map 41A/3, 41A/6, 1:50,000

Saugeen River–Map 3

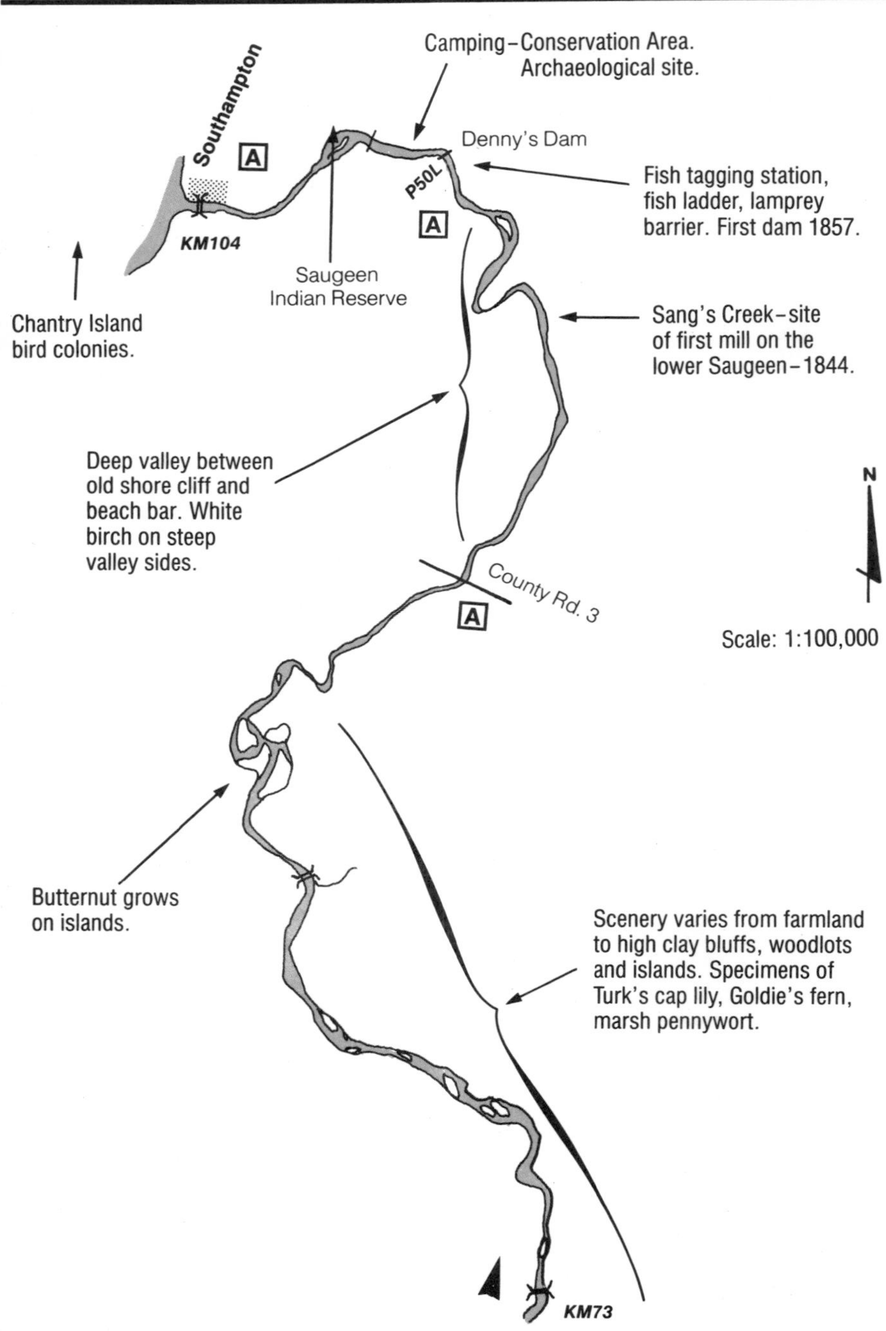

Ref: N.T.S. Map 41A/6, 41A/11, 1:50,000

The Rankin: A River Reprieved

Look at the early history of Grey and Bruce counties and one name soon seems to haunt the pages before you—Charles Rankin. One of that hardy breed of backwoods surveyors who preceded the flood of settlers into the Queen's Bush, it was Mr. Rankin who laid out many of the townships in this area. He left his mark in the rectangular, sometimes senseless gridwork of roads that cuts across hill and vale in this irregular landscape. He also left his name on the small river that drains the lower part of the Indian peninsula that his surveys helped "civilize."

Today Mr. Rankin's river flows quietly through the lakes and marshes that have marked its course for millennia. The coming of the settlers stripped the fine timber from its banks; the hordes of passenger pigeons no longer darken the sky above; but the desperate attempts to tame the river bed for agriculture failed, and the Rankin was eventually returned to the wildlife that it supports so abundantly. An 18-km paddle here, easily accomplished in a day, provides one of the best wildlife canoeing experiences in southern Ontario.

Along the trilogy of lakes known as Sky, Boat and Isaac, much of the lakeshore is now owned and managed jointly by the Sauble Valley Conservation Authority and the Ministry of Natural Resources. Some land is still private, however, so please respect the rights of these landowners. On a trip down the Rankin you can enjoy the feel of a productive chain of wetlands, safe from the forces that have destroyed so many of their kind across southern Ontario.

Wetlands along the Way

The waters of the Rankin rise as cool trout streams close to the abrupt easterly shore of the Bruce Peninsula, but our canoe route traces only the lower, slow-moving sections. The Bruce Peninsula is thought to have originated about 300–600 million years ago in the bottom of an ancient sea something like our Gulf of Mexico. Layer upon layer of sediments built up, often enriched by corals, and eventually these layers, like huge pancakes, compressed into the sedimentary rocks we see today. But because softer rocks are overlain by a cap of the harder dolomite, erosion of the edge of the pancakes has produced the dramatic cliffs found along the Niagara Escarpment.

A similar process on a smaller scale has produced the secondary scarp that acts as a dam for the Rankin. The river is underlain by the softer Amabel formation, which eroded away while the Guelph formation dolomite resisted. Another ridge of bedrock at the bottom end of Boat Lake held back the waters and allowed a thick mantle of organic matter to accumulate.

Between here and Lake Huron, a thick layer of sands has been sculpted into a series of beach dunes. The river cuts through these dunes, now mostly heavily wooded, in its lower reaches. However, the smooth bedrock is never far away, surfacing again at Sauble Falls.

It seems likely that these dunes originally supported stands of pine, but the shallow rocky soils of most of the watershed were clad in hardwoods when the first settlers arrived. The forest is still overwhelmingly deciduous, though a combination of indiscriminate logging and fires has reduced the present stands to a young state.

For much of this canoe route the trees are set well back and it is the marshes that occupy your attention. Nutrient-rich marshlands such as these are among the most productive ecosystems known to man, and that productivity is reflected both in the profusion of aquatic vegetation and in the wildlife. This area has yielded 126 breeding birds, the highest diversity of the Bruce Peninsula. Waterfowl are especially able to take advantage of the Rankin's riches. By April the bufflehead and scaup have returned to the open waters of the lakes, and the marshes are speckled with mallards, pintails, shovellers and teal. At least ten species of ducks remain to nest, an unusually high number for southern Ontario. And the fall brings migrants again, diving ducks such as ring-necked and scaup, and even the handsome canvasbacks.

Waterfowl are only one component of the varied bird life of a marsh. Virginia and sora rails lead their secretive lives among the dense vegetation, and there are some who say that the elusive king rail also lurks here. Isaac Lake is a consistently good spot to find both the American bittern and the less common least bittern. Marsh wrens chatter from their swaying nests among the reeds; black terns flock noisily above their simple mud nests.

Sadly the days of the passenger pigeon on the Rankin are gone forever, for the bird is one of a growing list of species recently extinct. But Sherwood Fox recalls the stories told by his father of vast colonies of the pigeons that extended in a broad sinuous line from the mouth of the Sauble River along the course of the Rankin all the way to Berford Lake, east of Hwy 6. What a sight it must have been, when with "a roar like Niagara" the birds rose to make their evening foray to the beech and oak woods for nuts or to the grain fields to feed on the bounty there.

The shallow waters of the Rankin today are home to a host of other creatures, such as the river otter, rare elsewhere on the Bruce, and an assortment of frogs, turtles and snakes. Pike, perch and largemouth bass are common game fish, and even the strangely shaped bowfin has been found here.

Along the Peninsula Portage

There is archaeological evidence of several thousand years of Indian use of Bruce County, and by the time of Champlain the peninsula was most likely inhabited by the semi-nomadic Ottawa tribe. Attracted by the abundant fisheries of the offshore islands in Lake Huron and the wildlife resources of the marshlands, these hunters ranged widely. The Rankin system, however, was of particular significance because it formed part of the Peninsula portage, cutting across the narrow neck of land from Wiarton to Boat Lake, and thence to Lake Huron.

It is clear from early accounts that many of the nearby tribes used this portage as a convenient means to avoid the long trip around the Peninsula in their trading and hunting forays. The route followed the present course of the Oliphant road from Wiarton to the Ministry access point at the foot of Isaac Lake. After a short paddle to the west side of Boat Lake, the canoeists would portage again to Spry Lake, and then across the dunes to the west.

An alternate route, down the Rankin past Sauble Falls, seems to have been used less often. However, the earliest known map of this area, left by a Jesuit father, François Joseph Bressani, in 1657,

Colonies of black terns are a common sight along the marshes of the Rankin; watch for their simple mud nests just above the waterline.
Hap Wilson

shows the Rankin as part of the route. A much later account, of the first settlers to Southampton, Captains Spence and Kennedy in 1848, also describes the use of the Rankin as part of the portage.

As a trade route the Peninsula portage survived the destructive Indian wars that swept across southern Ontario before colonization. The Iroquois, for example, used this route to take their furs for trade from their village at the mouth of the Saugeen across to the Nottawasaga en route to Montreal. Later the invading Ojibway would use a similar route. Few settlers came this way, however, since the late settlement of the Peninsula meant that access roads were already pushing up from the south.

It was 1854 when the surrender of the Bruce Peninsula opened the way for settlers and loggers, only 18 years after the Manitowaning Treaty had promised to protect the land "forever from the encroachments of the whites." By 1862 the first mills had sprung up at Sauble Falls and for a few years a thriving lumber community grew there. In 1905 the falls were harnessed for another use, producing the first electric power for the town of Wiarton.

One of the unusual historical features along the river is the remains of the *Waterwitch*, a 12-m steamer used for many years to haul logs along the string of lakes. Originally in use on the Saugeen, the *Waterwitch* was transported in the winter of 1883 on sleighs from the Saugeen to Boat Lake. By the turn of the century, victim of dwindling timber supplies and better roads, the *Waterwitch* had been abandoned, and its rotting remains still lie near the exit of Boat Lake.

In 1920 progress caught up with the Rankin in the form of a drainage scheme for the marsh lands for agriculture. A ridge of rock was blasted out at the exit of Boat Lake and a channel dredged though the silty bottom. Soon, however, the new farmland was found to be lacking in soil fertility and structure, and the project was abandoned. It was not until 1951 that requests from local people resulted in the first attempts to restore the former water levels, and in 1961 the present dam for that purpose was constructed.

Exploring the River

The 18-km trip down the Rankin can be made anytime during the canoeing season, although low water levels in late summer may slow your progress a little. This is an excellent route for novices, especially since it is possible to make short loops on the lakes from several access points.

Our starting point is the bridge on the Red Bay road, leading west from Hwy. 6 at Mar. As you park your car, notice the rock cut through the escarpment on the west side. The layers of soft limestone can be clearly seen, topped by the Guelph formation dolomite. Fossils are common in these rocks, and if you break a small chunk you can smell the low-grade petroleum locked within the sedimentary structure. A residue from ancient organic deposits, this oil is not concentrated enough for commercial extraction, although small amounts of natural gas have been tapped at Hepworth only 20 km away.

The forest along this ridge is mixed conifer and hardwood second growth, with a dense shrubby layer of round-leafed dogwood, buffalo berry, bush honeysuckle and several others. Like much of the western side of the Bruce, this woods has a northern flavour, enhanced by such wildflowers as large-leaved aster, twinflower, barren strawberry and green-leaved rattlesnake plantain.

To the north the marshy stretches of Sky Lake are a good spot to watch for painted turtles and bullfrogs, or for the common garter and northern water snakes. Massasauga rattlesnakes do occur on the Bruce Peninsula, usually along the edges of swampy areas, but they are increasingly rare and seldom seen. If you do see a rattler, respect its independence and leave it alone. In the very unlikely event of a bite, stay calm and head for the nearest hospital in Wiarton for a dose of the antivenin.

As you paddle the first kilometre into Isaac Lake, you are already within productive waterfowl marsh. In places wood duck boxes have been attached to trees to help our most beautiful species of waterfowl return from its former low numbers. These boxes are sometimes also used by other ducks, such as hooded mergansers, which have been known to nest along the Rankin, or even by other birds such as screech owls.

As you come onto Isaac Lake, you might notice that the forest along the edge is now largely deciduous, dominated by maple and birch on these shallow soils. Watch in these woods for leatherwood, a distinctive shrub with twigs that are very supple and tough. Early in the spring this shrub produces pretty yellow bell-like flowers. These limestone woods are excellent places to brush up on your violets, since at least four different kinds occur here.

Looking east across the lake, you can see several low whaleback hills known as drumlins, a legacy of the glacial times. Along the side of one of these, another access point leads to the Rankin Wildlife Management Area, along a pleasant laneway good for forest birds. A series of artificial ponds was built for a flock of giant Canada geese introduced in 1971, and geese still regularly visit. As well, this is a good place to watch for other waterfowl, including unusual breeding species such as green-wing teal. The goose pens are also accessible by a township road from Hwy. 6.

Back on the lake, a narrow channel leads you past the end of another drumlin into the marshy lower half. Hard-stem and soft-stem bulrushes are common in deeper water here, along with wild rice, pickerel weed, coontail and other underwater plants such as chara. Red-wing blackbirds, yellow warblers and black terns compete with the chattering of the marsh wrens.

As the canoeable channel narrows, the shrubby shores include sweetgale and meadowsweet, along with basket willow. In several spots the climbing vines of Canada moonseed, an unusual species this far north, sport their poisonous berries. This is a particularly good spot for ducks and rails, and least bitterns can be seen regularly here.

Just above the first bridge an access point on the site of the old portage leads to the Oliphant road. Another short marshy stretch, through the dead trees left by the return of water levels, brings you onto Boat Lake.

It is interesting to note how the rise in water levels 25 years ago has changed the aquatic vegetation of Boat and Isaac lakes. The pondweeds, bladderwort and milfoil that had been abundant have almost disappeared, replaced by bulrushes, water lilies and pickerel weed. Wild rice, which formerly grew along the edges of Boat Lake, now is restricted to a large patch in the middle.

Finding the exit from Boat Lake is sometimes tricky, for it is centred in the crescent of dead trees at the south end. The next 2 km twist through a fine red ash-silver maple swamp based on a deep pocket of organic soils. At times it seems that the river almost doubles back on itself as it loops and twists. Pussywillows and silky dogwoods occur in patches, along with the ubiquitous sensitive fern and the elegant royal fern. Tree swallows by the hundreds swirl through the forest above.

Eventually you reach the conservation authority dam, where a 30-m portage on the left is necessary. Botanizing in this area can be fascinating, with several rare ferns and orchids found nearby. To the west the wooded dunes begin, clad in maple and birch, beech and white ash. The forest floor is rich with wildflowers, including typical species such as white trillium and squirrel corn as well as more northern flowers like Canada mayflower, sarsaparilla and false Solomon's seal. The magenta blossoms of gaywings, or polygala, are a specialty of these sandy areas.

The river winds southwards among the dunes, sometimes blocked by fallen trees or small beaver dams. Watch for poison ivy if you have to scramble past any obstructions on shore. A shallow swift several hundred metres long may require wading if the water is low. And on a sharp bend, another small ledge may require lining.

Just before our end point, the Rankin joins the larger Sauble River. The first several kilometres upstream on the Sauble can make an excellent addition to your trip if you have time, for its quiet waters are undisturbed by cottages or houses. The woods around the junction are especially rich in wildflowers, with good spring displays of dogtooth violet and spring beauty.

Our trip ends at Sauble Falls Provincial Park, just above the county road bridge. Just downstream, the falls show good exposures of limestone bedrock, and at times a good view of rainbow trout, coho and chinook salmon ascending the river. None of these sport fish are native to Ontario; they have been introduced from the west coast and have successfully adapted to life in the Great Lakes. Only the rainbow trout, however, can reproduce under natural conditions in Ontario.

Camping is available at the provincial park or at several private campsites in nearby Sauble Beach.

National Topographic System Maps
Scale 1:50,000: 41A/11, A/14

Ministry of Natural Resources Office
611 Ninth Ave. E., Owen Sound, N4K 3E4

Rankin River–Map 1

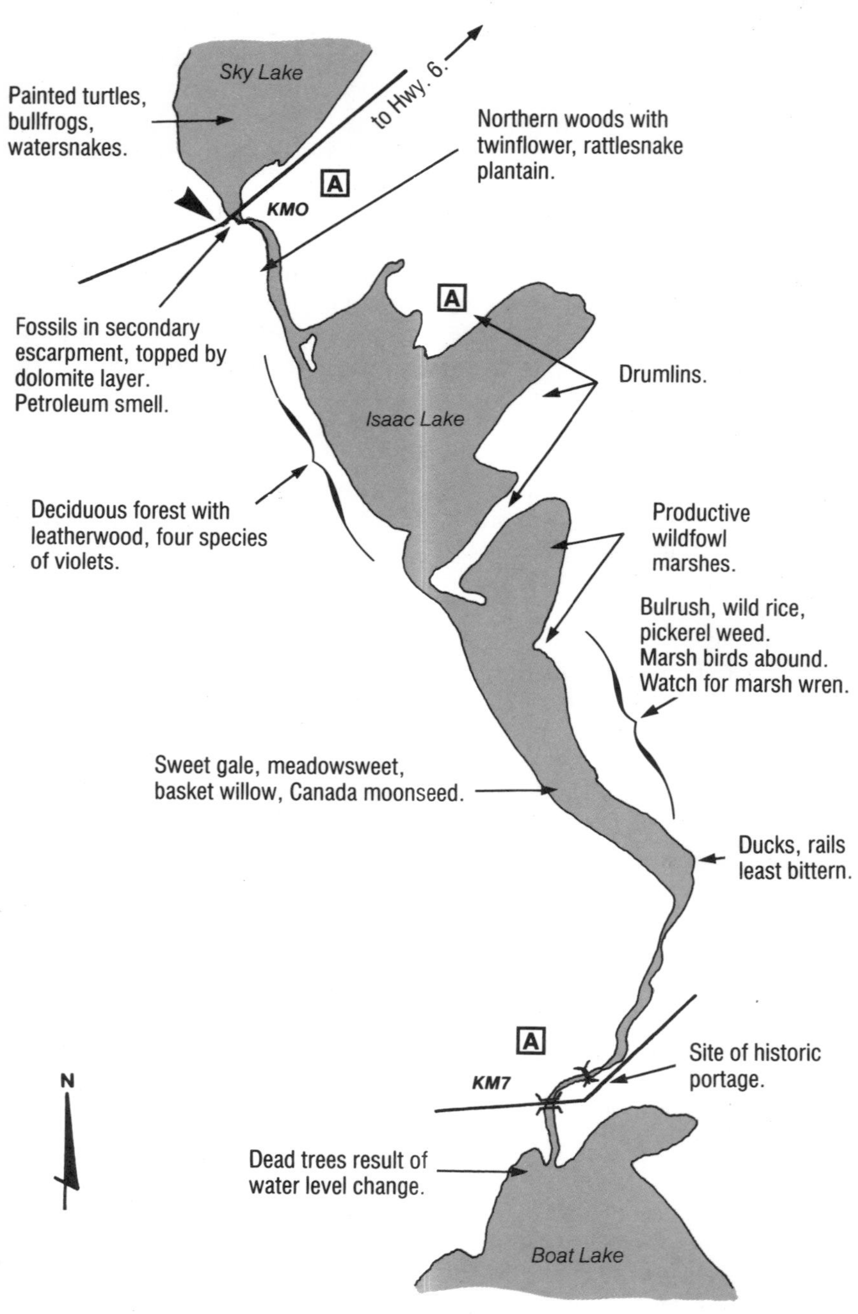

Ref: N.T.S. Map 41A/14, 1:50,000

Rankin River – Map 2

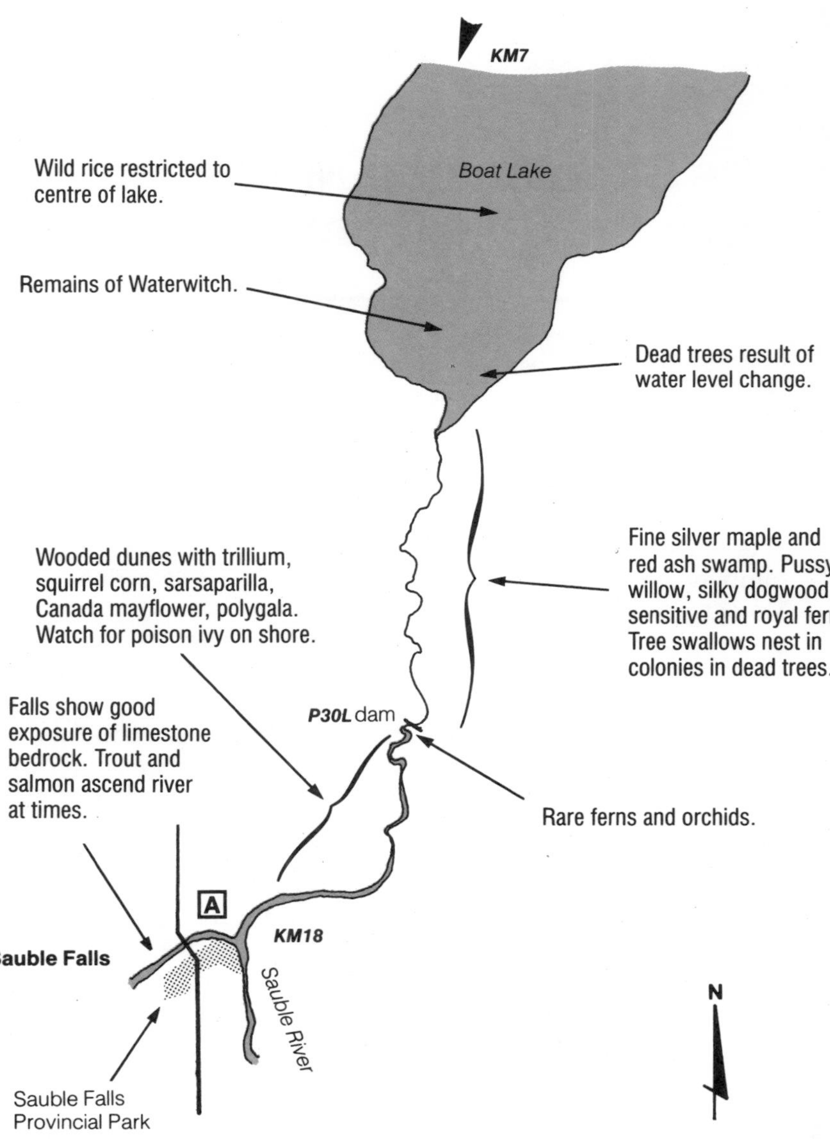

Ref: N.T.S. Map 41A/11, 1:50,000

The Skootamatta-Moira: From the Shield onto the Plain

If rivers were like people, then surely the Moira would be an elegant old matron, silver-haired and knowing, with a dignity born of long experience. For the Moira has the air of the matriarch about it—banks gracefully lined with stately silver maple trees, waters stitched into lacework by the white flecking of rapids, birds gossiping happily nearby like a mansion full of servants. The Skootamatta, on the other hand, is more the frolicking young lady, tumbling noisily down among the wild lands to add its flow to the Moira's.

Certainly both are experienced with the feeble whims of man. Here came the settlers to harness their waters for sawmill and grist. Here came the lumbermen, thrusting logs through the chutes and narrows in a maniacal rush towards the mill. Here came the miners in a fruitless search for gold, finding instead other sources of mineral wealth to fuel the industries of early Ontario. Here too came the distillers in search of pure water. And now, it is the canoeist who seeks the waters of the Moira, a suitor that treats the great lady more gently than those of the past.

Canoeing the Skootamatta-Moira is not for the faint of heart—close to 30 portages in five days. Even at that, some fast-water experience is necessary to run the longer, easier rapids. Despite these drawbacks, it is a river that is both accessible and interesting. The portages are almost all short and relatively level, and we find they greatly enhance the trip for they reveal much about the surrounding countryside.

The river drops 225 m from Skootamatta Lake to Cannifton, over a length of 105 km. It is best travelled just after the leaves are breaking, in mid-May to mid-June, for later in the season some stretches become shallow. Only the section above Slave Lake is

Crown land, so you must be aware of the rights of private landowners for most of the river, and respect any posted areas.

Water quality along the Moira is generally good, although we recommend that you boil any drinking water. The west branch of the Moira has been polluted by arsenic from the Deloro gold mine, but this does not, of course, affect the Skootamatta. Downstream of the junction the hazard appears minimal.

A Valley Divided

The scenery, natural history and land use of the Moira basin are overwhelmingly influenced by its alignment, crossing the boundary between the Precambrian Shield and the younger limestone bedrock. Thus the countryside that you experience along the Skootamatta is very different from the farmlands south from Tweed.

The upper parts of the route follow an uncertain course among the massive rock knobs of the Shield, which are up to 2000 million years old. In this part of the Shield, all the rock has been metamorphosed—that is, exposed to great heat and pressure so that significant changes took place. The ancient limestones were transformed into marble, for example, such as the crystalline stone that can be seen in the Actinolite church.

The southern third of the watershed is based on much younger limestones, laid down by a sea about 440 million years ago. The edge of this limestone is obscured by glacial drift, so you have to look closely for its presence. This Dummer moraine, deposited during a pause in the retreat of the glacier, contains both rounded granitic boulders and fragments of limestone, since it straddles the edge of the Shield. Its hummocky surface, in many parts converted to farmland, can be clearly seen along the east side of Stoco Lake and where the west and east channels of the Moira rejoin south of the lake.

Associated with the moraine is a glacial spillway leading along the valley floor where the Skootamatta and the Moira join. Below Chisholm the Moira crosses the easterly tip of the Peterborough drumlin field, a widespread cluster of these elongated hills that stretches from here to Lake Simcoe. Past Plainfield, the glacial till plain gradually thins until only a shallow cover is left over the limestone plains that enclose the river's mouth.

The vegetation of the Moira watershed has also been affected by its dichotomy in landforms. While many of the common trees,

Large bur oak trees found occasionally along the Moira can be identified by their rough corky twigs. **Ron Reid**

such as sugar maple on the uplands and silver maple along the floodplains, are abundant throughout the basin, others are less tolerant. Rock elm and red cedar, for example, occur only in limestone-based soils. Northern species, such as black spruce and balsam fir, are restricted largely to the Shield. For other species, such as the Carolinean shagbark hickory, the effects of climate may have been responsible for its appearance only in southern sections of the Moira Valley.

The forests you see today along the Moira, typical of those in the Great Lakes–St. Lawrence forest region, have changed mostly in quality since the days of the early lumbermen. The great white pines have long gone, but an article by John Macoun, a local schoolteacher, in the 1864 *Directory of Hastings County*, suggests that red pine had always been scarce this far south. The forests retain a good quantity of oaks, as he described, but the hickory, butternut and black walnut listed in early sawmill records are probably scarcer now.

Macoun described elms as abundant in Hastings County, with great quantities made into square timber and exported. You can still find occasional large elms along the river but the pernicious Dutch elm disease in the 1960s spelled the end of their abundance. Similarly, in Macoun's day tamarack formed extensive swamps, and its wood was exported for ship-building. But shortly after 1890 the introduction of the larch sawfly almost wiped out the species locally.

The wildlife of the Moira is one of its best features. A sudden meeting with a black bear and her two cubs along the upper Skootamatta sent us into frantic back-paddling, and the two cubs scuttling to the very top of a nearby pine. In these undisturbed sections even an occasional moose sighting is not out of the question. The 1950 Conservation Report lists marten as extinct in the watershed, but we were treated to a careful once-over by one of these curious little fur-bearers. Among the swamps of the Skootamatta, beaver and muskrat are abundant as well. The tepid waters of the Moira provide good fishing for bass, pickerel and pike, especially just below rapids or falls.

Loyalist Country

The early settlement of southeastern Ontario owes its start to the American Revolution. Thousands of settlers from the American Colonies remained loyal to Britain and drifted northwards to join British forces. Often their lands had been confiscated and their families forced into exile, leaving the British administration in Canada with a sizable contingent of "displaced persons" to support. As it became clear that these refugees could not return home after peace was restored, the authorities moved quickly to establish military bases as centres for settlement. From one such fort at Cataraqui, now Kingston, the first Loyalist settlers pushed westward to the better farmlands along the Bay of Quinte.

So it was that in October 1783, the small group of Mississauga Indians who occupied the lower Moira surrendered most of their lands within a day's journey of the lake. The following year the first of the Loyalists, who were a group of Mohawk Indians under

John Deserontyou, moved in. Most of the other early Loyalists were Scots or Dutch from upstate New York.

These experienced American settlers knew enough to avoid swamps, thin-soiled rocky lands or sandy barrens, and so progress in the lower Moira came slowly. Until 1800 settlement was concentrated around the mouth and in the Foxboro area, and by 1805 grist mills had opened near Corbyville and Cannifton. But it was 1826 before the first permanent settlers reached the south shore of Stoco Lake, and ten years after that before the first mill was built at Tweed.

In the upper sections of the watershed it was the lumbermen who led the way. Before 1826 only the British Navy or its representatives were officially allowed to cut pine, which was reserved for masts and spars. This was a source of much irritation for the settlers. However, a pioneer was allowed to sell any pine that had blown over naturally—hence the term "windfall profits." By the 1830s the square timber trade was well established, with trimmed timbers transported downriver, then rafted up and floated to the timber coves at Quebec City.

Twenty years later Belleville boasted some of the largest sawmills west of Ottawa. The 1856 *Directory of Hastings County* proclaimed the prosperity brought about by logging: "For some years past, the saw logs brought down the river here averaged from 150,000 to 175,000 [logs] a year." By mid-century the Honourable Billa Flint had pushed industry well up onto the Shield, with new sawmills at Troy (later Actinolite) and Flinton. But by the turn of the century the big timber was all gone, and the year 1908 saw the last log drive down from Skootamatta Lake to the mouth.

Exploring the River

The Moira and Skootamatta rivers are navigable in late spring from almost the head of the watershed, Skootamatta Lake, to within 5 km of the mouth. With a total fall of 200 m over 105 km, this is a relatively steep watershed for southern Ontario. Even though the gradient in the Skootamatta is nearly twice that of the lower Moira, much of the drop occurs at dams or falls, so that short portages are more common than runnable rapids. A detailed description of portages and rapids is available from the Moira River Conservation Authority, Box 698, Belleville, K8N 5B3.

A trip down the length of the Skootamatta and Moira from

Skootamatta Lake to Cannifton takes about five days in late May or early June. Later in the season some stretches are very shallow, especially above Flinton and from Chisholm's Mill to Latta, and your navigation is likely to include some wading. A variety of camping spots are available along the river, and supplies can be purchased at Flinton, Actinolite, Tweed and Latta.

SKOOTAMATTA LAKE TO HWY. 7

This first 50 km passes mostly through dense second-growth forests, with shrubby swamps and majestic soft-maple forests for variety. It involves at least 19 portages, the longest 800 metres, and several other lift-overs, so it is recommended that you attempt it only if you are in reasonably good physical condition. However, the frequent portages are not entirely a curse, for they force you out of your canoe to gain a fuller appreciation of the landscape around you. This is a particular bonus early in the season when the spring wildflowers are blooming.

The trip begins at the south end of Skootamatta Lake, accessible from Hwy. 41 by a twisty gravel road just north of Cloyne. As you pass through the first small lakes, the wilderness soon asserts itself. The gentle shores are covered in white birch and pine, with even a few of the infrequent red pine. In wetter spots the ubiquitous silver maple makes its first appearance. Mallards and wood ducks flee before your approaching canoe and a flicker hammers out his territorial rhythm on a dead tree stub. Among the frequent conifers on the first portage, watch for the waxy flowers and creeping, leathery leaves of trailing arbutus, one of the first northern wildflowers to bloom.

Through the next kilometre, you pass through the first of many swampy depressions, where the river steals its way quietly among dense thickets of speckled alder and sweet gale. In this sort of country the kingbird reigns from his regal perch, puffing out his white chest in song. At the lower end of the swamp the remains of a beaver dam at the top of a small rapid means another short portage or lift-over.

On these rocky portages several early-blooming shrubs frequently scent the air. The loose-clustered flowers of serviceberries wave in the spring breeze at the end of light grey twigs. On open knolls the shrubby mats of blueberries hang their lantern-shaped flowers. Further downriver, the white flat-topped flower clusters of alternate-leaved dogwood often dot the shore as you drift by. This species of dogwood is also known as the pagoda tree, because its branches fan out in parallel horizontal layers, like some out-of-place Japanese garden delight.

The next rapids are announced by massive steel Hydro towers and by the bridge which serves this right-of-way. An 800-m portage around this broken string of rapids can often be avoided by careful scouting of each step, running some and portaging others. Be careful though, for several blind corners hide steep drops, and even here the Skootamatta has enough power to be dangerous.

As you step out beside the first dam at Slave Lake, it is easy to see that the lake was once much larger. The two concrete dams were constructed about 1920 to provide electric power for the Ore Chimney Gold Mine across Hwy. 41 to the east. Neither the mine nor the power plant was long-lived, and a ring of second-growth forest has now invaded the former flood lines.

Half a kilometre after the Slave Lake portage, O'Donnell's rapids requires another short carry. The next 6 km of the Skootamatta winds through soft maple and shrub swamps, where the insistent ringing call of the northern waterthrush competes with the chattering burble of the winter wren and the endless "chebecks" of the least flycatcher.

Warblers are a specialty of the Canadian Shield, and they are here by the dozen, more often heard than seen. One warbler in particular is worth searching for in the shrubby alder swamps. A distinctive buzzy four-note song belongs to the rare golden-winged warbler, whose black chin and mask are set off by a golden crown and, as the name implies, golden wing bars. On a trip down the Skootamatta in 1984 we found five of these delightful warblers in successive alder swales along this stretch.

The swamplands are interrupted occasionally by outcrops of rock or sand. At one of these a sandy field on the left is the start of another short portage around a small falls. Since the beginning of the trip, the river has followed a band of metamorphosed volcanic rocks, and the pitted surface of ancient lava shows clearly at the base of these falls.

A little later an old farmstead is slowly reverting to the bush, the roof of the log house already gone and trees invading the hard-won pasture. We found wild oats along the river bank here, also called sessile bellwort, with a single creamy bell-flower hanging from each stalk of clasping leaves.

After a lift-over at a ledge, the next set of rapids can be missed altogether by a 400-m portage, or run by experienced paddlers after the first corner is portaged. As you approach Flinton, a pocket

While the coppice growth of both species of soft maple is similar, the blunt-lobed leaves of red maple differ from the delicate pattern of the silver.
Hap Wilson

of deeper sands produces noticeably better forests of pine, spruce and hemlock, with a few large yellow birch along the bank.

The Flinton mill pond provides a good view of an old frame church, and the portage through the town park takes you past the dam site first chosen by Billa Flint in 1853. Beside the bridge where you put in, you can see the remains of the mill building. From the round holes in its wall and the dam 100 m away, you can trace the course of the circular penstock that provided the water supply. Backwash from the dam has exposed good sections of the meta-volcanic bedrock here, tilted to an oblique angle and appearing quite different from that upstream.

If you are canoeing the Skootamatta later in the season and want to avoid the shallow stretches in the first 17 km, Flinton can be used as a starting point. Camping is not available here, but the small store can provide some basic supplies.

For the next kilometre the river flows fast and dark between rocky shores covered with hemlock and cedar. A short portage is necessary around a falls with a right-angle bend at the bottom, and another chute a short distance further on should be approached with caution. In no time at all, it seems, you are at the infamous "Mile Portage."

As the river tumbles down off the volcanic ridge onto the

granitic rocks that now form its bed, it channels into a canyon and becomes progressively faster and whiter. The portage is actually about 800 m, but a combination of poor markings and steep hills makes it seem at least a mile. The portage does show you a nice cross-section of mixed forest, with hemlock, pine, oak and birch overhead. The ovenbird is common here, another secretive warbler, whose signature call is often interpreted as "teacher, Teacher, TEACHER."

Several short portages and rapids later, the river flattens out again in a large shallow swamp. On the higher ground coniferous forests have dominated, but here in the lowlands the trees are entirely deciduous—silver maple, black ash, bur oak and butternut. These trees have adapted to life with wet feet, creating shallow, broadly spaced root systems. Even so, they need periodic drying of the surface layer to allow sufficient oxygen to reach their roots, a condition provided by the varying water levels in these floodplain forests.

The wetlands along the Moira perform a valuable role in moderating water flows, by storing spring floods in their spongy soils and releasing these cool waters throughout the summer. Because of the mineral sediments brought down by the spring flush of the river, the soils beneath these swamps are a rich mixture of organic and mineral materials.

At the next small falls, approximately 2 km past the road, experienced paddlers can use a short carry across the centre island as an alternative to a longer carry on the right. For the next 3 km short portages alternate with swampy stretches, with frequent beaver meadows off to the sides.

A small set of rapids brings you to the top of another dangerous rapids known locally as the Chute. The river here surges through a long fault in the granite, which has created a small cliff along the eastern side. A 200-m portage on the right rocky edge brings you safely past, and shows you colonies of the rich purple-fringed polygola or "gaywings" in the woods and the delicate pink corydalis on the open rocks.

Just downstream, barely after the boils from the Chute have settled, another poorly marked portage on the right bypasses Log Jam Falls. First, however, it's worth pulling in on the left for a better view of the falls. Iron pegs anchored in the massive rock provided an anchor for herding logs down this tumbled falls. As the river pushes over the crest, it splits, with the main force of the current cascading left over a slanted overhanging lip. After a clear

Once thought to be an Indian corn grinding hole, this feature is actually a kettle worn by the swirling action of stones in the current of a glacial river. **Ron Reid**

drop of some 4 m, this flow is suddenly reversed onto itself, as it batters onto an opposing slanted face before thundering down through a jumble of boulders. You can almost hear the splintering of the great bolts of pine and maple as they bounced over this confusion of granite and spray, and imagine the ringing curses of the lumberjacks as the logs lodged once again.

Having spent its energy, the Skootamatta now settles down to a quieter pace, with only one small rapids until Hare Falls is reached. Short portages here and just above Storring's bridge bring you to a rural road. The conservation authority brochure describes an Indian corn grinding hole about 200 m east along the road, but in fact the hole is a classic example of a "kettle" created by the grinding action of boulders in the current of some ancient river.

With a couple of more drops the river now descends onto the ancient metasedimentary (meta = changed) rocks. The banding characteristic of gneiss can be seen especially well at Varty's Rapids, where the Little Skootamatta adds its flow. This is also a good place to watch for marten; we spotted one near the top of the portage.

Below Varty's the character of the river changes as it enters a sandy plain left at the toe of the glacier. It now meanders through patches of farmland and camping sites are scarce, except for a commercial site 2 km before High Falls. The river has created many swampy backwaters as shifting sand bars build up on the inside of corners. In these quiet bayous, where silver maples line the shores, wood ducks and green herons are common. Many kinds of ferns are common here including ostrich, sensitive and the lovely royal fern.

After 8 km of quiet water, you reach the natural dam that has blocked the fall of the river at High Falls. Massive shoulders of granite have squeezed in on the valley here, and a tongue of volcanic rock from the west has added its influence as well. Through a break in this rock the Skootamatta tumbles noisily, creating drifts of foam in the pool below. The foam is not indicative of pollution but is simply the result of unusual aeration of the water.

A lift-over at the left end of the dam brings you to Hwy. 7, where you can take out. Just across the highway is the Price Conservation Area, which supplies picnic facilities but no camping.

ACTINOLITE TO VANDERWATER

The next 26 km to the Vanderwater Conservation Area requires from three to six portages, depending on water levels and your level of experience. As this is the country created by the Dummer moraine, most of the features you see are glacially related.

As you begin this section, you can muse on the rise and fall of Actinolite. In the mid-to-late 1800s this community, then known as Bridgewater, was a boom town, much larger than Tweed. It began with a sawmill but it was minerals that really shaped its growth. By 1865 marble quarries were operating near by, and lime was being burnt and exported. Later a small iron mine was opened in the vicinity and the Actinolite Roofing Works was established to exploit the fibrous asbestos-like material that gives the town its name.

But it was gold that fired the real boom for Bridgewater. In

August 1866 gold was discovered on a farm near Madoc, and gold fever swept across southern Ontario. Prospectors flooded into Hastings County; Bridgewater flourished. A large marble schoolhouse and church were built to service the doubled population. But four years later, as the gold proved elusive, only the speculators came away rich and the boom faded into history.

The initial stretch of river below Hwy. 7 is a bit tricky. After a short carry through the conservation area, you can put in near the old dam abutments. (The footbridge mentioned in the Moira River Conservation Authority brochure is no longer there, having been swept away twice now by high spring flows and ice.) A paddle across the river will bring you to a longer carry on the right, across the Actinolite road and below the rapids. Alternately you can carefully run the first set of rapids and take out just above the bridge on the left. Cross over the bridge and follow a steep trail on the right side of the river to a pool. There are good examples here of metamorphosed sedimentary rocks; the fracturing into layers can be clearly seen.

The river is now following an old glacial spillway so that the layer of soil and gravel is much deeper over the rocks. On your right you can see through the pines an esker that has been exploited for gravel, taking advantage of the well-sorted layers laid down by glacial water rushing through a crack in the ice. Much of this area of deeper soils around the junction with the Moira River has been planted with pine and spruce since it provides ideal growing habitat for these trees.

Several sets of abandoned bridge abutments in this area, well grown over with trees, are all that remain of the Bannockburn railway, constructed in the 1890s to serve Actinolite and points to the northwest during the mining boom. Experienced canoeists can usually run the several sets of rapids between here and Tweed, though an excellent campsite halfway down Squatting Bear rapids is worth checking. At the top of this rapid the "young" sedimentary rock, only 440 million years or so old, makes its first appearance. Reddish shaley banks occur in several spots, even though Precambrian rocks are still found in the same area. This is part of the outlier of limestone that forms a rough circle between here and Tweed. The limestone is better seen just below the dam in Tweed.

At Tweed the dam is best approached on the left, where a determined effort in high water will allow a short carry to the turbulent waters below (steer clear of the dangerous area at the base of dam). It is safer and perhaps easier to cross the footbridge

The quiet lower stretches of the Moira provide pleasant camping in a rural setting. **Ron Reid**

and carry your canoe below the mill for put-in. The Conservation Authority now recommends that the rapids here not be attempted and that you carry through the streets of town to Stoco Lake. Experienced whitewater paddlers, however, will find the rapids shallow but runnable in late spring.

A 2-km paddle across Stoco Lake is the only open water of the trip. There seems to be some debate between the geologists and geomorphologists about whether Stoco Lake is held back by the edge of the limestone plain or by glacial drift dumped into its exit valley. In any case the bedrock here is once again clearly Precambrian, glinting pinkly in the sun, and a tongue of these older rocks is exposed for 5 km downstream along the river.

Except for some excellent stands of soft maple forest, the well-cottaged route along the east side of Sugar Island has little to recommend it. The west channel, which is swampier but shallower, may be better if water levels are high enough to get you through. Although Sugar Island is now mostly farmland, it drew its name from the stands of great maples that once stood there, tapped each spring by the Indians for maple sugar.

Several sets of rapids later, the river rejoins, and almost immediately divides again in the Lost Channel area. Expert paddlers will enjoy the left channel, after a short portage at the old dam site at the top. The rest of us can work our way down the right, lining and lifting in several spots. Don't take the tempting middle channel—we did, and it led us through an old mill site that took several hours to negotiate!

The mill site in the centre of the island is worth a look though, if you pull out at the bridge and walk back along the road. Constructed in 1850 using machinery recovered from a Tweed mill that had washed into Stoco Lake, this mill (actually a series of five) was once a major centre of commerce.

Below Lost Channel, the Moira settles down to a more orderly pace across the gravelly moraine and sand plain that leads to the Vanderwater Conservation Area. From the trees along the river, northern orioles sing their syrupy song and hide their brilliant orange and black amazingly well among the few leaves at the top of the trees. Watch for pileated woodpeckers as well, crow-sized birds with a scarlet crest and white flashes along the wing. These shy woodpeckers normally obtain their food by hammering square-shaped holes into the heart of rotting trees; but we watched one feeding the lazy way, picking emerging blackflies off a waterside branch with sedate licks of his bristly tongue.

Vanderwater Conservation Area, directly east of Thomasburg, provides self-guided nature trails and picnic sites but no longer has provisions for camping.

VANDERWATER TO CANNIFTON

The first 4 km of this 28-km section are bounded by the wooded bends of the Vanderwater Conservation Area. On the west side of the river a shallow limestone plain provides the first extensive areas of Black River limestone. About halfway down the conservation area, a ragged shelf of this limestone extends across the river, requiring a short portage or lining.

Just before Chisholm the vegetation of two limestone islands show the changes here from the Shield. The untidy trunks of shagbark hickory are common. For the first time you also see a few scattered eastern red cedar trees, a member of the juniper family whose fragrant wood was used in the pencil trade. French settlers called this tree "baton rouge" or red stick, eventually giving the name to the state capital of Louisiana.

The next 8 km of rapids, from Chisholm to Latta, should be run only by experienced whitewater paddlers during high water. By summer, low water has reduced the danger but increased the difficulty as well, for shallow spots may have to be waded. A limestone ledge just around the first bend requires special caution, but most of the rapids are based on bouldery till and provide more chop than drop.

This section of the river cuts into a shallow till plain, littered with low glacial hills called drumlins. About 5 km down, the nature of the underlying limestone changes as the river passes into the Trenton limestone group. This rock is softer and more broken, with many layers and holes where the rock has been dissolved. The best example of this karst topography that we have ever seen is at the Scuttle Holes, where dissolution has produced a series of underground caves and channels. Follow the left branch of the river around the large islands to the southern tip of the channel, where a clamber up the bank will bring you to the holes.

The first thing you may notice here is that a good deal of the river's water is flowing through the collapsed caverns. Nearby in the karst area, a system of caves includes the Moira Cave, regarded as the largest in eastern Canada. The Moira cave is used for hibernation by five species of bats and has the largest hibernating population of little brown bats anywhere in southern Ontario.

Around the Scuttle Holes small hackberry trees attest to the southern influences here, and rye and wild garlic suggest that this area may have been an Indian campsite. Local legend has it that Indians fled down into the caves with a booty of gold, and that neither the Indians nor the gold were ever seen again!

The old stone mill at Latta provides another short portage and a good view of rounded Precambrian boulders left by the glaciers as "erratics" on the limestone pavement along the shore. By 1836 this dam supported a grist mill at one end and a sawmill at the other. The old grist mill is now well on its way to becoming a ruin, but note the unusual stone arches at the base of the building.

Below Plainfield a grassy knoll on the southeast side of the pool below the rapids provides a good campsite on Conservation Authority land. It is possible to leave the river at a boat ramp at the side of Hwy. 37 just downstream from here. Otherwise the next 13 km are flatwater canoeing, with a fringe of soft maple swamp and an increasing number of houses along the river's edge. As the river cuts across the gently rolling till plain, it passes the Thurlow Wildlife Area at the mouth of Chrysal Creek, a good area for waterbirds.

Corbyville provides another take-out point, or a short portage around the weir. The extensive buildings of the distillery on the banks of the river here date back to 1859, just two years after Henry Corby opened a grist mill on the site. An excellent historical brochure is available at the visitor's centre beside the river, and tours can be arranged.

The river now drops over the steps of a shallow limestone plain , and rapids are frequent for the last kilometre to the bridge at Cannifton. This marks the end of the trip, since the difficult rapids from here to the mouth are suitable only for whitewater enthusiasts with empty canoes in the spring.

National Topographic System Maps
1:50,000 scale: 31C/3, C/6, C/11, C/14

Ministry of Natural Resources Office
Box 70, Tweed, K0K 3J0

Skootamatta-Moira River – Map 1

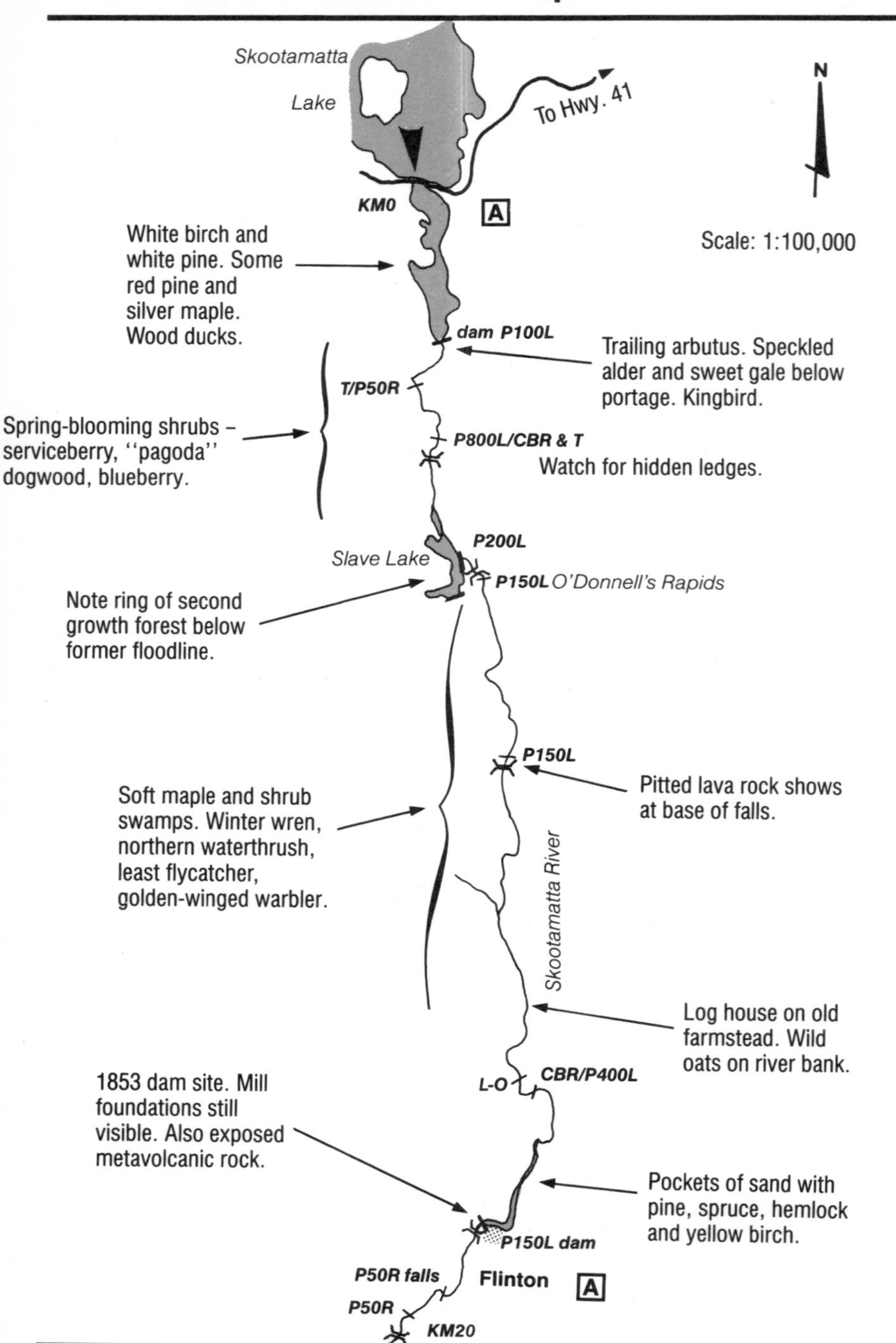

Ref: N.T.S Map 31C/11, 31C/14, 1:50,000

Skootamatta-Moira River – Map 2

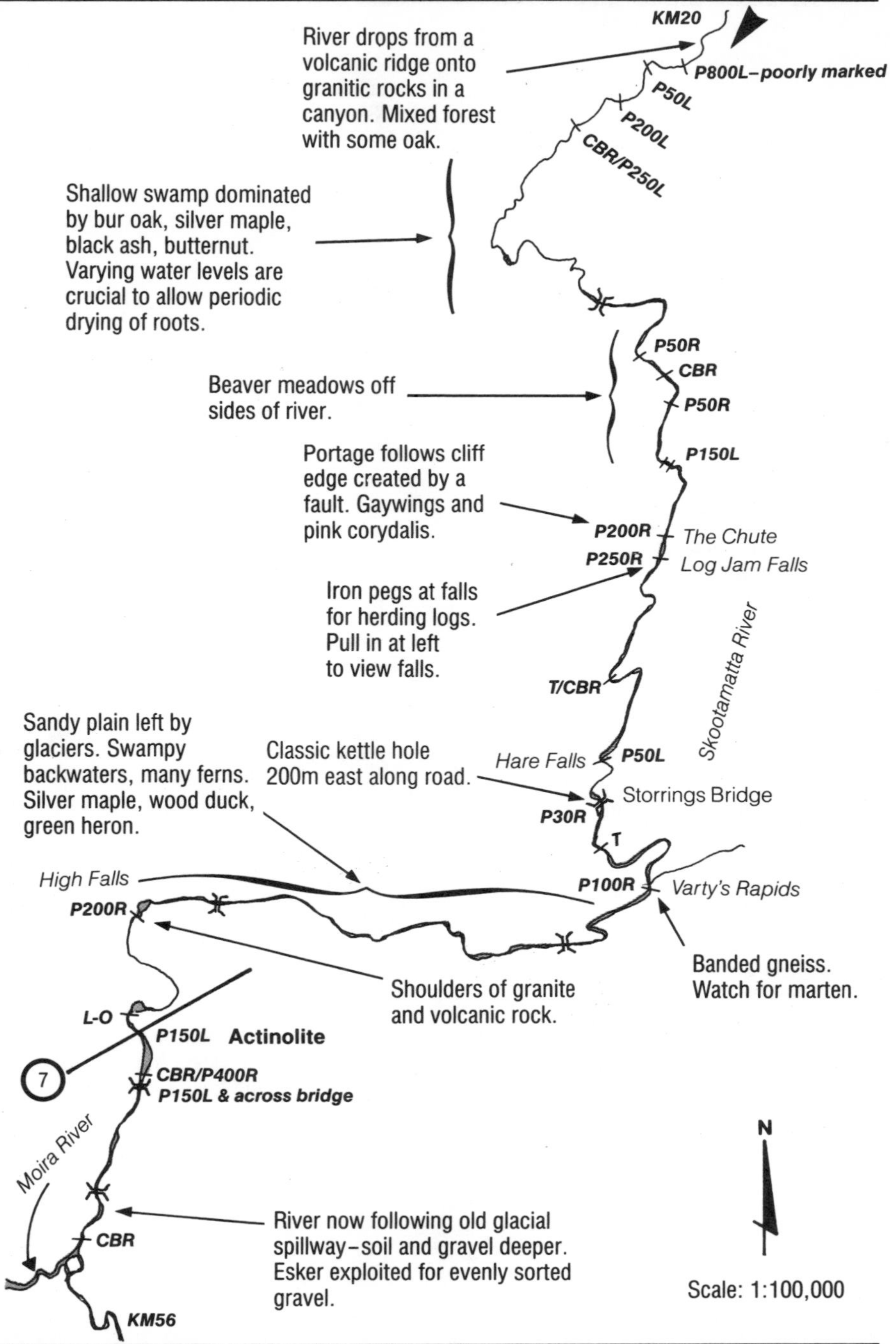

Ref: N.T.S Map 31C/11, 1:50,000

Skootamatta-Moira River – Map 3

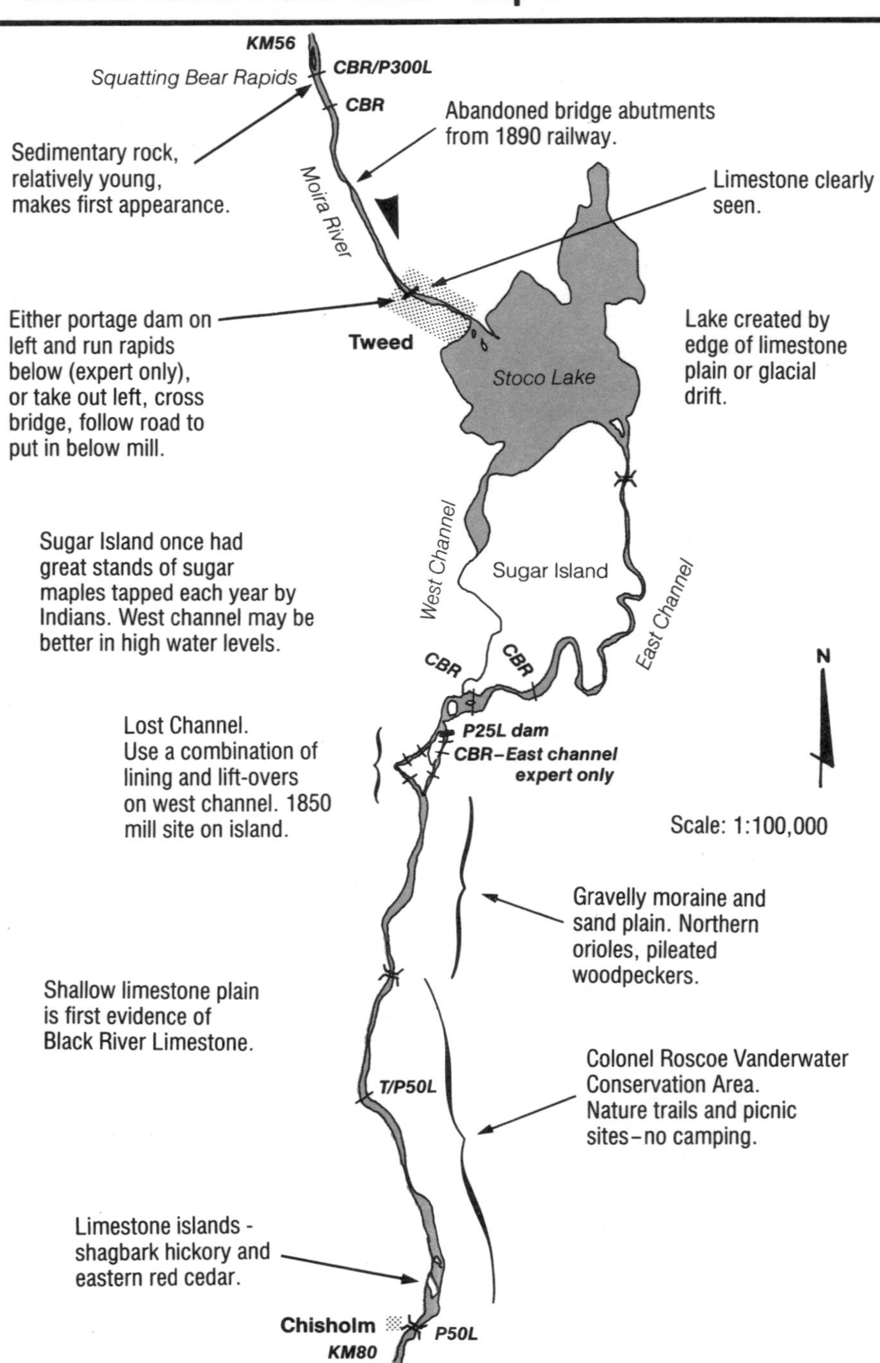

Ref: N.T.S Map 31C/6, 1:50,000

Skootamatta-Moira River–Map 4

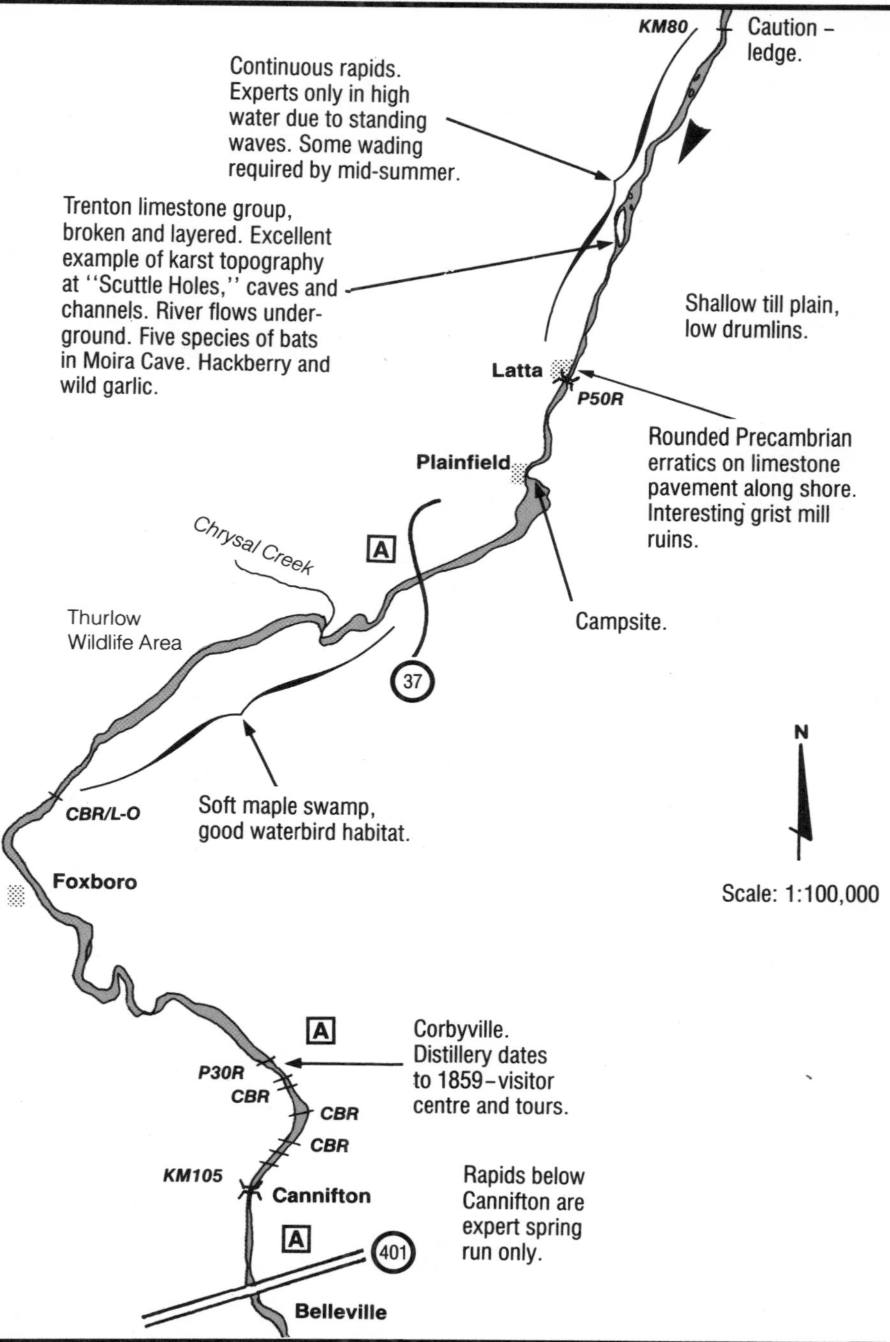

Ref: N.T.S Map 31C/6, 31C/3, 1:50,000

Other Rivers in Farm Country

Most southern Ontario rivers are at their best in late spring when water levels are still moderately high. Shallow water is not the only canoeing hazard—barbed wire fences to enclose cattle also cross some rivers and require a careful approach. Most of the land is private along these rivers, so take care to respect the rights of the owners.

Several small rivers in the heart of farm country provide relatively easy spring trips. The Maitland, in a 72-km trip from Wingham to Goderich, presents a variety of quiet stretches and rapids. Near its mouth the river passes through a 50-m-deep valley with steep clay banks and sections of exposed limestone. This route is described in a brochure available from the Ministry of Natural Resources, R.R. 5, Wingham, N0G 2W0.

Further north in Grey County, the Beaver River enjoys a dramatic setting in a notch of the Niagara Escarpment. A 20-km route from Kimberley to Heathcote passes through a large silver maple swamp with excellent wildlife viewing. Downstream from Heathcote, a further 13 km should be attempted only by experienced whitewater paddlers in early spring. A brochure is available from the Ministry of Natural Resources, 611 Ninth Ave. E., Owen Sound, N4K 3E4.

A 26-km route on the Nottawasaga River takes you past lime-rich marl lakes, sand dunes and sunken ships from the War of 1812. This is a particularly interesting river for history buffs, since it formed part of a major route from Lake Simcoe to Georgian Bay, linking up to the Toronto Portage. Further upstream, Minesing Swamp provides spring canoeing in a unique biological area, although care is needed to avoid getting lost. A brochure is available from the Ministry of Natural Resources, Midhurst, L0L 1X0.

A longer route can be followed on the Grand River, draining south into Lake Erie. A series of conservation areas permit camping for a four-day trip from the Elora Gorge to the river mouth. Along the way you will pass many historic sites in the towns that line the valley, as well as more natural sections of excellent Carolinean forest. A guidebook titled *Canoeing on the Grand River* is available from the Grand River Conservation Authority, Box 729, Cambridge, N1R 5W6.

In eastern Ontario several good routes lead from the edge of the Shield onto the farmland. The Indian River, from Stoney Lake to Rice Lake, passes two restored 19th century mills as well as dramatic cliffs and gorges. At one point the river disappears into an underground channel and a 500-m portage along the dry streambed is necessary. A brochure is available from the Otonabee Region Conservation Authority, 727 Lansdowne St. W., Peterborough, K9J 1Z2.

The Mississippi River provides an excellent eight-day trip from Bon Echo Provincial Park near its headwaters to the Ottawa River. The river is rich in history, from the pictographs on Bon Echo rock to the remains of logging slides and old mills along the lower river. A good brochure, titled "Pine Trees and Portages," is published by the Mississippi Valley Conservation Authority, Box 268, Lanark, K0G 1K0.

section 3

big pine country

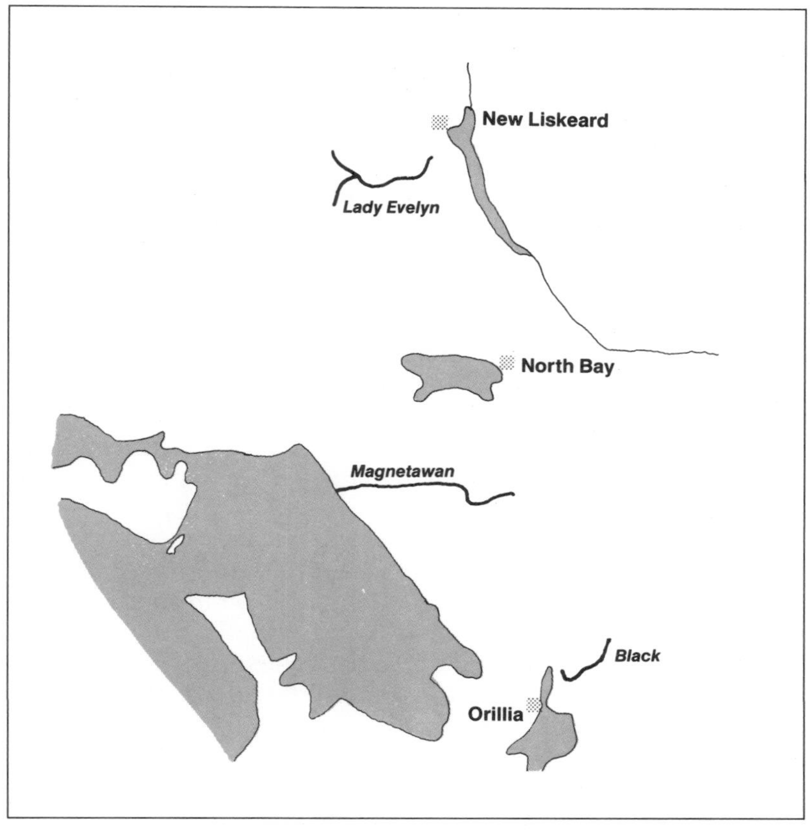

In a broad belt across the southern Shield, the glaciers left a mosaic of sand and stone, ideal conditions for groves of red and white pine. For the French voyageurs paddling across this landscape, the giant pines meant only occasional shelter for a camp or portage. But when the British took over the fledgling colony of Upper Canada, the pines became the foundation of an economy.

White pine, now Ontario's official tree, was the most sought after. On good soils, the feathery white pine would grow to 60 m and more, straight and true and free of knots. Such trees made masts for the Royal Navy, square timber for export and lumber for the new settlers. Pine wood had another desirable quality for these early loggers—it floated high and therefore was easy to herd downriver.

So it was that the rivers became the highways of this early industry. Armed with axes and adzes, crosscut saws and peaveys, the loggers swept first up the valley of the Ottawa, fanning westwards and north along its tributaries. By the 1870s the focus began to shift to the rivers of Georgian Bay, which by the turn of the century boasted a mill at virtually every river mouth. Later still, the lumbermen sought the last of the big pine in more northern watersheds.

All too soon the big pine was exhausted, and the commerce based on virgin pine shrivelled. The era of skidding trails and river drives ended as suddenly as it began, with the Dirty Thirties finishing off the last of the stragglers. But the memories of logging in a more romantic age can be found in the names along the rivers, and in the ruins of old shanties, timber slides and boom chains that line their banks.

The Magnetawan: Memories of a Logging Boom

"Daylight in the swamp!" Such was the morning call sung out by the surly cooks in the logging shanties along the Magnetawan. For 30 years and more, from 1870 to the early 1900s, this 4 a.m. refrain rang out along the river as the great forests were stripped away to build the cities of the American midwest.

In the short span of a few decades, the woods fell back before the ring of the timberman's axe, the squeal of heavily loaded sleighs on a frosty winter road, the roar and tumble of logs catapulting down a swollen spring river. Finally the last hill of virgin timber was felled, the loggers moved relentlessly on to some other frontier and the Magnetawan valley fell silent again.

Today the resilient forests have regrown, and you can paddle down the Magnetawan through a landscape that bears little resemblance to the wasteland left by the loggers. The river begins in the rolling, thickly wooded highlands of Algonquin. About 110 km downriver and 125 m lower, you will find yourself among the thin woodlands bordering Georgian Bay, with the bare pinkish whalebacks of the Thirty Thousand Islands just offshore.

Although an uninterrupted trip down the Magnetawan from Burk's Falls to the mouth can be rewarding, for most canoeists this is a river of parts. The upper stretch is a flatwater paddle, suitable for those relatively new to canoeing, where the tang of wilderness is largely replaced by the tamer flavour of cottage country. Then come "The Chutes," a long series of rapids and falls that make a fine playground for kayakers but usually mean a chain of challenging portages for canoeists. In its lower third, the river links up with more popular canoe routes, as part of several loops that can provide a diverse wilderness experience without the usual access difficulties.

The Magnetawan is a good summer river, though some might prefer its upper stretches in June or September, when the motorboat fraternity is less active. Most of the land along the upper half is private, and campsites there are sparse, but the lower half is mainly Crown land with many good camping spots. In any case, we found people along the river friendly and cooperative to canoeists, provided that you approach them in the same spirit.

A Land of Birch and Pine

A geologist would tell you that most of the Magnetawan valley is underlain by clastic metasediments, which might not leave you much the wiser. Simply put, that means these rocks were created by an accumulation of sand and other particles (hence the term clastic) about 2000 million years ago. Later these sedimentary rocks were metamorphosed, or changed, by tremendous forces of heat and pressure. Many of the resulting colour-banded rocks are classed as gneiss, but in some areas, such as in the vicinity of Britt, pinkish granite bedrock is common as well.

Much of the drainage pattern of central Ontario is controlled by the warping of these ancient rocks, creating a huge dome centred in Algonquin Park. The Magnetawan flows off the west side of this dome, against the direction of its waters' eventual destination in the sea. The orientation of the river in many areas is also controlled by extensive faulting in the rocks, where massive chunks of rock have subsided along a break line. This complex pattern of faults, which can be seen in many places along the river, has also created the odd elongated and cross-shaped lakes characteristic of this area.

The glaciers have left little mark on this landscape. Most of their action here was scraping, carrying away the thin covering of soil to areas further south. As well, all of the river valley from Burk's Falls west was submerged during the Lake Algonquin stage, so there was little opportunity for the creation of beach or shoreline features. In the area between Burk's Falls and the town of Magnetawan, a small clay plain developed in the floor of that lake, and a poorly developed sand plain reaching down to Britt from the north probably marks some ancient delta. Otherwise evidence of the retreat of the glaciers is restricted to small till deposits in the Maple Island area.

The hardwood forests of the eastern sections of the valley make this one of the most colourful areas of the province in the autumn.

Extensive stands of sugar maple and yellow birch associate with smaller numbers of basswood, beech, hemlock, and red and white pine. As soils become thinner in the Georgian Bay area, most of the hardwoods die out, and pine and hemlock become dominant. On bare ridges and very shallow soils, stunted red oak and jack pine may be the only trees tough enough to survive.

Wildlife in this part of Ontario is relatively rich, since forests are extensive enough to support northern species such as moose and marten, while the mixed deciduous-coniferous nature of the forest encourages southern species as well. Some animals are relative newcomers. White-tailed deer were unknown here until the 1880s, when loggers and the first settlers had opened the canopy enough to grow winter browse. In recent years moose have been making a comeback in central Ontario as the forest matures again.

Moose are unlikely to take over completely so long as the deer remain, however. In the 1960s wildlife researchers finally unravelled the mystery of "moose staggers," a fatal disease that appears only where deer and moose ranges overlap. The culprit is a tiny brainworm which passes its eggs down the bloodstream and out with the feces of the moose. A snail acts as an intermediate host, and the larvae are picked up again by the unfortunate moose in feeding. The worms can develop in deer as well but are only fatal to moose. Thus, when dense populations of the two animals come together, the deer act as a constant reservoir of reinfection, and the moose eventually are thinned out.

Abundant bird life also takes advantage of the mixed forests along the Magnetawan, with 200 species recorded for Grundy Provincial Park just to the north. For fishermen the river provides good sport, with bass, pike and pickerel throughout the watershed.

Sawmills and Settlers

While the Magnetawan no doubt served as a local travel corridor for prehistoric Indians and early traders, it does not seem to have played a major role in early history. Its potential was not forgotten, however. As early as 1837, demands for a canal between Georgian Bay and the Ottawa prompted a look at the Magnetawan and Petawawa as one of three possible routes. Upper Canada's Deputy Surveyor, William Hoskins, travelled these rivers but concluded that they were too narrow for the proposed canal project. The canal idea was to resurface periodically for the next 120 years, but

The steamship "Wanita" was one of many to carry visitors and goods along the Magnetawan early this century.

Public Archives Canada/C-38430

the Magnetawan was never again considered for such a use.

Some parts of the river, however, have felt the throb of steamboats. In 1879 the 34-foot *Pioneer* was launched at Burk's Falls to become the first of many steamboats to trace the river to the village of Magnetawan. A few years later, locks were constructed at Magnetawan to allow traffic all the way to Ahmic Lake. This service from the railhead at Burk's Falls to outlying settlements continued to 1934; in the first part of this century, the shuttling steamboats passed through the locks an average of 704 times every year.

The surrounding lands had been surrendered by the Indians as part of the massive Robinson Treaty in 1859, but it was not until 1868 that the first sawmill on the river was constructed at Magnetawan. By 1873 the Rosseau-Nipissing road had been pushed through in an ill-fated attempt to encourage settlement, and by the 1880s Purdy's flour mill was grinding away at the village as well.

The opening of the southern Shield for agricultural settlement in the 1870s and '80s must rank as one of the most monumental mismatches between bureaucratic hopes and the hard facts of life that Ontario has witnessed. Based on optimistic and inaccurate surveys of the farming potential of the area, government agents pushed through settlement roads and promoted the recruitment of new settlers from the crowded countries of Europe with free land grants. Fresh off the boat, these new Canadians faced a combination of harsh winters and thin soils which thwarted their best efforts.

Most soon became discouraged and moved on, often to western Canada. One group which largely remained was a Swiss colony founded in the Magnetawan area by Elise von Koerber, a Canadian immigration agent of German origin. By 1877 her settlement numbered several hundred German-speaking Swiss, whose descendants to this day give the area a special flavour.

But it was lumbering that really signalled the beginnings of the modern era for the Magnetawan valley. By the 1860s the easily accessible stands of pine along the edge of Lake Ontario and in the Ottawa Valley were dwindling, and the loggers were casting their eyes northward. The Magnetawan became one of the many rivers that transported the spoils of the forest down to the Bay for sawing or for transport to more distant markets. At first logs were floated in great rafts to the mills of Michigan, but in 1898 the Ontario legislature finally gave in to growing cries of indignation about the exports and ordered that all logs cut on Crown property must be sawn in Ontario.

Some mills had already been active for years. Prominent among these were the three at Byng Inlet, just across from the present town of Britt. In 1890 these mills cut more timber than any other point on Georgian Bay. The community here was so important that no fewer than three steamers, including one named the *Magnettawan*, competed for its trade with Owen Sound, Collingwood and Sault Ste. Marie.

All this mattered little to the logger in the bush. His annual routine was simple—cut logs and build roads in the fall, haul logs by sleigh to the edge of the winter ice and ride the spring freshet down the river to guide the logs to the mouth. This dangerous river drive was assisted by pointer boats, propelled by oars and with long upward-pointed bows and sterns to help ride up over the logs. It was a devil of a task—often the bravest (or most foolhardy) man of the crew would be called upon to pick out the key log of a jam and start the whole mass moving downstream again. Perhaps it's no coincidence that many of the bushmen were French, descendants of the hardy voyageurs.

Most of the logs to come downriver were pine, for the big

hardwoods were too heavy to float well to distant mills. Only with the coming of the railways and local sawmills would the big maple and birch become significant in the timber trade. All too soon the boom was over. In 1905, even then the declining years of the trade, the Parry Sound district produced 200 million board feet of lumber; in 1962 the equivalent yield was only 25 million.

Exploring the River

We suggest that a full Magnetawan trip will take an experienced canoeist five or six days depending on water levels. Of course, you can paddle only sections of the river, and the stretch from Wahwashkesh Lake to Miner Lake is often incorporated into loop routes beginning at the Harris Lake access point off Hwy. 69.

BURK'S FALLS TO HWY. 124

This first 36 km of canoeable river has very little fall and can provide a pleasant introduction for novice paddlers. A public dock beside Hwy. 520 in Burk's Falls makes a convenient put-in point, and the Ontario Provincial Police just south of town can provide useful suggestions on where to leave your car for extended periods. Before you push off downstream, you can take a quick look at the Burk's Falls dam, first used as a power source for a local sawmill in 1885 and site of a local electrical generator from 1923 to 1960.

You now follow the historic steamship route through low swampland for the next 14 km. You will see little exposed rock here; a mantle of clay soils and, in some areas, the mat of decayed vegetation that makes up organic soils cover the bedrock. These relatively rich soils support a lush growth of wetland vegetation, with soft maple, black ash, white birch and white spruce especially common.

Along the edges of the water, watch for sweet gale, a low shrub with leaves that have coarse teeth only on the end and that emit a characteristic sweet smell when crushed. Speckled alder and red osier dogwood are also part of this shoreline vegetation, as are both the northern interrupted fern and the more southern cinnamon fern. One specialty plant found in the sheltered swampy inlets here is the wild calla, in which a broad white "petal" or spathe provides a dramatic backdrop for the club-shaped flower stem crowded with tiny yellow flowers.

This slow-moving area of the river also provides some of the best birdwatching of the trip, especially in the late spring. North-

The showy white "petal" of the wild calla is actually a modified bract; the roots and fruits of this member of the arum family contain a burning poison. **Hap Wilson**

ern orioles are particularly abundant, their orange and black plumage flashing as they race past en route from treetop singing perch to suspended pouch-like nest. Occasionally you may find a hooded merganser, a fish-eating duck that takes full advantage of its swampy habitat by nesting in holes in trees. And of course the flycatcher and warbler families are well represented here, feeding on the prolific insect life.

Just past the river crossing of Hwy. 520, a good stand of yellow birch shows you something of the way these forests might have been before the depredations of the logger. In fact the upper part of the Magnetawan canoe route passes some of the best yellow birch stands we have seen anywhere in Ontario. Much valued as furniture wood, this species seems to do better on granite-based acidic soils, while sugar maple grows better on alkaline ground. Even so, yellow birch regeneration often loses out to maple because its seeds are so tiny, over 3 million to a kilogram.

At the entrance to Midlothian Lake lies a curious formation. Instead of entering directly, the river runs parallel to the lakeshore for a considerable distance, separated by only a thin spit of sand. We speculated that perhaps the opposing actions of the lake waves and the river current combined to create this unusual deposit. In any case, another, larger sand spit between this lake and Cecebe presents the first opportunity for camping, at a commercial site.

Cecebe and Ahmic Lakes are typical Ontario cottage country, temperamental in a wind and short of suitable camp spots. However, a few islands provide camping for small parties, with a welcome breeze for fly control and loons near by to sing you to sleep. Along the maple-lined shores you can also admire the architecture of an elegant age of cottaging that sadly seems to have passed. Just before Magnetawan, another commercial campground on the north side of the river provides accommodation in a pinch.

Take the right channel approaching the town and you will see the locks in the centre of the channel dead ahead. The present locks, rebuilt in 1911, are still operated, and riding through a lock in a canoe is reason enough alone to do this part of the trip. The locks are hand-operated, or should we say bum-operated, for the gates are opened by the attendant pushing backwards against a large timber. Magnetawan also has a small museum in the old mill-house at the end of the dam, several historical plaques, and an access point just below the bridge where cars can be left.

As you enter Ahmic Lake, the island straight ahead displays another quirk of nature. Even though the surrounding hills are forested in white pine and maple, with hemlock and yellow birch along the lake edges, this island is treed heavily with red pine. As you gaze at the rough reddish bark and clumped upward-pointing needles that mark red pine, can you avoid asking why, especially why only on this one island? The answer may lie in deeper better soils on the island, but more likely a different fire history is the answer. Logged-over lands, with their accumulation of dead slash, are notoriously prone to wildfire, but even a widespread fire on the mainland would likely miss this island.

As you come onto Ahmic Lake, you may also notice the "bath-tub ring" effect, with all the lower branches of the trees neatly pruned several metres above the water. This is the browse line, created by deer that winter in such sheltered areas. Deer need twigs and cedar leaves for nutrition, and when a combination of deep snows and forests growing out of reach caused a shortage of browse in the late 1950s, deer in central Ontario starved to death by the thousands. The herds in this area have never recovered from that crisis, although white-tails are still the most common wild herbivore.

Ahmic Lake seems to have been designed in such a way that it is impossible to avoid a head wind part of the time, though we still haven't figured out how we could have a head wind *all* the time on such a twisty lake. Nonetheless, after you have struggled your way into the northwest section, take the right-hand channel to Knoefli Falls. An abandoned roadway at the right side of the dam leads to a 100-m portage, and the end of this section of the river.

HWY. 124 TO WAHWASHKESH LAKE

Most of the Magnetawan's drop occurs in this 28-km section, and the resulting series of rapids means frequent portages. As it narrows to a river again, the change in character in the Magnetawan is quickly obvious. The river banks now are lined with hemlock and yellow birch, and these cool woods provide ideal habitat for such northern wildflowers as Clintonia, often called bluebead because of its bright blue seeds, and starflower, whose star-shaped blooms are matched by leaves in a similar pattern beneath. Bunchberry is here as well, its showy white bloom and red cluster of berries glowing in the gloom.

The first two sets of rapids along the route come in duets. At the Poverty Bay Chutes the river drops over the edge of a fault, the line of which extends westward through Love Lake and the top section of Whitestone Lake. A small cabin on the left marks the start of a 200-m portage, and a little further on another portage on the left takes 300 m to bypass the rapid. This trail features lots of hobblebush, easily recognized by its opposite heart-shaped leaves that ascend the sprawling stem like stair-steps. The common name for this shrub is derived from its ability to grow new roots from the tip of its stalk, thereby creating living loops to trip you up.

At Seller Rapids the glaciers left a heap of well-rounded boulders in the valley, and the river presents quite a different character. The first of this set can be portaged 75 m on the right, or might be lineable in low water. The second, however, is dangerous, and you should start the 300-m portage on the right well upstream from the fast water heading down the chute. In this area the forests are

The lower end of Seller Rapids tumbles over well-rounded boulders left by the glaciers. **Ron Reid**

mostly dryland hardwoods, with sugar maple, beech and yellow birch heading the list.

Another small cabin on the right announces the start of the 350-m portage around Ross Rapids. The river plunges through a rocky gut here, while the portage trail leads over a clay hill where partridgeberry, foamflower and broad-leaved aster distract your attention from the load on your back.

Just past the Magnetawan Whitewater Resort, an unnamed rapids demands either a 500-m portage, or a shorter 200-m carry if you are experienced enough to carefully run the first half of the rapid. Just downstream, the square canyon of Cody Rapids marks another local fault, necessitating a 250-m carry on the left side across the road and down a cottage laneway. Porter Rapids are smaller and can often be run or lined, though a 150-m portage trail is available on the left.

As you approach the gravelly hill that marks Maple Island, the nature of the valley becomes more southern with a soft maple swamp that you must negotiate. The left channel provides a good short cut, though the longer right channel would provide better access to the road in case of need.

Burnt Chutes would seem to be well named, for the area surrounding their entrance is covered in poplar and white birch,

Alligator tugs could walk themselves awkwardly across portages; their main use was winching spring log booms across large lakes.

Archives of Ontario/S.4852

both species that do well after a fire. These trees are called pioneers because of their ability to thrive in full sunlight in areas disturbed by fire or clearing. Later the shade-loving species characteristic of the more mature forests in this area, such as maple and yellow birch, will spring up in the shelter of these pioneers.

Upper Burnt Chute can sometimes be safely run but is otherwise portaged 200 m on the right; the Lower Chute must be portaged 750 m on the left. On the rocky hills next to the rapids, a good stand of the feathery white pine typifies the more coniferous forests that are beginning to occur as you head west.

The final couplet of rapids is the Needles Eye, where the layered rocks squeeze the river into narrow canyons. The first short drop runs fast and deep, and can be easily run, but the second series twists its way through a zigzag break in the rocks and must be portaged 800 m on the left. One final short carry past Lovesick Rapids and the easterly end of Wahwashkesh Lake is reached.

With its rocky, breezy shores and only a scattering of cottages, Wahwashkesh Lake is a good spot for a little relaxing and fishing. During the logging era the lake must have presented a different picture, with tugs pulling up to 25,000 logs across its expanse at a single go. Originally the "tug" was a large raft known as a capstan crib, on which a horse walked round and round to wind in the three-inch tow rope. Later the steam-boiler "alligator" tug became a common sight.

Basic provisions are available in the Indian Narrows area of the lake, and a public access road leads from there back east to Hwy. 520.

WAHWASHKESH LAKE TO BRITT

This 42-km section of the river is relatively well travelled thanks to a Ministry of Natural Resources canoe route loop which links up with Naiscoot Lake to the southwest. It includes some very pretty canoe country, mostly in small lakes and rivers that are suitable for beginning canoe trippers. Unfortunately it also includes several long portages, which caused us to wonder on occasion if this shouldn't be known as the Magnetawan Hiking Trail.

The toughest part of this section is near the beginning, to bypass the famous Canal Rapids, although some experts have been known to run this difficult set. At the very end of Deep Bay you will see the dock and buildings of the Deep Bay Hunt Club, where the portage starts. This is one of the largest of the many hunt clubs along the river, which in 1983 blocked plans to establish this area as a wilderness park by their vociferous protests.

Following a rough road for 1800 m brings you to the foot of Canal Rapids. This is one of the few visible sections of the old tote road which once paralleled the river all the way from Magnetawan to Byng Inlet. Established by timber operators in 1868, the bush road was the lifeline for several lumber camps until 1915, when cutting along the river ended.

At the end of the portage take a look back upstream at the Canal. With its square-cut rock banks reaching 15 m into the air, you might well imagine that this canyon had been made by man, but for the boiling waters below. How the adrenalin must have flowed when the logs jammed here and a logger had to be lowered over the cliffs on a rope to pick apart the jam!

You can follow the road for another 500 m to carry past Graves Rapids as well, or paddle downstream a little way until you reach another 200-m trail on the right. There is said to be a graveyard for river drivers drowned in the rapids here, but the rapids' name was more likely derived from one of the local timber companies, Graves, Bigwood, and Co.

The reward for all your work is Trout Lake, with its mosaic of rocky islands, inlets and points seemingly designed with a canoeist in mind. As you select a campsite among the red and white pines, watch for no fewer than three species of honeysuckle that thrive here. All are shrubs with opposite leaves, but in the common wild honeysuckle the top leaves are united to form a bracket for the orangy flowers. You may see only the smooth rounded leaves of fly honeysuckle, since the twin yellow blossoms occur in early spring. However, the tubular flowers of bush honeysuckle are common in early summer, along with distinctly toothed leaves which identify it.

You can continue to follow the North Branch of the Magnetawan through Island Lake, past Carve Island, where the loggers held up by westerly winds would whittle replicas of birds and animals. This route requires several portages, including one 2380 m long around Thirty Dollar Rapids, where the dollar-a-day loggers lost a full month's pay to some massive jam.

Our choice was to follow the slightly longer South Branch, a more intimate route where the pine and white birch crowd the shores of the narrow river. Initially this route follows another bedrock fault, where cedar waxwings trill their busyness, curious ravens sweep down for a closer look at you and phoebes guard their nest beneath the shelter of an overhanging cliff. Only one portage is needed here, a 300-m trail on the right just past the Hydro lines.

The rocks in this area have been much smoothed by the glaciers, in some areas leaving bare whalebacked hummocks known as rock drumlins that are more characteristic of the Georgian Bay coast. Just past the junction with Big Bay, watch on the right for a small cliff that displays the tremendous forces that must have gone into the warping of this sedimentary rock. In a great S-shape, the rock shows both the downward trough known as a syncline and the opposite ridge shape called an anticline.

On the south shore of this branch, an inlet leads to the Harris Lake access point, linking up to Hwy. 69. To rejoin the main river, follow a 1370-m portage past three sets of rapids. In high water it is possible, though difficult, to line through these rapids, but in our experience the portage trail will be easier on both your equipment and your temper.

The portage brings you out onto Miner Lake, where campsites are abundant. As the soil grows thinner, for the first time now we begin to see jack pine, as well as groves of stunted red oak. In these shallow acid soils, sweetfern also makes an appearance, its slender lobed leaves and woody stems emitting a pleasant spicy odour.

As the river begins its final descent through the Magnetawan Indian Reserve, four sets of rapids are presented in quick succession. The first three can be passed by relatively short portages, while the fourth is smaller and can usually be run. Just under the Hwy. 69 bridge, the river kicks up its heels for a final time before subsiding into Georgian Bay, and a cautious look is required before running through.

All that remains of the giant sawmills of Byng Inlet now are a few foundations and one old chimney. Along the river banks, however, you can spy the great iron pegs and rings bolted into the rock that were used as anchors for the log booms catching the winter's harvest coming downriver. There are several campsites and stores to serve you in the Britt area. One of the best is the New Magnetawan Hotel, on the north bank of the river, whose Scottish owners offer the best of hospitality.

Byng Inlet reaches eastward like a fiord to receive the waters of the Magnetawan, and the remaining 6 km to the Bay can give you a taste of the Thirty Thousand Islands, themselves a canoeing treat for those with the patience to wait out the weather. At the mouth of the Inlet, a picnic site on Clark Island makes a relaxing lunch spot. Just off to the southwest, on the tip of Gereaux Island, you can see one of the historic lighthouses that guard this part of the Bay. An American sailor named H.L. Hurley visited this lighthouse in 1898, and his description portrays a leisurely lifestyle that is still not unknown in this area:

"At the house we were directed to inquire at a boathouse near at hand by a stout, barefooted Frenchwoman. Upon opening the door we found the keeper, a most picturesque old child of the sea, reclining in a wonderful home-made hammock, smoking a short-stemmed pipe, and recounting early adventures to a black-eyed grandson. He acknowledged our arrival with easy unconcern, and in a few words of broken English made us feel quite at home."

National Topographic System Maps
Scale 1:125,000: Sundridge 31E/NW
Byng Inlet 41H/NE
Scale 1:50,000: 31E/11, E/12
41H/9, H/16, H/15

Ministry of Natural Resources Office
4 Miller St., Parry Sound, P2A 1S8

Magnetawan River – Map 1

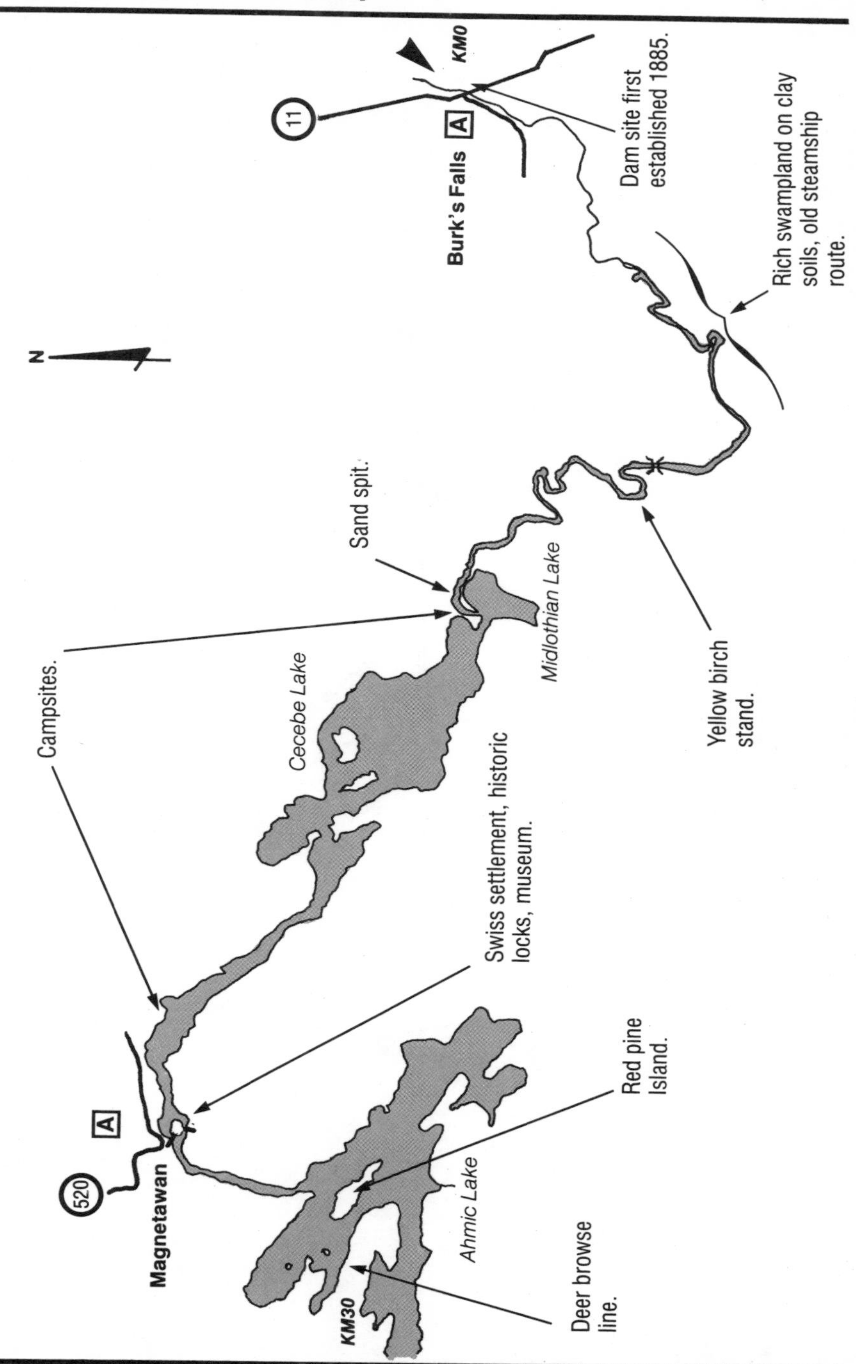

Ref: N.T.S. Map 31E/NW, 1:125,000

Magnetawan River – Map 2

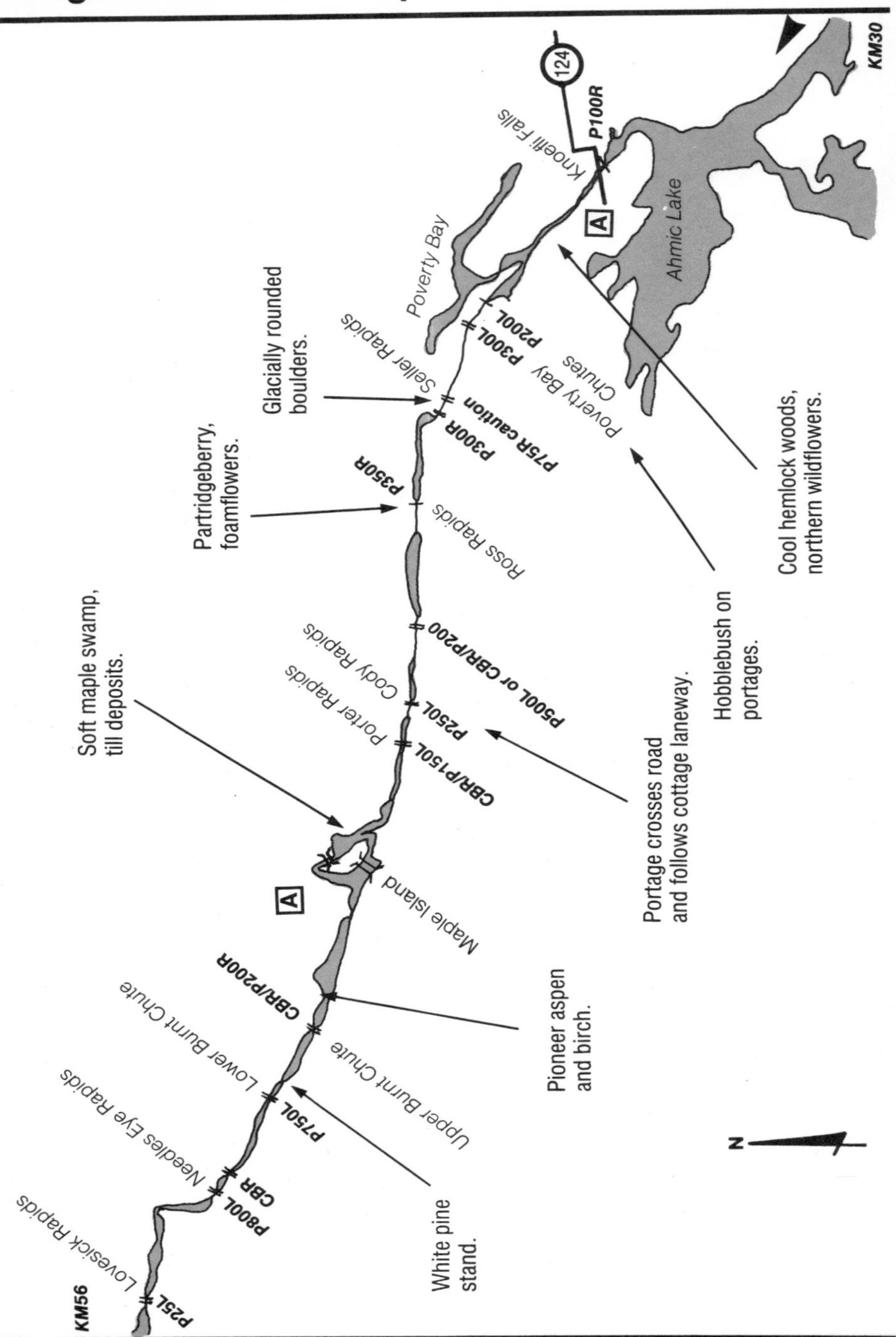

Ref: N.T.S. Map 31E/NW, 1:125,000

Magnetawan River – Map 3

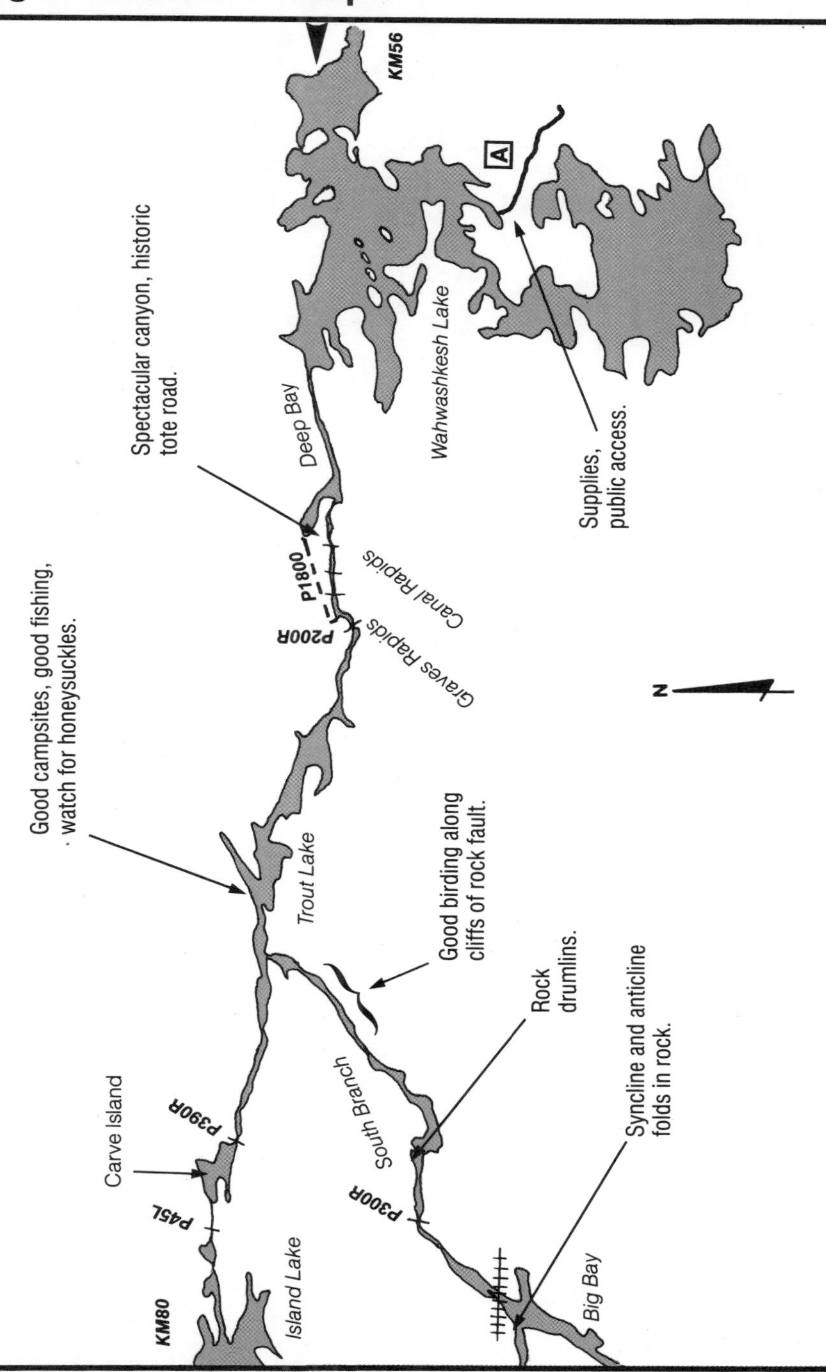

Ref: N.T.S. Map 41H/NE, 1:125,000

Magnetawan River – Map 4

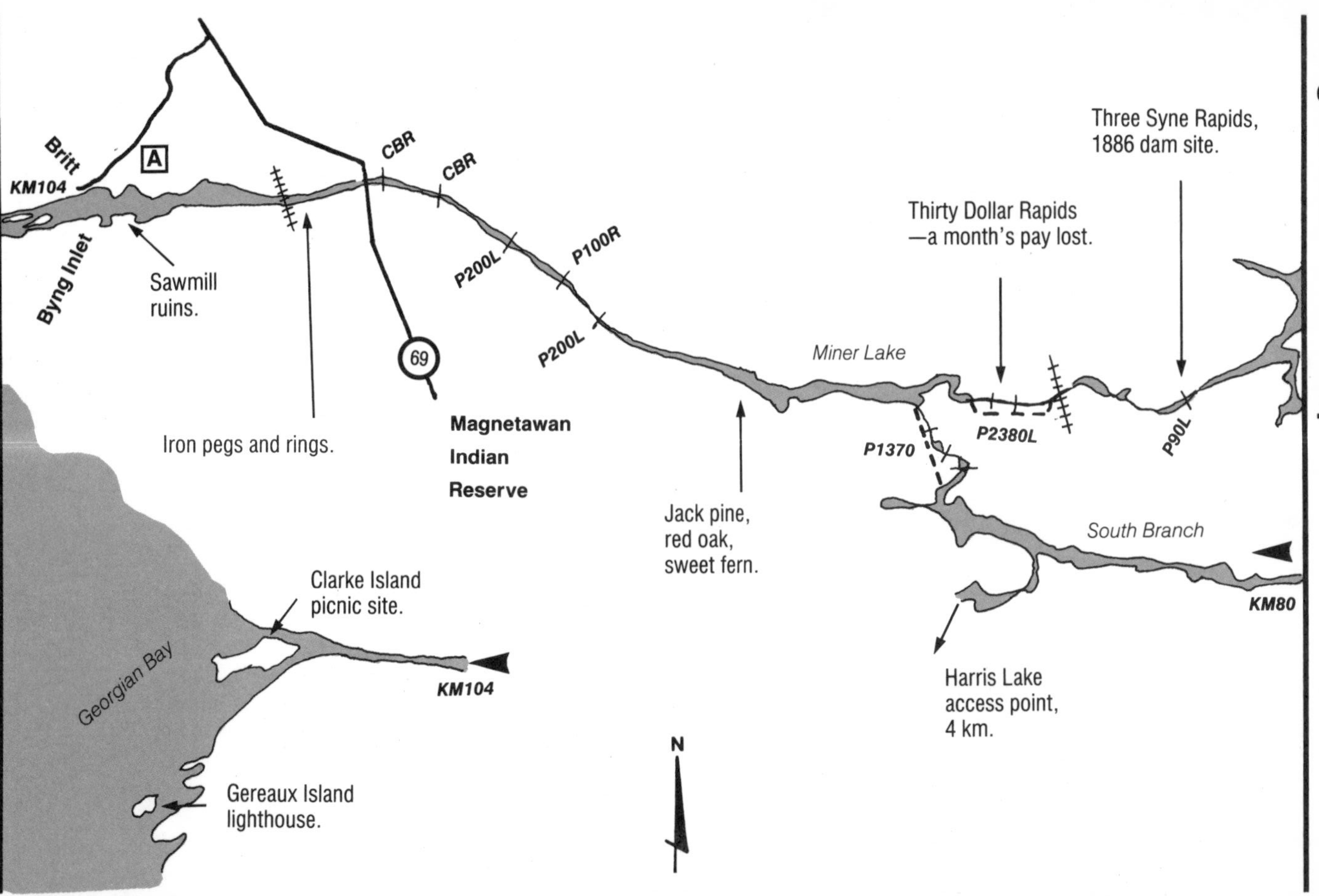

Ref: N.T.S. Map 41H/NE, 1:125,000

The Black: Forgotten Valley

Usually we think of the northern reaches of Ontario when we think of wilderness rivers, for the hand of man lies heavily on most waterways in the south. But here and there a river has escaped, hidden away among the inhospitable mounds of gneiss in the southern Shield. Often the natural character of these rivers has been protected more by oversight than by intent. Such is the case with the Black, nestled in the rocky country northeast of Lake Couchiching.

A local history of the townships surrounding the Black is called *The Land Between*, an accurate summary of its economic geography. Certainly the land and the rivers to the south have fallen under the wheel of "progress"—the mills and cottages of the Kawarthas, the long history of canals on the Trent and the Severn. To the north, cottage country has boomed over the lakes of Muskoka and Haliburton, lining the waterways with shacks and palaces. But the land between—the valley of the Black—has so far escaped most such developments.

Several factors have contributed to the quiet state of affairs along the Black. The valley had its pine—two-thirds of the original forest was white pine—but this dowry to economic development was squandered. When the loggers had stripped away the pine and whatever quality hardwoods they found convenient, they left no lasting developments in their wake. No new towns grew up along the Black; little land was found with soils deep enough to sustain permanent farms. Most of the crude roads built to service the logging were allowed to revert to the wilderness, and the valley slumbered once again.

A second factor played a more active role in protecting the

Black. Longford Township, one of the central townships along the river, is unusual in that it has been held continuously as a single block by various owners since its first sale in 1865. For the past 55 years it has been owned by an American company and maintained as a private hunting and recreational reserve. For this reason the 40 lakes in Longford, all part of the Black system, have not seen the intensive cottage development that otherwise would almost certainly have taken place.

The result of all this is a canoe route, barely two hours from Toronto, which provides an interesting and unspoiled natural setting for day or weekend trips. The Black River drops slowly, with few lengthy rapids, so it is an ideal trip for those who prefer flatwater or lack the experience to tackle more remote rivers. Since the Black holds its water well, it can be paddled at any time during the canoeing season, with the possible exception of late summer in dry years. In spring, however, the nature of the rapids changes dramatically, requiring more caution, and more portages, than those described here.

The route we outline here includes only the lower Black, from Victoria Falls to Hwy. 169, a distance of 30 km. The 25-km stretch from Vankoughnet southwards is also navigable by canoe, but its use is actively discouraged by the owners of the Longford Reserve. As well, it is possible to paddle through the more developed sections of the lower river to its junction with the Severn on the outskirts of Washago. This branch of the Severn is known locally as the Green, for its clear, limestone-derived waters contrast strikingly with the dark, organically stained water of the Black.

Snappers, Skinks and Squirrels

Trickling southwesterly off the great Algonquin dome, the Black traverses banded Precambrian gneiss so characteristic of this area. It comes teasingly close to the boundary between these Shield rocks and the younger sedimentary limestones, but at the last moment turns west and refuses to leave its ancient hard-rock bosom. The glaciers scoured deeply in the valley of the Black, especially when their flow matched direction with the grain of the rock, leaving a landscape of rounded edges and smooth flowing lines.

In most of this region the glaciers left only a thin veneer of ground moraine. However, at one stage of the glacial retreat, the Black valley became a long bay of glacial Lake Algonquin. Sands

Flying squirrels, rarely seen by day, are easily identified by their large bulging eyes, soft grey fur, and loose folds of skin along the legs. **Hap Wilson**

and clay deposits laid down in that period are common along the riverside, providing a more varied and rich woodlands there than in the surrounding uplands.

On many of the scoured rocky hills, trees are sparse and scattered blueberries, juneberry and sumac form the main cover. These barrens are likely the result of irresponsible logging and repeated fires in its wake as much as the earlier action of the glaciers. If you search carefully here, you might find more unusual species, such as the delicate corydalis, blue harebells or nodding ladies' tresses, in wetter pockets.

On the sandy areas along the river the forests are now mostly second-growth deciduous, with white birch and largetooth aspen leading the way. On moister sites silver maple, bur oak and basswood are common trees; in drier areas the birch is joined by hard maple, white ash and red oak. These forests provide shelter for a rich assortment of shrubs and ferns, as well as a varied bird life including several warblers, vireos and sparrows.

The river bank itself often creates a special type of habitat. Watch for the scarlet blooms of cardinal flower late in the summer along muddy shores. Higher up, a hanging mat of roots and vegetation often includes mosses and liverworts as well as the common sensitive fern and the uncommon long beech fern.

The Black River is an excellent place to watch for flying squirrels, easily identified by their soft grey fur, loose folds of skin between the legs and bulging black eyes. Flying squirrels are actually as common as their noisy cousin, the red squirrel, but the fliers emerge only at night. They spend their days snuggled in groups in woodpecker holes or tree crevices, where your search for dry firewood might rouse them to take a look. Flying squirrels don't actually fly, but rather glide on their outstretched skin, a technique that can take them as far as 45 metres.

On the aquatic side, the Black is a good spot for snapping turtles, Canada's largest turtle. Female snappers bury their leathery eggs in sand banks in early summer, sometimes travelling several kilometres from their home territory to make use of traditional nesting spots. Often you will see the remains of a nest dug up by raccoons. Those eggs that survive have a most remarkable peculiarity. Unlike most animals, the sex of the egg is determined not by its fertilization but by the temperature at which it incubates within the sand. Over the years, cool summers and warm produce a roughly even sex balance in these primitive reptiles.

A more uncommon reptile which has been found along the Black is the five-lined skink, Ontario's only lizard. Usually found around rock or log piles where insects are abundant, skinks can reach a length of 15–20 cm. Young skinks are especially visible, for their tails are a bright blue colour.

Few Came to Stay

The history of the Black is one of transience, for few settlers chose this watershed as a place to put down roots. Even Indian use seems to have been light, for no former village sites have been discovered. Undoubtedly the river was used for local trapping and hunting, but the transport of furs from the highlands appears to have mostly funnelled down the Gull River just to the east. The Black lay along the edge of the territory of the agricultural Hurons, but its poor farmland was largely spurned even by these early farmers.

In any case, the Hurons abandoned their lands east of Lake

Simcoe near the end of the 16th century, in response to growing Iroquois pressure from the east. Their retreat to fortified villages in Simcoe County did little to save the tribe, however, from the savagery of the Iroquois in their attack of 1649. No doubt the Black also saw the canoes of the Mississauga and Ojibway after these tribes had pushed the Iroquois southwards again after 1740. But this reign was to last only a short time, for in 1818 the countryside was handed over to the British government as part of a large treaty encompassing Peterborough and Victoria counties.

The first Europeans to travel the Black may well have been Lt. W.B. Marlow and Lt. Smith, who in 1826 examined it as a possible route for the long-sought canal to link Georgian Bay and the Ottawa. From their sketch map, it appears that their route took them up the river into Longford Township, and then up Anson Creek towards the east.

It was not until the 1860s that the townships in this area were laid out, and lots were offered for sale soon after. The Canada Land and Emigration Company, an English firm set up to encourage emigration (at a profit, of course), bought the whole of Longford Township in 1865 for 50 cents an acre. The company soon began to realize how little value this township possessed for settlers, and the land was sold outright to the lumber company of Thompson and Dodge.

For the next few years, thousands of logs moved down the Black River as Longford was stripped of its pine. The waste was enormous, for only the best logs were taken, the others being left to rot on the ground. Those logs that did make it down the river were herded into a canal that took them to Lake St. John. From there, a jackladder portaged the logs across a narrow neck of land to the company mills on the shores of Lake Couchiching.

For the few settlers who built their shanties along the Black in the late 1800s, the future must have looked promising. They were able to make a living selling oats, potatoes, hay and meat to the local lumber camps. The Victoria road, a rough track along the township line between Dalton and Digby, snaked northwards all the way to Vankoughnet, crossing the Black in the vicinity of Victoria Falls. At one time a rural post office opened at Ragged Rapids. Discovery of deposits of gold was reported along the river, though this later proved to be the iron pyrite "fool's gold."

But when the pine was gone and the lumbermen left, the community collapsed. The remote farmers on their poor soils could not compete for more distant markets. The little-used road was too expensive to maintain, or to guard against repeated forest fires, and it was soon abandoned. In a pattern repeated across the southern Shield, the end of logging meant the end of farming as well.

One community which did survive, at least partly, is Cooper's Falls. Founded in 1864 by Thomas Cooper, it once boasted a blacksmith shop, cheese factory, general store, two churches, a school and a small sawmill. Only a few remnants remain today in what has become a small cottaging community, although the Cooper family is still well represented in the village.

Exploring the River

A leisurely trip from Victoria Falls to Hwy. 169 takes two days, covering a distance of about 30 km. To reach Victoria Falls, follow the Riley Lake road east for 2 km past Cooper's Falls and turn right onto a dirt road when it bends north. Follow the dirt road, which parallels the river in parts, for approximately 14 km to reach the bridge just above Victoria Falls. No camping is allowed here.

Cross the bridge and portage 150 m to a small beach below the falls. The river here pours through a smooth notch gouged by the glaciers, creating spectacular scenery but dangerous swimming above the falls. Almost immediately after you begin, you will be stopped again by a small chute zigzagging through the rocks. This can be lined, or carefully run if water levels are low. As you go by, take note of the iron pegs anchored in the rocks, a memento of the days when the Longford pine had to be manoeuvred around this obstacle.

As you work your way downstream, notice how the contrasting forests relate to soil conditions. On the deeper soils, deciduous forests of birch and maple are characteristic, but whenever a rocky knoll presents harsher conditions, white pine makes its appearance. In these pine areas, you might find partridgeberry, wintergreen and shinleaf, a common type of pyrola. The spiky branches of the juniper shrub also sprawl occasionally across these knolls.

The forest floor of the sandy areas is more dense, with interrupted fern, ostrich fern, marginal wood fern and many of the common wildflowers occurring. Along the edge of the river, wetter conditions encourage the growth of high-bush cranberry, winterberry and mountain ash.

About 2 km from the start, a 1-m falls requires either a short portage on the right or a lift-over on the left. Another 2 km downstream, a large boulder in midstream marks the start of Ragged Rapids, the most difficult portage of the trip. Take out 50 m upstream of the boulder and portage 650 m on the right. Follow a bush road past the top of the ridge, take the left fork and then turn right onto another trail leading downhill past the falls.

At the top of the first ridge on this portage trail, you can get a fine view of the rocky gorge. On the barren rocks here, tough pioneering shrubs such as sumac and sweetfern have established a hold, and red oak trees have colonized part of this hostile habitat. Notice that the oak trees appear to be stunted, with their branches dwarfed. This is the result of decades of bear damage, since bears harvest the autumn crop of acorns by climbing into the centre of the tree and pulling all the branches inwards. In the long slow stretch below Ragged Rapids, the river often cuts into the sandy banks, exposing sand cliffs that can be used by kingfishers and several species of swallows for nest holes. If water levels are low, you may also see exposed banks of clay, cracked and folded in dense layers.

In quiet waters such as these, the spring birdsong can seem deafening. Yellowthroats call out their "witchity-witchity-witchity" from streamside thickets. Red-eyed vireos chirrup endlessly, invisible among the upper leaves. A pileated woodpecker drums out his territorial claim on a dead stub. In the warmth of the evening, a whip-poor-will sings out his name. Increasingly, naturalists involved with research projects such as the Ontario Breeding Bird Atlas are using the distinctive songs of the several hundred different birds that nest in Ontario to identify their presence.

Shortly after a bridge crosses the Black, you reach the rapid known as Big Eddy. This is actually a double rapid. The first small set can be run or lined, depending on your experience. The second set divides around a small island. The 75-m portage is on the island, starting from the head of the left channel. As you land, notice the glacial scours, nearly a metre wide, where great grooves have been created in the gneiss.

This island is often used as a campsite, since it provides a pleasant setting among the pines despite several nearby cottages. The end of the portage boasts a fine stand of royal fern, as well as sweet gale, speckled alder and boneset. The latter plant was used historically to help set broken bones, apparently in the belief that it would cause bones to join in a similar way to the paired opposite leaves of the plant.

Two km later, a 300-m portage starting left of the old bridge leads past Cooper's Falls. Just upstream, a quaint outdoor hockey rink stands on the site of an old sawmill. Unfortunately road access is difficult here, but it is possible to end your trip by clambering up a steep bank to a rural road just south of the village.

As the river heads southward now, hemlock and pine are more common along the shore, perhaps reflecting this area's proximity to richer calcareous soils. Canada yew, one of our few coniferous shrubs, is also abundant in some areas.

Another bridge marks the next rapids, a series of shallow shelves that can usually be lined with little difficulty. Unfortunately the lower sections of this rapid are often too shallow to run safely.

In quiet waters along the Black, a common sight is a cluster of dark, beetle-like insects on the surface of the water, which seem to explode into a frenzy of gyrations when you come near. Appropriately enough, these are known as whirligig beetles, and they have several other special adaptations besides their defensive strategy. Whirligig beetles are predaceous and can swim easily under water, a habit you can see if you watch closely. They are also one of the few animals with two sets of eyes, one for the air above and another for the water below. Small wonder they are so successful!

Around the confluence with the Head River, the landscape becomes more swampy, with silver maple a major component. A small shallow lake on the left bank provides good waterfowl habitat, since it has become virtually filled with aquatic vegetation.

The river now narrows and passes through a rocky gorge with several small swifts along the way. Just before Hwy. 169, it broadens again as the adjacent land flattens into open farmland. It is possible to take out your canoe at the highway crossing, or you can continue downstream past a small rapid to camp at the Black River Wilderness Park, operated by the Indians of the Rama Reserve. This band, of Ojibway descent, purchased land here in 1838 after they were pushed out of their former lands on Lake Scugog and at Atherley. Their leader at that time was a widely respected chief known as Yellowhead, or Mesquakie, from which the modern name of Muskoka was probably derived.

The river continues for another 8 km before its junction with the Severn, a pleasant paddle despite an increasing number of cottages along its shores. Several shallow rapids require lining or short carries. Easy access is available in the village of Washago from the centre channel of the Severn.

National Topographic System Maps
Scale 1:50,000: 31D/11, D/14

Ministry of Natural Resources Office
Minden, K0M 2K0

Black River – Map 1

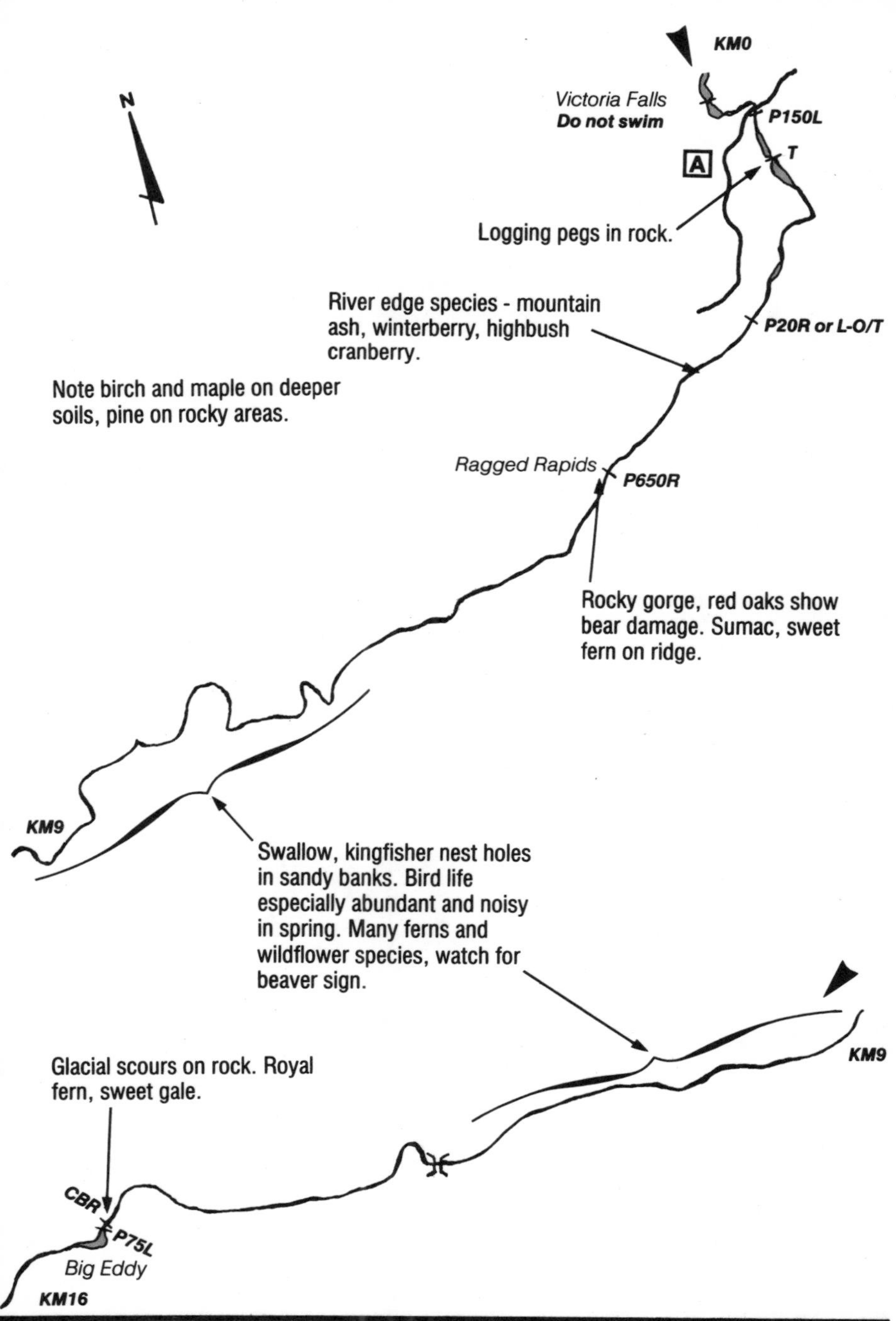

Ref: N.T.S. Map 31D/14, 1:50,000

Black River–Map 2

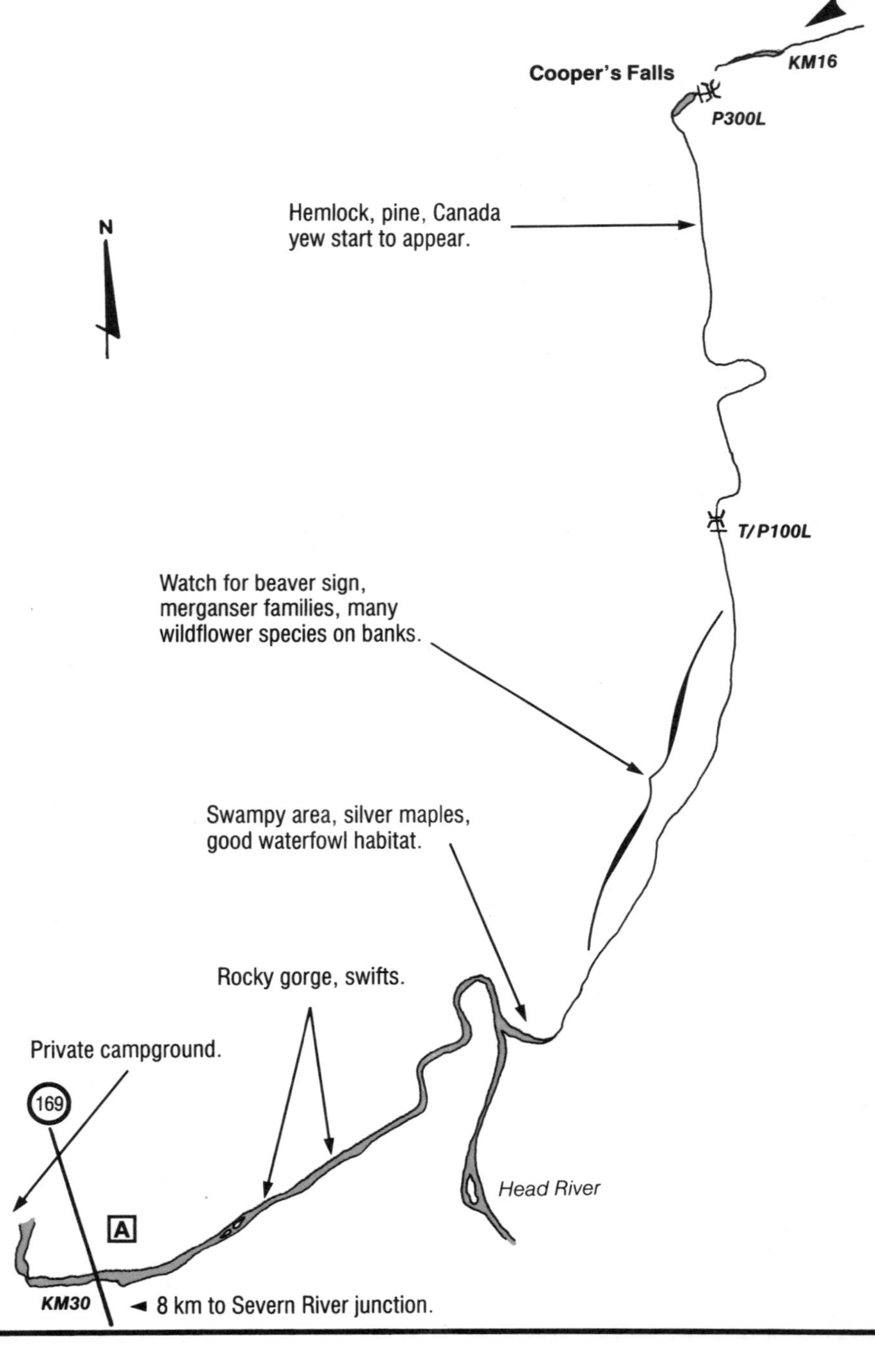

Ref: N.T.S. Map 31D/11, 1:50:000

The Lady Evelyn: Another Pretty Face

The Ojibway called it Ka-nah-nosing—"place of five little portages together." Where the cool trout waters of the Lady Evelyn River emptied into the lake, the Indian name changed to Monzkananing, or "haunt of the moose." But as European man planted his heavy foot on the north country, he chose to name this watershed after an English Lady. In all likelihood it was a staunch Orangeman touring or exploring in this country in the 1870s who pinned the name of the Earl of Erne's new daughter on these waters. You can be sure that the original Lady Evelyn never saw this rugged country, nor likely was even aware of her namesake. But we like to think that if the Lady were to visit now, she would approve, for it is hard to imagine a prettier piece of country than the green valley of the Lady Evelyn.

The foresters would tell you that this valley is near the northern edge of the pine belt. Its harsher climate and poor soils generally discourage the growth of giant red and white pine like those once so prevalent further south. But even here, large pine have been an important component of both the ecologic mosaic and economic history.

For canoeists Lady Evelyn is Temagami North, a natural extension of the canoe country centred around Temagami Lake. Indeed Lady Evelyn Lake serves as a second hub for routes in various directions. Detailed notes on route alternatives can be found in Hap Wilson's excellent book, *Temagami Canoe Routes*, which is available from Smoothwater Outfitters, Temagami, P0H 2H0.

The route covered here, down the Lady Evelyn River, is only one of many. However, it does give a general picture of the countryside, from which you can branch out to create your own route. The scenic falls along the river are often quite crowded in mid-summer, so those seeking solitude are advised to search out the back routes away from the main river.

The 102-km route outlined here can be covered in about a week. Two-thirds of that distance lies within the newly-created Lady Evelyn–Smoothwater Wilderness Park. The route is canoeable any time during the season, but more rapids can be run during spring water levels. Even then, the Lady Evelyn is only a moderately good whitewater river. Most of those who visit are relatively new to wilderness tripping and willing to walk the numerous portages.

A Ride through the High Country

The Lady Evelyn passes between the two highest points in Ontario. To the west, the massive brooding ridge of Ishpatina tops the provincial list; to the north, the conical bulk of Maple Mountain produces the second highest point. We are near the height of land here—the Montreal River system, which includes the Lady Evelyn, is the most northerly tributary of the Ottawa.

The rock in these highlands is mostly sandstone, lightly metamorphosed and broken into great slab-sided hills. Fault lines control the course of the drainage in places, especially in the north-south orientation of Lady Evelyn Lake. Near the easterly end of our trip, faulting also allowed the intrusion of younger rocks, which sometimes brought minerals as well.

The glaciers left few traces of their passing here, although the upper river shows the rounded boulders and gravels of a valley train, where rushing glacial waters dropped their load of sediments. Along the south branch to Florence Lake and on the north shore of Lady Evelyn Lake, deeper pockets of sand have also been laid down.

The forests reflect the cool climate and poor soils, with a distinctly boreal feel. Especially near the upper end of the watershed, white spruce and balsam fir are common, and the maples and yellow birch typical of this mixed-wood region are scarce. Lady Evelyn is still within the pine belt, however, and fine stands of red, white and jack pine form an important part of the landscape. The pine stems partly from a repeated history of fire. Much of the watershed here was burned over only three-quarters of a century ago, no doubt delaying the push of the loggers back into the area.

In the wake of those burns, white-tailed deer occupied this country briefly, but now the deep snows and lack of browse prevent that animal's habitation. Moose are the dominant large ungulate, although the generally broken topography, with relatively few extensive lowlands, keeps their numbers down. Even the moose are relative newcomers. Older Temagami Indians recall that moose replaced woodland caribou in the time of their grandfathers around 1880.

The larger lakes to the east support good populations of pickerel and northern pike, and the river itself is home to a natural population of speckled trout. Just to the west of our starting point, a handful of small lakes formerly supported the Aurora trout, a close relative of the speckled but with even more colour and fight. The Aurora is thought to be extinct in its native lakes, the only place on the planet where it was found. Fortunately a few were airlifted from the lakes and are being carefully reared in a hatchery to ward off final extinction.

The culprit in this story is a now-familiar one—acid rain. The tiny lakes around Lady Evelyn, surrounded by weather-resistant bedrock and with little soil to provide buffering, are terribly vulnerable to the industrial poisons that arrive with every shower of rain. Downwind from the Inco stacks at Sudbury and from the emissions of the American midwest that drift northeasterly, Lady Evelyn country has been among the first areas to show the ravages of acid rain.

In headwater lakes such as Florence, much of the damage is already done, and can probably never be undone. In other, larger lakes, the inexorable process is just beginning. The water is beautifully clear, is still safe to swim in and likely to drink, but its spark of life is missing. The frogs and crayfish and tiny aquatic invertebrates are missing, so are the fish, and the loons and herons and mergansers and otters that depend on the fish no longer find food here. When you return home from Lady Evelyn, we hope you take a store of pleasant memories. But we hope you also carry home a sense of outrage, that we could have allowed this to happen and that we allow it to happen still.

A History along the Edge

Scattered traces of Indian use along the Lady Evelyn date back several thousand years, but the river itself has never been searched for major sites. Evidence of native use has been found on Florence Lake and on the Makobe system, just to the north of the Lady Evelyn. When Europeans first arrived here, they found two distinct bands of Algonquin and Ojibway lineage, one around Lake

Collecting the pine logs on large lakes and guiding it downriver was the role of pointer boats, with distinctive prows to ride up on floating logs. **Archives of Ontario/S.16200**

Temagami and the other on Timiskaming. The early river often saw the hunting canoes of these tribes.

French fur traders entered this area in the early 1600s, but again the focus of their trade and transport was elsewhere, especially along the Montreal River. Early logging endeavours followed the same pattern, stripping first the easily accessible stands along Lake Timiskaming and the Montreal River. It was not until 1905 that the first cutting reached Mowat's Landing, at the easterly end of our route.

The main push into the interior began in 1916, with the Conkey and Murphy Lumber Company's quest for large red and white pine. Camps sprang up along Lady Evelyn Lake, and a logging dam to improve navigation was soon constructed near Mowat's Landing.

Through the 1920s and '30s, each spring saw huge log drives down the lake, assisted by a steel-hulled "alligator" tug. These ingenious inventions would anchor solidly to bottom, let out a kilometre or more of cable to the log boom, and then winch it home, a tedious but sure process for getting the logs across large lakes. Alligators could also winch themselves across portages, and their slow and awkward progress on land likely was the origin of this reptilian name. Soon the pine would be sliding its way past Mattawapika Falls on the timber sluice, then would be herded downstream to the company mills near Latchford.

Water transport of logs is now a thing of the past: it has been replaced by the ubiquitous logging truck, probing into the heart of the Lady Evelyn from Elk Lake to the north. Wild river park status was intended to protect the river itself from adverse effects, but several bridges scar the wilderness experience, and in places only a thin screen of trees masks the clearcuts.

In 1972 a different kind of threat hung over Lady Evelyn, in the form of a government-sponsored recreation development planned for Maple Mountain. Extensive lobbying by conservation groups and concerned local citizens eventually halted the project and provided a focus for the alternative, the creation of a wilderness park. Finally, in 1983, Natural Resources Minister Alan Pope announced the creation of the park, covering the area west from Sucker Gut Lake. Unfortunately several conflicting activities, including the road, will remain, but at least the park should be secure from major new intrusions.

Exploring the River

The Lady Evelyn River can easily be paddled in either direction, especially in the summer months when most rapids must be portaged in any case. Our trip, from the upstream end, includes an optional 40-km side trip to Florence Lake in its 102 km length. As well, the Lady Evelyn can be combined with a large number of other routes to produce longer trips.

TO FLORENCE LAKE AND RETURN

Our starting point, on Gamble Lake, is located 32 km south of Longpoint Lake off Hwy. 560. The logging road is rough and dusty, and you will have to watch your map closely to avoid missing the access point. Unfortunately you are not allowed to leave cars here, so it is necessary to arrange with one of the local outfitters or friends to deliver you to Gamble Lake.

The river's first 8 km, down to the forks, are marshy and generally flat, for this is an area of abundant soil. Along with the spruce and fir typical of this countryside, swampy pockets of black ash line the river. Reeds and sedges help to maintain the cool temperatures necessary for speckled trout, as well as serving the needs of kingbirds and other insectivorous birds. Only a few shallow riffles over the gravel disturb the river's smooth flow. A logging bridge reminds you that we have not yet left civilization, for this is the most recent cutting area within the park.

These boreal woods are especially fine haunts for the diversity of warblers which so enliven our Canadian avifauna. As you learn to pick out each warbler by its song or its colourful plumage, keep in mind that each has its own special place in the forest as well. Those marshy edges, for example, are just right for the handsome yellowthroat, and for the noisy yellow warbler if there is a bit of brush about. A water-logged woods might ring with the call of a northern waterthrush instead, a bird easier to hear than see. Even in the drier mixed woods, each species will specialize. The Nashville warbler, which is common here, nests on the ground and spends much of its time low. The dark and exotic-looking black-throated blue prefers a small shrub for its hidden nest. But in the same woods, the yellow-rump warbler builds its nest much higher, usually in a conifer tree.

The 20-km paddle upstream to Florence Lake is alive with birds, for the stream meanders endlessly through rich sandy banks. Speckled alder, highbush cranberry and groves of tamarack are abundant here, and the small ponds along the way are a good place to watch for moose. In late summer progress can be slow because of the density of the underwater vegetation, but no portages are necessary along this interesting stretch.

Duff Lake is little more than a widening in the river, but the pine-clad cliffs to the east and the promise of speckled trout in its depths make it an attractive wilderness setting. Shortly thereafter, you veer to the right up a shallow tributary to reach Florence Lake. Watch along the right close to the entrance for an active osprey nest. On the far side of Florence Lake, originally called Skim-Ska-Djee-Ashing or "lake that bends in the middle," a massive shelf of sandstone makes an excellent campsite.

PAST THE FALLS OF THE LOWER RIVER

After returning to the main river, you soon begin to enter swifter water. The first set of three rapids may have to be at least partly lined in summer, although they are usually runnable earlier in the season. Another 2 km of marshy river brings you to a small falls, which you must portage. A longer portage on the left bypasses the rapids below as well, or experienced paddlers can run or line these in high water.

You now enter a triangular-shaped, marshy lake that usually shelters a few pair of goldeneye and black duck, and perhaps a bittern. American bittern are very difficult to spot, since their brown-and-beige striping blends so perfectly with the marsh.

The vertical stripes of the American bittern provide ideal camouflage among the cattails of its marshy habitat. **Hap Wilson**

Indians call them stick birds because of their habit of freezing in place like a stick. However, at night they are easy to hear, and you can identify the "pump-er-lunk" song that earned the bittern the nickname of "stakedriver."

Five short rapids take you to MacPherson Lake, of which only the central one can be run even in high water. The sandstone cliffs in this area are quite dramatic, and the last portage presents a pleasant rocky campsite close to the base of the waterfall.

MacPherson Lake is marshy and shallow, but staying to the left of the large islands will bring you past two rapids that can be lined or run, depending on water levels, and into Stonehenge Lake. This small lake is marked by columns of stone along its edge, not so impressive as those of its namesake but interesting nonetheless.

The end of Stonehenge brings you to Shangri La, Ontario-style. This particular Shangri La is another portage, and one with rough footing at that! However, the 525-m portage also features a good campsite overlooking a very pretty falls.

Two more short rapids will likely have to be lined to bring you into Divide or Katherine Lake. From here it is possible to head down the south branch of the Lady Evelyn, past places with such evocative names as Bridal Veil Falls and Fat Man's Portage. However, our route continues along the north branch, starting immediately past the lake with a pair of portages 250 and 360 m long.

Close on their heels, the river narrows again into a rocky gut leading to Helen Falls. This portage, while only 500 m, has to rank among the worst in our experience. The river drops over a sandstone shelf, producing a fine spectacle, but the portage trail, dropping over that same shelf, produces only loose, ankle-twisting rock and a steep, treeless slope. On a rainy day it is almost impossible.

Past this obstacle, you can relax again for a moment, enjoy the scenery and listen to the busy melodies of the song sparrows. One of the commonest northern birds, this sparrow is easily identified by its boldly-striped breast, complete with a dark stickpin. Like all members of the finch family, the song sparrow thrives on seeds, and its thick bill is specially constructed for the task of extracting food from tough shells.

Your respite is short-lived, for after another short rapids comes Centre Falls, also affectionately known as the Golden Staircase. This 650-m ramble is laced with steep-sided ridges, most of them with steps just slightly higher than it is possible for most of us to reach comfortably. There are compensations, however. The setting is breathtaking, with scattered pines, smooth sculpted rocks and the falls themselves. Camping and swimming are excellent, with a natural water slide through the campsite. And the worst of the Staircase has been bridged by a wooden ramp, one of the few places where we have actually welcomed such an unnatural intrusion into the wilderness.

Finally, only one more short portage, past Frank Falls, takes you onto the start of Sucker Gut Lake.

SUCKER GUT LAKE TO MOWAT'S LANDING

Sucker Gut is hardly a charming name but in fact this rocky lake is a very attractive spot. Early in the summer the islands turn pink with the bloom of sheep laurel, a shrub sometimes called lambkill since it can be poisonous to livestock. This plant uses trickery to ensure its propagation, for its anthers spring out when an insect lands, dusting the intruder with a good dose of pollen to carry to the next flower.

This camp on Lady Evelyn Lake in 1897 was one indication of the growing popularity of this part of Ontario for early recreational canoeists.

Photo by Dr. W.H. Ellis/Public Archives Canada/ PA-121320

If you have the time and energy for more hiking, an 8-km detour up Hobart Lake into Tupper Lake will bring you to the Maple Mountain trail. Three km of steady climbing will earn you a magnificent view of the surrounding countryside from the bald top of this massive hill. This open area was created by an accidental burn several decades ago. It is interesting to note the stands of black spruce on top of the hill, created in part by the freshwater springs there but also by the harsh climate. This high land is known locally as Ghost Mountain.

Back on the lake, you will see pockets of dead trees, killed and left standing when Lady Evelyn Lake was dammed in the 1920s. These dead stubs are a good place to watch for woodpeckers, and you may be treated to a flight of the pretty blue-backed tree swallow here.

Lady Evelyn Lake is an excellent spot for watching loons, especially in the late summer when family groups gather on large water bodies, with flocks of 40–50 birds often occurring. You might even have a chance to see the loons "dancing"—splashing along the surface while calling wildly. Such displays are likely part of the courtship ritual in the spring, but their role in the autumn is less clear. Some researchers have suggested they are merely a result of increased hormone levels in the fall birds, produced as part of the preparation for migration.

Our course takes us across the northern end of Lady Evelyn Lake, a speedy trip if the winds are right. The lake squeezes along a fault line at Obisaga Narrows. A little further on, in the area of golden beaches, another Indian name is preserved in Obawanga Narrows, meaning "sandy narrows." Indeed this is a very special area, for the curious patterns of swamp and ridges along the south shore here are the remains of sand dunes. The finger-like projections were created long before the existing Hydro dam flooded the base of the dunes, and scientists think that these parabolic dunes may even be unique to Ontario.

As you enter the final narrows heading northward, you might notice that the rocks along the west shore have a different character from most of those we have seen. This dark rock is gabbro which intruded in liquid form into the sandstone at a much later date and hardened. In this area the gabbro has yielded samples of cobalt, copper, lead and zinc, but it does not seem to contain the valuable concentrations found in the mineral-rich areas to the east.

A final 270-m portage past the dam at Mattawapika Falls brings you onto the Montreal River. Mowat's Landing is just upstream, but across the river on the west side is the old homestead of Charlie Mowat, a well known pioneer of the area. As loggers, farmers, guides and outdoorsmen, the Mowats saw the development of this area from their arrival before 1900 until the demise of the older generation a few years ago.

A well serviced access point brings you back into civilization via Hwy. 558 to Haileybury.

National Topographic System Maps
Scale 1:50,000: 41P/7, P/8, 31M/5

Ministry of Natural Resources Maps
Scale 1:126,720: Maple Mountain 41P/SE
Haileybury 31M/SW

Ministry of Natural Resources Office
P.O. Box 38, Temagami, P0H 2H0

Lady Evelyn River–Map 1

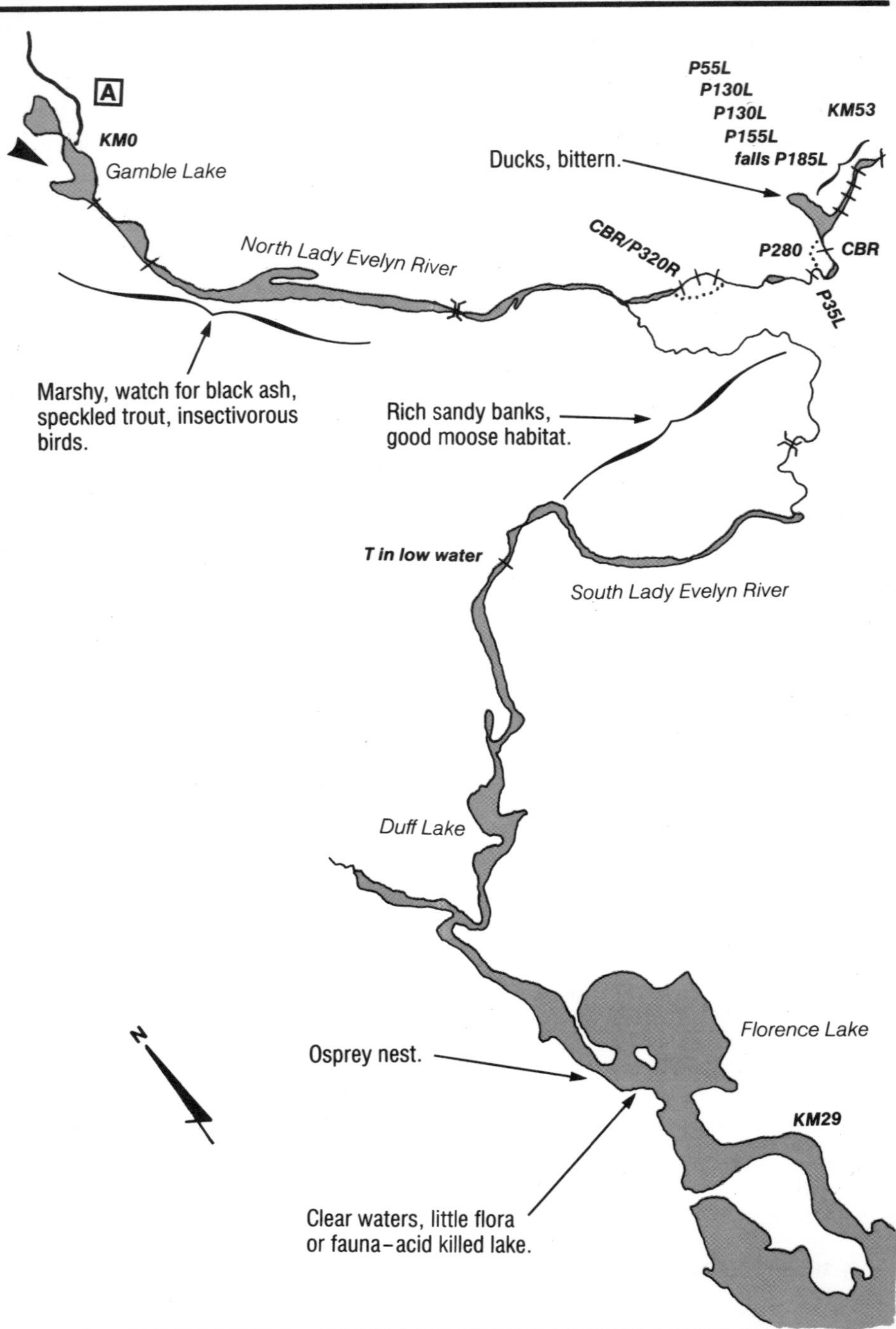

Ref: M.N.R. Map 41P/SE, 1:100,000

Lady Evelyn River–Map 2

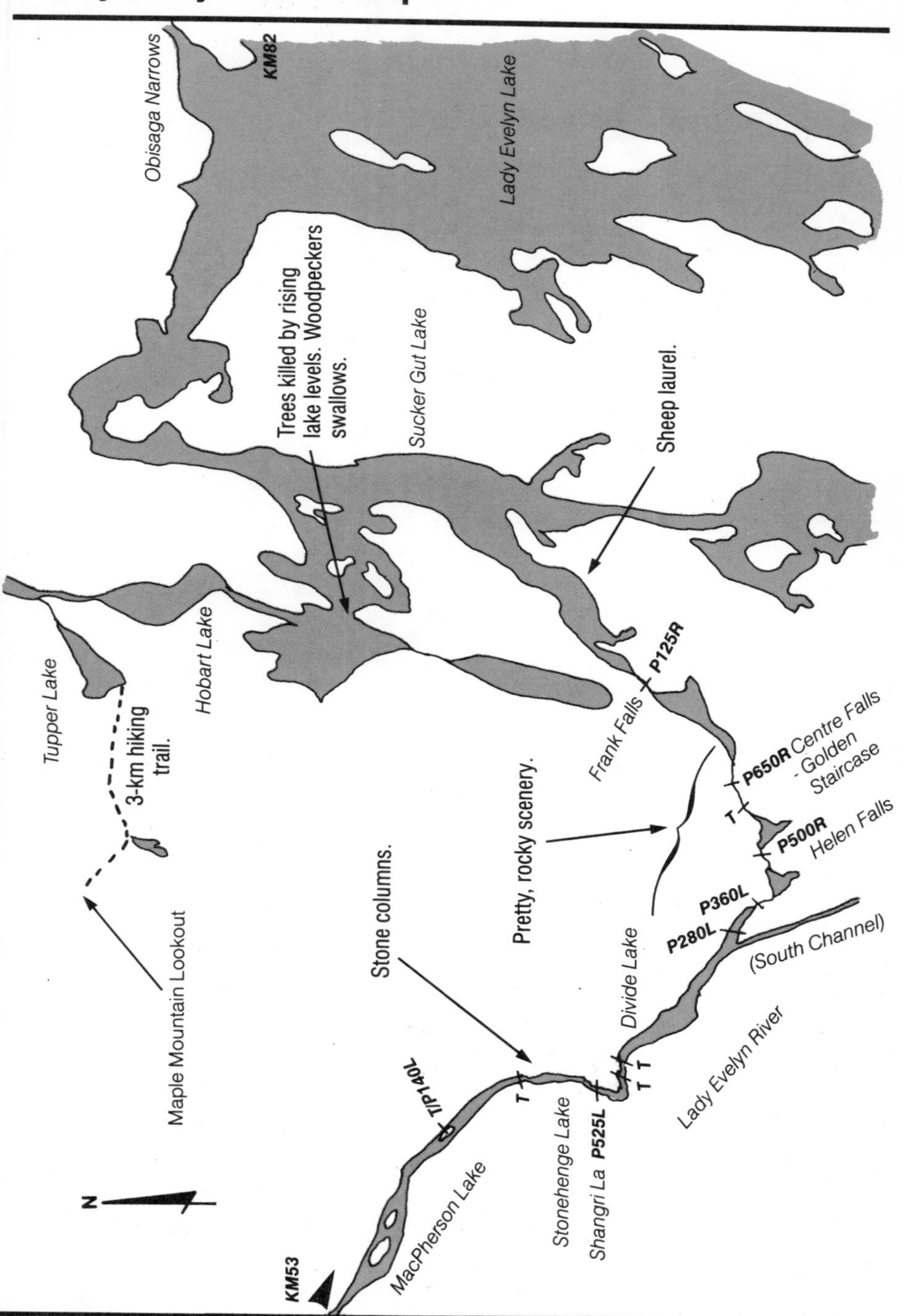

Ref: M.N.R. Map 41P/SE, 1:100,000

Lady Evelyn River – Map 3

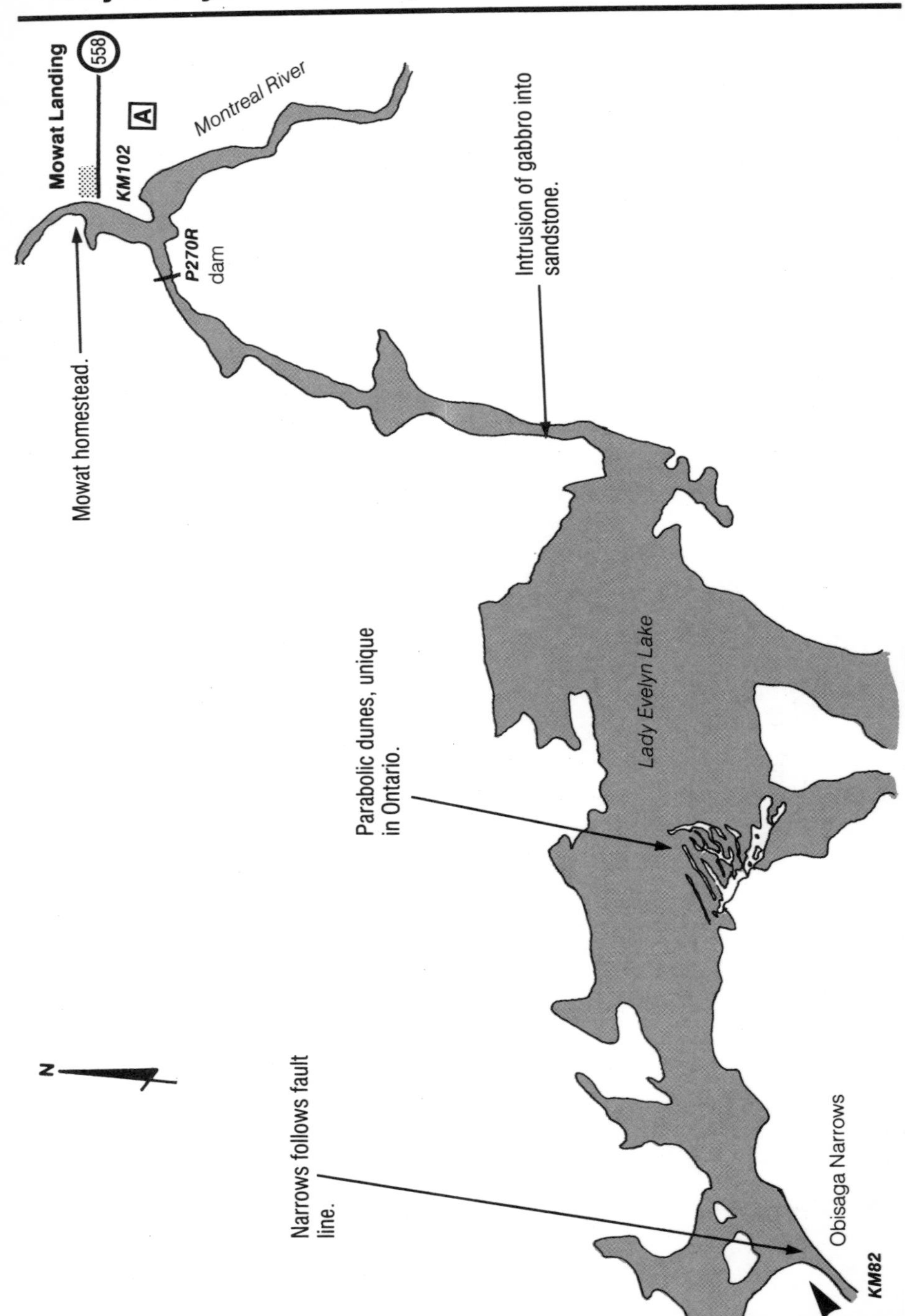

Ref: M.N.R. Map 41P/SE, 1:100,000

Other Rivers in Pine Country

Across the southern Shield, dozens of rivers served the timber industry during the rush to harvest the pine. Some, such as the Ottawa, are now dammed and altered almost beyond recognition; many others have been extensively developed for cottages. But many remain as potential canoe routes, with a diversity of history and wildness that only enhances their attraction.

For canoeists seeking short trips close to cottage country, several routes are described in a Ministry of Natural Resources brochure called "Canoe Muskoka-Haliburton" (available from MNR, Box 1138, Bracebridge, P0B 1C0). Perhaps the best is a 42-km route along the South Branch of the Muskoka River between Baysville and Bracebridge. Long used by the Indians as a route to their hunting grounds, this river was visited by the famous western explorer David Thompson in 1837, in search of the elusive Georgian Bay–Ottawa canal. Most of the 11 portages along this two-day route are short.

Further to the north, the Wolf and Pickerel rivers also drain westward into Georgian Bay. A combined route of 51 km, with only two portages, is described in another MNR brochure (available from MNR, 4 Miller St, Parry Sound, P2A 1S8). After the pine had been stripped from the French River, many of the loggers turned their attention to the Pickerel, and from about 1912 a steamboat worked Dollars Lake, towing logs downriver.

Algonquin Park lies within the heart of pine country, although only a few examples of the original big pine have survived a century of logging. Dozens of interconnected canoe routes penetrate every corner of the park, and a descriptive map is available from MNR, Box 219, Whitney, K0J 2M0. One of the best river routes is the Petawawa from Traverse Lake to McManus Lake in the northeastern section of the park. In late spring the Petawawa is a challenging and beautiful whitewater river, although overcrowding can spoil your experience somewhat.

The same periodic overcrowding can be a problem on the central section of the Madawaska River from Palmer Rapids to Griffith. Nonetheless this is an excellent stretch often used for teaching whitewater skills, since short rapids of varying difficulty are spaced closely together. No brochure is available on this route, although part of it will soon become a provincial park, so further information should be easier to obtain.

In the northern reaches of pine country, many of the rivers are still in a wild state. One of the less-travelled short routes is the Boland River, a 55-km combination of lakes and river off Hwy. 546 (brochure available from MNR, Box 190, Blind River, P0R 1B0). Although this route has been used extensively for the transport of logs, several virgin stands of red, white and jack pine remain along Rawhide Lake.

Finally, several branches of the upper Montreal River in the Gowganda area provide excellent small-river canoeing with lots of logging remains (brochure from MNR, Box 129, Swastika, P0K 1T0). Sydney Creek passes the remains of a sawmill and is an especially good route for wildlife. On the West Montreal just above Matachewan, the ruins of an old Hudson's Bay Post are found on the west shore.

section 4

land of grey owl

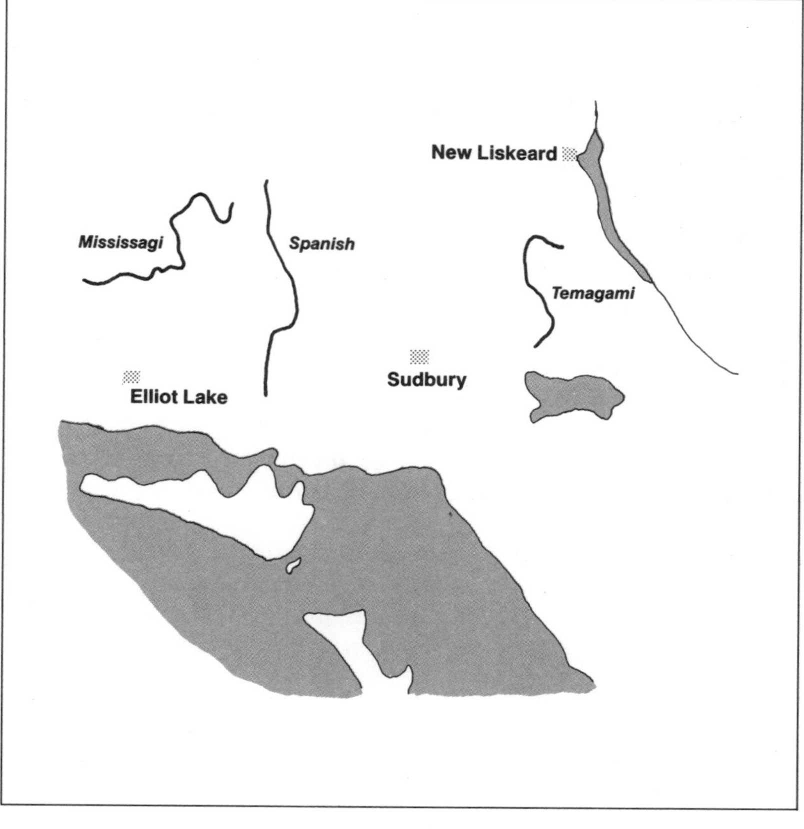

Few of us are able to shape our lives completely to meet our childhood dreams. Yet for an unhappy English lad named Archie Belaney that is exactly what happened. He dreamed of being an Indian, of joining the faraway wilderness society of Indians in the Canadian woods. His first steps were halting, but through determination and good luck he learned the skills of a master canoeman and became adept at the wilderness occupations of trapping and guiding. He was accepted by the Ojibway of northeastern Ontario, who gave him the name that was to become famous—Wa-sha-quon-asin, translated as Grey Owl.

As trapper and fire ranger, Grey Owl travelled widely on the rivers of his adopted country. But under the tuition of his native wife, Anahareo, he befriended two orphaned beaver kits, and as he watched them grow, his attitude towards the wildlife around him began dramatically to change. Obviously a man of great passion and intellect, Grey Owl found himself unable to stand by as irresponsible trapping practices exterminated the wildlife he had come to admire, and which he vowed never to kill again.

His first article, published in England, met a warm reception, and a book soon followed. Other tales of wilderness adventure, laced with straightforward pleas for conservation, were published in two further books. After several rigorous years of films, lecture tours and writing, Grey Owl died prematurely in 1938. Only after his death did his fans discover that this remarkably articulate Indian was actually an Englishman who had fulfilled his dreams.

Today you can follow the rivers so familiar to this first great advocate of Canadian conservation, and compare your own impressions with his written descriptions. And if you hear the far-off slap of a beaver's tail some gentle summer's eve, you can thank the idealism of Grey Owl for the salvation of a species.

The Spanish: An Uncertain Future

A gentle mid-summer trip down the Spanish—a trip to introduce yet another group of outdoor enthusiasts to the excitement of whitewater and the mosaic of landscapes and wildlife that makes a beautiful river. Most of their questions are easily answered. What fruit is this? And what bird slipping from sight beyond the tree? Who placed these rocks here? But one question, posed by almost everyone over the course of the week, is not so simple—how did the name Spanish arise?

True, Ontario has an English River, and several French, reflecting the twin elements of our cultural roots, but the attentions of Spain's colonial days were directed far from the chilly woods of Canada. A search of the history books revealed little, except that the town of Espanola, meaning "little Spain," had taken its name from the river. Finally, archaeologist Thor Conway came up with an answer, based on his research into Indian oral history. To the Indians this river was known as the Kingfisher, but the name changed in honour of a dark-skinned Ojibway, nicknamed the Spaniard, who trapped here. This historical figure is mostly lost in the past, but one of his descendants, Jimmy L'Espaniel from Biscotasing, would be affectionately described by Grey Owl as "brother."

But if the river's name is mysterious, its attractions are not. One of the most popular "beginner" whitewater rivers in the province, the Spanish each year hosts dozens of canoe parties. Yet with an abundance of good campsites along its 142-km length, few portages and attractive scenery, the Spanish seldom seems crowded.

There are good reasons for the river's popularity. First, with easy accessibility by road, rail and air, it is one of the most readily available in northeastern Ontario. Second, the waters of the Spanish proceed from mere riffles near its headwaters to progressively more difficult rapids, making it an ideal learning river. Third, no roads cross its course from its headwaters to well below Agnew Lake. Finally, at times shallow and marshy, at times sandwiched between massive buttresses of rose-pink rock, the Spanish offers a diversity of countryside and wildlife few other rivers can match.

Sadly, the Spanish is also the waterway most under threat by the avaricious side of industrial man. Since 1977, the Inco mining company of Sudbury has been talking of two new hydro-electric dams on the Spanish, dams that would eliminate most of the white-water and about 50 km of the productive valley. Through the efforts of the Wilderness Canoe Association and other conservation groups, Inco has agreed to submit its plans to environmental assessment, and tougher economic times have lessened the immediacy of the threat. But like storm clouds muttering low along a distant horizon, Inco's plans continue to cast a shadow on the river, and it is likely that the efforts of every canoeist who has ever paddled and grown to love the Spanish will eventually be needed to defend its honour.

Past Buttresses of Rose Granite

Ask a group of naturalists why they enjoy the Spanish and they will praise its diverse range of habitats. This is the edge between the boreal forest of spruce and balsam fir and the hardwood bush of maple and birch, and the diversity of wildlife, from hawks to hummingbirds, reflects this transition.

In some ways this diversity is surprising, since most of the river lies on bedrock of a single type—massive domes of early Precambrian granite. Often these "plutons" of solid rock rise out of the surrounding landscape as towering pink hills, warming your senses with their reassuring solidity. Occasionally other rocks are found—the darker mass of gabbro at the head of Agnew Lake, a few remnants of sandstone around Graveyard Rapids, a vein of ancient volcanics near the Mogo River, but it is the granite, its rose-coloured bulk topped by the green mantle of pine, that gives the Spanish its character.

For much of its length, from Duke Lake down to the Elbow, the river follows a trough in that granite created by a massive fault eons ago. In that trough the glaciers have left their spoor, for this natural conduit served as a channel for the tumultuous flow from the retreating glacial front. The evidence can be seen in the clusters of rounded boulders that line almost every rapid, and in the layers of sand and gravel laid down along the valley by an ancient stream.

Where the river slows, these deeper soils often create ideal conditions for the beaver which supported Grey Owl in his trapping days here. As this early naturalist was to discover, the beaver is an animal of many interesting ways, as well as the most important mammal in Canada's economic history. Its ingenious habit of building dams to alter and extend its habitat is well known, but did you know that the beaver also often construct canals, sometimes complete with "locks," to provide access back into low wooded areas? Researchers estimate that a typical beaver cuts 216 trees a year, mostly trembling aspen if it is available. You might remember that the fur trade was based on the demand for beaver hats, but did you realize that these were not fur hats, but rather made of felt derived from the thick pelage of the beaver?

Because beaver are tied to one obvious home base, it is relatively easy for trappers to take entire families. With few controls, and with an influx of nomadic, opportunistic trappers along with the logging boom, beaver were almost exterminated in the wild by 1930. That destruction became the cause of Grey Owl, trapper turned conservationist, and his dramatic cry of conscience helped turn the tide of public and government opinion. Starting in northern Ontario, a closely regulated system of quotas allowed the beaver to come back, and today populations are likely as high as they have ever been.

Only the Echoes Remain

This is Ojibway country, and the tradition of pictographs and spirit rocks attests to their regular use of the Spanish. When the fur traders came, the river played its part as a transportation route to the North West Company post at La Cloche, near its mouth. Grey Owl also regularly plied the clear waters of the Spanish in the dozen years that he used the great canoeing crossroads of Biscotasing as his base.

With the coming of the Canadian Pacific Railway in 1883, the river was viewed in a different light. No longer needed for the transport of men, it became a transporter of logs instead. Soon the river swarmed with lumberjacks, armed with pike poles and axes and hobnail boots to strip the Spanish of its pine. Hundreds of men put in 15-hour days from break-up to freeze-up to herd the pine downriver to the mouth, where great booms would float it away to the mills of southern Ontario or the U.S.

By 1900, 25 companies were cutting in the Spanish watershed,

Sorting jacks, probably near the mouth of the river, channelled the pine that had come down the Spanish into various uses.

Public Archives Canada/PA-123809

operating more than 100 camps and producing more than two and a half million pieces per year. In such a competitive atmosphere, with minimal government involvement, abuses were perhaps not surprising. By 1920 the Spanish River Lumber Company, one of the largest in the area, had been convicted of a range of offences, including the appointment of men who couldn't count to report the cut to government, the skidding of timber from expensive licenses to cheaper ones before counting, and just plain false reports of the amount being cut.

By 1930 most of the pine was gone, even pulpwood spruce was becoming scarce, and only a few camps remained. Once more the river flowed in silence, counting the seasons that nurtured a cure to its wounded banks, slowly recovering from the avarice that had scarred its beauty.

Exploring the River

The Spanish is accessible by road at Duke Lake, 1.6 km west of Hwy. 144 in Arden Township. Regular train service can also take you and your canoe to Biscotasing, on the West Branch. Agnew Lake Air Services, near Webbwood, will fly you either to Biscotasing or to Pogamasing Lake, where a short portage brings you onto the river at Sheahan. This latter arrangement allows you to paddle back right to your car, well worth the cost if your time is limited.

The Spanish can be canoed anytime from late spring to the crisp months of autumn, since it holds its water well except in very dry years. You should allow five days from either Duke Lake or Bisco to Agnew Lake, or three long days from Pogamasing.

While either branch of the Spanish can be canoed, we have chosen the East Branch from Duke Lake, a route of 142 km. This trip combines a series of scenic small lakes, some good introductory swifts, and the best of the swift water for a diverse and interesting trip. Anyone with a good command of flatwater paddling and some understanding of river canoeing should be able to negotiate this route successfully.

DUKE LAKE TO THE FORKS

At the starting point on Duke Lake, two campsites feature an abundance of pin cherries in late summer. From the north several tributaries drain a sand plain deposited by a glacial lake known as Ostrom. The shores of the upper lakes in the string of ten that you

The petals of the deep blue flowers of closed or bottle gentian never open, for they are joined along the edges by a fringed membrane.

Hap Wilson

paddle first are lined by poplar and birch, with boreal elements such as spruce occurring frequently. This is a good area for ducks such as goldeneye, which nest in holes in trees. Late in the season, watch for the blue, bottle-like flowers of closed gentian, unusual this far north.

On a cliff face near the northeast corner of Ninth Lake, a small group of Indian pictographs includes the thunderbird figure, a powerful symbolic bird that lives in the sky above the sight of man, and has only to clap his wings to produce thunder, or blink his eyes to flash lightning.

In the narrows between lakes, a series of bouldery swifts gives you the first taste of fast-water canoeing. Red and white pine commonly occur along these lakeshores, making them a good area for cedar waxwings, white-throated sparrows and white-winged crossbills. As you count your way southwards, notice the swampy area produced by a small moraine at the mouth of Paudash Creek.

A colony of beaver harvest the birch and aspen along the shore here, creating open habitat suitable for meadowsweet, a common shrub from the rose family with a sweet-smelling cone-shaped bloom.

Below Third Lake there are good exposures of layered sand alongside the swifts, laid down when the East Spanish acted as a spillway for meltwater from the glaciers. Watch for nest holes dug by kingfishers. Along First Lake, where the Snake River enters in a noisy rapid, listen at night for barred owls, identified by their signature "I cook today, you cook tomorrow" call. You can try imitating the call, as barred owls often can be lured closer.

The high cliffs along the edge of Expanse Lake support pure stands of jack pine on shallow rock. An old river drive camp on the east shore probably dates to about 1920 when the pine here was logged. You follow the path of the logs down a longer series of bouldery swifts to the Forks, parallel to an esker on the west side. This gravelly ridge was created by the rushing waters following a crack in the glacial ice.

At the junction with the West Branch from Biscotasing, there is a good marsh, rich in birdlife, including northern waterthrush, flicker, ruby-throated hummingbird and black duck. Common moisture-loving plants such as sensitive fern and square-stemmed monkey flower are also found here.

THE FORKS TO AGNEW LAKE

Your first major rapids is 4 km downstream. Portage 210 m on right, or run empty through the first set, but the lower part can usually be run. Two km later, another rapids should be checked before running, or portage 150 m on right if necessary. There is an interesting association of jack pine, sweetfern and blueberries here, all of which like dry, acid soil. Sweetfern is actually a shrub with scalloped leaves; it has long creeping roots to help survive frequent fires.

Swift water continues in short stretches through to the Mogo River, usually presenting few problems except in very dry weather. Where the Pogamasing Lake trail joins the river, several old shacks mark the old sawmill site of Sheahan, built in 1929 to saw pine from the "Charlton Limits" around Pogamasing Lake. These operations ceased in 1939–40, but pilings in the river for the headpond boom are still visible.

Pogamasing translates from Ojibway as "where water flows over gravel," which is appropriate since the river now follows water-deposited sands from the Wisconsin glacier. In places a myriad of islands create good areas to watch for moose. The rocky hills or "plutons" of pinkish granite are especially impressive, contrasting with the low sandy shores of the river itself. Along the way you might notice the dozens of dead fir caused by spruce budworm.

A silver maple swamp, sandy spits and pockets of marshland create a very different environment where the river crosses a moraine just before Spanish Lake. Moose, otter and beaver make good use of this wetland habitat, and the floating teacup blossoms of fragrant water lily are common.

Below Spanish Lake, Zigzag Rapids require a 230-m portage on the right, or they can be run after checking carefully. There is swift water from here to the Elbow as the river follows a gravelly outwash channel. The path of this glacial outwash continues southwards from the Elbow, indicating that the original river had a different course. Note how the river is re-sorting gravel and boulders along its edges, often creating gravel bars in the centre.

Just past the Elbow, the most dangerous part of the trip begins in the series of rapids known as the Graveyard. You can portage 500 m on the right around the first two sets of swift water, or carefully run the first set after checking, though it is more difficult than it first appears appears, so check carefully. The second set must be portaged 150 m on right or lined.

The next small chute can usually be run, leading you into a pool where you take out on the left for a short portage around a falls. Shortly after, a lift-over takes you past another small ledge. Across from the mouth of the Agnes River, portage 350 m on the left, or line down the left channel in low water. The rock dyke at the head of these rapids was constructed by lumbermen to direct logs away from the troublesome shallows.

The two final shallow rapids in the Graveyard series can be run in high water or waded in low water. At the campsite below the final set, the log walls of the shantymen's cambooses (bunkhouses) are still visible, littered with bits of harness and other remnants of the river drive days. The mixed woods here feature pioneer species such as pearly everlasting, fireweed and raspberries in the old clearing.

Cedar Rapids, next in line, are normally runnable but watch for a large boulder around the bend at the end of the first set. The Spanish gives you a royal ride on swift water from here all the way to the mouth of the Wakonassin River, where a broad grassy delta makes good habitat for waterfowl and moose.

A series of marshy islands at the head of Agnew Lake also makes a good wildlife area. Watch for arrowhead, an aquatic plant with arrow-shaped leaf and white blossom. The entrance to this large lake is guarded by Eagle Rock, a massive granite cliff that has religious significance for the Ojibway. Its name marks this as a spiritual place, for the eagle was believed by the Indians to be a symbolic messenger between earth and sky. Eagles are seldom seen here, but red-tail hawks have nested on the cliff recently. This site is on one of the oldest canoe routes on Lake Huron, for archaeological investigations on Agnew Lake have revealed Indian campsites dating back 7000 years.

Another reminder of the logging days, anchors for a holding boom are set in the masses of gabbro where the lake narrows. Agnew Lake was created in 1920 by Inco's Big Eddy hydro-electric plant, but the reservoir is still in the process of stabilization, with active shoreline erosion and creation of sandy islands. As you reach the south end of the lake, the hardwoods typical of more southerly forests become common. Agnew Lake Lodge provides access to Hwy. 17 at Webbwood, as well as a float plane dock for those flying in.

National Topographic System Maps
1:50,000 scale: 41I/5, I/12, I/13
41P/4, 41P/5

Ministry of Natural Resources Maps
1:126,720 scale: Westree 41P/SW
Cartier 41I/NW
Espanola 41I/SW

Ministry of Natural Resources Office
Box 129, Gogama, POM 1W0

Spanish River–Map 1

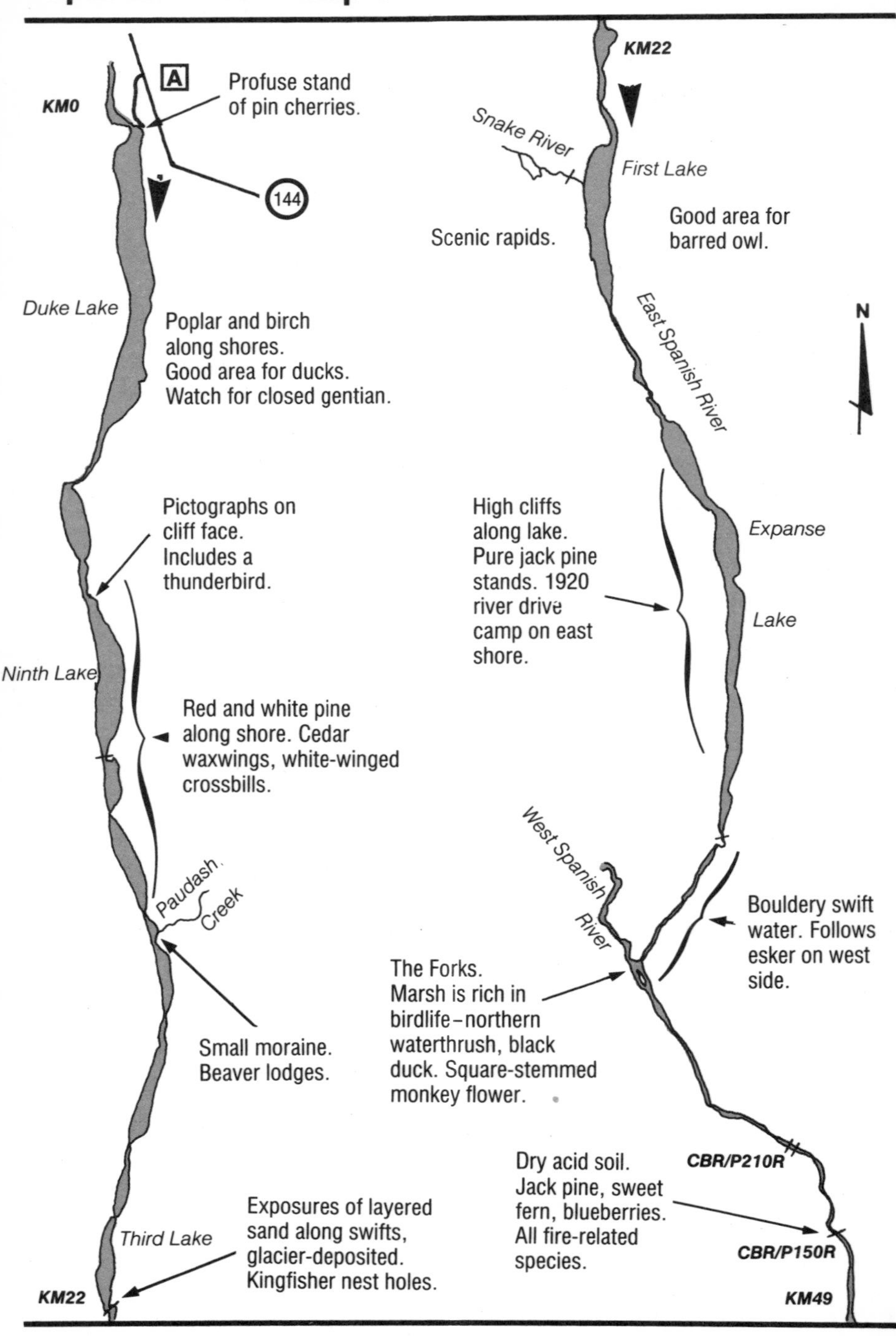

Ref: M.N.R. Map 41P/SW, 1:126,000

Spanish River – Map 2

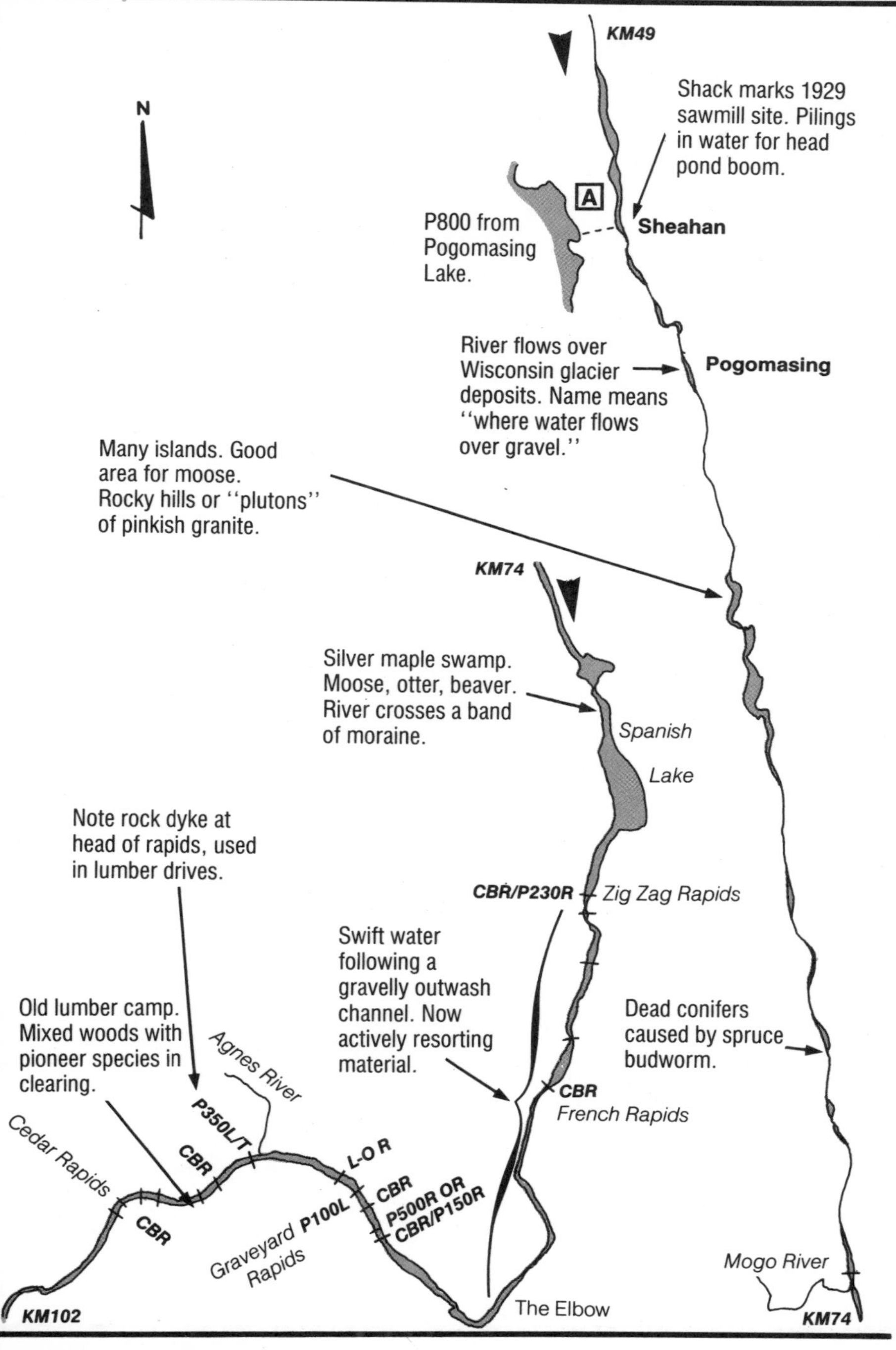

Ref: M.N.R. Map 41I/NW, 1:126,000

Spanish River – Map 3

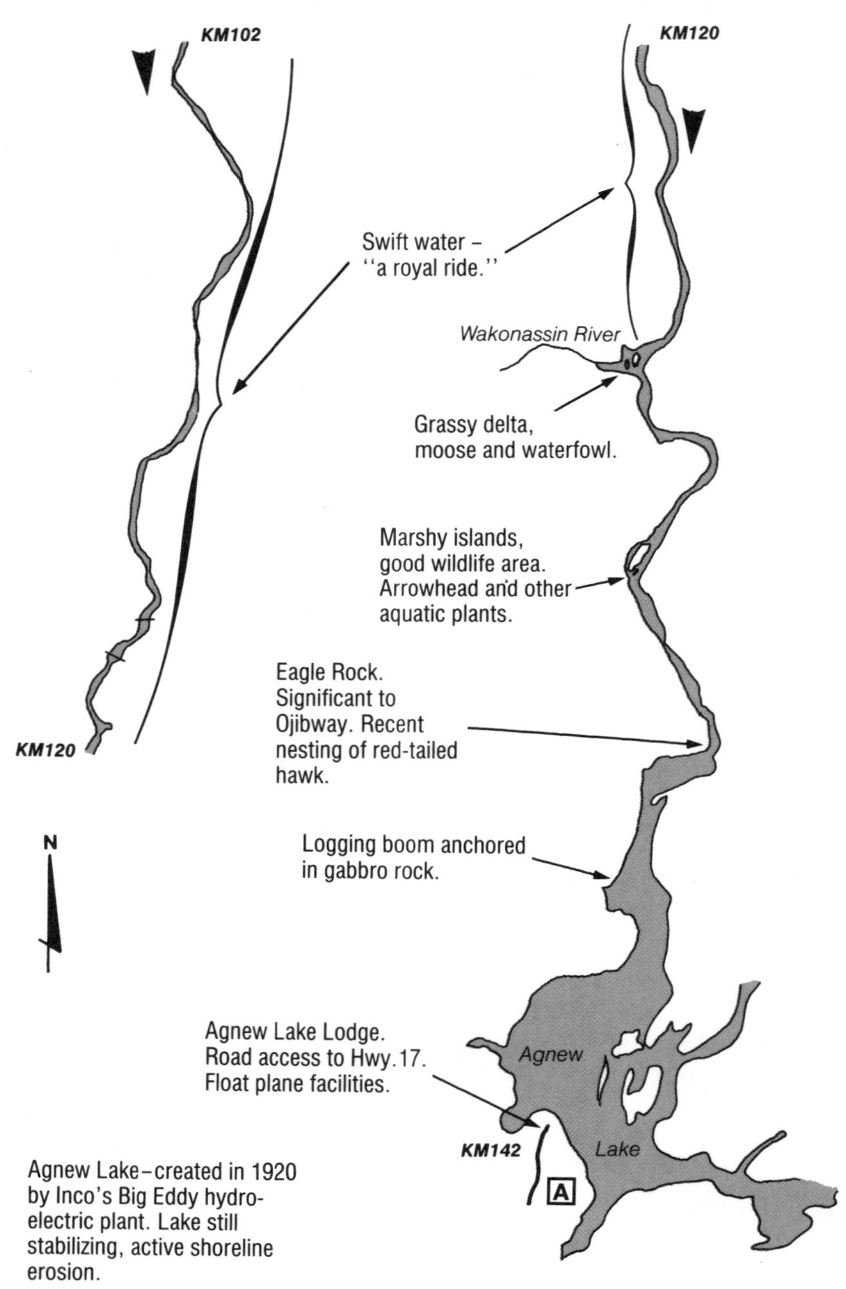

Ref: M.N.R. Map 41I/NW, 41I/SW, 1:126,000

The Mississagi: King among Rivers

Early in the summer of 1914 an unlikely pair left the Forestry Branch headquarters in Biscotasing. In the tradition of Ontario's summer forest rangers, a familiar sight in the woods for almost 30 years now, these two men were to fight fires, run off unlicensed prospectors, cut portages and generally spread the message of conservation across the north. Their route this summer took them down the Mississagi to the Aubinadong, across its headwaters along an old Indian route to the Goulais, and eventually back to Bisco. Their isolation was so complete that they did not know war had broken out until their return to headquarters in September.

What made this pair unusual was not their route or their isolation, for that was a standard part of the canoe patrols. Rather it was the individuals. The senior ranger was a formidable character named William Draper, former light heavyweight champion in the British Navy and an enthusiastic participant in the Boer War and World War I. As a youth Draper had smuggled ivory out of the Congo, an unlikely background for a protector of Canada's wild country.

For his partner the Department chose a lanky young Englishman named Archie Belaney, a trapper and guide with extensive knowledge of the waterways of this area. It was Belaney who would rise from his humble beginnings to become one of Canada's most eloquent wildlife conservationists, under his Ojibway name Grey Owl. Of the Mississagi he had this to say:

"For this is no ordinary stream, but a very King among rivers... the Grand Discharge of Waters of the Indians, pouring its furious way between rock-bound shores, sweeping a path for twice a hundred miles through the forest lands, levying tribute, in all its branches, from four thousand square miles of territory, untamed,

In his later days, the conservation writings and lectures of Grey Owl would take him often into the public limelight, far from his beloved wilderness. **Hap Wilson**

defiant and relentless, arrogantly imposing its name on all surrounding country; so that a man may travel many a day by canoe and portage through an intricate network of stream and lake and forest, among a rich infinite variety of scenery and still be within Mississagi's far-flung principality. . . ." (Reprinted by permission of Macmillan of Canada, A Division of Canada Publishing Corporation.)

Unfortunately the inexorable march of man has robbed the Mississagi of some of its arrogance in the years since Grey Owl, but the upper sections have been protected in a Provincial Wild River Park, and canoeing there is still an experience to be savoured. The best of the river, from Biscotasing to Aubrey Falls, covers 177 km and takes at least seven days, but several shorter routes are possible. The timing of your trip on the Mississagi is not crucial, since the river holds its water well through the summer.

Because of its remoteness and some difficult rapids in the central portion, canoeists contemplating the Mississagi should have well developed wilderness skills.

Skirting along the Height of Land

The Mississagi rises along the backbone of northern Ontario—the height of land that divides the Atlantic watershed from the Arctic. Like its sister river, the Spanish, the Mississagi meanders among a confusing mosaic of lakes before striking southward. In fact the first third of this route lies within the Spanish watershed, and the countryside shares many similarities with that basin.

The glaciers left few marks of their passing here, only a thin veneer of sandy moraine. In most places it is the underlying rock that determines the landscape—massive rounded rocks of pink and grey granite. Often the granite has been split by the pressures of a continent in the making, and molten rock has filled the cracks and cooled into crystals. In Rocky Island Lake most of these "dykes" are filled with a dark-coloured stone known as diabase, a common source of economic minerals.

The red and white pine along the Mississagi represents the remnants left by the logging era. Another man-related factor has been even more significant here—fire. With the entry of trappers, loggers, tourists and railwaymen, fire became much more frequent along the river. The first major recorded fire was a monster that stretched from Temagami to Michipicoten in 1885, but no doubt there were others before then. Fires continued intermittently until 1948, when the vast Mississagi fire burned over half-a-million hectares of pine.

The result can be seen in the second-growth stands of poplar and birch in many parts of this route, and in patches of fire-generated jack pine. In recent years the die-back of birch and balsam fir has created "weedy" forests of mountain maple, hazel and other shrubs instead of the valuable softwoods that the forest industry would prefer.

Wildlife along this route is typical of central Ontario, with several good marshy areas that often shelter moose and other northern mammals. This is also a good area to listen in the late evening for the howls of timber wolves, for these magnificent predators range throughout the back country. There are few wilderness sounds so sure to give you the shivers as the distant music of the wolves, but our natural fears of the creatures have been greatly exaggerated. It's hard to argue with the northern sage who declared, "Any man who claims he's been et by a wolf is a liar." Nonetheless wolf predation on moose calves is thought by wildlife managers to be a serious problem in some areas, and the temptation to fiddle with this natural equation is great, especially to counter an excessive slaughter by hunters.

Fishing is generally good along the Mississagi, with lake trout found in Upper Green and Bark lakes.

Two Centuries of Canoes

How important was the Mississagi River as a travel corridor for the prehistoric Indians? Without extensive archaeological research, we will likely never know, but there are hints that the delta, where the river enters Lake Huron, was an important camp. There are records of Indian encampments and graveyards as well at Bark Lake and Rouelle Lake, now submerged within Rocky Island Lake. These traces of the past indicate how thoroughly native people had settled areas of Ontario now considered remote.

From the location of these camps, and the decision of the Montreal traders to establish a trading post on Upper Green Lake sometime late in the 1700s, we can assume at least that the route was well known to the native peoples. Unfortunately information on the operation of the Green Lake post is scanty until after the Hudson's Bay Company took it over in 1821. The HBC continued to operate the post until about 1892, supplying it by brigades up the river until the railway provided easier access in the mid-1880s.

Eventually the new post at Biscotasing made Green River redundant. When the Forestry Department erected the log buildings at the exit of Bark Lake to serve as their base about 1908, they made use of some of the lumber from the Green River post for their construction. Materials that had served well in one era were soon put to use in another.

The river was not to remain quiet long. By 1895 pine logs were tumbling down the river, helping to fuel the logging frenzy that would grip northeastern Ontario until the 1930s. Despite the creation of the Mississagi Forest Reserve in 1904, the cutting reached a peak about 1910, for the reserves were to discourage settlement and fires, not logging. The great fire of 1948 brought an end to most commercial logging, although pulpwood cutting still goes on in much of the surrounding area.

Exploring the River

Under ideal conditions it is possible to paddle the 177 km from Biscotasing to Aubrey Falls in a week. However, there are several large lakes on this route which often cause wind delays, and you may want extra time to enjoy the wilderness, so ten days is a more realistic time frame.

Your starting point, Biscotasing, is accessible by road from Hwy. 144 to the east or Hwy. 129 to the west, or by rail from Sudbury or Chapleau. The road is rough, both physically and visually. One canoeist summarized his reaction to the clearcut scars this way: "My God, what are we doing to our country?"

If your time is limited and you want to cut off the first 44 km, all of it lake travel, you can take the logging road south from Ramsey and put in at Spanish Chutes. Or, for a shorter trip yet, you can start from Hwy. 553 at Lac aux Sables and portage across a series of small lakes into the south end of Bark Lake.

If you are on your own, or if you dislike the thought of duplicating lengthy car shuttles, you can make arrangements to be transported from Aubrey Falls to your starting point. Contact the Aubrey Falls Trading Post, Box 7, Thessalon, P0R 1L0, for details.

BISCOTASING TO BARK LAKE

Our trip begins in a series of giant loops on the Spanish River, working gradually westward from Biscotasing. The forests here are second-growth poplar and birch, with smaller amounts of spruce and soft maple. Watch along wet edges for Joe-Pye-weed, tall herbaceous plants whose flat-topped pinkish blooms form large patches in the late summer. Joe-Pye is said to have been an 18th century Indian who cured typhoid with an extract from the plant. One of the species of Joe-Pye-weed is still used by Indian medicine men to ease childbirth. Its Ojibway name, Mem-skhoo-nah-kuck, refers to the "thousand roots" of the plant's large underground system.

Fourteen km from the start, you must portage around a small dam into Boyuk Bay. Careful navigation is needed to keep your bearings on Ramsey Lake, for its many bays and islands can be confusing. At the north end of Cat Bay a large marsh gives you the first good opportunity to watch for moose, as well as a welcome change in the bird life. A few kilometres later, a lift-over up a small rapids brings you to the logging road from Ramsey that serves as an alternate access point.

Under low water conditions, a soggy, difficult portage is necessary for 500 m into Spanish Lake. A second short portage at the south end of the lake takes you around a dam into Bardney Lake, where several islands provide excellent campsites. Among the mixed forests in this area, watch for kestrels, small falcons easily recognized by their rusty-red backs. This is also a good lake for otters, usually found in sheltered spots along the shore.

A steep uphill path takes you over the divide between the

Spanish and Mississagi watersheds. The string of portages leading from this point into Mississagi Lake is a difficult challenge on a hot day, especially since the stagnant water in the ponds along the way is of questionable quality, and you are well advised to tote along some drinking water.

You might notice that some of the more southerly vegetation elements have begun to show, with hard maple and yellow birch present near Sulphur Lake. After an initial short portage into a pothole, a steep, up-and-down path leads for a kilometre past a stream to Circle Lake. This boggy lake is another good spot for moose, partly because the obnoxious portage provides a degree of isolation. Two more short carries and you finally reach the open waters of Mississagi Lake.

Progress is considerably easier now, for the river is mostly slow past cedar-lined banks, with a few swifts that can be easily run. The country shows more evidence of the large white pine that once dominated this land. In these mixed woods both solitary and Philadelphia vireos, small insect-eating birds easier to hear than see amongst the dense foliage, are commonly found.

A modern lodge now sits on the shores of Upper Green Lake, once the home of a North West Company post. A pair of portages brings you to Shanguish Lake, where you should watch for an osprey nest. Another short rapid, and past a logging bridge, and you enter Limit Lake.

Much of the balsam fir in this part of Ontario has been killed by an epidemic of spruce budworm. The insect is a natural part of the boreal ecosystem, but its numbers have been intensified by the abundance of balsam fir resulting from poorly managed logging. Since fir is not as important to Ontario's forest industry as other species, we have not faced the same pressures for hazardous spray programs as the Maritime provinces, but the losses of standing timber have been substantial. For canoeists the dead fir trees are a nuisance, since they often block portage paths, but for at least some birds the budworms are a bonus. Populations of Tennessee, Cape May and bay-breasted warblers have increased greatly in recent years because of the budworm infestation.

Our route continues past three short portages into Upper Bark Lake. The river swings to the east here, but most canoeists opt for a shorter passage, down a narrow bay to the southwest. This is a good spot to watch in the evening for beaver, particularly later in the summer when the fur-bearers are busy stockpiling branches for winter.

A 500-m portage into a small lake, followed by a 100-m carry, brings you onto Bark Lake, near the cabins that once served as the base for the Mississagi Forest Reserve. If you look closely in one of the cabins, you can still find the autographs of William Draper and Archie Belaney—Grey Owl—from that summer of 1914.

BARK LAKE TO AUBREY FALLS

The first half of this 80-km stretch contains the rapids and falls that make the Mississagi a special challenge for whitewater canoeists; the second half is all flat water. The dancing water begins almost immediately with a small swift, and a series of riffles adds spice as the river swings southwards around the first bend.

Red and white pine are common now, mixed with the poplar and birch. As you paddle along, listen for the haunting songs of the thrushes from low in the woods: the ethereal, bell-like notes of the hermit thrush, the rising song of the Swainson's thrush, rolling upwards, or the "drainpipe" song of the veery, spiralling downwards.

You have come almost 14 km from Bark Lake before the rapids begin in earnest, just as you enter Shulman Township. A 160-m carry on the left avoids a steep 2-m drop. Over the next 2 km, the river twists through a series of rapids, which the experts might want to try running if water conditions are suitable. For the less experienced, a combination of lining and two short portages will get you through.

The next two rapids definitely require portages. A short portage to the left leads around the narrow gorge known as Split Rock Rapids. Again on the left, a 680-m portage leads around Hellgate Rapids and Falls. Be sure to hike off the trail to have a look at the falls—deep within a trench in the rock, they are a spectacular sight.

As the countryside becomes more rocky and shallow, jack pine and black spruce become more common. The river remains rambunctious and three portages may be required, depending on your skill. However, the last of the swift water is soon passed, and the access point from Hwy. 546 appears on the left.

Two km further on, an active beaver pond blocks the entrance of the creek from Army Lake. The river now flows between barren rocky uplands, but the floodplain itself has been enriched by a layer of sand deposited by the meltwaters of the glaciers. The channel meanders through these deposits, doubling back on itself, and in places even cutting off loops known as oxbows. Such conditions are productive for wildlife, so it is not surprising to spot another osprey nest along this stretch, or the trapper's cabin at the edge of one of the marshes.

The scenic splendour of Aubrey Falls has diminished greatly from its former grandeur, thanks to a hydroelectric development here.
Archives of Ontario/3-E-255

Below the mouth of the Abinette or Spruce River, a short rapids requires a lift-over, and a massive logjam where the river forks may also need to be carefully negotiated. The right fork leads you into the most productive wildlife area along the entire river, Majestic Marsh. The river winds through an extensive flat marshy area, with the surrounding rocky knobs providing several excellent campsites with a view. Not only is this a dependable spot to see moose, but the marsh has also been known to yield sightings of sandhill cranes, rare this far south in the breeding season.

Our course now takes us onto Rocky Island Lake, one of the prettiest of the northern lakes. Dozens of islands are strewn across its irregular surface, often highlighted by stands of red and jack pine. Watch among the pinkish rocks and you will see the intrusive diabase dykes characteristic of this formation. The only blemish on the tranquil beauty of this setting might be the wind, for a westerly wind can pick up a great sweep on Rocky Island Lake and leave you windbound for days.

You now have your choice of end points. To reach Rouelle Landing on the Peshu Lake road, follow the channel to the north of the large central island. For the Rocky Island Lake access point, follow south of the island for another 17 km, bearing left to the southerly end of the last bay. If you are going on to Aubrey Falls, portage 720 m left of the dam and follow Aubrey Lake to the northwest.

You might notice that you are now in much more sandy country, for this is part of the Wenebegon spillway, a glacial valley that drained a large lake known as Sultan. The spillway continues down the Mississagi, but rather than following the present course past Aubrey Falls, it cuts across along Black Creek. The old outlet of the spillway is now blocked by a man-made coffer dam. To the north, on an island in Wenebegon Lake, archaeologist Thor Conway found a 16th-century Indian campsite. Excavations revealed a diet as rich as the country, with remains of beaver, muskrat, fisher and woodland caribou.

At Aubrey Falls a 1-km trail across the island between the two dams leads to the parking lot. If you are continuing downriver, the portage trail cuts down the hill past the footbridge. The river's 30-m plunge into a rock-fault canyon at Aubrey Falls has been much reduced since the days of Grey Owl, who described how "the echoing, red walls of the gorge and the crest of the looming pines that overtop them, and the all-surrounding amphitheatre of the hills, throw back and forth in thunderous repetition the awe-inspiring reverberations of the mighty cataract." Ontario Hydro's dams are not the first development to mar the beauty of the Falls; in 1929 a huge log flume was constructed here to allow passage of the valuable pine from upriver.

A route description of the 145-km lower section of the river is available from the Ministry of Natural Resources in Blind River. However, several more power dams create obstacles to your progress, and their peaking operation creates drastically fluctuating water levels. Sadly, the lower Mississagi is no longer "untamed, defiant, and relentless."

National Topographic System Maps
1:50:000 scale: 41O/1, O/2, O/8
41J/14, J/15, J/16

Ministry of Natural Resources Maps
1:100,000 scale: Biscotasing 41O/SE
Bark Lake 41J/NE
Wakomata Lake 41J/NW

Ministry of Natural Resources Office
34 Birch St., Chapleau, P0M 1K0

Mississagi River–Map 1

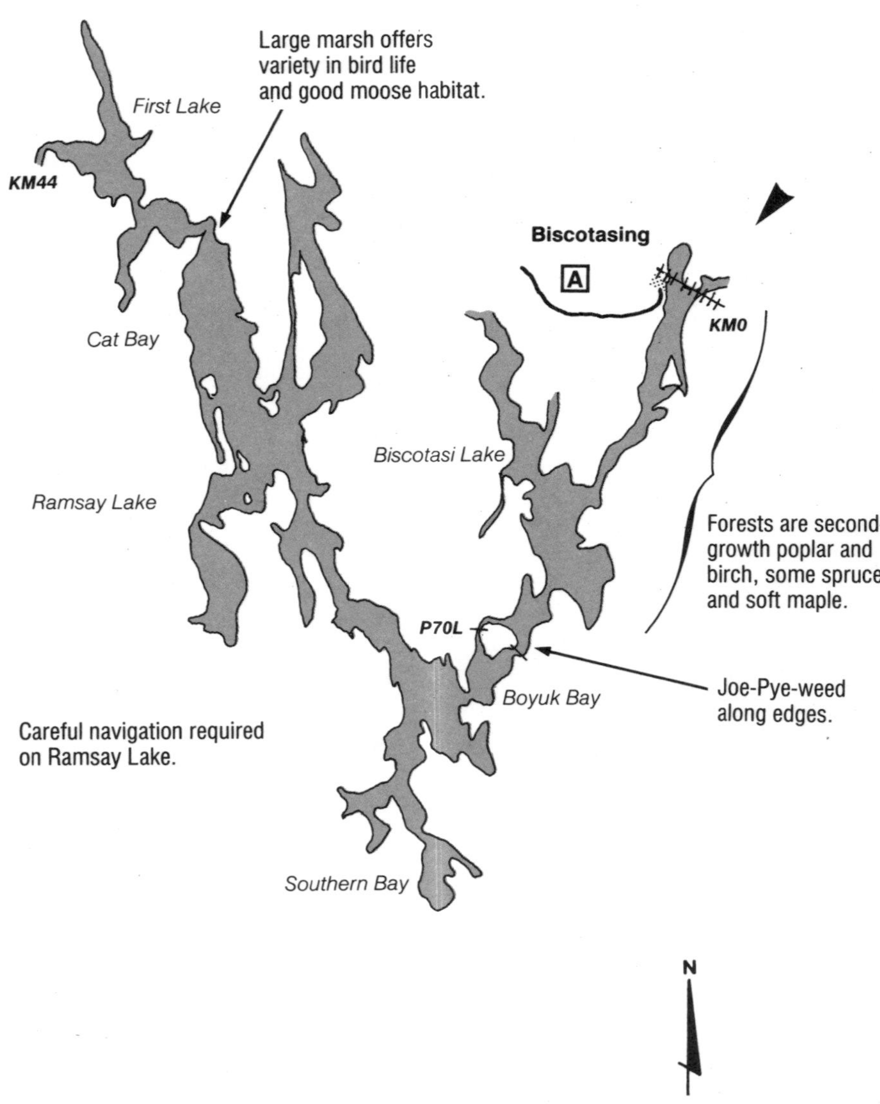

Ref: N.T.S. Map 41O, 1:250,000

Mississagi River–Map 2

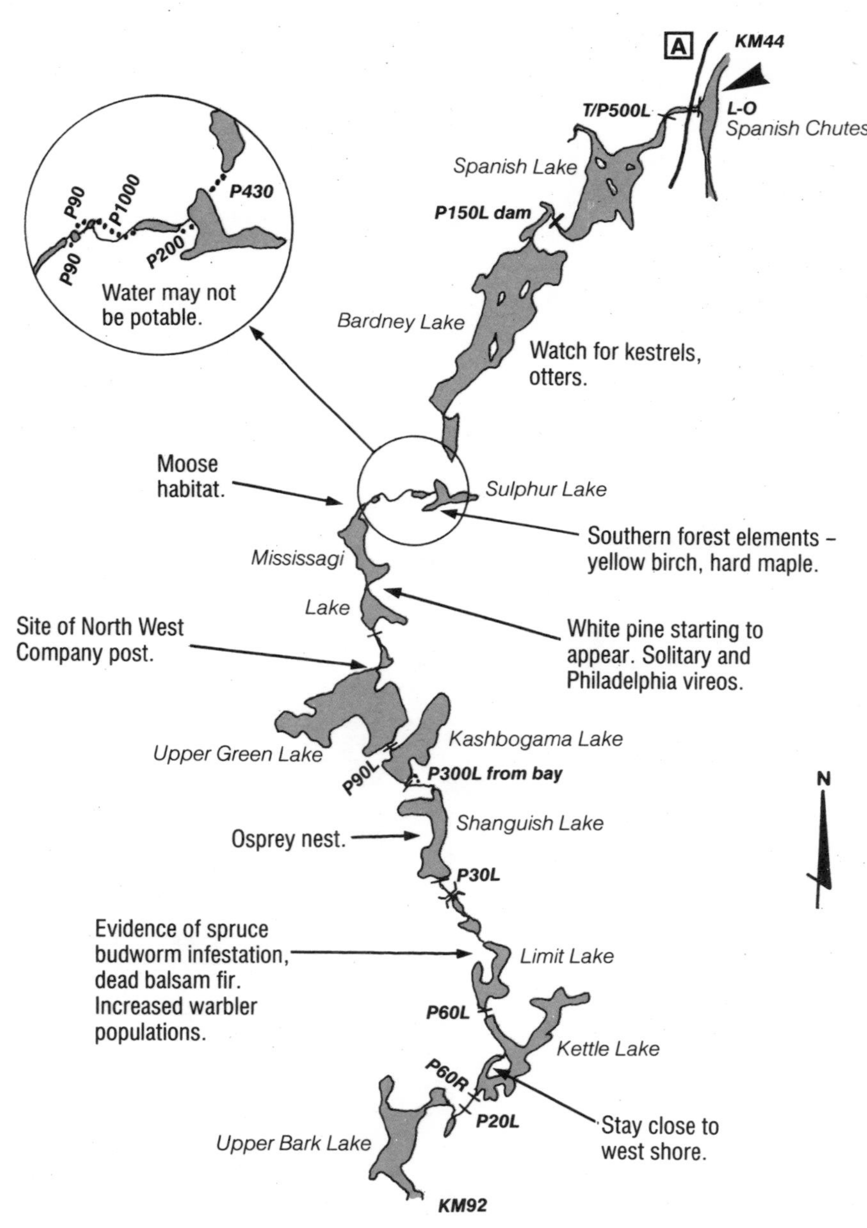

Ref: N.T.S. Map 41O, 1:250,000

Mississagi River–Map 3

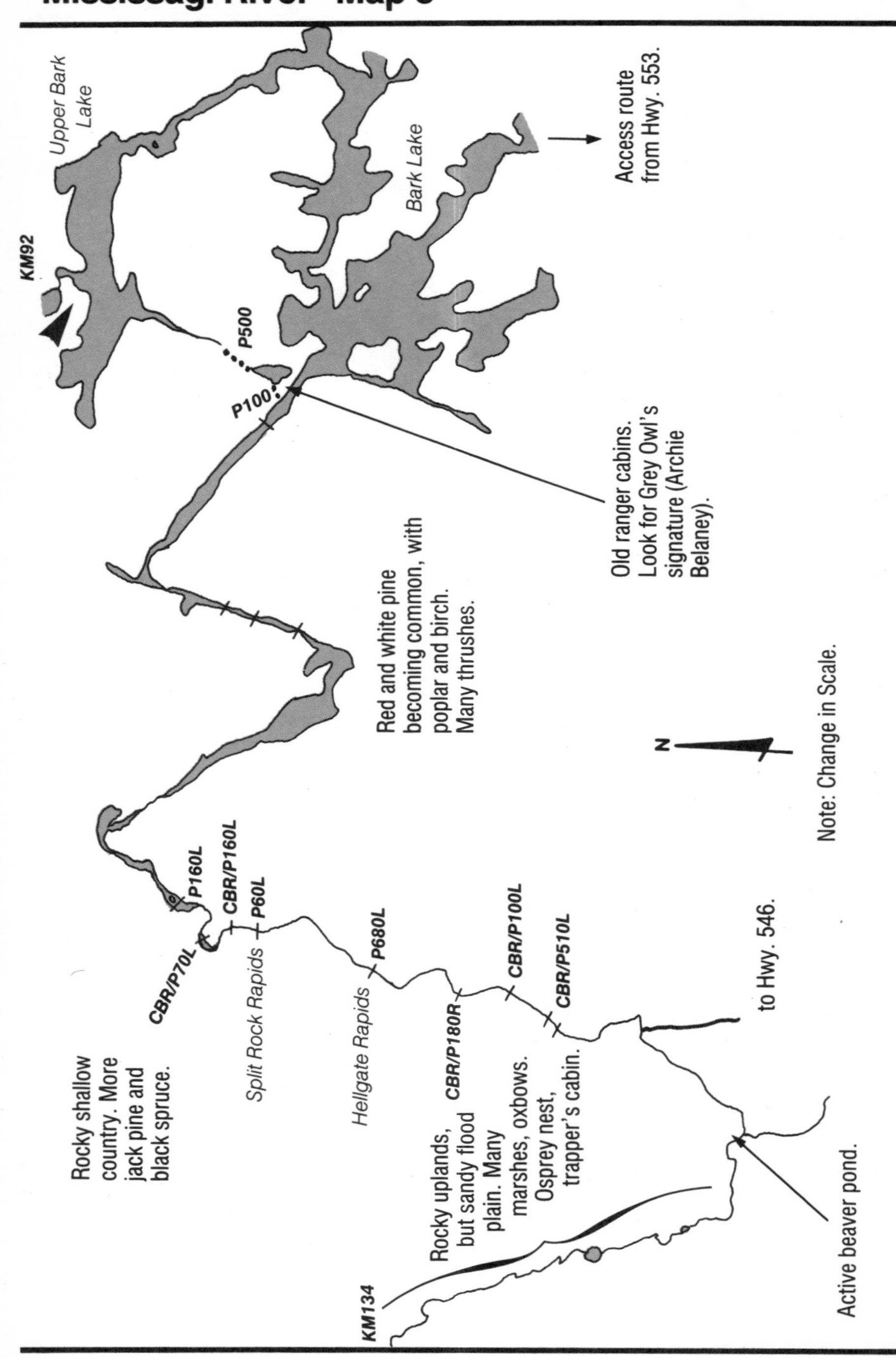

Ref: M.N.R. Map 41J/NE, 1:126,000

Mississagi River – Map 4

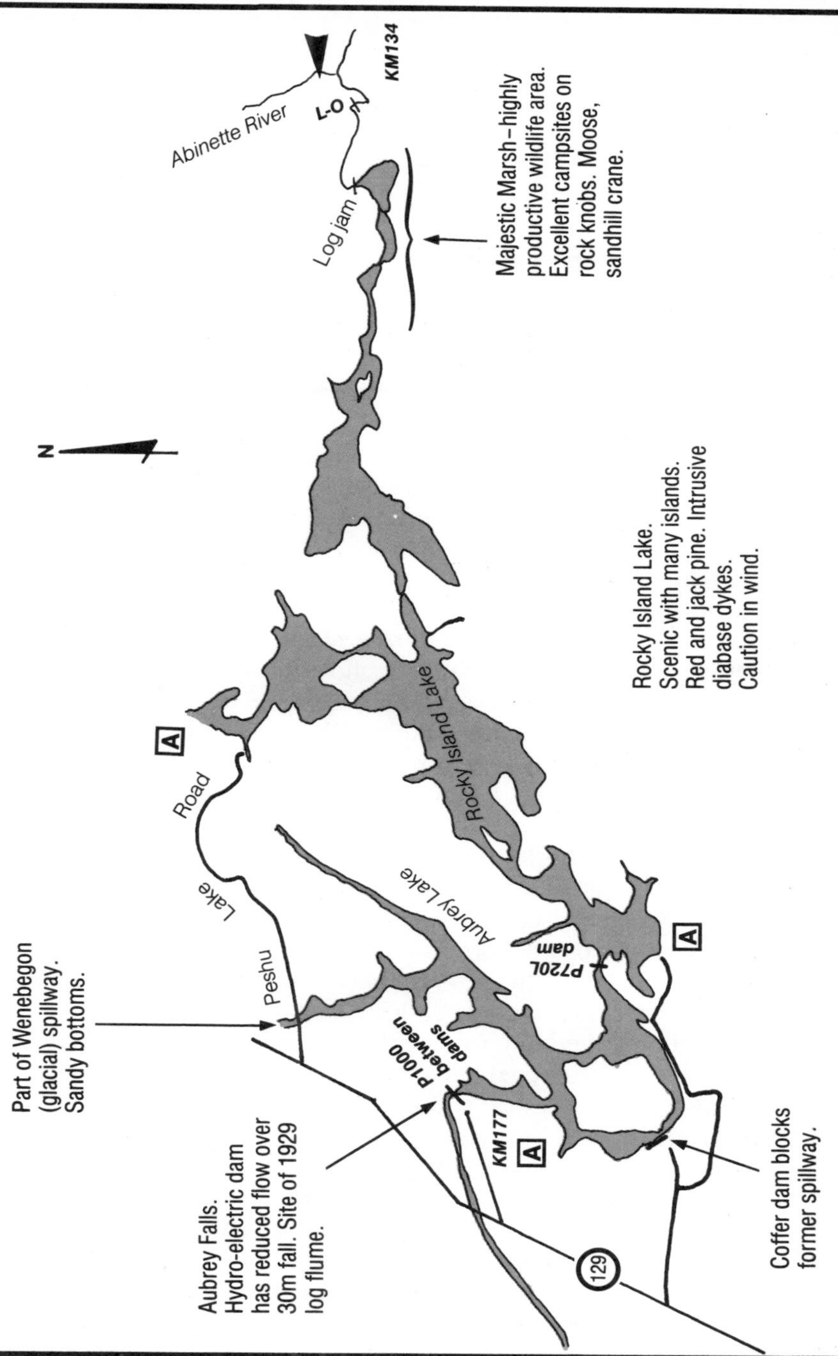

Ref: N.T.S Map 41J, 1:250,000

The Temagami: Place of Deep Waters

"The Temagami country, as an objective point for the canoeist, is a peerless region, offering pleasures unobtainable in any other part of America. There is not only one canoe route but dozens of trips that can be taken, all magnificent in their scenic attractions, and where the fishermen or hunter will find an abundance of game."

As this excerpt from a 1909 Grand Trunk Railway brochure shows, not only modern advertisers are guilty of hyperbole. Nonetheless its central message is valid—the web of canoe routes radiating out from Lake Temagami makes this an area unexcelled for the novice and seasoned lake paddler alike. Even in the days when Grey Owl began his northern career serving as a packer and a guide here, this corner of Ontario attracted canoeists as did few other areas.

Lake Temagami itself offers a shoreline of nearly 4800 km and a mosaic of 1400 islands to tempt the canoeist. A skyline of white pines, waters so crystal-clear that the bottom seems to reach up towards you, portages short and long that connect you with other watersheds and other routes—all have combined to make Temagami one of the premier canoeing areas of Ontario.

The logistics of getting from one place to another on dozens of Temagami canoe routes are described in a brochure available from the Ministry of Natural Resources, or in a more comprehensive book by the dean of Temagami canoeists, Hap Wilson.

In this chapter we have chosen only one of those route possibilities, to give you a sample of the countryside that is typical of Temagami. Our 77-km route begins outside the central watershed, at Jumping Cariboo Lake, traverses the swampy ponds over the height of land, and then follows the large lakes to the Temagami River. Most of this route is suitable for relatively new canoeists, provided that care is taken to avoid windy conditions on the larger lakes, but the lower Temagami River includes a series of rapids and should only be attempted by experienced paddlers.

Temagami country is at its best in the summer, when the clear waters beckon you for a swim and the loons frolic in the quiet backwaters. On the larger lakes you may have to tolerate an occasional motorboat and you might find a camp spot occupied by one of the children's camps that specialize in canoe trips in this area. But for the most part, the traffic is light and easily avoided by exploring away from the main lake.

On a Bed of Greywacke

Most of the shores of Lake Temagami and the surrounding area are composed of ancient sedimentary rocks called greywacke, so designated because they contain pebbles among the consolidated layers of sand and silt. As you sit on the glacially smoothed mounds of rock, it is easy to find nuggets of pink granite or white quartz gleaming in the otherwise dull bedrock, placed there by a sedimentary process 2000 million years ago.

As you move southwards, below Cross Lake, the bedrock changes to solid pink, marking the intrusion of younger masses of granite and the closely related migmatite. This is the area of the Grenville Front, the geological boundary between the mineral-rich Southern Province and the younger rocks of the Grenville Province. Along this boundary the rocks have been altered and faulted by being thrust up against the rigid older strata, helping to create the frequent rapids and falls in this part of the river.

In the final stretches of the Temagami the sedimentary bedrock has been metamorphosed, making its appearance quite different from the rocks of similar origin around the lake.

The forests of Temagami country have a northern flavour, with white spruce, white birch and balsam fir taking over from the maples and other hardwoods of the south. But the climate is still southern enough to encourage the growth of pine, and it is the large red and white pine that give the area much of its charm. Fortunately much of the pine along the shores of Lake Temagami has survived within a "skyline reserve," even though virtually all the valuable timber in the surrounding countryside has been stripped.

The presence of large pines along the lakeshore may be partly the result of a happy circumstance. An 1894 report by the Commissioner of Crown Lands reported that the timber around the shores was small, following a burn. Early visitors had to walk into the back country to see the big virgin pines. Now, with the back country reduced to young forests by logging, the pines along Lake Temagami have matured, and the efforts of the Temagami Lakes Association and many others are helping to stave off the never-ending demands of the loggers.

Wildlife along this route is typical of the mixed forest, with a varied bird life taking advantage of the abundant insect populations of early summer. Moose is now the dominant large mammal, a change from the early days when white-tailed deer were recorded as common (possibly in response to the favourable habitat provided by the burn). Another mammal listed as abundant in 1894 was the caribou, and the 1909 Grand Trunk brochure declares that "signs of [caribou] are seen everywhere." Today the nearest caribou are close to James Bay.

White Pine and Wanigans

The early history of the Temagami area lives on in the legends of the local Indians. Archaeologists have found numerous Indian campsites dating back as far as 6000 years along the lake and river, and a recent project documented Indian knowledge of over 1200 portages in the Temagami area. In the Ojibway language, this area was Temeagama, or "deep water lake."

The river played a role in the epic flight of a party of Nipissing Indians from the marauding Iroquois in 1650. Driven from their native Lake Nipissing by a massacre of their tribesmen, the Indians fled up the Sturgeon River and then up the Temagami. Even in those distant days, canoe trails must have been well known, for the party was able to make its way across the headwaters into the Abitibi system, down to James Bay, and back up the Albany River to Lake Nipigon, an incredible journey even by today's standards.

Iroquois war parties also reached the Temagami area, and Michael Paul, an elder from Bear Island, tells of an ambush on these intruders on the Temagami River below the lake. A floating lynx skin was pulled across the river to draw the Iroquois into a portion of the river where the strong current carried their canoes swiftly downstream. Only one Iroquois survived the raid that followed.

Other early records mention a well used portage at the present site of Temagami village. By 1834 the Hudson's Bay Company had recognized the trade potential of the lake with a trading post on

Temagami Island. The post was moved to Bear Island in 1870, since this now served as a base for the local Indian population with the surrender of their lands as part of the 1850 Robinson Huron treaty. The validity of that surrender is now being contested by the Bear Island Band, who are claiming control of a large area in this vicinity.

By the 1890s the first surveys were being carried out in this area, and by 1904 the railway had reached Temagami. But it was not only farmland that these tentacles of civilization sought; it was also wood. Lumbermen had been pushing up the Ottawa Valley to the east for decades, but it was not until 1908 that the mills on Lake Nipissing began reaching back up the Sturgeon for fresh supplies.

The first wave of logging around Temagami was delayed by declaration of the area as a Forest Reserve, where cutting and settling was prohibited, but by 1920 these protective measures had been set aside. Logging peaked in the 1925–35 era, but logs were still sent spinning down the Temagami River in the 1940s and '50s. As you canoe the river today, you can still see many remnants of this relatively recent logging, with boom logs and chains still in place along the side of the fast water.

Recreation was to make a more lasting contribution to the Temagami area. As early as 1894, in a letter to the *Empire*, Mr. T.A. Gregg was suggesting setting aside Lake Temagami as a national park. With the coming of the railway, the first cottagers came too, and the first of the camps that were to train generations of youngsters in the ways of the wilderness. Canada's first boys' camp was established on Lake Temagami in 1900 by A.C. Cochrane, and others were soon to follow.

Archie Belaney began his career as a guide at Camp Wabi-kon in the 1920s. It was here that he met the Indian girl, Anahareo, who was to become his wife and eventually to change his life work by encouraging his conservation activities and his writing.

Even now Temagami camps are steeped in tradition. This is one of the few areas in Ontario where the use of the cedar strip canoe and the dreaded wooden pack box known as the wanigan is still a regular feature of camp life.

Exploring the River

You can expect to spend four or five days on the 77-km route we describe here. Again we emphasize this is not necessarily the best Temagami route, but merely one that demonstrates the opportunities present on dozens of different options. We urge you to study the maps and route descriptions provided in Hap Wilson's guide book to create your own Temagami experience.

JUMPING CARIBOO TO TEMAGAMI LAKE

Jumping Cariboo Lake lies just west of Hwy. 11, 15 km north of Marten River Provincial Park. Local legend says that its name comes from the caribou driven off the cliffs at its south end by packs of wolves. You can get to the lake from the side of the highway, or take the gravel road just past Olive Lake to gain access from the side of this quiet roadway.

Scattered among the dense forests of pine, spruce and birch along the shore of Jumping Cariboo are dead conifer trees, mostly balsam fir killed by spruce budworm. The budworms eat the growing tip of the spring buds, preventing the production of seed by spruce, but killing fir outright.

A 70 m portage leading to Ingall Lake can be lined upstream. At one time this small rapids did not exist, for the lake level had been flooded 3 m higher to allow logs to float through.

The entrance to Ingall Lake is a narrow bay edged by a rich bog community with black spruce, larch, white cedar, sheep-laurel, sweet gale, labrador tea, pitcher plant, buckbean and round-leaved sundew—a very good place to poke around with your field guide to wild plants.

Ingall and Waha lakes provide good spots for camping, and access is also available where the gravel road crosses the river again. A short portage may be necessary here in low water, and the next stretch is shallow and swampy until you reach the 100-m portage into Brophy Lake. Watch for starflower, bunchberry and lily-of-the-valley along the trail. Cedar waxwings and evening grosbeaks are common breeding birds in this area.

Careful navigation is required on Brophy Lake, for the low wooded hills can be confusing. There are few campsites from here to Wasaksina, and the terrain becomes increasingly swampy as you cross over from one watershed to the other.

A 600-m portage with bad footing in black spruce swamp takes you into Greenlaw Lake. Sensitive fern and interrupted fern along the way attest to the poor drainage conditions in these water-logged soils. Another short but soggy portage brings you into an abandoned beaver pond, very shallow in midsummer, but with excellent views of the beaver lodge, now standing high and dry in the middle of its former pond.

This sheltered inlet to Shiningwood Bay has been modified by an impressive beaver dam, but provides a nursery for bullfrogs.

Ron Reid

Past the old beaver dam, a short paddle down a winding channel in shrubby swamp brings you to the final 60-m portage into Wasaksina Lake. This lake's name refers to the white peeled beaver sticks often seen along the shore, but it could well have spelled relief, for its breezy expanse is a welcome change from the swampy tangles to the east.

The pine-clad points of Wasaksina have several good campsites, and an evening here is a good spot to listen to the wilderness symphony. Out on the lake the loons herald the dusk with maniacal wails and laughter. An osprey passes by, whistling its alarm at your presence. Among the trees the thrushes take up the chorus—the flute-like phrases of the Swainson's thrush sliding upwards; the contrasting song of the veery wheeling down.

At the far end of Wasaksina a series of three portages takes you across Denedus and Olier lakes into Shiningwood Bay. The third portage is particularly interesting. From its start in a bay to the right of the river, it follows an old lumber road past excellent specimens of red and white pine, with solid stands of largetooth aspen growing up in places where the pine has been removed. In early summer this walk is also enlivened by the blood-red berries of the fly honeysuckle, a shrub that grows commonly here.

Shiningwood Bay is one of the far-flung arms of Lake Temagami, but it has very little development along its shores. Near its east end a small inlet leads off enticingly towards a large beaver dam. This inlet serves as a nursery for tadpoles, by their size probably bullfrog tadpoles. Your progress here will be preceded by the constant splashing of partly-transformed tadpoles, as they dive off the lily-pad stems where they have been sunning.

Several islands in Shiningwood Bay are used by herring gulls for nesting, and their rocky surfaces have been liberally whitewashed by the roosting gulls. Good examples of greywacke with granite pebbles can be found along this stretch.

As you enter Lake Temagami, notice how the rocky hills around the lake have red pine on sheltered lower slopes and white pine on the ridges. Many of the birds you will hear in this habitat are especially adapted for conifer woods, especially the red-breasted nuthatch and black-throated green warbler.

LAKE TEMAGAMI TO RED CEDAR LAKE

From the entrance of Shiningwood Bay it is possible to loop back along the Northeast Arm to the village of Temagami, or to link into dozens of other routes radiating out from the lake. Our route, however, takes us into the sheltered waters of Portage Bay. As the name suggests, a short portage over a ridge of rock is necessary at its southerly end. A set of pictographs can be seen on the lower east side of Portage Bay.

At the outlet of Lake Temagami you may encounter two swifts, both easily run. However, if the water level has been raised by the control dam on Cross Lake, this fast water disappears entirely. On earlier maps this place was marked "Temagami Falls," with a small dam at the first swift. The forest is noticeably more diverse here, with pockets of spruce bog that shelter clintonia and snowberry.

This stretch is known locally as the "S Narrows," and it was an important hunting site for Indians from a village at nearby Austin Bay. Woodland caribou regularly crossed here, and were speared. As well, this was a favourite spot for deadfall log traps, weighted with rocks, to capture black bears that crossed to avoid the large lakes.

From this point it is possible to loop northwards through Cross Lake to rejoin our original route. However, we turn southwards down Cross Lake through a shallow bay. In low water it may be necessary to head northeastwards around the large island to get through. Cross Lake is one of the prettiest spots along this route, with rocky shores and good camping spots.

Surveyor Lake is simply an extension of Cross, but at its south end a steep 260-m portage around the control dam is necessary. Run the small rapids below the portage, and soon you will begin to see the pinkish granite islands that mark the intrusions associated with the Grenville Front.

Portages become more frequent now, beginning with a 600-m walk just past the logging bridge. The next carry, this time 250 m, can sometimes be avoided by carefully running the rapids, so check first. One and a half km later, a triple set of rapids requires careful negotiation. The first set can sometimes be run, but both the second and third must be portaged on the left. The loggers must have had difficulty with these rapids as well, for you can still see the chains and boom logs along the shore at the lower end. Across the river you can also see exposures of glacially deposited gravels, characteristically sorted into layers.

These deeper soils along the edge soon exert their influence in the forest cover, which now includes sugar maple, yellow birch and white spruce.

Running a set of small swifts now brings you into Red Cedar Lake, featuring good campsites on rocky points or sandy beaches. If you want to create a loop route, you can follow Red Cedar Lake to the north to connect with Hangstone Lake and a route back to your starting point. Only experienced whitewater paddlers should proceed down the Temagami River.

RED CEDAR LAKE TO RIVER VALLEY

A short portage around the outlet dam takes you into Thistle Lake, a good spot for common mergansers and loons. Towards its west end, smooth fingers of rock, scoured by the grinding action of glaciers a kilometre or more thick, provide conditions suitable for jack pine. A swift at the end of the lake can usually be run.

Three km later, as the river bends to the west again, another short portage, or tracking down the rapids, is required. Along the slower stretches, watch for the pockets of black ash that thrive where soils are deeper. These deciduous swamps are good areas to listen for the "che-buk" calls of the least flycatcher and for the ringing calls of the northern waterthrush.

Island Portage is the most difficult in a series of carries along the river, both because the path is steep in places and because it is so easy to lose your way. Do not take the well trodden path to the left as the portage begins; it is well trodden from the disgruntled canoeists coming back (including us!) who have discovered at length that it leads nowhere. The correct path heads uphill, and becomes more clear past the top of the ridge.

After this long carry you are in the river again for only a short distance, past two swifts, before you must carry again, this time 490 m on the right. This is an excellent area for jack pine and blueberries, and expert whitewater paddlers might want to dally to play in the lower rapids if water levels are right.

There are two steep rapids at Ragged Chute. Lift-over the first 25 m on the left, and line or carefully run the lower part. Note the small kettle hole in the rocks by the rapid, worn by small rocks swirled by floodwaters. Portage 75 m on the left around the second rapid. Cedar waxwings are often present, feeding on insects above the rapids.

A triple set of rapids completes this turbulent stretch of river. The first two sets can be lined or tracked, but the third must be portaged 140 m on left. There is lots of evidence of log drives here, in the form of boom logs, chains and other debris along the shore.

After the next bridge the river runs very swiftly over gravel shallows for the next 6 km. Forests are mostly aspen and birch, with some farmland making an appearance. Watch for exposures of gravelly, water-lain deposits, and for varved clays along the shore, whose regular dark layers indicate a marine origin.

The royal ride ends just above the River Valley bridge, where a difficult rapids requires a 350-m portage. A word of caution—while the upper part of this rapids might look runnable to experts, it ends in a falls just past the railway bridge, so it must be portaged.

It is possible to end your trip here, or to continue a few kilometres more to Hwy. 539. This final stretch includes an exciting ride through large standing waves in a rapids that is usually runnable, and a calmer paddle past a series of swampy ponds. Just after the mouth of the river is reached, a few hundred metres on the Sturgeon brings you to the take-out point at the bridge.

National Topographic System Maps
1:50,000 scale: 41 I/9, I/16
31 L/12, L/13

Ministry of Natural Resources Maps
1:100,000 scale: Tomiko 31L/NW
1:126,720 scale: Capreol 41 I/NE

Ministry of Natural Resources Office
Box 38, Temagami, P0H 2H0

Temagami River Map – 1

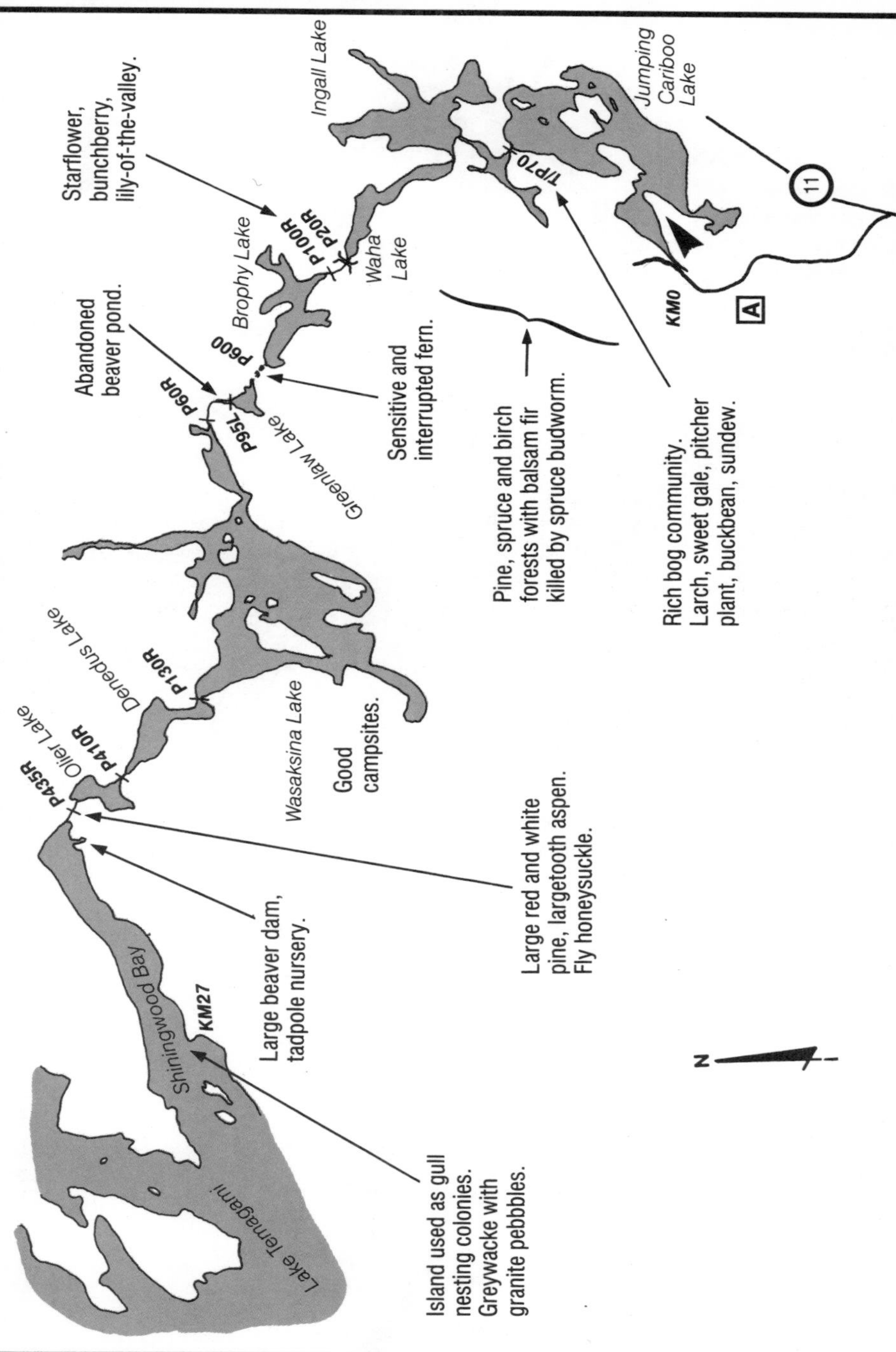

Ref. M.N.R. Map 41I/NE, 31L/NW, 1:126,000

Temagami River Map–2

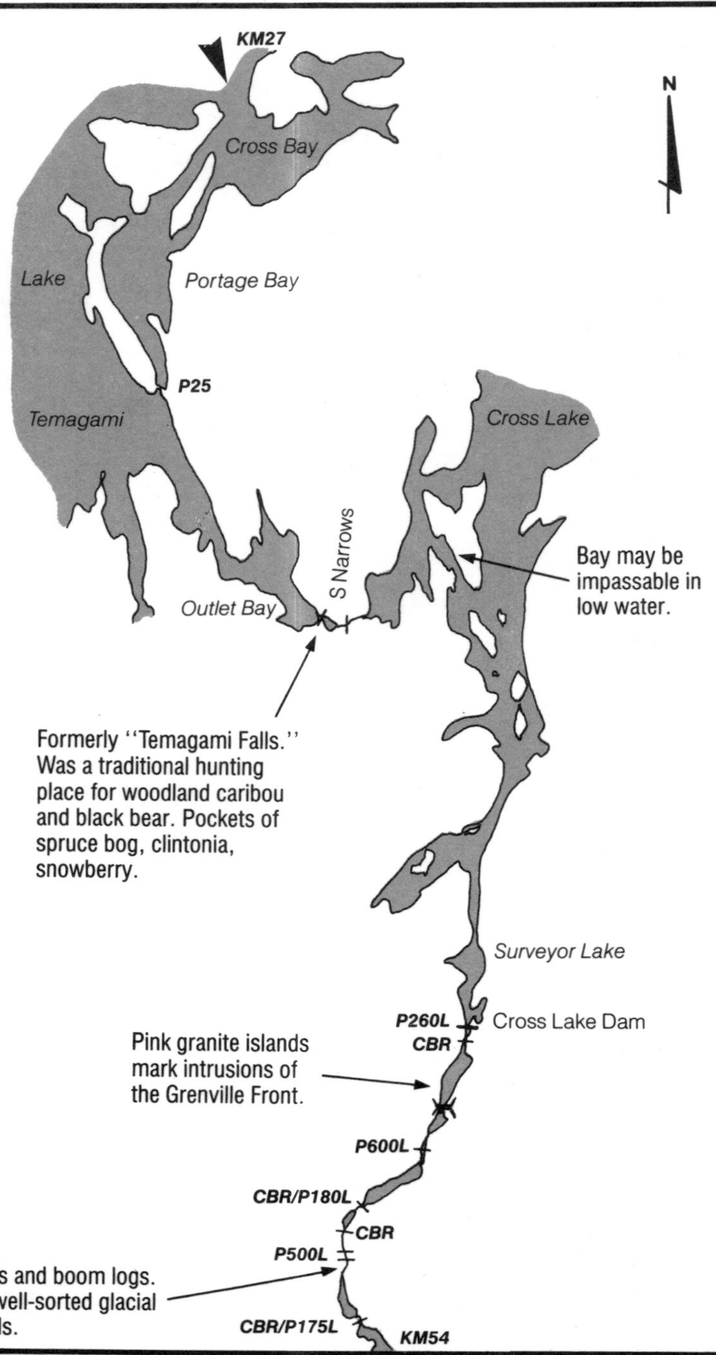

Ref. M.N.R. Map 41I/NE, 31L/NW, 1:126,000

Temagami River Map – 3

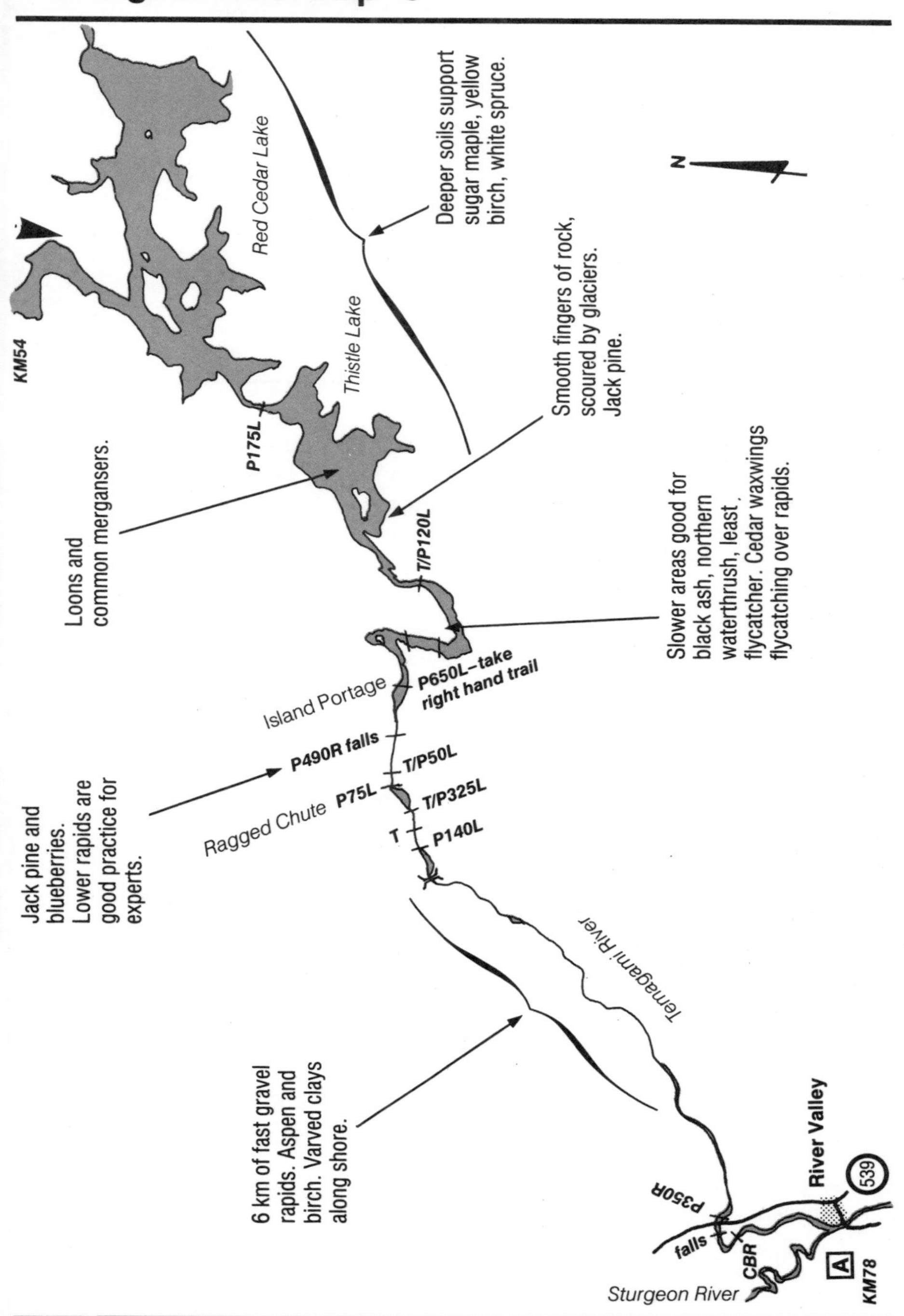

Ref. M.N.R. Map 41I/NE, 31L/NW, 1:126,000

Other Rivers in the Land of Grey Owl

To follow in the footsteps of Grey Owl is difficult, for he left only a sketchy record of his travels. But we know that he acted as a guide for several years in Temagami, and then spent more than a decade as a trapper based in the Biscotasing area, so his knowledge of the surrounding rivers must have been considerable.

One thing is clear from the writings of Grey Owl—he was a connoisseur of white water and went out of his way to run exciting rapids. In the Temagami area, as well as the rivers described in the section on Big Pine Country, this would include the Sturgeon River, which is described in Hap Wilson's *Temagami Canoe Routes*. Further to the west, the Wanapitei River also provides challenging stretches of whitewater. A brochure on this 200-km route is available from the Ministry of Natural Resources, Box 3500, Postal Station A, Sudbury, P3A 4S2.

Several routes lead north from the Biscotasing area. The Wakami River offers turbulent whitewater early in the season, though summer water levels are often low. This 124-km route begins at Wakami Provincial Park, which features a logging museum, a replica of a trapper's cabin and the ruins of a Hudson's Bay post. Another traditional route leading north from Bisco is known as the Sakatawi. As well as many relics of the logging days, this route includes the ghost town of Jerome.

In his days as a forest ranger, Grey Owl travelled extensively in the Mississagi Forest Reserve. This area includes a number of excellent routes, among the best being the Wenebegon, which joins the Mississagi at Aubrey Falls. Running along an old glacial spillway parallel to Hwy. 129, this 104-km route has several good rapids, as well as several log jams that resulted from the debris of a disastrous 1948 fire.

On the west side of the highway another tributary is the Aubinadong River, usually passable only in May and June. This route is dominated by high rock faces along the river and lots of white pine. It is also a good wildlife river, with moose, lynx and osprey reported along its length. Brochures for the Aubinadong and Wenebegon are both available from the Ministry of Natural Resources, 34 Birch St., Chapleau, P0M 1K0.

Traditional teepees clad in sheets of birch bark provided shelter for the Temagami Indians for hundreds of years.

W.H. Ellis/Public Archives Canada/ PA-121317

section 5

trails of early traders

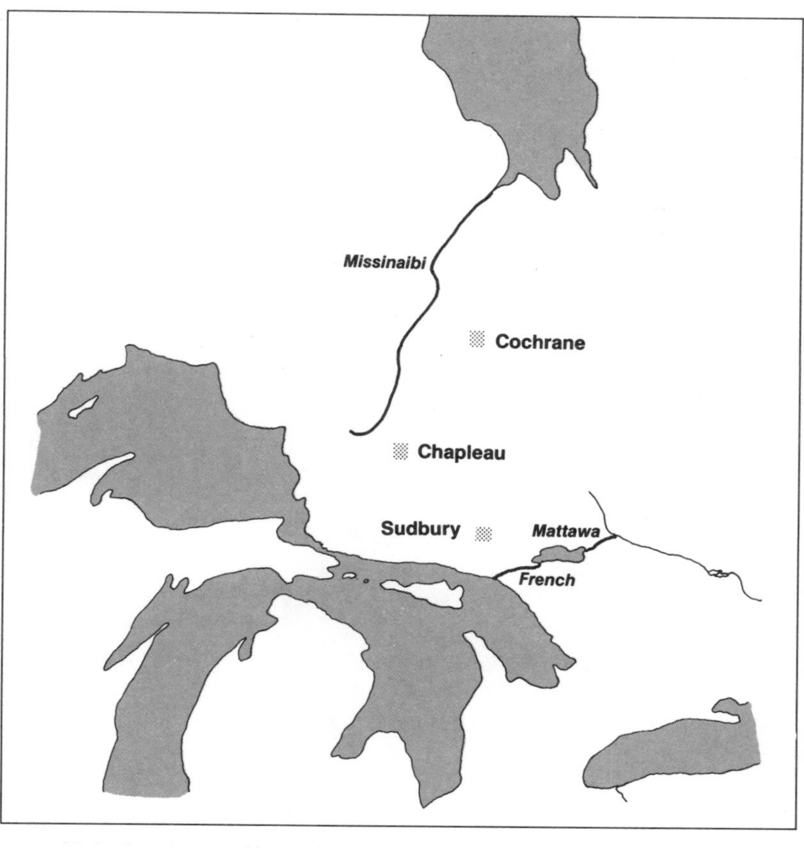

Hidden at the base of many a waterfall lies a treasure of trade goods—beads, trinkets, metal pots and flintlocks. This is not a treasure carefully buried for later retrieval, but rather the result of accidents two centuries ago which sent men and goods to the bottom of the swirling waters. Along the rivers of commerce that served Canada's fur trade, the voyageurs led a perilous life, coping with dangerous rapids, abundant insects and back-breaking work in fragile birch-bark canoes.

Spurred on by competition, two great companies probed westwards along the waterways of an unknown country. From Montreal a group of French-Canadian traders joined forces to form the North West Company, using the traditional Ottawa-French River route to reach westwards, eventually extending their trade routes an incredible 5000 km. From the north, the rival Hudson's Bay Company sent their agents up the Missinaibi and the Albany. Competing posts sprang up alongside each other, each enticing the local trade in beaver trapped by the Indians with a mixture of European goods and heavy-handed coercion.

The birch-bark craft used for this trade were a perfect example of adaptation to a harsh environment—light enough to be carried across rocky portages, strong enough to survive the turbulent seas of the Great Lakes, simple enough to be repaired with materials gathered along the way. Though the grand adventure of the voyageurs is long behind us now, some of their romance lives on in the names and the portages along their rivers.

The French: In the Wake of the Voyageurs

Robert McIntosh is a river man, one of a dying breed whose lives are intertwined with the history of their chosen river. For Robert, it is the lower French that stirs the blood, for this is the river not only of his life but of his father and grandfather as well.

We met Robert as he hailed us from his dock on the main outlet of the French, his gap-toothed grin inviting us in for a cold beer and a chat. Though neat as a pin inside, his house looked a little down at the heels from the water, with good reason, for it is one of the few survivors of the only major settlement that ever graced the banks of the French.

It took little encouragement for the river man to haul out his treasures—scrapbooks of photos showing the river in winter, the old wooden hotels and houses, the fishing boats and lumber tugs, the steamer pushing down through the rapids so it could be moved to Collingwood, and on and on. And other treasures too, like the original survey map of a fairy-tale town called Coponaning, all laid out in straight roads and square lots across a landscape that is anything but straight.

It took little encouragement on Robert's part to "save you that first portage," to have us pile our packs and canoe inside his homemade fibreglass boat, and go bucking and splashing our way up the lower reaches of the Dalles Rapids.

Perhaps our enthusiastic welcome to the French should not have surprised us, for this has always been a welcoming river, since the days when the voyageurs danced on La Prairie des Français, at its westernmost mouth. And it has long been a river of history, at first thought to lead to the Orient, then recognized as the route to the riches of fur in the Canadian west. Now, with the proposal of the French as both an Ontario waterway park and a Canadian heritage river, history can be fully explored, and how better than by canoe?

The 80 km of the French is a canoe route with many possibilities but few portages, suitable for the beginner as well as the seasoned pro. One of its many advantages is a relative freedom from insects; in peak bug season, when we paddled the river, insects were hardly noticeable. To avoid numerous motorboats, a June or September trip might be more enjoyable, though water levels are good throughout the summer.

A Land of Rock and Pine

One of the most striking aspects of the French was well expressed by the explorer Alexander Mackenzie as he passed on his way westward: "There is hardly a foot of soil to be seen from one end of the French River to the other, its banks consisting of hills of entire rock." Most of this exposed rock is metamorphosed sandstone and siltstone dating from the Precambrian age. Around the river's mouth larger areas of the pinkish granite have intruded.

The French follows a massive fault in the bedrock. Dipping into that valley, the glaciers were able to grind smooth the southern shore, and in many places steep northern walls were formed as the glaciers "quarried" out huge blocks, plucking broken pieces from the face and carrying them away. Around the river mouth, where the flow of the glaciers was aligned with old drainage channels, the ice was able to scour deeply and the tracks of the glaciers are exceptionally clear. Along with channels and grooves, watch for "chatter marks" left by boulders buried in the ice and skipping along the bedrock surface.

With this legacy of scoured rocks from glacial times, forests along the French developed thinly. For the most part the shoreline trees are limited to white and jack pine, red oak and hemlock, with a few pockets of hardwoods on deeper soils on Eighteen Mile Island and eastwards. You don't have to go far to return to a forest more typical of this part of Ontario. If you take the portage into the Restoule River, even a few hundred metres will bring you into deeper sands and a rich forest of sugar maple, basswood, yellow birch and white pine.

It is tempting to blame the loggers for the thinly stocked, short pines along the river, but it would be a mistake to do so. Even in 1788, a report by Deputy Surveyor-General Collins described the

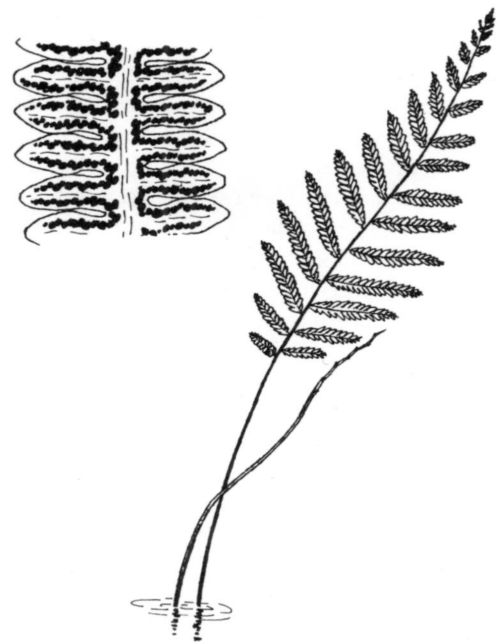

Virginia chain fern, rare in Ontario, is found in the pockets of bog north of Dalles Rapids; look for the chain-like spore pattern under the frond. **Hap Wilson**

country around the river mouth as "a rocky desert, nothing growing but small scrubby bushes and pine trees not 30 feet high—the same dreary prospect continues, I am informed, all the way up to Lake Nipissing."

Dan Brunton points out that some of the unusual vegetation found along the valley reflects the past. For example, the maritime influences of the Champlain Sea, which brought salt water up the Ottawa Valley, left eastern species such as Virginia chain fern, still abundant in the bogs near the mouth of the French. From the other direction, glacial Lake Algonquin brought the seeds of western plants, a few of which survive. The cold-tolerant plant communities that developed as the glaciers withdrew persist in the wetter areas, where boreal specialties such as nodding trillium and coltsfoot can be found. And from the south, relative newcomers such as cardinal flower are following the Georgian Bay shoreline to invade northwards.

Two species of wildlife more typical of western Canada are also found in the western sections of the French. Both the wapiti, or elk, and American bison were part of the original fauna of Ontario, but both were exterminated early by the pressure of guns. In the 1930s both species were reintroduced here, and small herds are occasionally spotted. Ironically, in the 1950s provincial wildlife authorities were convinced that elk harboured a liver parasite harmful to sheep and tried unsuccessfully to wipe out the species a second time. They were unable to do so, the parasite connection was eventually proved false, and finally in 1981 the Ministry of Natural Resources declared a ban on hunting the remaining elk.

The other notable form of wildlife here is the endangered Massasauga rattlesnake, which is abundant around the mouth and on the offshore islands. Ontario's only poisonous snake, the Massasauga usually frequents areas near swamps and bogs where it can catch frogs, but it can also occur in rocky areas, where it searches for mice. Even so, the rattlesnakes are timid and difficult to find, so your chances of running across one are minimal. If you are accidentally bitten, keep calm, use a snakebite suction kit if one is available to extract some of the poison, and head immediately for the nearest antivenin depots, in Sudbury or Parry Sound.

Bird life along the French is generally disappointing, due no doubt to the impoverished woodlands. However, a few osprey are known to nest along the river, and unusually high numbers of pine warblers are found in some areas.

The most important sport fish is the yellow pickerel, which spawns at the base of most of the rapids. Dalles Rapid is especially important in this regard, and the myriad of channels around the mouth of the French are regarded as some of the best pickerel-fishing areas in the province.

Gateway to a Continent

Mention almost any aspect of early Canadian history and the French River has played a part. Before the coming of road and rail, river travel was the lifeblood of the emerging nation, and the French was a critical link in the main artery to the West. Even before extensive use of the river by early French traders gave the river its name, the Indians had recognized its value as a connecting link. In the early days of the fur trade, Indians of the Huron and Ojibway tribes brought furs along this river en route to Montreal, and doubtless it had been used for some time previously as part of the extensive trade between the native tribes of Ontario.

This painting by Francis Hopkins is titled "Lake Superior", but the same canoes, handmade with a birchbark skin, often travelled the French. **Archives of Ontario/3-E 255**

The French was the pathway of the early explorers as well. Etienne Brulé used this corridor to discover Georgian Bay in 1610, as did his employer, Samuel de Champlain, five years later. Champlain tells of meeting a group of 300 Indians at the mouth of the French, probably from the Ottawa tribe further to the southeast, who came here regularly to gather huckleberries (more likely blueberries?) for winter use. These men were completely naked, their bodies tattooed extensively, their faces painted in diverse colours, their noses pierced and their ears bordered with trinkets. Small wonder they were looked down upon by the agricultural Hurons, who considered themselves more civilized.

In names such as Recollet Falls and Cross Island, the French reminds us that this was the route too for the early missionaries, men such as Brébeuf and Lalemant who were to meet a cruel death at the hands of the Iroquois. Here too came the *coureurs de bois*, independent traders such as Jean Nicolet, Pierre Radisson, des Groseilliers and la Verendrye. Short-tempered and rough-mannered as these early explorer-traders may have been, they were skilled in wilderness living and altered the course of history.

Almost a century later, in 1761, Alexander Henry passed through the French on his way westward. Recognizing the potential of this southern route, he and the other independent traders of

Montreal banded together to form the North West Company. At about the same time, the Hudson's Bay Company began its push inland from the northern coast, no longer content with the furs that trickled down to their river-mouth posts. So the stage was set for the great rivalry between the two giant fur companies that would rage over the next half-century.

For the North West Company, transporting furs and trade goods the 5000 km between Montreal and the prime fur country of the Athabasca was an enormous logistical problem. The answer lay in crews of voyageurs, tough French Canadians who paddled 16–18 hours a day, carried 80-kilo loads over portages, and steered fragile birch-bark canoes capable of carrying four tons. For these voyageurs, the 105 km from Lake Nipissing to Georgian Bay was an easy day's paddle, especially on the outward spring journey when all but two of the rapids could be run.

With the coming of larger, steam-powered boats on the Great Lakes, demands for conversion of the old fur trade route into a modern canal began. As early as 1837, investigations of the feasibility of a French-Ottawa canal were carried out. As recently as 1959, proposals for its construction were made, but the canal was an idea whose time was never to come.

The loggers came briefly to the French, beginning in the 1880s, but their stay was temporary. Farmers found little soil to attract their attention along the river, but recreation has become an important industry, with some 800 cottages now lining the shores of its central sections. Travel the French outside the cottaging season, though, and you will understand why it has been called a perpetually delayed frontier, always seeming on the verge of greater importance, but seldom fulfilled.

Exploring the River

The voyageurs paddled the French in both directions, and with a drop of only 19 m in its 80-km length, you will find it relatively easy to do so as well. In fact, there is some logic in paddling the French upstream, since the prevailing westerly winds can be more of a problem on the broad reaches than the current.

Approaching the French from the easterly end, the usual access points are at Chaudiere Dam, at the end of a secondary road from Monetville, or at Wolseley Bay, off Hwy. 528A. It is possible to arrange a shuttle service to Wolseley Bay with the French River Supply Post, located just east of Hwy. 69. Another popular access point to the east is Restoule Provincial Park, located just south of Lake Nipissing. An easy one-day paddle down the Restoule River, punctuated by several portages, brings you onto the French just downriver from Chaudiere.

Some canoeists make use of the irregular shoreline of Eighteen-Mile Island for a circle trip, taking about four days. Most, however, continue on downriver, past the Hwy. 69 access points, to the myriad of channels that form the river's mouth. Road access is available here at Hartley Bay, or you can loop back on the Pickerel River to Cantin Lake. Here a short portage along Little French Rapids brings you back on your original route, just upstream of Hwy. 69. Combined with a lift to Wolseley Bay arranged with the marina at French River, that happy circumstance makes the French one of the most accessible rivers in Ontario for "lone wolf" canoeists.

The route possibilities don't stop there, however. Since the French has no less than four exits to Georgian Bay in its rocky delta, any number of loops are possible there. Some canoeists continue westward from the mouth to Killarney. Others choose an easterly course, threading among the islands of Georgian Bay to Key Harbour, a beautiful route. The exposed waters of Georgian Bay can be extremely dangerous, and foul weather has a habit of brewing rapidly here, but the hundreds of small islands do provide shelter from the worst of the wind. Armed with a detailed map (we found 1:50,000 to be sufficient), a compass and a generous dose of patience to wait out windy weather, you can safely experience the unsurpassed beauty of the Georgian Bay islands.

CHAUDIERE TO HWY. 69

This first 50 km combines the best of the French's rapids with long stretches of island-studded flatwater, more like a lake than a river. In the vicinity of Chaudiere Falls, where the dam is bypassed by the 900-m Champlain Portage, watch for the kettle-shaped holes worn in the rock by the rush of glacial waters. These "chaudieres" (French for kettles) gave the area its name. Thor Conway reports that Indians passing the kettles toss in tobacco as a religious rite, a tradition recorded for over 300 years.

As you thread your way westwards among dozens of pine-clad islands, the shoreline on both sides belongs to the Dokis Indian Reserve. Local tradition has it that this band took their name from a chief who had difficulty pronouncing the plural of duck, which came out as "dock-ees." Nonetheless the tribe turned out to be

This simple wooden cross is one of several marking Cross Island, but the true origins of the name are lost in time. **Ron Reid**

astute businessmen. In 1910 they sold the rights to the last great pine stand along the French, located in their reserve, for $1.2 million, a sum that made them the wealthiest band in the province.

Soon you arrive at the northeast corner of Commanda Island, where the French loses much of its fall in a series of seven drops known collectively as the Five Mile Rapids. Often used as introductory training for whitewater paddlers, these rapids are relatively tame and most can be run down or lined up by experienced paddlers, depending on water levels. The Ministry of Natural Resources brochure provides a good synopsis of the conditions at each step. In this vicinity, as elsewhere along the upper river, camping spots are abundant and excellent.

As you shoot out past the inevitable fishermen in their motorboats at the base of Crooked Rapids, you enter another long stretch of flat water. The tree cover now begins to show more clearly the stress of shallow soils. The red pines and cedar become less common and in places even the hardy white pine is replaced by the tougher jack pine. One such area is on the west shore opposite Cross Island. You can see that all the trees of this extensive stand of jack pine are of similar age, almost certain testament to a fire which swept through the area, opening the cones of the jack pine as it went.

Cross Island is marked by a white wooden cross erected by the local Knights of Columbus and by several more rudimentary wood and stone crosses higher up. Local legend has it that the priests were burned alive at the stake here, but it is more likely that the island is simply a burial site for those drowned in the rapids above.

Westward you go, past a pair of steep-sided islands known as the Haystacks, past an abandoned sawmill site on the north shore, past another high island called the Owl's Head, where legend says a fleeing owl and her brood were turned to stone. Pockets of deeper soil along the north shore support mixed stands, with birch and hemlock among the pines. These richer sites support a more diverse understorey as well, with spinulose wood fern, northern beech fern and the rare maidenhair fern found among the plant roster.

At Lost Child Bend the spirits have been active again, stealing away a legendary Indian child whose cries were heard for six days while searchers combed the woods in vain. Just to the south, a bay in Cantin Island supports one of the the most biologically significant sites along the river. Among the beautiful pink islands and points, swampy backwaters provide habitat for a community of pondweeds and milfoil very unusual in Ontario.

The cottages and lodges are thicker now, and a short paddle brings you to the marina and store at French River, in a bay just past the railway bridge. Basic supplies and access facilities are available here, only a few kilometres from Hwy. 69.

HWY. 69 TO GEORGIAN BAY

In the 30 km from here to the mouth, the riverside becomes more steep and rocky, the trees more stunted, the channels more complex and the opportunities for campsites more limited. Despite the occasional motorboat and cottage, this area has the unmistakable imprint of wildness upon it; untamed by the pursuits of man, it remains a sanctuary of rough-hewn beauty.

Even before Hwy. 69 crosses high above you, the river begins to funnel into a steep-walled canyon. The scouring effect of the glaciers is clearly seen, contrasting with the steeper north walls where ancient ice plucked away great chunks of Precambrian rock. In the spring, the walls of this canyon are enlivened by dozens of small streams which spray, drip and chatter their way down to the mainstream. Along these moist shady walls, white cedars line the shore, and delicate oak ferns can be found in the rich green carpet of moss.

Recollet Falls is the only major drop along this section, its name derived from the priests who passed here. The voyageurs would doff their red caps and murmur a prayer before the crosses erected here—as many as 30 on one bank, according to a traveller here in 1800. Even today, the Falls still drown the unwary, so be particularly careful, especially in high water, in approaching the portage on the south bank very close to the top of the falls. There are Indian pictographs on the canyon wall above the Falls, but when we passed by in high water, we were too fully occupied dealing with the boiling eddies and powerful current even to attempt a search.

Further down the fault line that has captured the French, a side channel leading into Flowerpot Bay marks the beginning of a stand of almost pure red oak on the eastern shore. On the bare acidic rocks beneath this stand, rocks that hold the heat of the sun, specialized species such as the feathery clumps of the rusty woodsia fern grow. Here also is found the rare pinesap, a parasitic plant that feeds off the roots of the oak.

At Ox Bay the river branches out into a confusing array of channels and islands, offering opportunities for leisurely exploring. Don't be surprised if your campsite here is serenaded by a whippoorwill, or the evening air is disturbed by the flappy flight and raspy calls of a nighthawk, for this rocky terrain provides ideal nesting places for these night-foraging members of the goatsucker family.

Your choice of route will likely be determined by your eventual destination. The Pickerel River flows in from the east here, and the Pickerel River exit will lead down to Georgian Bay close to the entrance to Key Harbour. The Western Channel, thought to be the one most frequently used by the voyageurs, provides extra shelter on the route to Killarney. It is on this route that the Petite Faucille or "little sickle" rapids referred to in several early journals is found, requiring a lift-over of 25 m.

Two channels lead south from Ox Bay to another crossroads at the Elbow. A straight run down the eastern outlet provides a good look at the glacial scars near the tramway, but the main outlet is more interesting. On the north shore here, above Dalles Rapids, several small bogs nestled in hollows in the bedrock contain spectacular concentrations of Virginia chain fern, a species seldom found in Ontario. The rapids themselves require careful scouting, and often a short portage, as a historic account from David Thompson's journal attests:

"They preferred running the Dalles; they had not gone far, when to avoid the ridge of waves, [to] which they ought to have kept, they took the apparent smooth water, were drawn into a whirlpool, which wheeled them around into its vortex; the Canoe with the Men clinging to it, went down end foremost, and all were drowned; at the foot of the Dalles search was made for their bodies, but only one Man was found, his body much mangled by the rocks."

On the channel below the rapids, only a few traces remain of the village of French River, developed briefly on the site that was to be Coponaning. An old mill foundation just north of the existing lighthouse remains to show that this country was not always wilderness. Along the water's edge several old boilers rust away; they were never used but were too difficult to remove when the mills were dismantled. But of the two mills that worked here in the 1890s, the houses for 300 people, the two hotels and the matching churches, Roman Catholic and Anglican, very little remains. Most of the buildings were torn down and shipped to Toronto for reassembly in the 1930s; almost all of the others gradually fell victim to fire and rot.

Still it is a place of romance and legends, a place where you can picture the barges being loaded in "the Creek," the shingle mill whining away in the Loading Cove; the rotted roads created from wood slabs and sawdust in a land where no gravel was to be found. The frontier once more delayed, the promise of settlement once more defeated, the mouth of the French now reverts back to the alders, sand cherry and pine of the wild.

National Topographic System Maps
Scale 1:50,000: 41 I/1, I/2
41 H/15

Ministry of Natural Resources Maps
Scale 1:126,720: Sudbury 41I/SE

Ministry of Natural Resources Office
Box 3070, North Bay, P1B 8K7

French River – Map 1

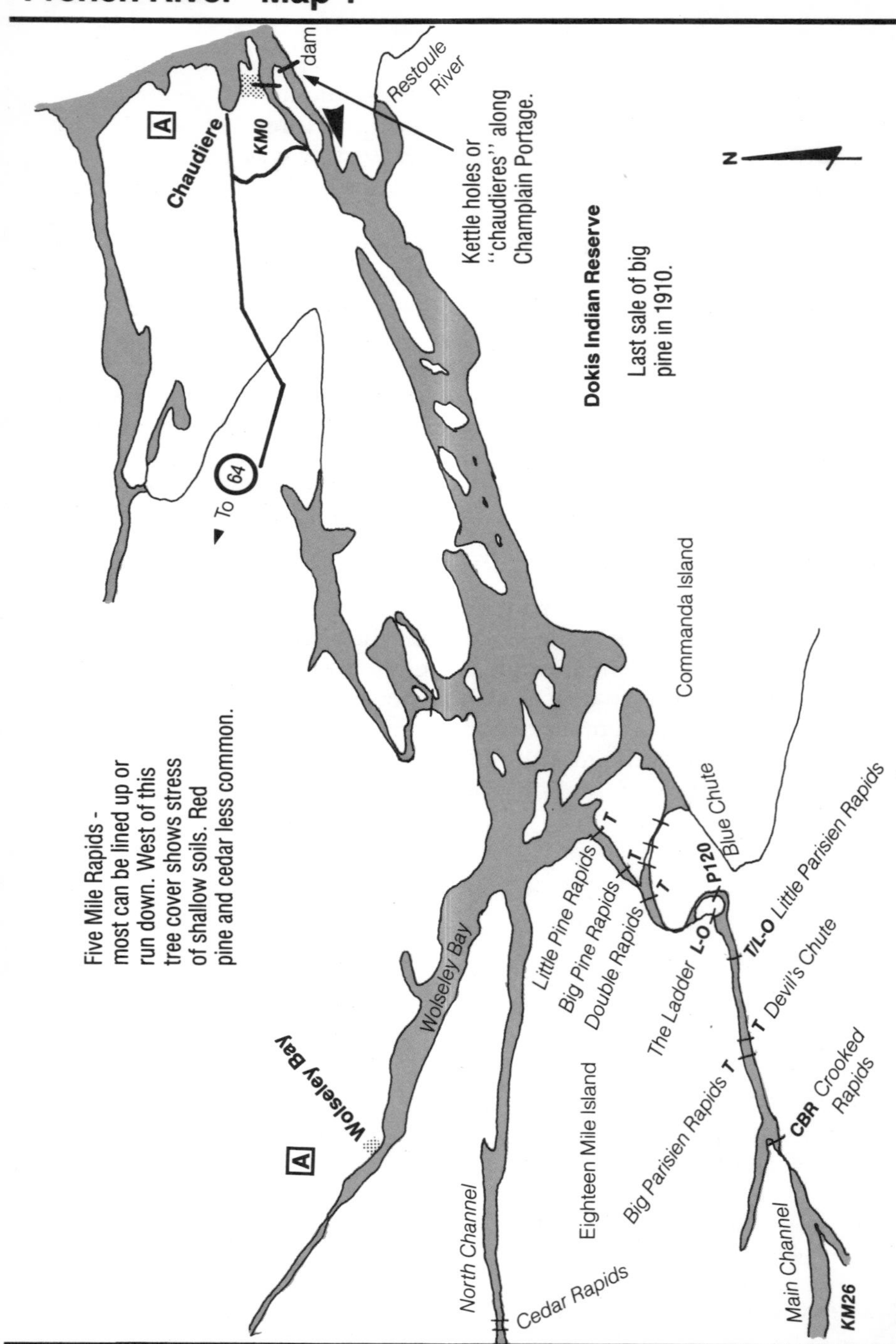

Ref: M.N.R. Map 41I/SE, 1:126,000

French River–Map 2

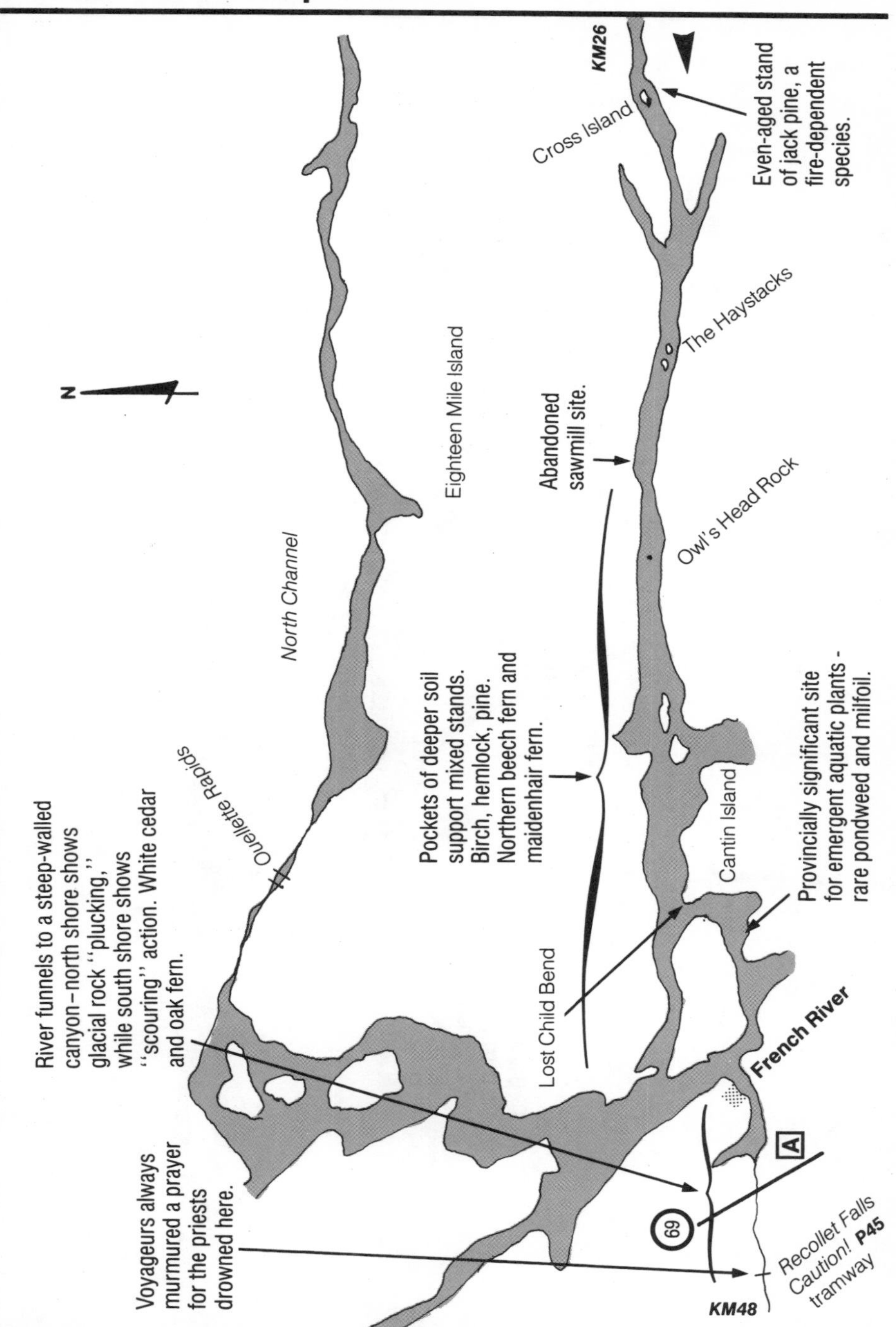

Ref: M.N.R. Map 41I/SE, 1:126,000

French River–Map 3

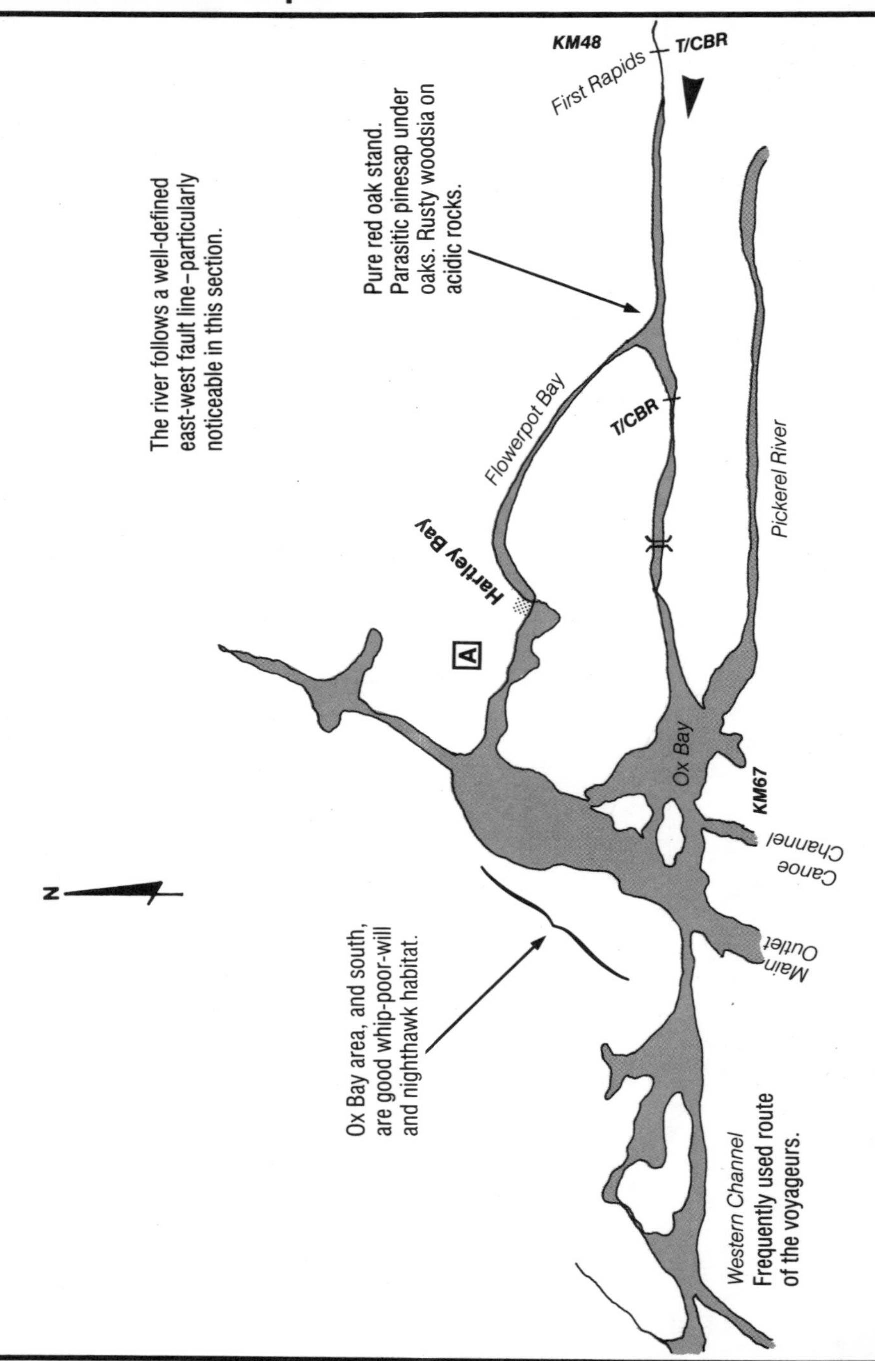

Ref: M.N.R. Map 41I/SE, 1:126,000

French River – Map 4

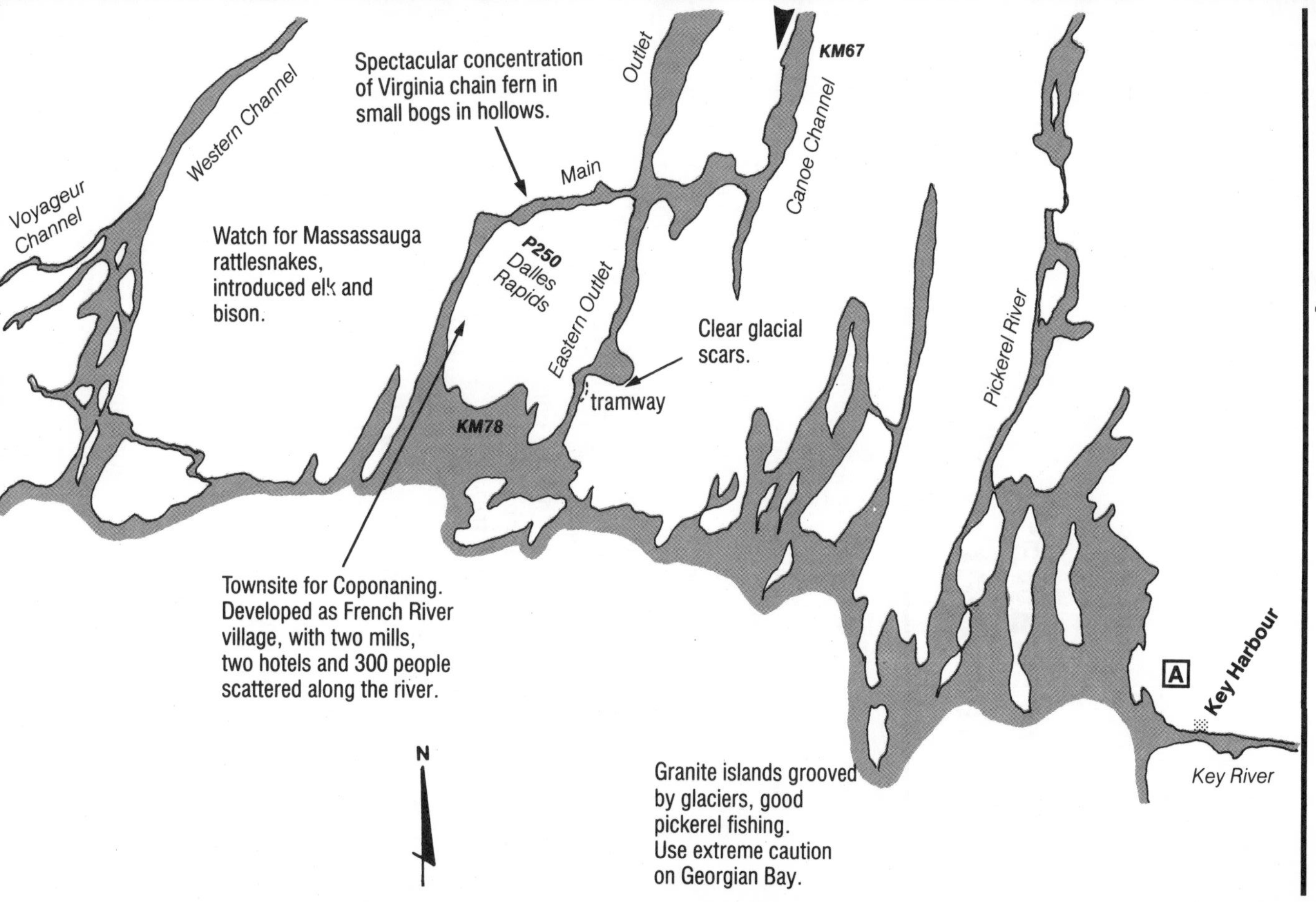

Ref: N.T.S. Map 41H/NE, 1:125,000

The Mattawa: A Little Gem of History

"The Mattawa is a little gem of history: rocky and rugged for nearly all of its forty miles, it has defied cultivation or settlement, and remains for most of its length unchanged in every way."

Eric Morse's introduction to this segment of the great fur trade route summarizes a delightful canoeing experience, even though the Mattawa is considerably less remote than most rivers of its nature. With two provincial parks protecting most of the river, and the voyageur portages once again regularly used, the Mattawa is a vivid reminder of the romance of our history.

The Mattawa Wild River Provincial Park covers 32 km on the central section of the river, but the complete trip from North Bay to the town of Mattawa on the Ottawa River encompasses 58 km, an easy three- or four-day trip. The voyageurs must have known this river well, for 11 of the 38 portages on their three-month trip to Thunder Bay were concentrated in this short stretch. All of these 11 are still known by their original French names, although two portages have been obliterated by the construction of small dams.

In the height of summer it might be difficult to describe the Mattawa of today as wilderness—there are too many visitors and too many motorboats. Some of the campsites are likely to be crowded, and natural firewood in their vicinity is scarce. This is a route where a small gas stove would be a welcome addition. Or, if you just can't give up the flavour of pine smoke, collect your firewood along the way before you camp. A more pleasant alternative is to paddle the Mattawa in late September, about the time when the voyageurs would be returning along its course in their hasty retreat back to Lachine before the winter frosts.

This is the season of a thousand colours: the scarlet slash of a maple sapling among the pines, the burnt sienna of royal ferns reflecting in dark waters, the speckled yellow of a fallen aspen leaf. You might have paddled by shrubby shores of winterberry a hundred times and never known it was there until the autumn extravaganza of orange berries announced its presence. Or missed the clinging vines of Virginia creeper intertwined with the trailside saplings, until frost revealed the rich purple of its autumn leaves.

Autumn canoeing can mean crisp clear days that send sunshine down into your very soul. But it can also mean even crisper nights, or days filled with north winds and sleety rains, so go prepared with clothes to withstand the worst. One advantage of this river is that its rocky portages with good landings mean that you will probably never have to cope with wet feet.

Whenever you go, you will find the Mattawa an ideal river for canoeists with limited experience. Portages are short and well marked, there are easy rapids to try as well as a few more difficult ones, and access is easy. What fledgling voyageur could ask for more?

Only a Stream Remains

The Mattawa today is quite a small river; in places it seems little more than a stream. Yet at one time it was a torrent that rivalled the present St. Clair River in size, draining all the upper Great Lakes through its course. This outlet began as a lobe of ice that had blocked the valley withdrew, allowing the waters of glacial Lake Algonquin to rush down a new course. This sudden release left its mark along the Mattawa in the form of rounded boulders and scour marks. As the immense weight of the glaciers was lifted, the earth's crust rebounded, raising the Mattawa basin at least 150 m. As the land rose and the clay deposits blocking the St. Clair River eroded away, the drainage pattern of the Great Lakes switched to the one we see today.

The Mattawa had been preordained to fulfill this brief role by the development of an enormous fault in the ancient gneiss bedrock, extending down the Ottawa Valley. As well as determining the course of the river, this fault created several very deep lakes along its length. Trout, Turtle and Talon lakes are all greater than 60 m deep. These cold, nutrient-poor lakes are ideal habitat for lake trout, which occur in all three. An introduced population of

Atlantic salmon also thrives in Trout Lake, the only place in Ontario where this species now is self-sustaining.

In the central section of the river, between Talon Lake and Samuel de Champlain Park, a massive "pluton" of granite-like igneous rock has intruded. Cracks in this pluton contain calcareous marble, which creates a much richer habitat for plant life, especially along the cliffs, where such unusual species as wild columbine, fragrant cliff fern and smooth cliff-brake occur.

The marble also contains crystals of brucite, a mineral used as a colouring agent in paper production. In the 1950s a brucite mine north of Boivin Lake extracted the mineral, bringing it out across a bridge beside the Talon Chutes dam. Further to the east, the Purdy mine extracted crystalline mica from cracks in the rock, selling most of it to the U.S. government during the Second World War.

It was pine that attracted the first industrial attention to the Mattawa, and stands of white and red pine still line most of the valley. On deeper soils, mixed stands with white spruce, white birch, largetooth aspen and other hardwoods provide richer wildlife habitat. The pioneering birch and aspen are found especially along the south shore, which has entirely burned since the days of early logging. Parts of the north shore have been spared from fire, and on the hills there are rich stands of sugar maple and associated hardwoods.

The Mattawa is not a spectacular wildlife river, although a good sampling of birds and the more common northern mammals can be found there. In the winter, however, the central section does act as a yarding area for white-tailed deer from surrounding areas.

The Meeting of the Waters

Mattawa is Ojibway for "meeting of the waters," an appropriate appellation for this crossing point from Lake Huron to the voyageurs' Main Street down the Ottawa. But even before Etienne Brulé turned left on his way up the Ottawa in 1610 and made history, the Mattawa had been an Indian trade route for centuries.

Archaeologists have recovered evidence along the Mattawa of Indian use up to 6000 years ago. On favoured campsites, such as the sandy shores on the east end of Camp Island, there is clear evidence of extensive use by Middle and Late Woodland Indians. In several places on Trout Lake, mysterious stone structures, thought to have had some Indian ceremonial purpose, have been

During the brief period of logging along the Mattawa, structures such as this timber slide, photographed in 1897, sped the logs on their way.

W.H. Ellis/Public Archives Canada/PA-121268

discovered. And at Porte de l'Enfer, an Indian ochre mine is one of only two known in the province.

We know that the Hurons and the Ojibway travelled along this route to Lachine to trade their furs with the early French. When the explorers arrived, they had only to follow the well-worn paths of the Indians in this part of their travels. And arrive they did—the list of explorers who passed through the Mattawa on their way westward is a veritable Who's Who of Canadian exploration.

With the formation of the North West Company in 1784, and the gradual extension of their trade routes westward to such incredible lengths, the role of the Mattawa changed. The canoes along its course now belonged not to explorers poking their way into the dark unknown, but to the voyageurs, hired muscle for a cross-continent assembly line based on fur. For close to 40 years the cliffs along the river rang with the songs and curses of the French-Canadian voyageurs, but after the merger with the Hudson's Bay Company in 1821, the importance of this river as a commercial route rapidly declined.

By 1850 the first loggers searching for virgin pine began their short-lived invasion. Shortly thereafter, the arrival of the railways ended the era of the Mattawa as a transportation route forever.

Exploring the River

The 58-km route along the Mattawa can be paddled in either direction, although most canoeists begin in the west, making both current and prevailing winds work to their advantage. A car shuttle is straightforward here, as the river ends in the town of Mattawa and four buses daily can ferry you back to North Bay.

The most frequently used starting point is Armstrong Park, on Lakeside Drive just off Trout Lake Road (Hwy. 63) in North Bay. As you leave behind the suburbs and travel along the shelter of the south-shore islands, you might be in Algonquin country were it not for the cottages along the way. The hills around the lake are clad in pine and spruce, birch and aspen, with even the occasional specimen of maple, yellow birch and hemlock.

A short paddle brings you to Dugas Bay, where you join the route of the voyageurs. From the south tip of this bay, a short walk across Hwy. 17 follows the start of the famous La Vase portage over the height of land to Lake Nipissing. The route followed down La Vase Creek is about 14 km long, but only about 3 km actually had to be carried, for a series of beaver dams helpfully converted the tiny stream into a canal. The old route is still traceable today, but be warned: La Vase translates as "the muddy," a reflection of portage conditions along its length.

On the rocky sides of Dugas Bay, relics from an earlier era pose mysteries yet unsolved. Archaeologists Allen Tyyska and James Burns discovered several sites with low stone walls and steps, pathways and pavements, and primitive figures etched into the rock that suggest some kind of Indian ceremonial use. Just when or by whom they were developed remains unknown.

Near the east end of Trout Lake, a similar structure, with several pictographs, has been found on Camp Island. Among the fine stand of red and white pines at the east end of the island, the Woodland Indians also camped from 700 B.C. onwards. Remarkable as it may seem, that means that some form of canoe had to be regularly in use over 2600 years ago, well before the time of Christ.

Although it is private land, Camp Island (also known as Kirkwood) is heavily over-used for camping, and firewood is almost impossible to find. The central part of the island harbours the rocky bottom of a former river, part of the glacial outwash that once flowed here. In an ironic twist of geomorphology, the river has now become the island.

The end of the lake is marked by the Stepping Stones, a band of boulders stretched most of the way across the river. It would appear that a glacial moraine once crossed here, but centuries of flow removed all the finer materials, leaving only these large, water-rounded boulders. A second access point is located here. If you want to miss Trout Lake, drive north from Corbeil Corners on Centennial Crescent, then follow MacPherson Drive 6 km to the road's end.

At the Narrows, 2 km further along, the historic Portage de la Tortue has been blasted and flooded out of existence. It had never been a major carry, for in high water the canoes could squeeze through the rocky gut, but in summer the short trail would be used.

Along the broken rocky shores in this area, the mossy boulders support lush stands of polypody, a common fern along this route. Polypody is easily identified by its single fronds, each about 15 cm in length, and by the "teeth" that are offset rather than directly opposite each other. In September you might also notice the bright orange-red berries of winterberry, a member of the holly family, along the shore. While these persistent berries provide winter food for birds, they are too astringent to be eaten by humans.

At Turtle Lake you can choose to follow the river through a series of five short portages to Talon Lake, or to follow the fur trade route through Pine Lake. The latter leads through a small marsh at the east end of the lake, where beaver have cut canals through the sedge meadows to reach their favoured poplar. In summer the channel is thick with fragrant water lilies and the purple spikes of pickerelweed, but in autumn the marsh has settled into a more subdued beauty.

Just past a lift-over around a small beaver dam, you find the Portage de la Mauvaise Musique, an easy 200-m walk through rich woods. At some point in its history this portage has been considerably improved, with rocks placed to bridge the wet spots and provide more level footing on side slopes. Along the way you can see a good selection of typical understorey plants of the mixed forest region—wintergreen, trailing arbutus, lily-of-the-valley, broad-leaved aster, clintonia and partridgeberry.

Pine Lake, full of islands, used to be known as Robichaud, but somehow its name has fallen victim to the more mundane nature of our times. It now drains to the west, the way you have come, but along the portage trail at its end you can see the evidence of earlier times when it flowed northwards. The characteristic rounded boulders of an ancient stream line the path, especially as it descends to McCool Bay on Talon Lake.

This is the Portage Pin de Musique—the singing pines—although now most of the pine is replaced by a stand of large-tooth aspen. Along the autumn path you are likely to run across a phenomenon peculiar to fall migration—mixed bird parties. For some reason birds of several species often group together at this time of year for their flight southwards. Early in the fall, the winter calls of chickadees might lead you also to kinglets and various warblers; later in the season the chipping of song sparrows could also reveal white-crowned and white-throated sparrows, nuthatches or even downy woodpeckers.

You must look several kilometres to the north to see one of the most interesting areas on Lake Talon. At the mouth of the river a sandy delta has built up a series of meanders, oxbows and channels that provide excellent wildlife habitat. Silver maple thrives on the levees, and the shallow bay provides a foothold for wild rice as well as several rare species of underwater plants. This is the place along the river to see muskrats, hard at work building their winter "push-ups"—hollow mounds of vegetation that will provide breathing holes at regular intervals once the lake is frozen over.

As you paddle down Lake Talon, or perhaps sail before a northwesterly breeze, take note of some of the interesting glacial features around you. At the mouth of Spottiswood Bay a small gravelly ridge marks the northerly limit of one of southern Ontario's longest eskers, stretching 160 km south from here almost to Washago. On the opposite side of the lake, Grasswell Point acts as a recipient for fine sands washed down from glacial debris. Its point, still being shaped by the wave action of the lake, provides an excellent camp spot.

The sand has taken another form at Shields Bay, where a rocky island has been joined to the shore by a sand bar known as a tombolo. Near Blanchard's Landing on the south shore, another marsh at the mouth of Sharpes Creek marks the edge of the Rutherglen moraine, pushed up at the end of the glacial lobe that blocked this valley so long ago.

As you pass through the narrows into Boivin Lake, the influence of the Bonfield Batholith, a massive intrusion of granite-like rocks, becomes obvious in the square cliffs surrounding you. At the top of one of these cliffs on the right, you can see a jack pine stand, an unusual feature along this river. Ecologists think that jack pine is so rare here, in spite of the fires that usually favour the species, because the original stands of conifer had to contend with few fires, and jack pine seed was scarce.

At Talon Chutes the 330-m portage leads right of the dam over a series of difficult rock ridges. You can almost smell the salty sweat of the voyageurs as you descend the rocky path to a small beach at the bottom. But the effort is worth it, for the river here plunges into a narrow canyon that casts you into the perpetual shadows of these reddish cliffs.

Here the influence of the brucite-bearing marble sandwiched in the rock makes itself felt. Look closely at the vegetation and notice how many new species you see. Bristly clumps of juniper poke from the hillside, and mats of the creeping bearberry adorn its top. Here too the royal fern grows richly along the water, and the rare cliff-dwelling ferns make their first appearance.

The soft veins of marble are easily eroded by water, as you can see here in the southern "flood channel" that starts at the head of the portage. This channel is actually a marble vein scoured by the glacial river, and in places the swirling action of water and rocks has scoured potholes. Other water wear marks can be seen along the portage trail itself, but the most impressive potholes, some 2 m across and 5 m deep, are above the cliff on the north side of the river and difficult to find.

The cliffs provide nesting spots for birds such as the raven, phoebe, and rough-winged, barn and cliff swallows. There was also a pair of peregrine falcons nesting on these cliffs until about 1945. Sadly, like others of their kind, these birds fell prey to pesticide poisoning as contamination levels destroyed the vitality of their eggs. Peregrine falcons, whose predatory "stoop" can top 280 km/hr, are now listed as endangered, with captive breeding programs being used to try to rebuild their numbers.

The bird life of the Mattawa is relatively well known, thanks to Louise de Kiriline Lawrence, an amateur naturalist and author who has been observing birds in the vicinity of her home at Pimisi Bay over the past 40 years.

Public access is also available at Pimisi Bay from Hwy. 17. Just downstream, the river turns northward over the remains of an old logging dam at Decharge des Perches. This shallow rapid, which can usually be run, marked a point of celebration for the outward-bound voyageurs, for it was here that they threw aside the metal-shod poles (perches) that had helped them up through the shallow rapids below.

A series of short rapids now takes you northwards, either run if your experience and water levels permit, or portaged along the historic ways. The mixed woods are richer here, with the lime-loving white cedar making an appearance along the shores, and green ash, basswood and yellow birch adding to the roster along the trails. Watch as well for the white "doll's eye" berries of baneberry, but keep in mind that these attractive berries are poisonous.

When you reach Portage de la Prairie, more caution is necessary, for the swift waters lead to a small falls. Under some conditions expert canoeists could get through, but for most of us the portage trail is safer. There is no question at the next portage, around the 8-m Paresseux Falls. In any case the 400-m portage is made more interesting by its route along the abandoned river bed, littered with smooth boulders.

Just around the corner, the river leads by the Porte de l'Enfer, a dark crevice some 5 m above the water's level. Scramble up

The shadowy opening of Porte d l'Enfer is unmistakable, making this historic site a place of the spirits. **Ron Reid**

inside and you can see how the Indians worked several veins of the iron oxide hematite to extract the ore. Archaeologists have also found a refinery area directly above the cave, where the rocks were broken more finely. Just why this site was chosen for the mine, rather than one of the other frequent exposures of hematite along the river, is a mystery.

No doubt the site had a deep symbolic significance, for the red ochre produced was the basis for the paint used in pictographs. The choice of mine site might relate to the proximity of Paresseux Falls, for the Indians believed that spirits at the base of the falls were responsible for their noise. These legends may also explain the French name for the mine, since the superstitious voyageurs naturally associated talk of spirits with the Devil, and the "gates of Hell" followed naturally.

Two km downstream, a lone elm tree marks Elm Point, an excellent camping spot. Here you can trace the perambulations of a delta in the process of formation, as sand from a small stream is deposited in the quiet waters of the Mattawa.

Les Epingles is nothing more than a small swift leading into Bouillon Lake, but Des Roches Rapids, at the other end, is more

Fort Mattawa in 1876 was a thriving Hudson's Bay post, located on the spit of land that now forms Explorer's Park.
Public Archives Canada/PA-28725

difficult and should only be attempted by experts. Again, the remains of a moraine washed clean by the river can be seen here. Along the side of the river in this area, bur oak can also be spotted. The bridge leading to the Purdy Mica Mine is now gone, but you can still follow the logging trail several kilometres north if that endeavour interests you.

The next portage in line, Portage Campion, is worth a visit even by those expert enough to run through the rapids. The voyageurs carried their 180-lb loads across this portage, but ran the canoe through empty, a manoeuvre known as "decharge." Along the portage trail now, there stand several displays associated with Samuel de Champlain Provincial Park, including a full-sized replica birchbark canoe and various trade goods retrieved from the bottom of treacherous rapids.

From here eastwards, the river settles into a long narrow lake held back by the Hurdman Dam in Mattawa. Along the rocky sides, clad in pine, several rare shrubs including bittersweet and narrow-leaved New Jersey tea have been found. Towards the east end, the southern shore becomes level, perhaps accounting for the origin of the name Chant Plain. Eric Morse suggests that the name should actually be Champ Plain—flat field.

As you pick your way across the boardwalks at the south end of the dam, watch for several small potholes created by water action. You might also notice the pioneer species typical of disturbed ground: chickory, viper's bugloss, mullein, staghorn sumac and pin cherry, along with various grasses.

Four km downstream, at the junction with the Ottawa River, a newly built museum stands on the site of a Hudson's Bay post at Explorer's Park. The HBC took advantage of this traditional campground to open its post in 1837, the site chosen by Governor George Simpson. For most of its 71-year existence, the post did a good business, but now little remains but its memories. Considerable credit must go to the people of Mattawa for preserving Explorer's Park, a lonely point that stands sentinel for the little river that provided a pathway into an unknown continent.

National Topographic System Maps
Scale 1:50,000: 31L/6, L/7

Ministry of Natural Resources Maps
Scale 1:100,000: North Bay 31L/SW
Mattawa 31L/SE

Ministry of Natural Resources Office
Box 3070, North Bay, P1B 8K7

Mattawa River – Map 1

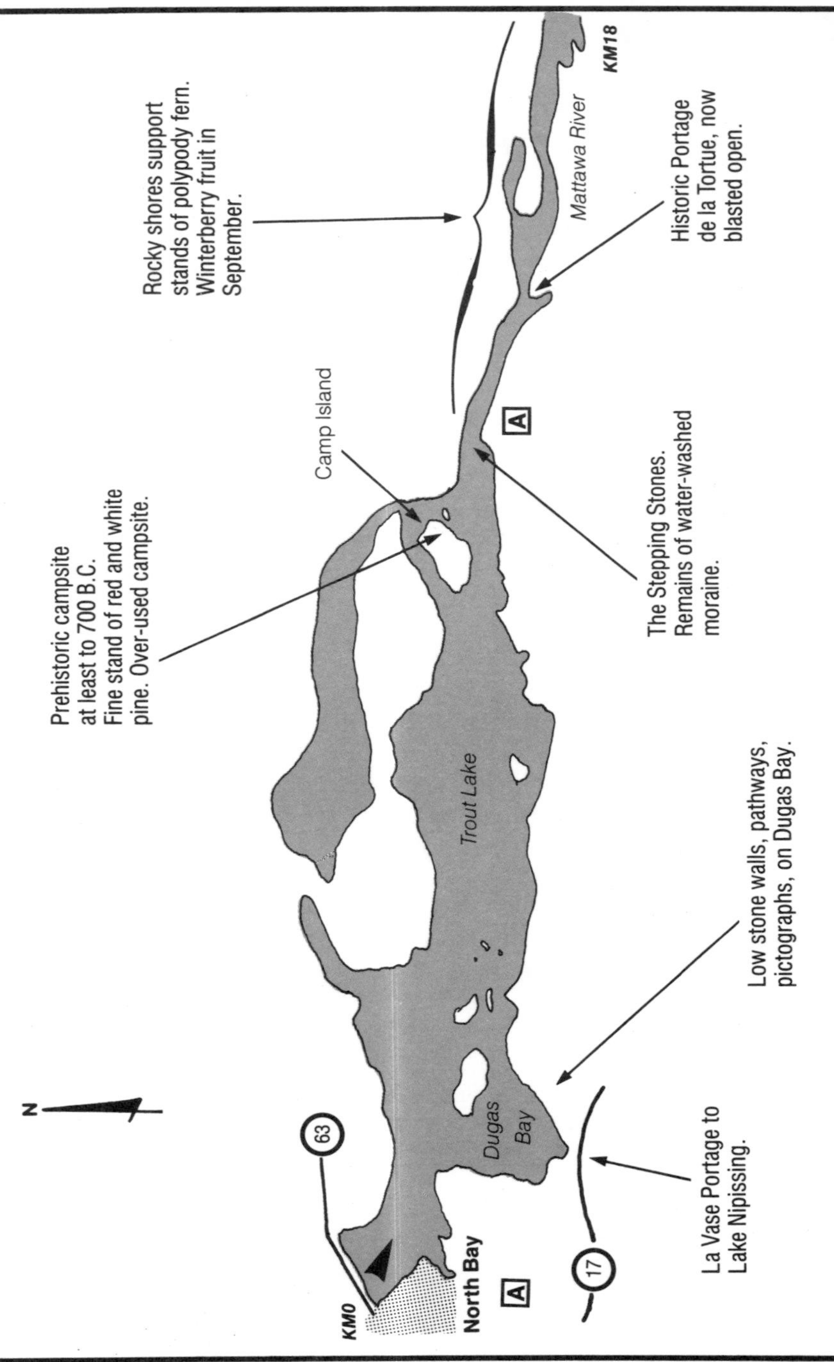

Ref: M.N.R. Map 31L/SW, 1:100,000

Mattawa River–Map 2

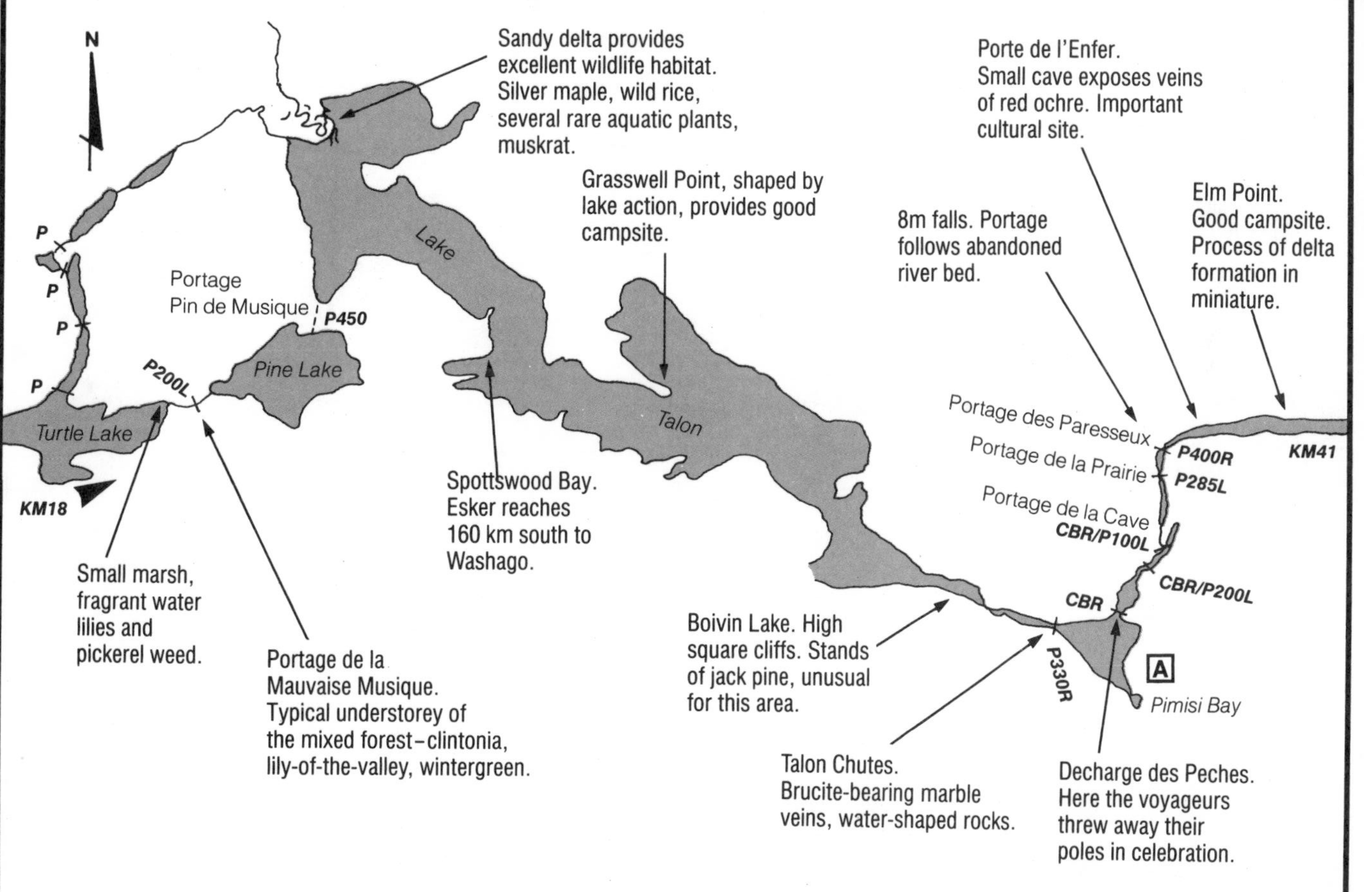

Ref: M.N.R. Map 31L/SW, 31L/SE, 1:100,000

Mattawa River – Map 3

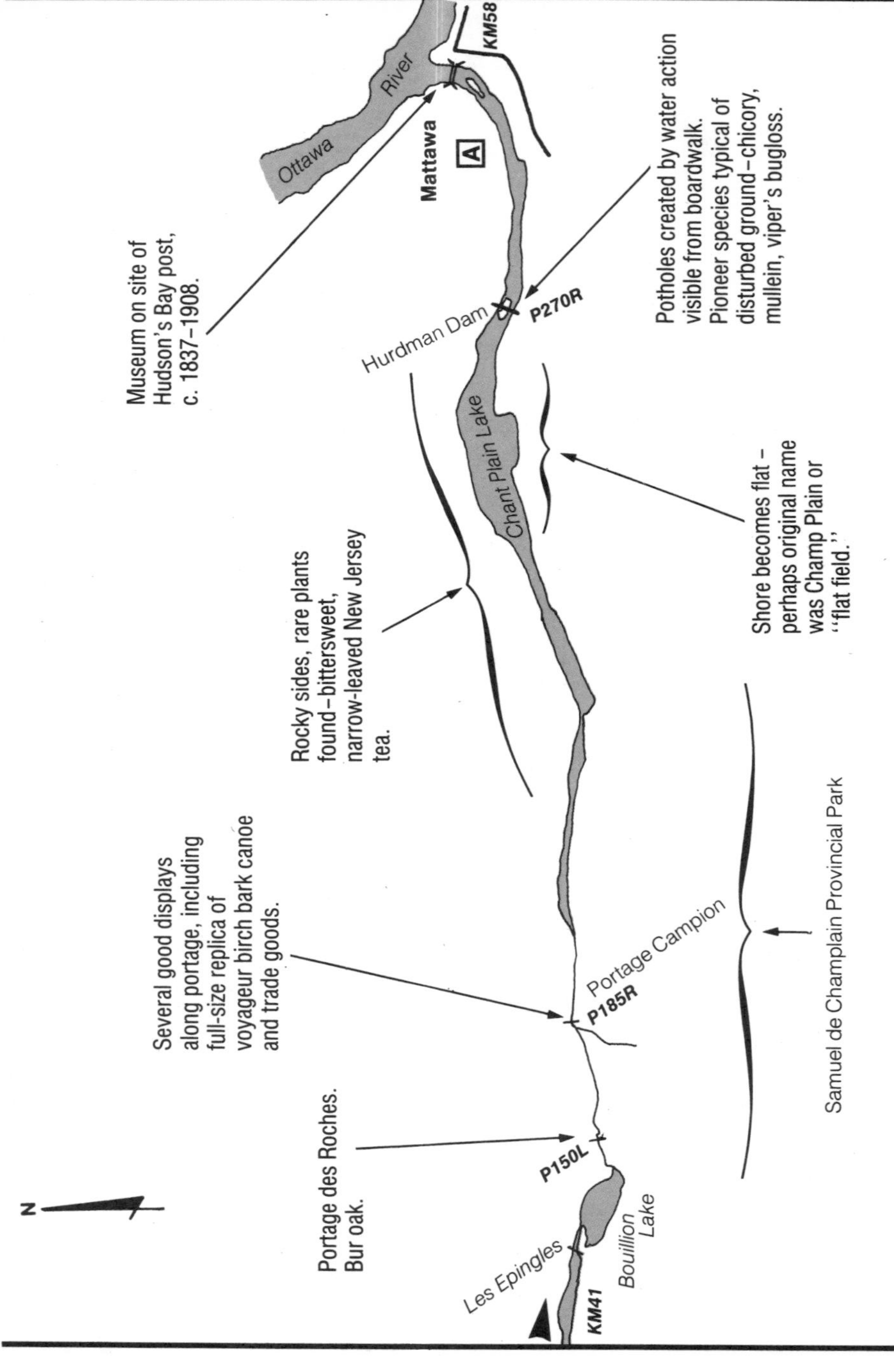

Ref: M.N.R. Map 31L/SE, 1:100,000

The Missinaibi: Valley of Pictured Waters

George Luste is a man of many rivers, a canoeist who has seen the best of Canada's wilderness. He knows well the weight of a heavy pack on a long portage, the fickle pull of current on paddle in a boiling rapid, the welcome coolness of a dawn mist. Yet if you ask George Luste to choose a favourite Ontario river, his answer is immediate—the Missinaibi.

What is it about this river that attracts the devotion of such a discriminating and experienced canoeist? Perhaps it's partly the fact that the Missinaibi is one of the few river systems still unspoiled along its entire length. Listen to George's recollections of other experiences:

"Almost every other river I have been on was despoiled. There was something about every trip that reflected misuse. The Abitibi was filthy. We had to boil our water, but even then we didn't know what was in it and had to hold our teeth tight when we drank.

After travelling the English River I learned it was among the most mercury-polluted on the continent. Pulp and paper activity was heavy on the Coulange River and in places the forests were decimated right to the water's edge.

"The lower part of the South Nahanni River in the Northwest Territories is protected but well travelled by tour boats. The headwaters are beautiful but not protected. Adjacent to one of the most picturesque sets of falls on the river is a mining development.

"It gets depressing. Your keep wondering whether your children will have the chance to use an unspoiled river."

In its 550 km from Missinaibi Lake to the salty estuary of James Bay, the Missinaibi River presents a silver strand of unspoiled wilderness. In that entire length the river has been spanned by man in only four places—twice by road and twice by rail. In that same length a canoeist will pass more than 75 sets of rapids and falls, the remains of five historic fur trade posts, several remnants of pre-European native culture, and dozens of tributaries large and small leading enticingly back into the wilderness. He will experience the intimacy of cedar-clad shores crowding over the growing stream, the spectacular roar of a falls aptly named Thunderhouse, and the windblown expansiveness of an estuary 3 km wide. Best of all, the canoeist will find the time and space to absorb the flavour of a true northern wilderness.

The Missinaibi is not a river for beginners, but neither is it necessary to be an Olympic champion. All of the rapids and falls are portageable, and access points are well spaced to allow trips of one to four weeks duration. Since all access points are near a railway, no expensive flying is required.

July is the month for the Missinaibi—river levels are moderate, the bugs have abated from their earlier fury and the water temperature is pleasant for wading or swimming.

Butterflies and Bedrock

From end to end, the Missinaibi creates a ribbon across Canada's shirtwaist—the narrow neck of land between James Bay and the Great Lakes. At its source the river is within the transitional forest, with elements of the Great Lakes hardwoods, such as ash and elm, still influencing the tree cover. Through much of the river's length, the surrounding forest is classic boreal—white spruce, balsam fir and jack pine on upland sites; black spruce and white cedar in wetter areas. Where fire or past logging has created a disturbance, white birch and trembling aspen are often present.

Below Thunderhouse Falls the character of the landscape changes; the Precambrian Shield is left behind and the broad expanse of the James Bay lowland begins. The underlying rock is now sedimentary, covered by clays left some 8000 years ago by the Tyrell Sea. While the river valley is treed to the coast, the effects of the harsh northern climate are more evident here, and it is interesting to note the decrease in height of black spruce as Moosonee is approached. Beyond the silty banks of the river, the landscape is dominated by the endless patterns of bog and fen on northern muskeg.

Along its course the Missinaibi gives many clues to its geologic past. Near the southern end the massive smooth outcrops of granite are joined by ancient volcanic rocks in a few places, Split Rock Falls and Devil Shoepack Falls for example. Above Mattice, in a series of rapids with sharply fractured bedrock, sedimentary rocks from the early Precambrian era are much in evidence.

In places the effects of centuries of erosion have produced strange shapes in the rock, such as the Conjurer's House pinnacle which rises 13 m from the middle of the river below Thunderhouse Falls. In this area the edge of the Tyrell Sea is reached, and from here to James Bay marine fossils are abundant. In these northern stretches the glacial deposits overlying the bedrock are exceptionally well preserved. Some of the oldest glacial features in Ontario, believed to be almost 200,000 years old, are exposed here.

The wildlife of the Missinaibi basin is as diverse as its geology. Moose is the most common large mammal and sightings are especially frequent in the Missinaibi Lake–Peterbell area. In the same vicinity there is also a small herd of elk, the result of a reintroduction project in the 1940s. In the far northern stretches of the river, a rare stroke of luck might show you one of Ontario's woodland caribou. Many other mammals typical of the boreal forest, from black bear and beaver to marten and mink, are also found along the river.

Little comprehensive work has been done on the birds of the Missinaibi, but one survey recorded a very respectable 135 species in a summer. On the James Bay lowlands sandhill cranes are often sighted, joining the great blue herons common further south. Surprisingly the Missinaibi rates as a good area for butterflies, with 68 species recorded along the valley.

The aquatic life of the Missinaibi is rich as well, with northern pike, yellow pickerel, sturgeon, whitefish and yellow perch found in various places. Brook trout are not found in the river itself but do inhabit many of the tributaries. One unusual fish found in the river's waters is mooneye, a silvery, herring-like species rarely found in the north.

A Route to the Interior

For centuries the Missinaibi valley was the homeland of a thinly scattered population of ancestral Ojibway and Cree. Most Indian sites are on the larger lakes or at the mouth of tributary rivers, such as the village site discovered at the mouth of the Brunswick River. These cultures left their mark in the form of pictographs on Fairy

The Ojibway and Cree Indians had been carrying trade goods on the Missinaibi for almost 300 years by the time of this photo at Island Portage in 1901.

D.B. Dowling/Public Archives Canada/PA-40033

Point, near the west end of Missinaibi Lake, and at nearby sites on Whitefish Bay and opposite Reva Island.

The Fairy Point pictographs, some of the best in eastern North America, are likely the source of the river's name, for the word Missinaibi is close to Ojibway for "pictured waters." No reliable date can be put on the origins of these iron oxide paintings, but we know that the name Missinaibi was applied locally as early as 1777, so they must be older than 200 years. It is interesting that one of the pictographs clearly shows a caribou, an animal that has been absent from this area for many years.

The Missinaibi was part of an Indian trade route well before Radisson and Grosseilliers descended it in 1662. One of the travel routes of the Nipissing tribe in the early 1600s has been documented along the river, and the discovery of ceramics from southern Ontario Iroquois at archaeological sites along the river further confirms this early trade.

By 1776 the Indians of the Missinaibi had begun to share their river with European man. The British Hudson's Bay Company had established a post at Moose Fort at the mouth of the river over a century earlier, attracting Indian trade from upriver. But declining fur trade there forced the HBC to send its traders into the interior. The Missinaibi soon became one of the most important fur trade rivers in Ontario, a role that it maintained for the next 140 years. Provisions from England were sent upriver from Moose Fort to Missinaibi Lake, and sometimes over the height of land to the Michipicoten River and down to Lake Superior, with furs returning along the same route. Most of the portage trails along the river today are the same ones used by the fur traders and by the Indians before that.

The Missinaibi valley was also central to the conflict between the Hudson's Bay Company and the rival North West Company over control of the fur trade. The Bay was more active in building posts along this route, with a post established at Wapiscogamy House in 1777, a short-lived attempt on Missinaibi Lake the same year, and another on Brunswick Lake in 1789. The North West Company, supplied from Montreal, fought back with a rival post on Brunswick Lake in 1796. It was so close to the HBC establishment that the Company had to erect a special house just to get a clear view of the lake. Other NWC posts appeared briefly at the mouth of Wapiscogamy Creek and near Moose Fort, but by 1821, when the rival companies finally merged, most of these outposts had been abandoned.

New Brunswick House remained until 1879 as a strategic centre for the fur trade, considered so important that the Company's governor often wintered there to better direct the rich yield of local furs. Missinaibi Lake House was rebuilt in 1873, and even though the arrival of the railway in that same decade signalled the end of the old-style fur trade, this post remained open until 1917. Standing today on its ruins, it is sobering to realize that so many generations lived and fought and died at these isolated outposts in the wilderness. In the woods behind Missinaibi Lake House, a lone marker dated 1897 stands at the grave of a five-year-old child, adding further to the sense that there are tales of tragedy and romance here that will forever remain hidden.

By 1900 the busiest years on the Missinaibi were over. Some local logging took place along the river after the First World War, feeding the sawmill at Peterbell, but eventually that too fell quiet. In the early 1970s the river was set aside as a park reserve, and interest and pressure from the Sierra Club of Ontario to secure its future is helping to bring about its revival as a canoe route.

Exploring the River

Since the Missinaibi is a river trip, with a total fall in its 550 km of 330 m, route options are limited to one—downstream.

MISSANABIE STATION TO PETERBELL

For those travelling by rail, this 90-km section begins at Missanabie Station, a dusty remnant of the railway days. Missanabie Station is also accessible by the dead-end Hwy. 651. The hamlet includes an intriguing, if somewhat dilapidated, hotel, which the owners can tell you began as the residence of the Hudson's Bay manager. The old Campanelli store down the street was the HBC post. On the other side of the hotel, a Paris fur company known as Revillion Frères, which founded Moosonee, competed for local trade early in this century. Some locals claim that Missanabie Station draws its name not from the river, since the spelling is different, but from a popular railway nurse known affectionately as Miss Anabie, but others scoff at such a tale.

Your trip begins behind the hotel on Dog Lake, which is actually part of the Michipicoten system. Dog Lake is a fascinating place to poke about for a few days, for its native history is particularly well documented by Thor Conway, including pictographs, a 15th-century fishing camp and a traditional Ojibway canoe building site on Carpenter Island. If you especially want the feel of history, you might stop at Little Stony Portage leading to Manitowik Lake, which has seen continuous use for over 2000 years.

A few short and soggy portages from the east end of Dog Lake bring you through Crooked Lake to Missinaibi Lake. This body of water is the largest of the trip and one of the most dangerous. Since it lies in line with the prevailing winds, fair weather can mean two days of unforgettable sailing (or easy paddling for the purists in the crowd), but foul weather means heavy seas and wind-bound delays.

Whatever the weather, Fairy Point should not be missed. The pictographs make this a place of the spirits, a place to be treated with reverence. They are best seen late in the evening, when the lake breezes have mellowed and the rays of the setting sun paint the rocks in warm tones. As you trace the pattern of symbols of the sun-god, ancient wildlife and long-departed war canoes, perhaps you will catch a fleeting glimpse of the spirits that moved native warriors hundreds of years ago to mark this as a place of special meaning.

Perhaps the name Fairy Point seems curious until you understand the Indian legends often associated with pictographs. Deep within the crevices in the cliff, so the legends say, there live small hairy-faced men who can paddle their stone canoes out mischievously to rob fish from nets or create bad weather. These are the May-may-gway-shi, which translates from Cree as "fairies." Also at this site is a depiction of Mishipizhiw, the mythical great lynx with spines along its back that was believed to be the evil spirit in rapids and troubled waters. This figure appears often in pictograph sites across the north.

Whitefish Falls is another enticing spot on the south side of the lake. Here the Little Missinaibi River enters over a 5-m drop, creating an excellent fishing hole. On a warm summer day this is also an ideal place to pause for a swim and natural shower. The attractive sandy beach across the cove is a protected area and should not be used for camping.

Missinaibi Lake hosts another road access point at the provincial park campground, for anyone courageous enough to drive the 93 km of gravel roads from Chapleau, and astute enough to figure out how to retrieve his car at the end of the trip. Access by this route cuts 51 km off the trip.

At the northeast end of the lake the ruins of Missinaibi Lake House sprawl over a grassy area with a fine view back down the lake. Besides a lesson in historical humility, this is an excellent area to watch for moose. Since the upper Missinaibi lies within the Chapleau Game Preserve, moose are both more abundant and tamer here than elsewhere.

Across this narrow part of the lake, in a larger clearing, lie the remains of a steel-bottomed barge used by the early logging operators. In an earlier age, handmade York boats had been used along the river by some of the traders, partly because of their capacity, but partly because the Scottish traders, recruited from the Orkney Islands by the Hudson's Bay Company, didn't trust canoes.

The last few days of this section are a pleasant river paddle, with tranquil cedar-lined banks and occasional rapids to add spice. Quittagene, Cedar, Long, Sun and Barrel rapids—all may be run, depending on water levels, or all can be portaged with ease. For those just beginning whitewater canoeing, the upper Missinaibi can be an excellent training ground under expert guidance. For the more proficient, these first few sets of rapids are a chance to reawaken your skills before the more serious challenges ahead. A word of caution, however—Quittagene has claimed at least one life, and advance scouting is essential on all rapids in this remote setting.

The waterlogged remains of a trapper's cabin mark the mouth of the Hay River. An exploratory paddle up the Hay offers an excellent opportunity to see wildlife, for the narrow creek winds through marshy terrain. This area also hosts a large number of unusual plants such as thimbleweed, yellow bedstraw, checkered rattlesnake plantain and small purple-fringed orchis. Watch also for bald eagles and for signs of elk.

If you have only a week, your trip ends in Peterbell, where the Canadian National Railway crosses the river. As George Luste points out, the railway and bridge here seem so hopelessly incongruous in the wilderness that coming upon them can be a rather bizarre experience. Occasionally a train will thunder by, but when the last rattles have died away the wild closes in once again, making the train's very existence seem impossible.

Despite its attractive name, Peterbell is not a village, so don't expect the neighbourhood grocery store just yet. Arrangements to have a train stop for pickup must be made in advance, but there is a railway telephone in a little concrete pillbox by the tracks in case of emergency. While you wait, you can explore downtown Peterbell (a grassy clearing with the ruins of an old sawmill) or paddle just downstream to poke about in Peterbell Marsh.

Many canoeists choose to spend two weeks on the upper Missinaibi, travelling the next section downriver to Mattice as well.

PETERBELL TO MATTICE

If you are looking a trip that specializes in whitewater, it is possible to arrange train passage with Via Rail into Peterbell as a start point. However, you will have to wait a little before you begin running rapids, for just downstream is one of the richest wildlife areas on the river, Peterbell Marsh. Here the river cuts through broad stretches of low flooded vegetation. Several excellent campsites are found on the rocky bluffs along the edge, giving you a lookout for moose or otter and a spot to admire the spaciousness of a night sky unconfined by trees. You can also explore the marsh for its crop of botanical specialties, such as bugleweed, narrow-leaved gentian, leafy white orchis and fragrant water lily.

The river banks along the 146 km to Mattice are generally well endowed with rich soil and lie between low hills covered in cedar, aspen and spruce. Only at the rapids and falls does the Precambrian rock show in an assortment of boulders, ledges and outcrops that create spectacular canoeing. Most of the 30 rapids in this stretch can be run in moderate water levels; a few must be portaged, and all can be portaged if necessary.

A few spots deserve special mention. Allan Island, where the river splits and rushes over dual waterfalls, provides an idyllic spot for a campsite or rest day. Downstream a little, Greenhill rapids pose a dangerous guessing game for those who thrill to whitewater. The portage is relatively long (about 1 km) and steep in places, and the five closely spaced sets of rapids are among the best on the river, but... in high water, or even moderately high water, the rapids can be very dangerous and more than one party has lost a canoe there. What's more, it's almost impossible to scout Greenhill from the shore, and once started, you are committed. If you are at all in doubt, take your lumps on the portage trail and hope for low water the next time.

From here the Missinaibi probes its way northwards through a series of rapids, the most notable being Split Rock Falls, where the river plunges through a cleft in the rock beside yet another spectacular campsite. By the time the Fire River is reached, the river has settled down to a leisurely pace, and the rocky shores are largely replaced by the clays deposited by glacial Lake Ojibway.

You now have a choice. If you stay with the river, you face at

At Split Rock Falls, the river cascades through a slanting fault in the bedrock. **George Luste**

least a day of fairly monotonous paddling between dense cedar-lined banks. The alternative is a 1600-m portage to the south end of Brunswick Lake, a pretty lake with rocky islands for camping and another historic fur trade post for exploring. Brunswick Lake also has a fly-in outfitter and several private cabins, useful neighbours in case of an emergency.

The site of the Hudson's Bay post, on a high point along the west shore of the lake near its north end, is now mostly grown over, but archaeologists find it a rich treasure ground. New Brunswick House, as it was called, began modestly enough with several log tents, but by the time of the 1821 union it boasted a master's house, a forge, a store, a cook house, a fish shed and barns for hay and cattle, all fenced within a stout stockade.

An active logging road crosses both the Missinaibi and Brunswick rivers near their junction. While some evidence of logging activity can be seen along the river banks in this area, Spruce Falls Pulp and Paper Company have generally reacted constructively to proposals for a waterway park through their licensed area.

A short paddle now brings you to the three devils—Devil Cap Falls, Devil Shoepack Falls and Devil Rapids, where a combination of portages and lift-overs are necessary over these ancient volcanic rocks. Through much of the next stretch, the river is rocky and shallow. Albany Rapids are a special challenge, for the river disappears into a 3-km rock garden that can reduce even the most expert navigator to wading through the shallow spots.

The last group of rapids before Mattice is very different in character. At Beaver Rapids and Sharprock Falls, the sedimentary bedrock has splintered into thousands of sharp-edged fragments. Portages are usually necessary over the lunar landscape along the river's edge, although a combination of lining and lift-overs can sometimes be used to advantage. This is an especially interesting way to get through Beaver Rapids, because you pass through an unusual box canyon in the middle of the river.

One more portage brings you past Glassy Falls and soon you are in sight of Mattice. Pass under Hwy. 11 and continue downriver for close to 1 km to reach the boat ramp. The town has a range of accommodation and restaurants, as well as transportation connections to points south.

MATTICE TO MOOSONEE

This last 316-km stretch is a route only for the experienced. It takes at least 10 days, includes a series of more challenging rapids and has considerably more difficult portages. It also includes some of the most spectacular river scenery anywhere in northern Ontario and is a wilderness experience never to be forgotten. In late July or August low water levels may make this route impassable, so it is prudent to check with the MNR office in Moosonee before setting out.

Fast water begins almost immediately downriver from Mattice, as the river winds northward through a series of rapids of varying difficulty. Some of the area around Black Feather Rapids is shallow and rocky, as the river passes through bouldery till left by the glaciers. At least one portage is required, around Kettle Falls, where the action of centuries of flow has carved kettle-shaped holes in the rock.

Gradually the signs of civilization fade away, the water once again becomes fit to drink without treatment, and the wildness returns. Forests of aspen, spruce and birch line the low valley; shrubby patches of alder and shaggy ninebark crowd the shore. Just past Alice Island, a small community of black ash and large

The Indians associated spirits with tumbling water, so it is not surprising that the spire of rock below Thunderhouse is known as Conjuror's House. **George Luste**

white elm, unusual this far north, is found. A closer look here will turn up plants familiar to a southerner but rare this far north, including red baneberry, wild ginger and hairy Solomon's seal.

Beyond Alice Island a long string of navigable rapids must be treated with caution in their last kilometre because of their proximity to Thunderhouse Falls. Several canoeists have been killed in this area through straying too far from shore and being swept over the falls. The portage trail begins well above the falls, cutting across a bend in the river and presenting little difficulty other than its length, about 2 km. The rewards are worth the effort, as a page from George Luste's diary attests:

"The Thunderhouse Falls area is the highlight of the entire river, and central to it is the falls itself. The water actually falls in three distinct drops, separated by two short gorges. Of these the first is the most impressive, and it is to this that the name Thunderhouse refers, a name well deserved indeed. The entire volume of river water roars between parallel, glistening rock faces a few feet apart in a chaos of white spray, and holds the observer spellbound by its energy. Even at low water, and even though made familiar with rushing water by three weeks on the river, I found it a splendid sight, and my poor words do it scant justice.

"The rock formations below here are quite striking, in particular there being a tall vertical cliff on the left, and on the right, a solitary pillar of rock known as the Conjuror's House."

Turbulent waters through impressive rock gorges continue for several kilometres beyond Thunderhouse as the river completes its descent off the Canadian Shield. Several long portages are required around Stone Rapids and Long Rapids. The gorge of this second set, which includes Hell's Gate, is a scenic feature that ranks alongside Thunderhouse Falls, but it takes a determined effort to see it, since the portage trail is set well back.

As you sweat your way across the portages, don't lose sight of the ecological significance of this area, where the Precambrian rocks give way to the younger bedrock of the Lowlands. The canyons and forests here provide a rich habitat for ferns and other vascular plants. One brief survey recorded 14 new plants for this part of the province, along with 33 others considered rare. Bird life is rich too—species such as merlin, kingfisher, boreal chickadee, brown creeper and red-breasted nuthatch.

During the fur trade era, brigades from up and down the river often met here to exchange goods, and there are even records of a store set up at Stone Rapids to facilitate this trade. Archaeologists have recently discovered an alternate route around Thunderhouse that was often used, starting in the rapids above the falls to the east and following a small stream known as Coal Creek to avoid the long series of rapids on the Missinaibi. At the mouth of Coal Creek a small cellar may represent the remains of a North West Company outpost.

Immediately following Long Rapids portage is Four Mile Rapids, which can be run or lined in good water conditions. Towards the end of these rapids, the rocky cliffs give way to eroded clay bluffs, a feature common in the next stretch of river. The last of the major rapids has now been passed and the river settles into a fast-flowing pace over a gravelly bottom.

Just upstream from the Pivabiska River is the site of Wapiscogamy House, the fur trade post that marked the beginning of the Hudson's Bay Company's push into the interior in 1777. Although the post was in operation only 30 years, it became a sizable establishment, with even a blacksmith's shop for the repair of guns and traps. Cattle and hogs were kept here, with "marsh hay" harvested along the banks of the river for a considerable distance each summer. One of the most reliable sources of food was a fish trap in the sparkling shallow waters of the Pivabiska, operated at night to capture fish on their way upstream.

Midway between the Pivabiska and the Soweska, a series of steep cliffs along the east shore provides an exceptional record of the last 350,000 years of physical evolution of northern Ontario. Five beds of till, laid down by five glacial advances, are separated by layers of darker non-glacial sediments richly spiked with organic fossils of peat, wood and buried soil.

At the mouth of the Soweska River the cliff shows an unusually thick layer of interglacial peat, technically known as the Missinaibi Formation. As you gaze at the half-metre layer of peat, reflect on just how long it took for these organic soils to develop between glaciers, certainly a span measured in tens of thousands of years. Within the compressed peat, flattened logs and branches are present in abundance, fossils of another age preserved by the acid organic bed in which they lie.

Downstream of the Soweska River, the steep banks become gentler and the river gradually begins to widen. In this area another gravesite overlooks the river, again that of a child whose fate has become an enigma. Good campsites on gravel bars or the riverbank are frequent, and the monotony of spruce and poplar is relieved occasionally by immense individual trees of cedar and white spruce. This area is rich in wildlife. Flocks of Canada geese become common, woodland caribou and sandhill cranes are possible sightings, and even the endangered golden eagle has been thought to nest here. Watch also for the common birds such as sparrows—white-throated, song, vesper, tree and swamp sparrows might all be found in this vicinity.

Eventually the river is joined by another large tributary, the Mattagami, to form the Moose River. A few kilometres downstream you arrive at a small native settlement known as Moose River Crossing. While this settlement does not boast a store, it does provide a stopping point for the Ontario Northland Railway, which can be taken back to the town of Cochrane on Hwy. 11.

If you decide to continue downriver to Moosonee, you face 72 km of a wide, almost featureless river that often divides among many islands. Just below Moose River Crossing the river has carved a series of caves in the soft gypsum along the shore. About half-way to Moosonee, the Abitibi adds its murky flow, and for the final few kilometres the effects of the James Bay tides can be felt. Shoreline vegetation is reduced in height and diversity in these subarctic conditions; semi-palmated plovers and least sandpipers rule over the gravel bars, and the river is so broad that the landscape seems "all horizon, as if you could paddle right into the sky."

Moosonee is a thriving town of 3000 with complete facilities for the tourist trade and rail connections back to Cochrane. For a final night's camping, there is Tidewater Provincial Park on one of the islands opposite the town. And in Moosonee, for those that just can't end the trip without glimpsing the salty waters of James Bay, you can hire a guide and motorboat to take you the last few kilometres onto the open ocean.

National Topographic System Maps
1:50,000 scale: 42B/5, B/6, B/11, B/14
42C/8
42G/3, G/6, G/11, G/14
42J/2, J/3, J/7, J/8, J/9
42I/11, I/12, I/14
42P/2, P/3, P/7

Ministry of Natural Resources Maps
1:126,720 scale: Goudreau 42C/SE
Missinaibi Lake 42B/SW
Fire River 42B/NW
Opasatika Lake 42G/SW
Hearst 42G/NW
Smoky Falls 42F/SE
1:100,000 scale: Thunderhouse Falls 42J/SW
Schleivert Lakes 42J/NE
Coverage incomplete; use NTS 42P for lower section.

Missinaibi River–Map 1

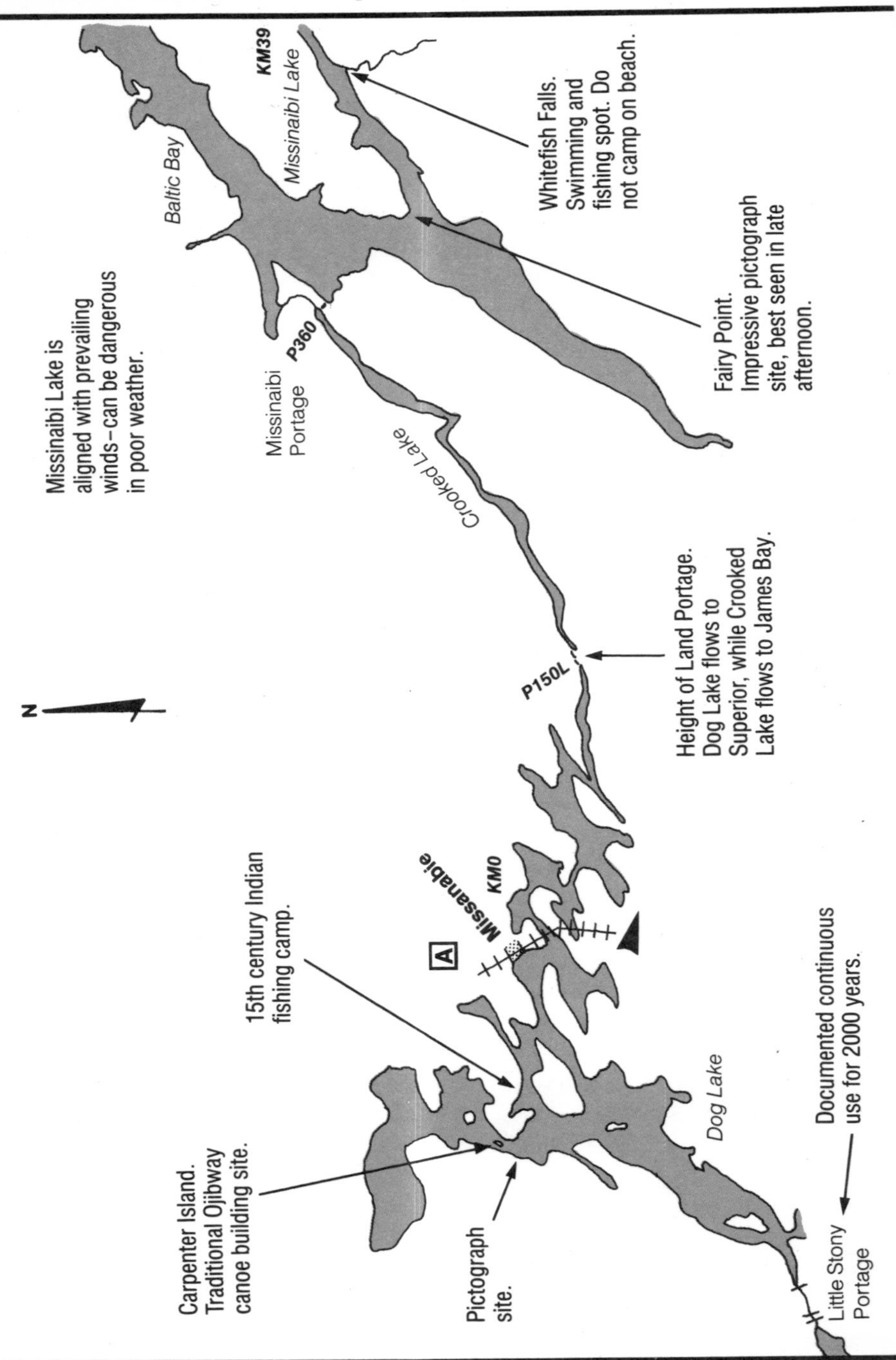

Ref: N.T.S. Map 42B, 42C, 1:250,000

Missinaibi River – Map 2

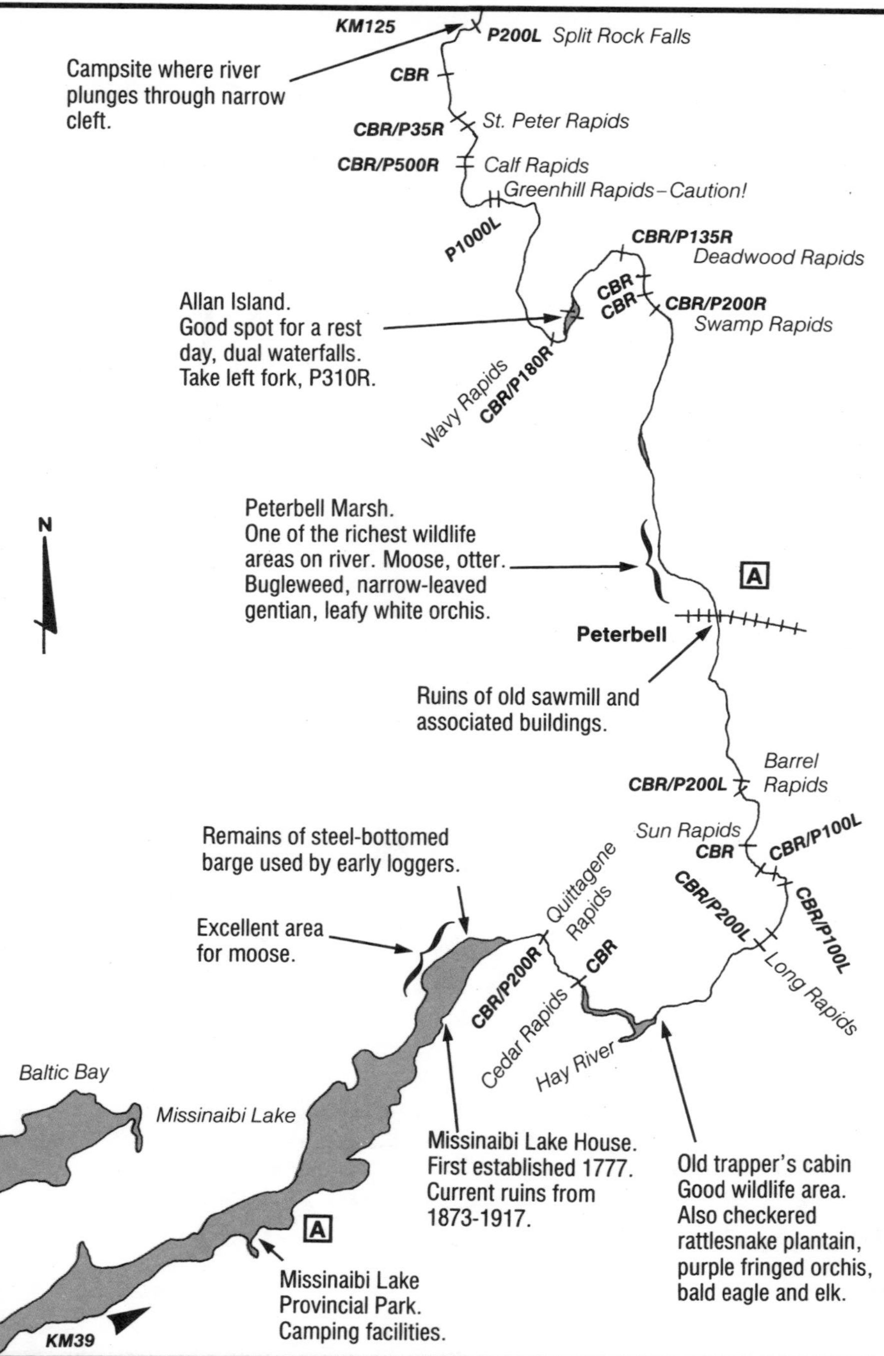

Ref: N.T.S. Map 42B, 1:250,000

Missinaibi River – Map 3

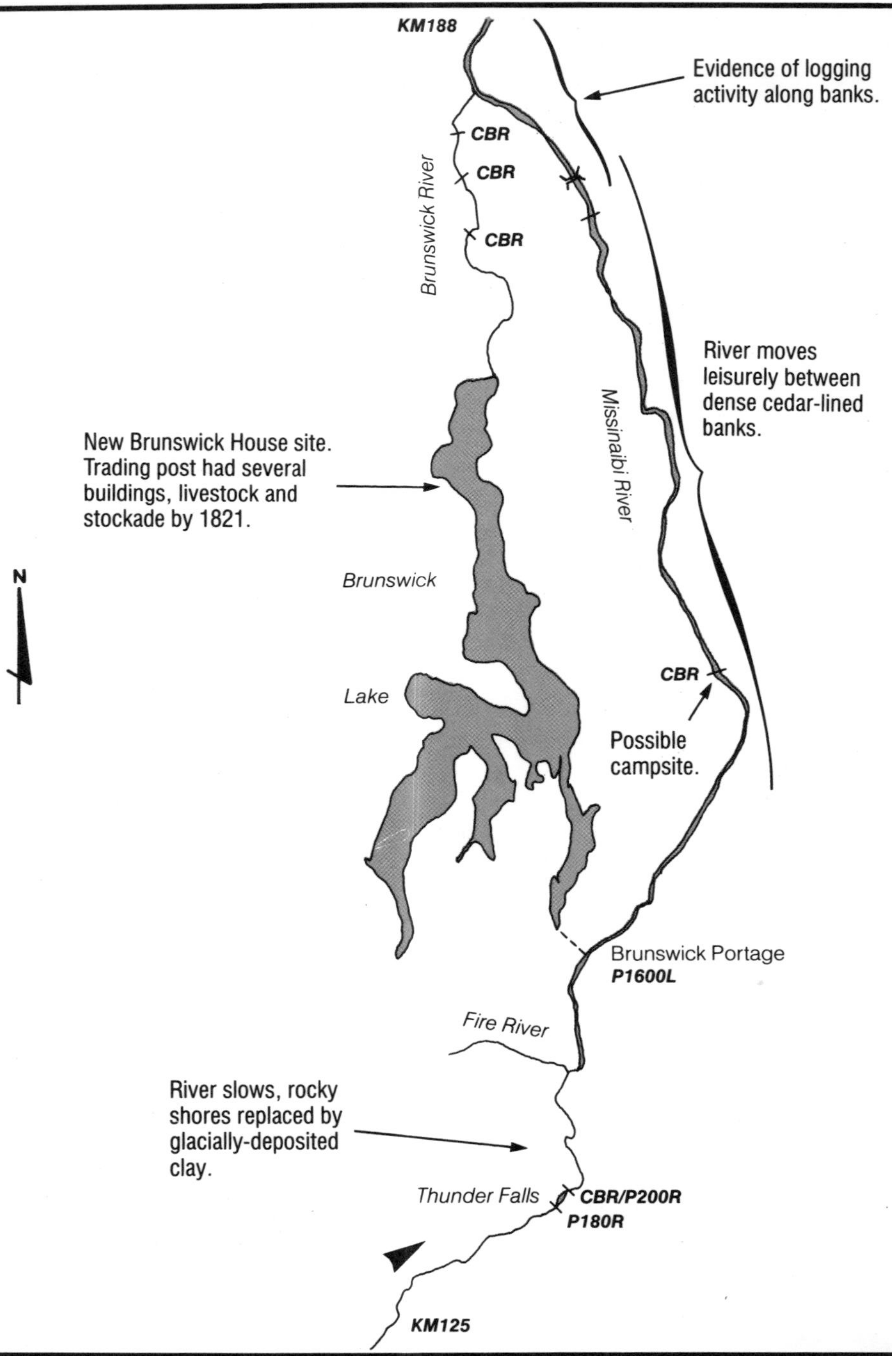

Ref: N.T.S. Map 42B, 42G, 1:250,000

Missinaibi River–Map 4

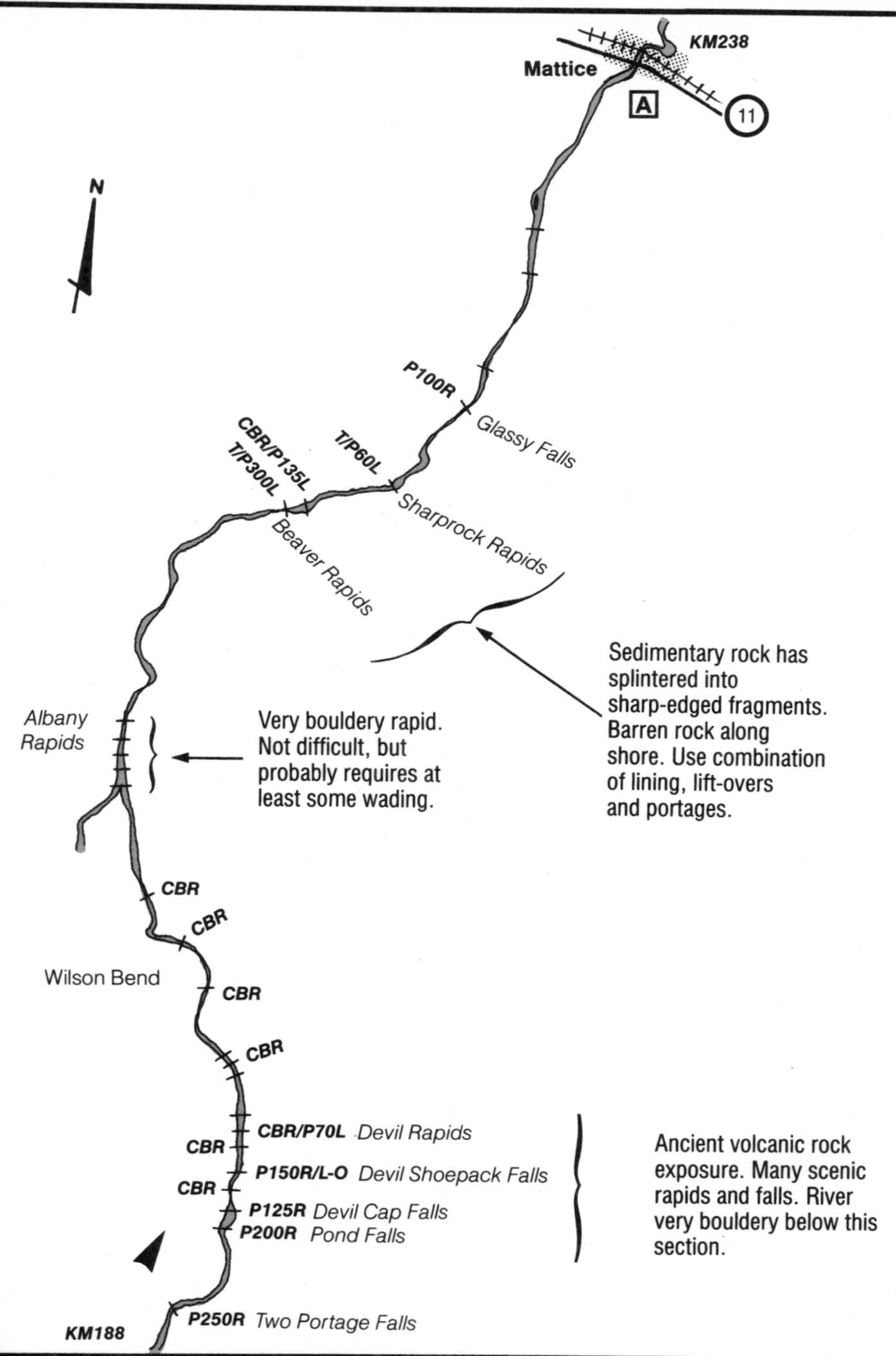

Ref: N.T.S. Map 42G, 1:250,000

Missinaibi River – Map 5

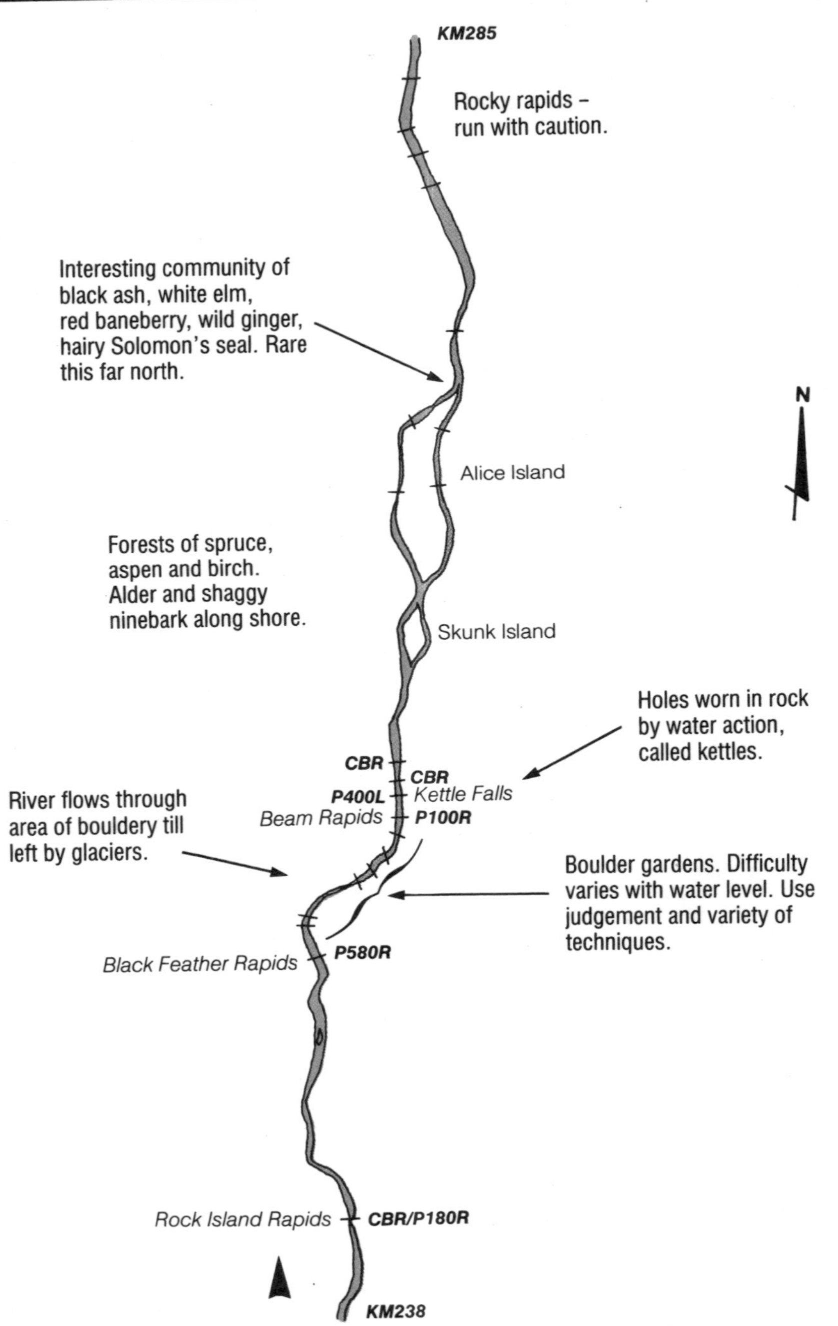

Ref: N.T.S. Map 42G, 1:250,000

Missinaibi River–Map 6

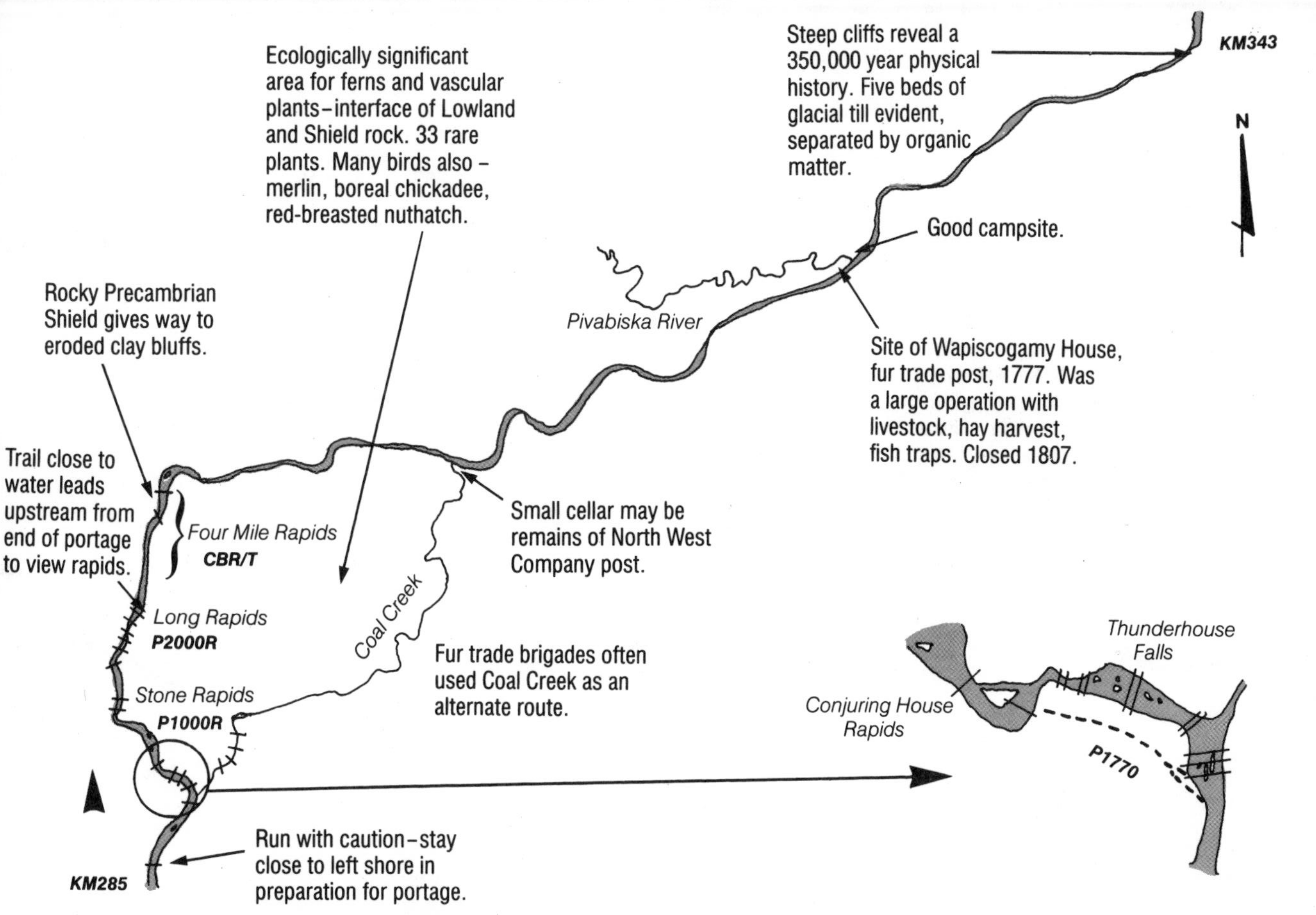

Ref: N.T.S. Map 42J, 1:250,000

Missinaibi River – Map 7

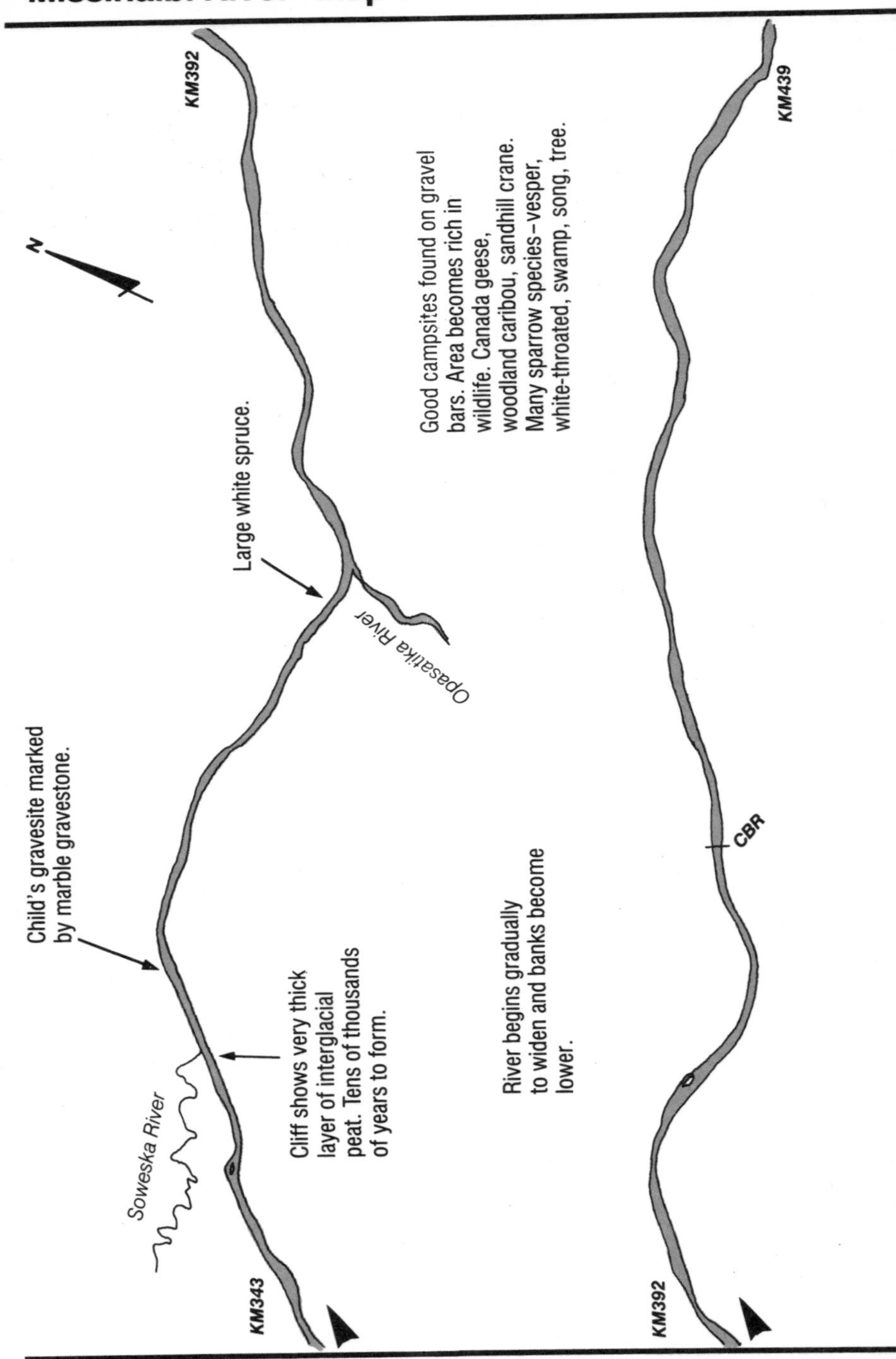

Ref: N.T.S. Map 42J, 42I, 1:250,000

Missinaibi River–Map 8

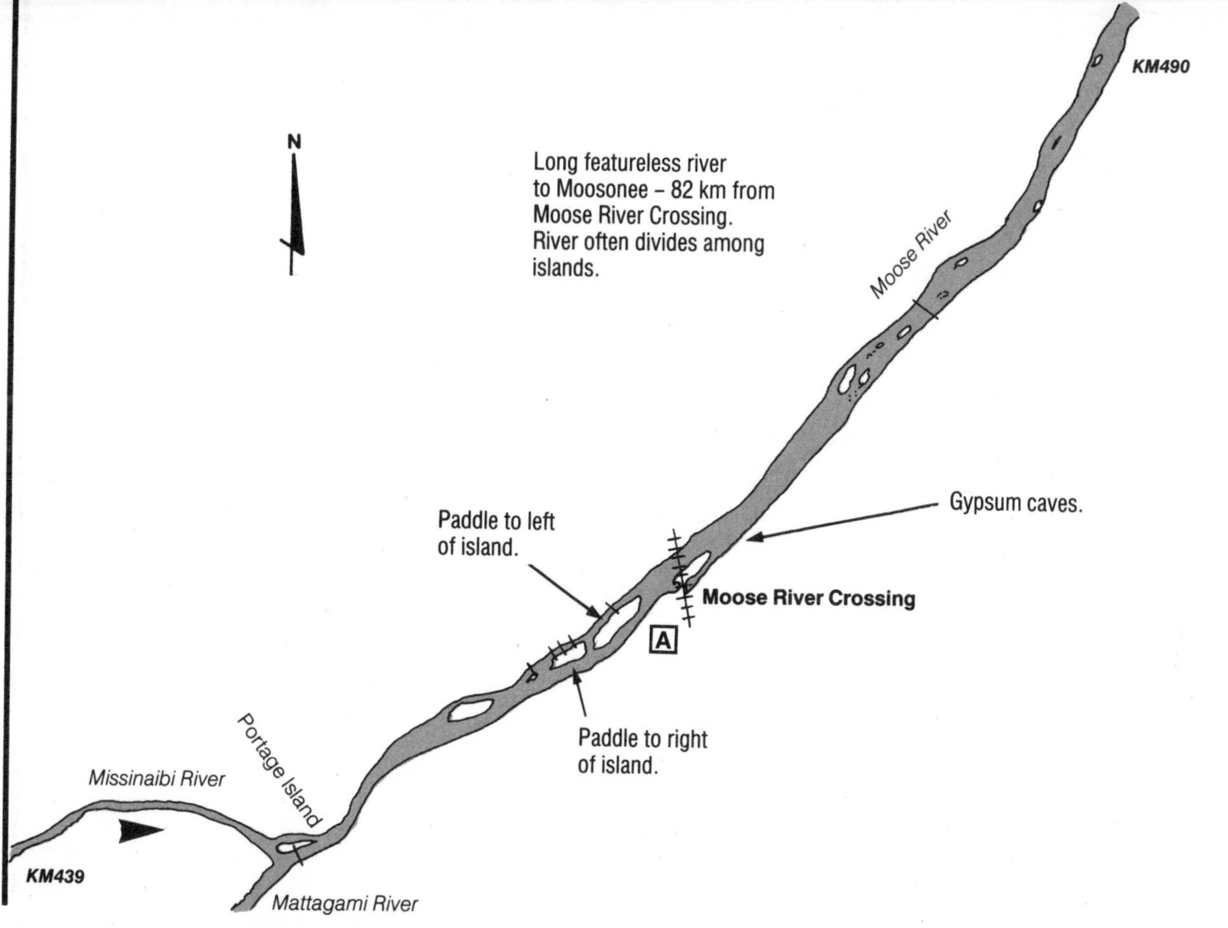

Ref: N.T.S. Map 42I, 1:250,000

Missinaibi River–Map 9

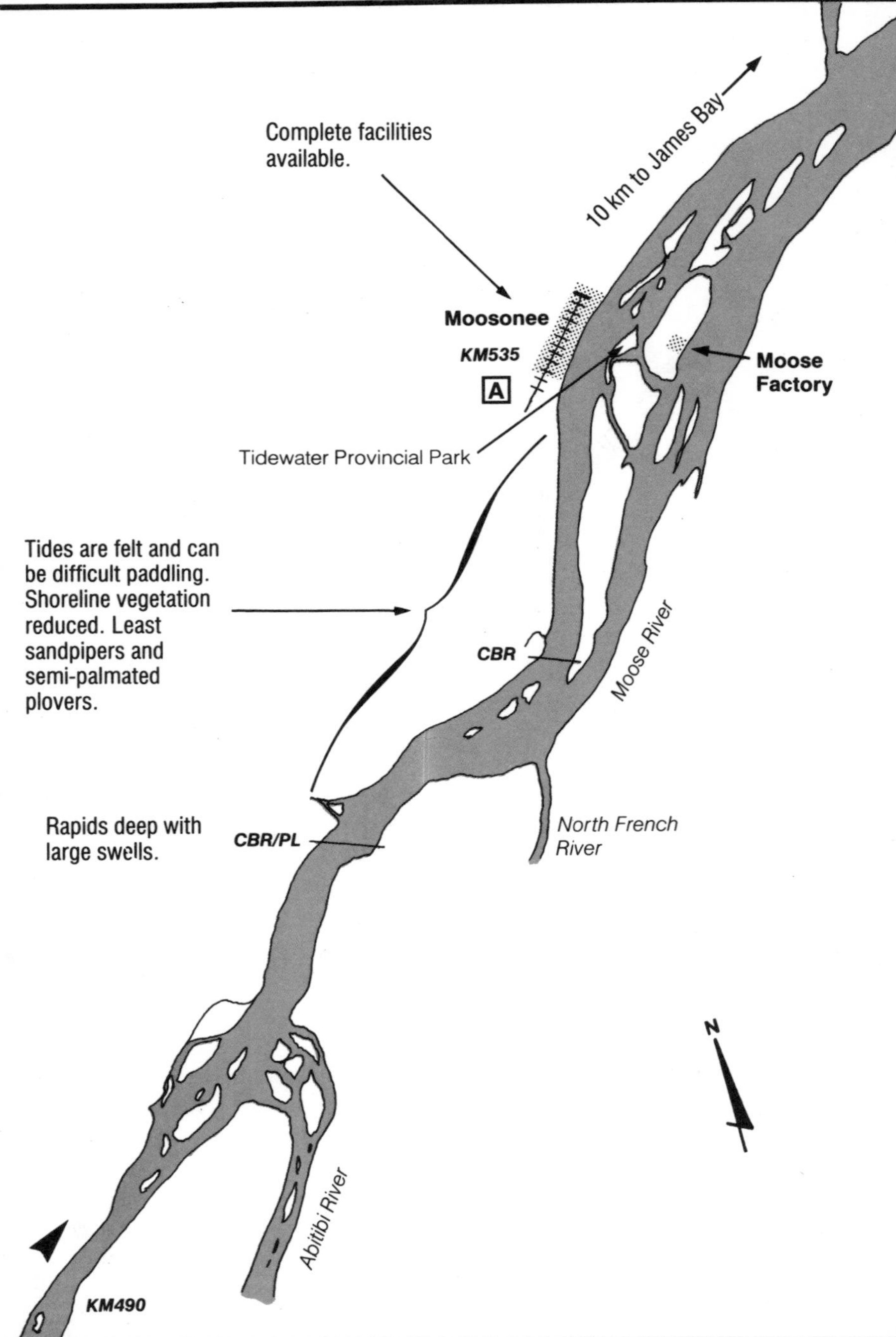

Ref: N.T.S. Map 42P, 1:250,000

Other Fur Trade Routes

Unfortunately only a few of the original fur trade routes in Ontario have survived without alteration. Some of the best are in northwestern Ontario, stretching west from Lake Superior towards the Manitoba border through Quetico country.

The Boundary Water route begins with the arduous Grand Portage, and follows the Pigeon River past impressive geological features and beautiful hardwood forests. After passing through the island-studded lakes of Quetico, this 520-km route continues westwards through the farm country of Rainy River, eventually leading to Lake of the Woods. This trip is rich in history, both of the fur trade era and of Indian settlements before that, and in wildlife.

A later trade route begins at Thunder Bay, following the Kaministikwia River upstream to Quetico Provincial Park, where it joins the Boundary Waters route. Highlights of this historic route include the restored Fort William and scenic Kakabeka Falls. Unfortunately parts of this route have been altered by Hydro dams and logging activities. Brochures describing both of these northwestern routes are available from the Ministry of Natural Resources, Box 5000, Thunder Bay F, P7E 6E3.

Further east most of the traditional routes have suffered badly. We had hoped to include the Michipicoten River in this guide, but a quick exploration revealed that very little of this route, used to link the Missinaibi corridor with Lake Superior, has been left in a natural condition. Despite the dams which now flood the valley and alter the river's flow, the Michipicoten does include several attractions along its length. Little Stony Portage, near its head, has a history of 2000 years of use. At the river's mouth Michipicoten Historical Park preserves the site of an important trade post.

Detailed trip information is not available for most of this route, but the bottom section is included in the route descriptions of Lake Superior Provincial Park, available from the MNR, Box 1160, Wawa, P0S 1K0.

Another commonly used trade route extends from a former Hudson's Bay Post on Lake Timiskaming down the Ottawa River. Since much of this 226-km route is on large bodies of water created by Hydro dams, caution is necessary on windy days. A route description extending as far south as Driftwood Provincial Park on the Ottawa is available from the MNR, Box 3070, North Bay, P1B 8K7. Below that point most of the Ottawa has been altered so much that virtually all traces of the voyageur days have been eliminated.

section 6

northward to the coast

Few of us think of Ontario as an Arctic province, yet well over half of its area lies within the watershed of the Arctic Ocean. Radiating southwards from the salty waters of Hudson Bay like the spokes of a wheel, dozens of rivers reach back into the forest. The rivers gave access to the interior by the Orkneymen of the Hudson's Bay Company in search of furs, and their banks hold the memories of trading post and York boat, bales of prime beaver and laden freighter canoes.

This is a young land, some of it released from the grip of the glaciers only 6000 years ago. Along the coastal edge a thin strip of treeless tundra, complete with polar bears, gives the Arctic a toehold in the province. But almost all of the rock and muskeg beyond the height of land is boreal forest, clad in the black spruce and jack pine that can survive the icy blasts of the subarctic wind.

This is not a gentle country, for the wilderness holds sway. Only along the rich clays of its southern fringe, created by a massive glacial lake, have the works of modern man intruded. Along the larger rivers, especially at the coast, small native communities struggle with the conversion to a society characterized by bush planes and television. But in the bush, the traditional ways continue, the eternal struggle of trapper and hunter against cold in the winter and mosquitoes in summer.

For the canoeist this is river country. Relatively few lakes dot these northern reaches, and the endless stretches of muskeg make portaging difficult. Here the rivers become the focus, rivers at first turbulent and challenging as they tumble northwards off the Shield, then swift and smooth as they cross the muskeg plains of the lowlands. Here in the remote north country the rivers capture your soul with their haunting blend of beauty and history.

The Chapleau-Nemegosenda: A Wild River Loop

Portaging can be fun, a facet of wilderness canoeing that most beginners find hard to believe. But wearing the *chapeau vert*—the 16-foot green canoe that serves as a portaging hat for one of us—sometimes means that we miss the best of the action around us. Such was the case on one of my carries on the Nemegosenda, when I tromped on by, oblivious to a chocolate-brown marten that had whisked up a tree just to one side of the trail.

Fortunately Janet's field of vision was not so restricted, and she soon laid down her pack for a better look at one of the north's most common yet most elusive fur-bearers. When I returned for my second load, they were still there, face to face a few metres apart, and it was hard to tell which of them was the more curious. Twitching with uncertainty, the marten would peer down from the safety of its cedar tree, occasionally venturing closer for a better look, then scrambling back to a safer height.

It is this curiosity that has been partly responsible for the decline of the marten in the southern parts of its range, since it is easily trapped. Habitat destruction has taken its toll as well, for marten prefer mature conifer forests and avoid recently burned or cut-over areas. This handsome little member of the weasel family, its rich brown fur and bushy tail set off by an orangy throat patch, feeds mostly on mice and other small mammals.

A close look at a marten is unusual on most canoe routes in Ontario, but it is not all that exceptional for the Chapleau-Nemegosenda. Snuggled against the side of the Chapleau Game Preserve, the river showed us an unprecedented array of wild creatures—moose, bear, skunk, otter, beaver, muskrat and marten, not to mention a diversity of bird life. If you are looking for a relatively easy trip that will give you a good cross-section of the wildlife of the boreal forest, this could be the route for you. Chapleau-Nemegosenda offers another advantage—it is possible to cover the entire route of 206 km in a loop, making the logistics for your trip simple.

Timing of a trip on this route is not critical, although the insects might be bad in June and early July. For a trip with a different flavour, you might consider going in early September. The autumn air has an invigorating crispness (another way of saying that the nights can be cold), and you will be free from crowds, both of other canoeists and of insects.

September is the fruiting moon, and everywhere the fullness of nature is displayed in colourful fruits. One portage trail might feature succulent late blueberries, the next raspberries that glow in their redness. Mountain ash berries hang in orange clumps, dogwoods are laden with white fruits, and highbush cranberries ripen from yellow to crimson with the first frost. The woods know no famine in September, and even the thought of approaching winter cannot curb the enjoyment of the fruits of summer.

Though the Chapleau River has a few exciting rapids, it is too small and bouldery to provide very good whitewater canoeing. There are many portages, but most are relatively short and all are well marked. Because of its remoteness and several fairly difficult portages, however, we would recommend it only to moderately well experienced paddlers.

Wetlands and Waterfowl

Both the Chapleau and the Nemegosenda rivers flow to the north before uniting to form the Kapuskasing River. Along much of their parallel courses, the rivers' direction is controlled by fault lines in the early Precambrian granite that underlies this area. Most of the time, however, those faults are not obvious, for the banks of the river are covered in a mantle of glacial ground moraine.

Only in a few places do more interesting glacial deposits make their appearance. In several locations the gravelly ridges of eskers appear, cutting lakes almost in half and affecting the course of the river. Around the northerly turning-point for this trip, at Kapuskasing Lake, a thick layer of varved clays surrounds the lake, part of a broad clay belt laid down between the face of the retreating glacier and the high ground to the south.

Tree cover along the rivers reflects these landforms and the boreal climate, with spruce and white birch common in most areas, jack pine in drier places, and white cedar in the damp. The effects of past logging can often be seen, with extensive stands of aspen and poplar in disturbed areas.

The most remarkable feature of this route is its wetlands, which range from small pockets to vast stands of sedges running for kilometres along the side of the channel. Often the wetlands are in the form of reed-swamps, where emergent marshy vegetation rises above the surface of the flowing water. Especially when combined with rich submergent (underwater) plant growth, these areas provide excellent waterfowl habitat, and the river sometimes seems to be full of black ducks, goldeneye, mallards and mergansers.

The other common type of riverside wetland is known as fen. These mats of solid grasses and sedges often are very extensive, with little open water, even though the underlying peat soils are continuously waterlogged. These fens do provide habitat essential to some birds, such as marsh hawks and common bitterns, but in general they are less productive for wildlife than their wetter counterparts.

The Chapleau Game Preserve, for which the Chapleau River provides the eastern boundary, was established in 1927 as a result of concern about the fate of the beaver. Since no hunting or trapping has been allowed in the area since then, populations of beaver and moose, and probably other animals as well, are unusually high and the wildlife is easily seen.

The lakes along this route provide fine fishing for northern pike and pickerel, and lake trout are found in Nemegosenda Lake as well. Nemegos is an Ojibway word for "trout," and the tributaries of the Nemegosenda ("home of the trout") River live up to their name, with excellent speckled trout fishing still to be found in that watershed.

No One Stays but the Wildlife

The Chapleau-Nemegosenda watershed has a history of transient use. Early Indians used the rivers as trapping areas and transportation corridors. Archaeologists have uncovered a 4000-year-old beach campsite from early Indians on Racine Lake, one of the tributaries of the Chapleau, and you can find pictographs midway down the river, but other signs of Indian use await discovery.

The towns that developed here were linked to more modern transportation. Chapleau developed as a node on the Canadian Pacific Railway, burned to the ground in an 1885 fire and grew again with the establishment of its first sawmill in 1899. The village of Elsas, where the two rivers join, sparked into life after the arrival of the Canadian National Railway in 1912. Continental Wood

Products opened a mill there in 1923, mostly to harvest the jack pine along the river valleys. For a few years logs rolled downriver from as far away as Schewabik Lake and Westover Lake, and for a short period Elsas became one of the largest sawmills in the north, but by the mid-1930s the mill was closed and the village returned to slumber.

By the early 1970s only a handful of private cabins and fishing lodges remained along the rivers. In 1973 an area of 8158 hectares, including a strip of 122 m on either side of the rivers, was set aside as the Chapleau-Nemegosenda Wild River Provincial Park.

Exploring the River

The entire 206-km loop covered on this route will take about 12 days to paddle comfortably. However, it is possible to do shorter trips in several ways.

Many groups start from Racine Lake, at a forestry road access point, and cover several portages from there down to the Chapleau River to shorten the distance of lake paddling. From here to Elsas is about five or six days. Rail transport out of Elsas is available, although you are advised to check timetables first to avoid a long wait. At the upper end of the Nemegosenda River you can end your trip at the start of Westover Lake, cutting off several long portages. From this point it is about 25 km back to Chapleau on Hwy. 101.

CHAPLEAU TO ELSAS

The easiest starting point in Chapleau is the government dock on the Kebsquashing River. The first 7 km is marshy, with few campsites. However, the marshes provide good waterfowl habitat, especially for goldeneye and mergansers.

A narrow swift between rocky points provides several good campsites at the 7-km mark, ironically known as Seven Mile Rapids. Henderson Lake provides a change of scene, with a pleasant array of islands and late summer congregations of loons. Some of these shores are clad in jack pine, but along others the large aspens have been felled by beaver, releasing solid stands of spruce. It is easy to see the exposed edge that marks the limit of beaver activity, where the risk of predation outweighs the need for food.

At the north end of D'Arcy Lake note the small black spruce and larch bog along the right shore, an uncommon wetland type in this area. Portage 225 m on right. (By our measure, portages on this

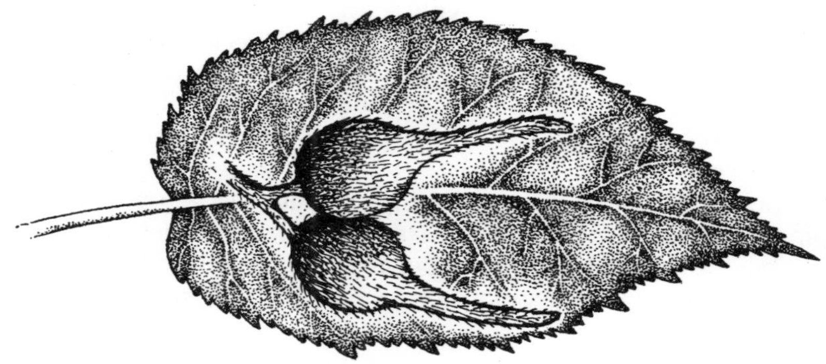

In late summer, the small shrub known as beaked hazel produces distinctive trumpet-shaped fruit, which yield an edible kernel.

Hap Wilson

route are consistently longer than the distances given; however, we are using the MNR figures to avoid confusion.) The portage leads through a mature aspen stand with typical understorey—large-leaved aster, clintonia, lily-of-the-valley, bunchberry, sensitive and interrupted fern. Listen for the repetitive "I see you, see me?" song of red-eyed vireo.

Past Robinson Lake, the first small chute can usually be run. Portage the second rapids 270 m on left or line down four narrow sets of rapids. Just downstream, the alternate route along Racine Creek joins in.

The next rapids can often be run after checking, except in very low water. You now come within the boundary of the wild river park. A grouping of five rapids begins with a portage of 250 m on the left to avoid a falls. Mixed woods dominate here, with a few old pine and spruce poking through the canopy to give an idea of what the original stand must have been like before logging.

The three central portages in this group can sometimes be run or lined, but the portages are preferable if your canoe is sensitive to rocks. The final rapid must be bypassed with a 585-m portage. This forest has a well developed shrubby layer, with moose maple, beaked hazel, creeping snowberry and partridgeberry common.

Two km later, portage 215 m on right, or line down the bouldery rapids. Another carry of similar length just downstream avoids a steep gorge with a falls. Along the trail a remnant stand of overmature white spruce and trembling aspen is beginning to fall down, an unnatural condition created by the suppression of fire. It looks untidy but makes great raspberry country.

The river now quietens, with 5 km of marshy sides along a stretch historically known as Narrow Lake. This is a good area for moose, especially near the campsite at the south end. Watch along the wet edges for the metre-high red seedheads of great water dock and for other aquatic specialties such as water smartweed and pondweed.

The end of the lake features a good campsite among the jack pine at the start of the portage. This portage around Island Rapids has been disrupted by a new logging road. If in doubt, bear left towards the log bridge and watch for a trail on the right side of the road.

The next two rapids are best portaged, although the second can be lined with difficulty. Between the rapids, fish-eating birds such as osprey, kingfisher and great blue heron seem to be especially abundant in the marshy ponds. An esker densely wooded with jack pine runs across the end of the main pond, showing typical steep sides where the river cuts through.

Two short portages on the right or a double exercise in lining brings you onto Schewabik Lake. A few white pine can be seen in this area, along with spruce and birch. Watch for clumps of royal fern along the water's edge.

Schewabik Lake is one of the most fascinating examples of landforms in the making in our experience. Its sandy shores are still quite active, with a series of sand spits being built by sediments carried parallel to the shore by wave action. About a third of the way along its length, beach bars have been deposited between the shore and a former island. The island was part of an esker that stretches away to the south—notice how the beach on its shore is pebbles, not sand. New sand spits provide ideal beach camping, as well as rooting habitat for black ash, but the trees never grow very large, probably because of climate. Bald eagles are often seen on this lake.

At the north end of the lake, the river leads into an impressive rock canyon, with a portage beginning on the right just above a falls—be careful! The trail is only 125 m long but very steep—now you can believe that a bedrock fault is present, for you climb up out of it, and then back down in again. Watch for oak fern and polypody fern along the portage trail. There are lots of blueberries here and a few red pine. Just around the corner, watch for an overhanging rock that shelters the faint red ochre pictographs.

A triple set of short portages bypasses the next set of rapids. The middle portage, over an island, passes among large white pine and cedar, making this a pretty walk. Among the underwater rocks in this moving water, watch for the bright green patches of freshwater sponge, and for the small nets woven by a species of caddisfly larvae.

Where a small esker divides the river a few kilometres downstream, keep right to stay on course. Earlier paddlers once portaged from this area to Bonar Lake, on a tributary to the west, to avoid the frequent rapids along the river. The next two rapids might be run by expert whitewater paddlers under favourable conditions, though the second set has several tricky ledges. Portages are available for those less experienced, and the second portage ends at an excellent campsite. Note the labrador tea among the spruce along this trail.

The following stretch of river is slow and swampy, with extensive stands of bulrush. Watch for the two different forms of arrowhead, with wide and narrow arrow-shaped leaves. These plants produce potato-like tubers in autumn that were much used by Indians as a food source. The rootstock of the wild blue iris, however, is poisonous, though it was used in small quantities for medicinal purposes.

Just before the confluence with the Makonie River comes 3 km of fast water, with the more difficult sections avoided by a series of five portages, all on the right. These rapids are shallow and bouldery; in moderate water levels they can often be run by experienced whitewater canoeists.

The final three rapids leading into Kapuskasing Lake can also be run by experts, or portaged if necessary. This mixed woods is a good area to watch for sharp-shinned hawks, aerial predators of small birds. A fishing camp is on the right at the entrance to the lake.

Kapuskasing Lake takes its name from the Cree word for "place where river bends" or "marshy river." It can be very rough in a wind so use caution in crossing. Watch along the shores for exposures of deep clays, with darker layers or varves. The lake has a good community of aquatic plants such as coontail, recognized by its fluffy round tail-like appearance. Otters make a home here in sheltered bays.

Your trip can be ended at the railway village of Elsas, continued on down the Kapuskasing River or looped back up the Nemegosenda River. No supplies are available at Elsas.

ELSAS TO WESTOVER LAKE

The 88-km return journey up the Nemegosenda River traverses a long stretch of slow water at first, before climbing in a series of progressively more difficult portages to the nearest road access at Hwy. 101.

Little evidence remains of the sawmill operation at the junction of the rivers that stripped much of the wood from these watersheds in the 1920s. A short cut into the Nemegosenda is available 500 m north of the railway bridge through a man-made canal, if you don't have the time to poke about the sawmill grounds at the forks.

The first 30 km of the Nemegosenda River was once known as Pine Lake, although there is precious little pine to be seen there now. Instead the river winds an often deceptive course through a broad floodplain of marsh and fen. Two good campsites overlook the marshes just past the railway bridge, virtually the only sites available from the rivers' junction to Frog Lake. Notice that the water in the Nemegosenda River is considerably clearer and cooler than the Chapleau, creating favourable conditions for speckled trout.

The forests along the river's edge, beyond the grassy fens, are mostly deciduous, reflecting deeper soils and a history of disturbance. Most of the stands, with tall "lollipop" trees, are trembling aspen. In some areas, darker bronzy leaves identify clusters of balsam poplar, a related species.

In the centre of Pine Lake a few red pine adorn an island. Both red and white pine are near the northern edge of their range here; perhaps it is the slightly milder microclimate created by the Nemegosenda that allows their presence here.

As you approach the fish camp and portage at Twenty-foot Falls, several rock outcrops provide small campsites. As the country rises into low hills, a more mixed forest with white spruce and pine replaces the deciduous woods.

When you enter the marshy expanses of Frog Lake, you have to watch carefully for the right-hand channel that takes you upstream. A point on the right side of Frog Lake still has the remains of a cabin where an Indian family was completely wiped out by influenza in the 1930s.

The swift water in the 4 km above the lake is avoided by a series of five portages, all well marked. The last swift can be lined upstream. Watch along the portage trails for small heath shrubs with leathery leaves, such as trailing arbutus, wintergreen and creeping snowberry. It was in these coniferous woods that we came face to face with our curious marten.

South of Alcorn Lake the countryside presents more classic

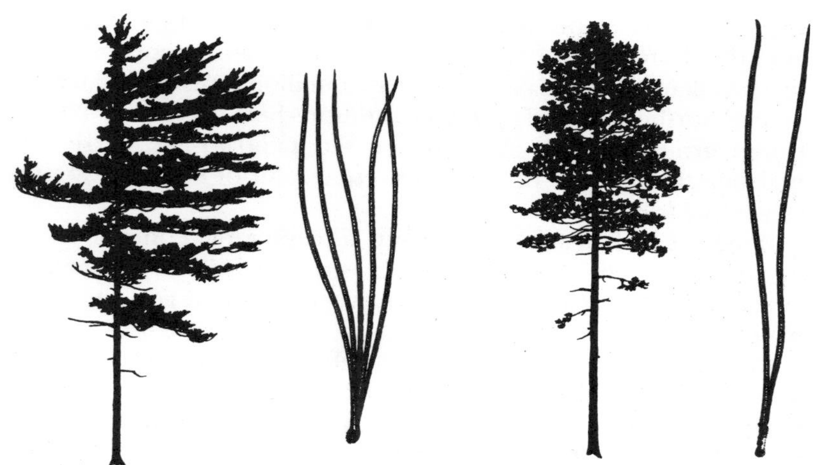

The feathery silhouette of white pine, with its clusters of five needles, contrasts with the whorled branches and paired needles of red pine.
Hap Wilson

northern scenery, with very pretty campsites under the large red pines. But just upstream the river again twists into sections with small channels and small backwater marshes very good for wildlife. Watch especially for the dark bodies and contrasting white underwings of black ducks, a species that has declined in Ontario due to overhunting, hybridization with mallards and possibly acid rain. Watch also for the solitary sandpiper, a medium-sized shorebird that lays its eggs in trees in the abandoned nests of other birds.

The remains of an old dam from the logging era mark the end of the park and the entrance into Nemegosenda Lake. Caution is necessary in a wind on this broad lake, since its rocky shores offer few sheltered harbours. Along its westerly shore, a candidate nature reserve has been identified to protect samples of several types of unusual alkaline rocks.

At the end of the lake lift over a beaver dam to start the portage just upstream on the left. Note the productive marshland created by beaver, with patches of cattail, marsh marigold and aquatic beggar-tick. The portage is 1 km long, uphill but mostly with good footing.

The trail leads through what foresters would call a "forest slum," with a few ancient aspens the only trees left standing in a sea of shrubbery. These conditions were created by poor logging practices some 40 years ago or more, yet regeneration into a commercially valuable stand still hasn't taken place. Despite increased attention to forest management, poor regeneration remains a serious problem in a good part of the half-a-million acres clear-cut each year in northern Ontario. Open conditions here are favourable for ruffed grouse. Watch also for the red pendant-like berries of nodding trillium, the boreal forest equivalent of the more southerly white trillium.

Borden Creek is small and twisty, a pleasurable contrast to the expanses of Nemegosenda Lake. Its shores are lined with white cedar and sweet gale; its waters are very clear and good for fish-watching.

After passing the remains of two abandoned logging bridges, you reach Mate Lake, cut in two by a high esker. Note the vegetation bands along the esker—white cedar along the damp lake edge, white spruce and birch along the side, and red, white and jack pine on the well-drained, gravelly top. The 450-m portage to Waweya Lake climbs the steep side of the esker, giving a close view of the rich understorey layer of honeysuckles and boreal flowers. Note especially the drooping scarlet seeds of the rose twisted-stalk. These are sometimes called "scoot-berries," because they cause diarrhea.

Waweya Lake is an aquamarine jewel set within the diverging arms of the esker—a kettle lake created by the slow melting of a block of ice left in the glacial debris. Since it has no inlets or outlets, its water is very clear and nutrient-poor, suitable for species such as the wild calla. On the 125-m portage out of Waweya, another small depression contains a sphagnum bog dominated by labrador tea and black spruce typical of these acidic habitats.

You can gain access to Hwy. 101 to end your trip here from the east end of Westover Lake, or the portage trail can be reached by car on a logging trail, leaving the highway 500 m east of the lake.

WESTOVER LAKE TO CHAPLEAU

If you want to follow the loop back to your starting point, it is possible to reach Chapleau through a series of lakes and four portages. Portage 90 m from the far end of Westover into Le Blanc Lake, following a bush road to the right on the portage trail. A longer walk takes you into Emerald Lake, so named because of its beautiful greenish colour. From there a 250-m carry across the highway takes you into Borden Lake. Despite many islands which can make navigation tricky, Borden Lake can be dangerous in a wind and should be treated with respect.

The final 1.5-km portage leads from Heckler's Bay into Mulligan Bay along logging roads. Mulligan Bay was once the site of a small Hudson's Bay post, so this portage must have seen much more frequent use in the past than it does now. In 1910 the same site played host to a pulpwood mill for a time, so nothing remains of the historic post. From this point a 6-km paddle along flat water will return you to your starting point at Chapleau.

National Topographic System Maps
Scale 1:50,000: 41O/14
42B/3, B/6, B/7, B/10

Ministry of Natural Resources Maps
Scale 1:100,000: Chapleau 41O/NW
Missinaibi Lake 42B/SW
Foleyet 42B/SE
Elsas 42B/NE

Ministry of Natural Resources Office
34 Birch St., Chapleau, POM 1K0

Chapleau-Nemegosenda Rivers–Map 1

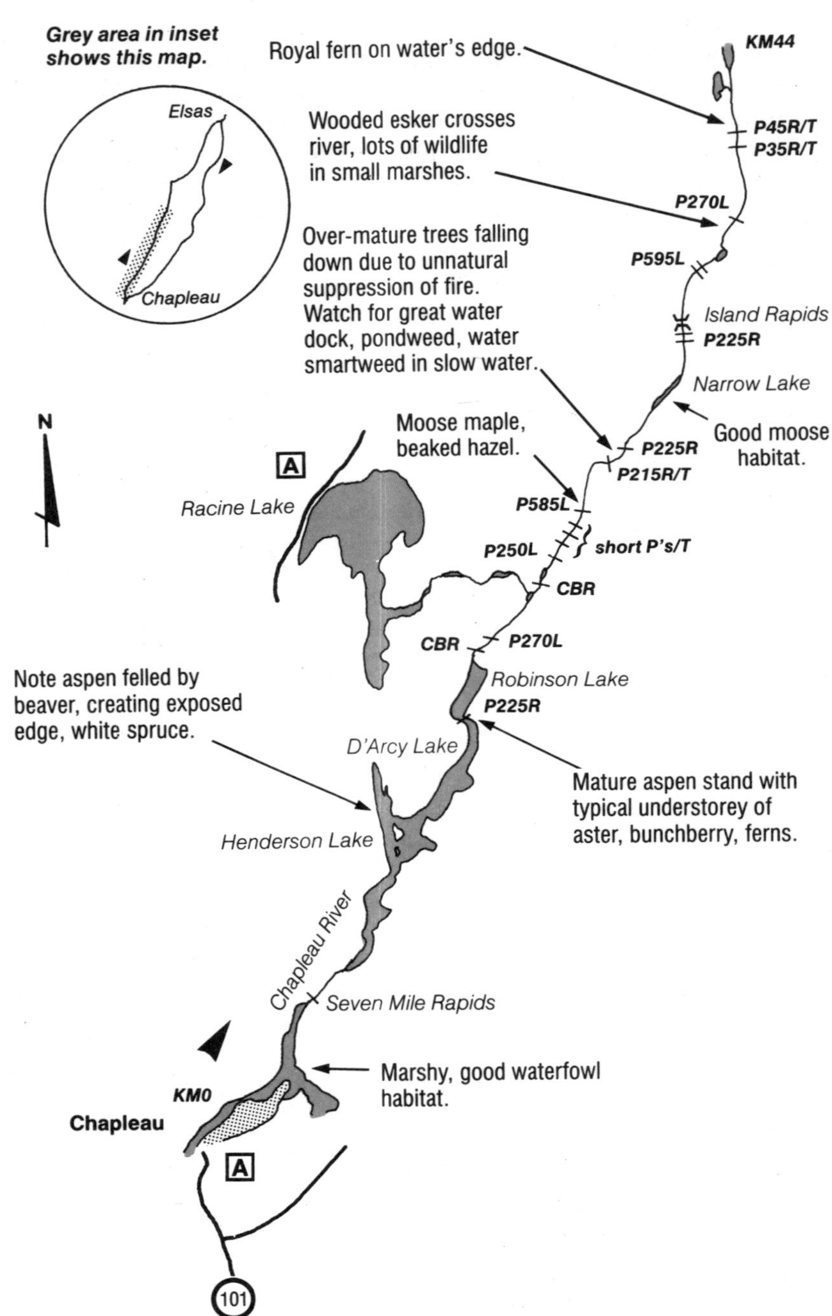

Ref: N.T.S. Map 41O,42B, 1:250,000

Chapleau-Nemegosenda Rivers–Map 2

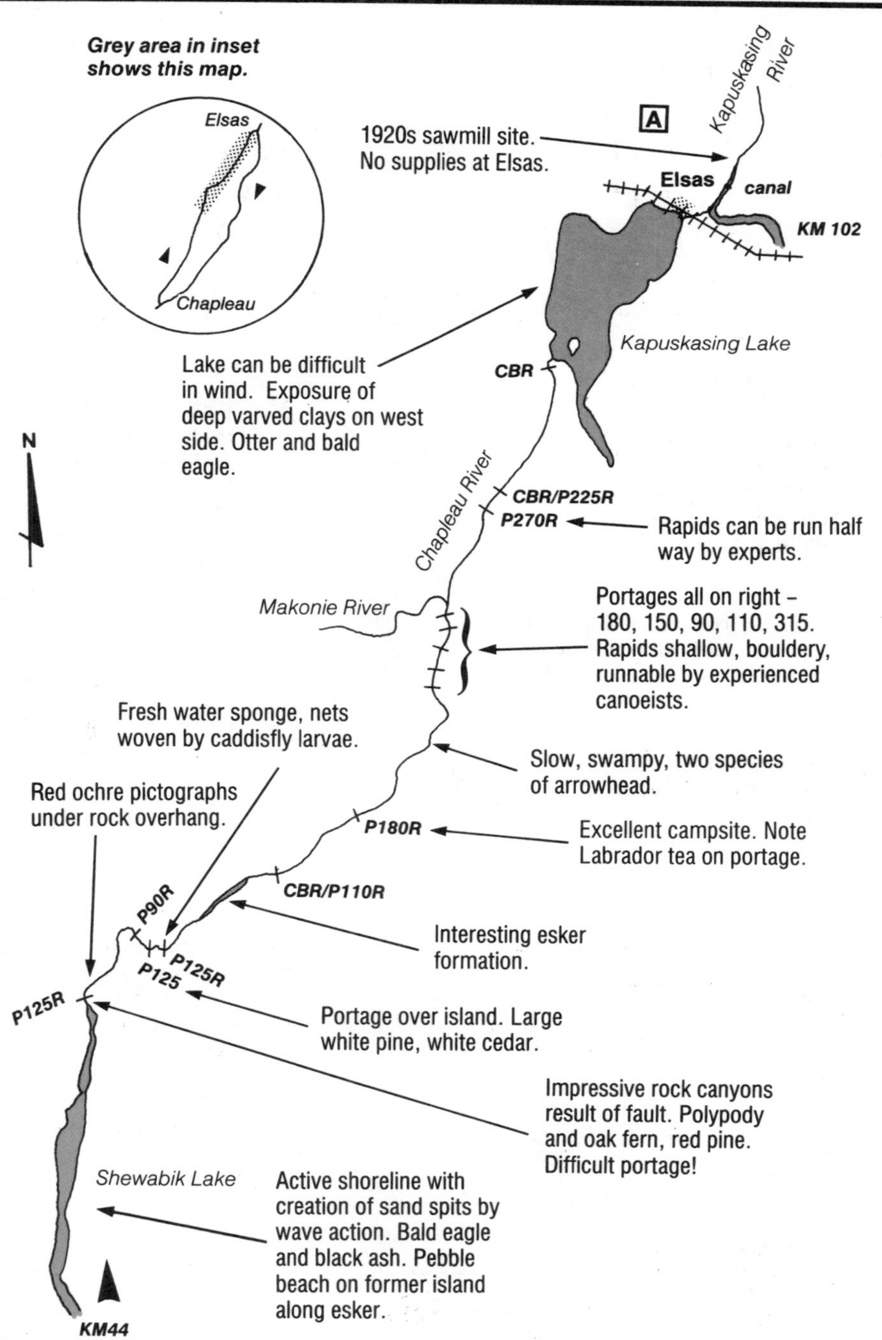

Ref: N.T.S. Map 42B, 1:250,000

Chapleau-Nemegosenda Rivers – Map 3

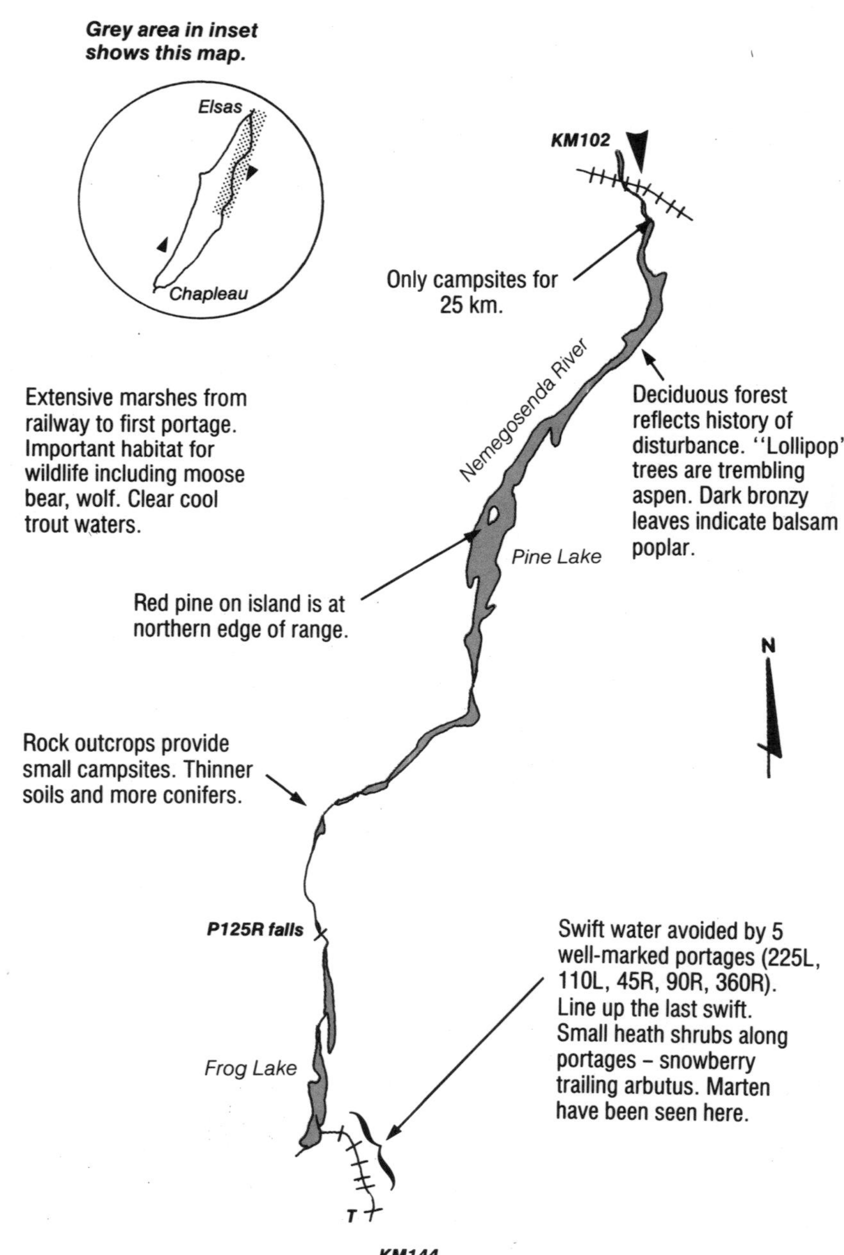

Ref: N.T.S. Map 42B, 1:250,000

Chapleau-Nemegosenda Rivers–Map 4

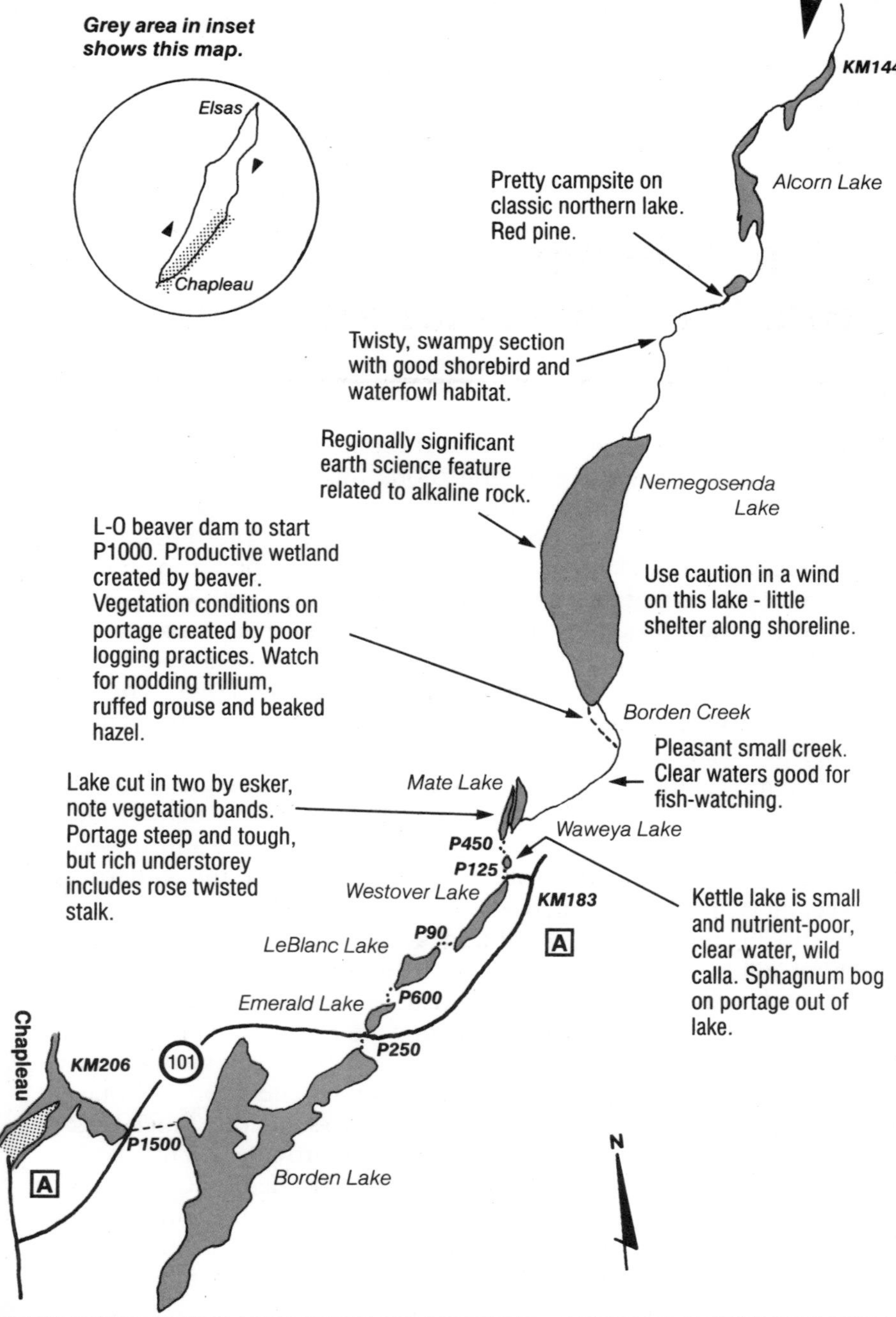

Ref: N.T.S. Map 42B, 410, 1:250,000

The Misehkow: Half the Fun Is Getting There

On the surficial geology map for the country north of Thunder Bay, a wash of green covering thousands of square kilometres shows the thin mantle of soils left by the retreat of the glaciers. Here and there the map breaks into darker green, blue and purple, where deeper pockets provide better growing conditions for the conifer forests that thrive here. But in the corner northwest of Lake Nipigon, the map shows almost all brown—an area of shallow and eroded bedrock where virtually all of the soil has been removed.

Such areas are a forester's bane: trees grow slowly and are difficult to regenerate. But if water is present, the smooth, shallow bedrock can create ideal canoe country. Fortunately water is present in abundance here, in a labyrinth of lakes and tumbling rivers that would take decades to cover completely. This is wilderness canoeing at its very best—portages are short, campsites are frequent and scenic, the waters teem with fish, and the wilderness feeling is unsullied by roads or crowds of competing users.

In 1983 the core of this wilderness area was designated as Wabakimi Wilderness Provincial Park. To the north, the Albany River corridor was identified as a candidate for future park status.

But these accomplishments, gained after years of fierce controversy, were a bitter disappointment to conservationists. Led by Bruce Hyer, a local canoe outfitter, and the Federation of Ontario Naturalists, wilderness enthusiasts fought to set aside a much larger park, including the Misehkow River to provide a link to the Albany. On the other side, the forest industry, led by Great Lakes Forest Products, poured tens of thousands of dollars into an anti-park campaign, including a series of public advertisements designed to undermine local support. Their investment paid off.

After the most bitterly fought wilderness controversy in Ontario history, the compromise solution heavily favoured industry.

Only in the most southerly sections of this route, however, are the threats of new roads and new logging immediate. For many years, you should be able to savour the untouched boreal flavour of a wilderness where caribou, golden eagles and timber wolves proclaim the wildness of the north woods.

The route we have outlined is one of dozens of possibilities, and we would urge you to study the maps to create your own loops or extended trips. While much of the canoeing in this area is exploratory, the Ministry of Natural Resources in Nipigon has detailed maps on portages that cover most route possibilities. As an alternative, several canoe outfitters, including Bruce Hyer of Wildwater Outfitters in Thunder Bay, specialize in trips to this part of Ontario.

The 330-km route from the CNR tracks near Armstrong to Fort Hope will take 15–20 days, depending on how much time you have to enjoy the countryside as you go. For the most part the canoeing is not particularly arduous, though good whitewater skills are necessary in the central and upper parts of the route. It is remote, however, especially on the rarely visited Misehkow, so this route cannot be recommended for travelling on your own unless you are experienced in wilderness survival. Generally the two summer months are preferable for a route this far north.

The Misehkow, which forms the connecting link in the central third of this route, is actually quite a small river. However, since it is only accessible after you canoe across the interconnected watersheds of the new Wabakimi Park, half the fun is getting to its headwaters. At the other end the most logical end point is at Fort Hope, 125 km down the Albany, so this trip gives you a taste of that large river as well.

The Land of Boreas: God of the North Wind

Our route takes you through the heartland of the boreal forest, that circumpolar belt of conifers named after the mythical Greek god of the north wind. Unlike routes further to the south, there are no transitional forests here—this is the true boreal state, undisturbed except by the forces of nature.

Canoeists accustomed to the boreal forest of northeastern Ontario may notice some major differences here. In the east, jack pine grows on dry ridges of sand or rock, while black spruce occupies the wetter lowlands. But here, mixed stands of jack pine and black spruce typically occur on upland sites. White spruce, normally a dry-land species further east, is relegated to a minor role on wetter sites here. The reason for this initially confusing ecological switch lies with the climate, for northwestern Ontario is both cooler and drier than similar latitudes to the east. The dryness restricts white spruce and deciduous trees and shrubs, allowing the versatile black spruce to colonize the mossy ridges commonly found here.

The second result of the drier climate is a high incidence of forest fires, so that even natural stands are usually kept in an immature state. Dry lightning storms are a frequent weather pattern in summer, and the resulting patchy burns favour "pioneer" communities such as jack pine and black spruce, or aspen and birch colonizing from root suckers on deeper soils if the burn is not too severe. Even within this dry boreal forest, however, there is considerable variety related to the underlying landforms. Our route crosses three broad belts, each with its own special characteristics.

In the south, around Smoothwater, Wabakimi and Kenoji lakes, the bedrock is granite. For the most part the soil is very shallow, having been scraped and smoothed by the glaciers. Few shrubs can survive in the bed of feather moss under the canopy of spruce and pine here, although a few northern specialties such as mountain cranberry and Labrador tea occur occasionally. This is also good habitat for the pink, or stemless, ladies' slipper, which is easily identified by its pair of broad basal leaves and its wrinkled pink flower pouch.

In more open stands the ground is often covered by carpets of whitish "caribou moss." This plant is not really a moss at all, but rather a lichen, composed of algae and fungi living in a partnership called symbiosis. The fungi, which give the structure to the plant, tend to hold water which can be used by the small algae. In fact you might be surprised to feel a clump of the lichen after a rain, for its normally crunchy texture is changed to a cushiony softness. The algae, in turn, are able to produce carbohydrates through photosynthesis. Their host fungi lack this ability, so they rely totally on food produced by the algae.

Along the Palisade watershed and Rockcliffe Lake, the underlying stone changes to metamorphosed sedimentary rock, sometimes covered with a mantle of poorly drained peat. In these boggy areas pure stands of black spruce, with the accompanying heath shrubs, are common. It is interesting to note that as early as 1535 the explorer Cartier used a tea from the boiled leaves and bark of

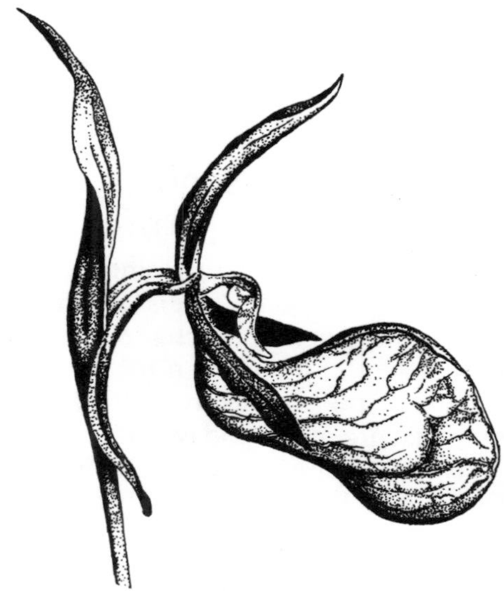

The deep pink, heavily-veined flower pouch of the stemless ladies' slipper is commonly seen in the mossy forests of the boreal zone.

Hap Wilson

black spruce to cure his men of scurvy. Later explorers, including Champlain, apparently had no knowledge of this cure and lost many men to the disease.

The most northerly belt, lying along the Misehkow and Albany rivers, has a more complex geology. Along with patches of granite and sedimentary rocks, the ancient volcanic rocks known as greenstone are present here. Besides containing many potentially useful minerals, these greenstone belts are relatively rich in lime, providing a strong nutrient supply for plant growth. As well, the Agutua moraine rises in gravelly hills up to 150 m above the Albany River. As the glacier receded, this area was submerged for a time by Lake Agassiz, and the hills are interspersed with finer deposits of rich sands laid down on the lake floor.

This combination of deeper soils and higher availability of nutrients has created a more mixed forest here, with aspen and white birch accompanying the black spruce and jack pine. A dense shrub layer of dwarf birch, prickly wild rose, green alder and pin cherry is also common. Here too you can find some northern specialties, such as squashberry, a member of the viburnum family that makes delicious jelly.

Fishing is excellent along this route, with large northern pike and pickerel in the lakes and rivers, and speckled trout found in the Misehkow. Along the Albany, you might be startled by the rolling of huge sturgeon.

A History Buried in the Sand

With a low population dispersed over thousands of kilometres of waterways, perhaps it is not surprising that few details of the history of this area are known. What is known relates mainly to the Albany corridor, and much of that has come from recent archaeological digs. Archaeologists in the north work on the reasonable theory that ancient peoples likely used the same portages and camping spots that are in use today. Indeed, sample digs beneath the surface layer of humus often yield fragments left by these earlier travellers, which can be gradually accumulated as evidence to postulate the story of the past.

Working on this theory, in 1978 and 1979 an archaeologist named David Riddle explored the shores of the Albany River. His research turned up evidence of prehistoric use along the length of the central river, especially at campsites along the major lakes. For example, significant sites were uncovered on Minimiska Lake, both at the entrance to Curry Bay and on a small island near the exit of the river.

The fragments found can be grouped into three general time periods. The oldest, of the Archaic period, fall between 5000 B.C. and 500 B.C., when Indian families moved seasonally within their traditional territory. Since no food supply remained constant, these Indians would move from fall fowling camps to winter hunting and trapping sites, and then in the spring to fishing grounds along the lakes. They gradually became more adept at hunting and fishing, developing bone harpoons and the bow and arrow, with stone arrow points often found on their sites. This was also the great age of copper, with the metal used for a variety of tools and decorations. The only known native copper mine from this era is located along the east coast of Lake Superior at Mamainse Harbour.

The second period of Indian occupation, from 500 B.C. to 800 A.D., is well represented in the archaeological finds along the Albany. Riddle found stone scrapers, presumably used for scraping hides, and shards of the decorated pottery typical of these Laurel people. During this period the Indians learned how to fish with nets, and campsites on points suitable for shallow-water seining often yield flat notched stones used for weighting nets.

Some of the lakeshore sites also yielded evidence of the Terminal Woodland period, which stretched from 800 A.D. to 1600, when the influence of the fur traders caused a dramatic change in the lifestyle of the northern Ontario Indian. In this Terminal period the Indians had developed a more stable lifestyle, returning repeatedly to the same coastal villages for deep-water fishing in the summer months. Trade with neighbouring tribes, extending even to the Hurons in southern Ontario, reached an advanced stage. No doubt the Albany served as an important trade route during this era.

Without doubt the other lakes and rivers of the area along our route also were occupied by Indians in prehistoric times, though little archaeological work has been done. However, you can find evidence of their passing in several pictograph sites and in traditional grave sites. The local Indians from Osnaburgh still come seasonally to some of the lakes along the upper Misehkow to trap and harvest wild rice, and native use of the Albany River is substantial.

The Albany also served as a fur trade route for the Hudson's Bay Company, linking the main post at its mouth with trading posts along the river from 1777 onwards. A major post existed at Osnaburgh House, and other temporary posts have been recorded on Eabamet Lake and Triangle Lake.

Exploring the River

The local base for trips into this area is usually the village of Armstrong, 241 km north of Thunder Bay on Hwy. 527. It is possible to enter the southern section of this route from Caribou Lake, beginning from an access point 10 km north of Armstrong. However, the preferable starting points are located along the Canadian National Railway line west of that village.

Our route begins at Schultz's Trail, but good routes also lead northward from the Boiling Sand River, Nemo River, Allanwater and the Flindt River. The Albany River portion of this trip can also be started at Osnaburgh House, on Hwy. 599 north from Ignace.

At the end of your trip, it is necessary to fly out from Fort Hope. This can be arranged through outfitters in the Armstrong area. Contact the Armstrong Outfitters Association, Armstrong, Ontario, for a listing of outfitters offering this service.

SCHULTZ'S TRAIL TO BURNTROCK LAKE

This first 100 km covers a series of large lakes and small connecting rivers in the Ogoki watershed. From the train's "request stop" at Schultz's Trail, it is a short walk down a trail to the north to reach Onamakawash Lake. Pine-clad shores and rocky points beckon you to the northwest, providing scenic paddling and easy camping.

A few kilometres later, a channel to the right leads you to the first portage on the Lookout River. This picturesque little stream leads past characteristic spruce-pine feather moss forests in a series of short portages into Spring Lake. At its exit, your gentle introduction to the trip is ended with a 900-m portage into Smoothrock Lake. Seldom is portaging such a pleasure though. The granite bedrock is covered here with a gravelly deposit, likely an old beach ridge or low esker, so the path leads through an open stand of birch and aspen. White caribou moss, punctuated by large purple and orange fungi and the scarlet clusters of bunchberries, carpets the ground. The whole effect is a kind of fairyland, leading to the apt local name of Fantasia Portage.

Smoothrock Lake is also aptly named, for its many islands have been caressed by the glaciers into flowing whaleback shapes. Around its southern end Smoothrock was subject to a patchy forest fire in July 1981, a natural phenomenon that temporarily mars the scenery but has its essential role in the ecology of the north woods.

As you paddle up the west arm of Smoothrock, you are now along the boundary of the new Wabakimi Wilderness Park. These woods are the home of the goshawk, a forest predator that feeds mostly on other birds. Camped on Smoothrock, you might see the wavering flight of a barred owl in the evening gloom, another predator adapted to the boreal forest.

The most exciting wildlife in this area, however, is the woodland caribou. A small herd of a few dozen roams the open woodlands from here to Wabakimi Lake, a remnant of a once-widespread animal that now depends on isolation for its survival. The appearance of caribou bones in archaeological digs revealed that northern Ontario Indians coexisted with this herbivore, using it as a food source, for over 9000 years. A change in technology, the introduction of firearms, seems to have been the factor that tipped the delicate balance between hunter and prey, and from 1700 onwards the caribou rapidly declined.

At the top of Smoothrock Lake three channels lead northward.

Primitive stone paintings known as pictographs are usually found in the shelter of overhanging rocks, and often depict animals, spirits, and men. **Hap Wilson**

The centre passage, down the Berg River, is perhaps the most interesting biologically, since it meanders through flat sandy country to produce superb wildlife habitat. Our route branches to the left, however, leading to Wabakimi Lake. Along the way, short portages bypass a scenic waterfall and several rapids. All the portages are necessary since you are now facing into the current.

The west end of Lower Wabakimi Lake appears to have had special significance to local Indians, who in this area are a mixture of Ojibway and Cree. Pictographs are found on the cliffs and an Indian grave site is near by.

Wabakimi Lake presents the largest stretch of open water on the trip, and a strong wind could easily leave you unable to cross for a day. Soils in this area are somewhat deeper than further south, so that deciduous trees become a more noticeable component of the forest on the surrounding hills. Like Smoothwater, Wabakimi is a major hub for canoe routes in this area. The turbulent Allanwater, which provides excellent whitewater canoeing, enters from the south, and the similar Flindt River marks the west end of the lake.

Our travels take us back out the northeast corner, down River Bay, but you might want to spend a day or two first poking about the islands along Wabakimi's northern shore. Besides offering good fishing and dozens of sheltered passageways to explore, these islands are thought to be the summer calving grounds for the caribou herd, so your chances of catching a glimpse of one are at a peak here. Wildlife biologists think that the caribou choose island sites for their calving to lower their vulnerability to wolves and other predators. Since caribou can readily swim, the channels around the islands present little barrier to their own movement.

The Ogoki River, leading downstream into Kenoji Lake, presents a fine series of bouldery rapids that can usually be run by experienced canoeists. Under high water conditions, a 600-m portage along the left shore provides an alternative. As you pick your way downriver, listen for the shrill whistles of an osprey to alert you to the nest of a pair of these large fish-eaters on the right shore. In quiet stretches you might also hear the resonant singing-down-the-drainpipe song of the veery, a common northern thrush that often nests on the ground.

Kenoji Lake is well named, for in the local dialect it means "pike lake," and the game fish is found in abundance in this relatively shallow water. Campsites are less frequent here, but rocky points provide excellent camping both where the river enters and on the western arm.

With your entry into the Palisade River system, your surroundings change considerably. The rock now is sedimentary, laid down by some ancient sea, and as the name suggests, it is broken along the river's edge into square cliffs. Just before the entrance of the Slim River, another set of pictographs, faint but still powerful in spirit, graces the cliffs. An impressive rock-fall just around the corner up the Slim River is also worth a visit.

A chain of short portages now leads northward and then west, linked sometimes by small rocky lakes, sometimes by shallow marshes floored with the organic debris affectionately and universally known as "loonshit." Your progress may slow a little, but ascending this remote watershed has its compensations. A family of mink may tumble through the rock-fall, more curious than afraid. Or you might catch sight of one of the endangered bald eagles known to nest in the vicinity.

A final 250-m portage brings you to the more open expanses of Burntrock Lake, where rocky shores offer some of the best camping spots in this generally swampy countryside. A compass might come in handy here, for the numerous arms of Burntrock, coupled with its large central island, can be confusing.

BURNTROCK LAKE TO THE ALBANY RIVER

The central 105 km of this route is remote, unspoiled and beautiful. However, as you cross the height of land, it starts off boggy, buggy and arduous.

A series of short portages brings you to Muskiga Lake, a shallow, reedy lake surrounded by black spruce peatland. At its far end the 1000-m portage can only be described as a stinker—flat but very wet, with bogholes up to your knees and spruce roots everywhere to trip you up. And at its end, there is only a puddle, from which another 300 m trail of similar disrepute leads to Timon Lake.

Timon Lake is also undistinguished, except that its low swampy shores support a breeding colony of Bonaparte's gulls. These small handsome gulls nest in trees across the coniferous forest belt from Ontario westward, but they are rarely seen in breeding season by birdwatchers.

Near the exit of Davies Lake, the next in line, an Indian trapper's cabin shows signs of active use. Amid the jumble of discarded clothes and food tins, wooden hoops for stretching beaver pelts and a pair of 2-metre snowshoes attest to the more traditional side of the winter trapline in this part of Ontario. Keep in mind the firm rule of wilderness travel, that such cabins be left undisturbed.

From this point onward you are actually on the Misehkow River, but here in the headwaters it could be more accurately classed as a stream. Several portages pass the shallowest spots, although wading might be a better alternative.

Rockcliffe Lake, as the name suggests, is bounded by abrupt buttresses of metamorphosed sedimentary rock along its 14-km length. At the southern end a gravelly island is surrounded by wild rice, and the harvesting nets used with the Indians' canoes await their yearly use at the campsite. In this area as well, a pair of infant graves are marked by a blaze at the top of the bank. In traditional native fashion, the graves are enclosed by low wooden fences, and the twin tikinogans, or cradle boards, hang forlornly in nearby trees.

The clear waters of the Misehkow now flow over gravelly swifts and a few larger rapids, necessitating some portaging or lining. The bedrock changes to ancient volcanic debris, in some places broken into sharp wafers. Sand beaches on small lakes have been created where the sediments of former glacial lakes are deeper.

This is good beaver country, and otter are common too. It is also a good place to spot moose, for the narrow twisting stream often takes you close before your presence is sensed. Even then, most of the ten moose we saw were decidedly casual about fleeing, presumably since they are seldom disturbed by man.

The only major portage on the Misehkow is at Iron Falls. You must watch carefully not to miss the beginning of the portage trail on the right, for the first part of the rapids looks deceptively easy. However, it soon grows into a swift rapids, leading inexorably to a series of chutes and falls. The portage trail cuts across a bend in the river, but an excellent campsite can be found at the falls themselves. Amateur botanists will delight in exploring this area, for the mixed woods host pink ladies' slipper, Hooker's orchis, mertensia and harebells, as well as the more common boreal wildflowers.

Below the falls the river winds for many kilometres between low muddy banks. Occasionally higher ridges of gravel will provide fine camping sites, with well worn game trails leading enticingly back among the scattered trees. Several short portages are available towards the lower end of the river, but most of the rapids can be run by experienced paddlers in normal water. The river now passes through another burn site, this one regenerated with a fine growth of spruce and tamarack. Finally a progressively faster set of rapids between high banks gives you a fine ride, then spills you out onto the Albany.

THE ALBANY RIVER TO FORT HOPE

After so many days on the intimate waterways of the Misehkow watershed, the broad expanse of the Albany, several hundred metres wide, is a refreshing change. Suddenly you feel exposed to the sky and the wind again. Even more, you suddenly feel vulnerable to a very powerful river, for the first bouldery rapid is immediately downstream and the treeless stretch of gravel along the sides attests to the power of the Albany in flood.

Even on the Albany, the aquatic highway of central Ontario, you are 125 km and four or five days travel from the nearest town at Fort Hope. But this is not just the tail end of your trip; the Albany is an experience in itself. Rising hundreds of kilometres to the west, most of the way to the Manitoba border, this river cuts across the grain of Ontario's north. Below the Albany watershed the crazy quilt of lakes and rivers flows southward to Lake Superior. Above the Albany the peatlands soon begin, drained in a more orderly pattern north to the sea. But the Albany charts its own course, an easterly flow that has provided a travel corridor for fur trader and Indian alike. Today it is often used by canoeists coming downriver from the old Hudson's Bay post at Osnaburgh.

As the river twists among the moraines left by the final push of the glaciers, exciting canoeing is provided by the bouldery rapids and braided channels, separated by gravel islands. In slower areas, such as the mouth of the Shabuskwia River and at Howell's Lake, the rich sediments help in the establishment of productive marshes.

It is not unusual to find evidence along the river bank of native fishing activities, including the shells of Ontario's largest fish, the sturgeon. A very primitive fish, sturgeon have no interior bones, relying instead on the hard shell-like plates on the outside for support. A large sturgeon, which could easily weigh over 100 kilos, is likely to be over 150 years old. This long life cycle, with sexual maturity not reached for 15–20 years, makes the sturgeon very vulnerable to overfishing and pollution. Over the years the range of the sturgeon in Ontario has shrunk drastically, and they are now found only in a few larger lakes and rivers.

At Upper Eskakwa Falls the different nature of canoeing the Albany strikes you again, for the portage seems a veritable expressway, wide and well trodden. This pattern continues at Eskakwa Falls, where an excellent campsite overlooks a barren area of volcanic rocks sculpted by the water. Snake Falls, the third in this trio, requires another short portage, although it is sometimes possible to run empty canoes down the turbulent waters of this long rocky funnel. Watch for golden eagles along this stretch of the river.

On your way to Miminiska Lake, watch for another grave site on the left bank. You might also notice evidence of the mineral exploration carried out at Howell's Lake, one of the threats to the future sanctity of this part of the river. On the north shore of Miminiska Lake, a fishing lodge could provide emergency assistance if required.

Below Miminiska Falls several stretches of fast water bring you to the start of Petawanga Lake. Near the entrance, a cluster of buildings includes an icehouse. Again, a combination of an old idea with modern materials prevails. The ice, presumably used for packing fish, is insulated by moss held down by branches. The building, however, is constructed of modern aluminum, enhanced by axe holes hammered throughout.

The rocky shores of Petawanga are often hidden by a mantle of lacustrine sand, producing some spectacular beaches. The finest is a narrow point at the easterly end, reaching two-thirds of the way across the lake. The point has been a traditional Indian camping site, as well as a modern one.

A 600-m portage on the right side of the river bypasses the challenging rapids leading to Kawitos Lake, though they can often be run by experts. On the other side of this small lake, the rapids will at least require lining in parts. Take the southerly channel around the island; a 180-m portage on the left avoids the worst of the rapids.

From here, it is a flatwater paddle to Eabamet Lake, broken only by the pull up a small swift on the Eabamet River. The native community of Fort Hope has moved to a new site, very visible from the lake, with only an old church and cemetery to mark the former village. Some supplies, communications and medical facilities are available here, along with good docking facilities for your flight homewards.

National Topographic System Maps
Scale 1:50,000: 52I/5, I/12, I/13
52P/3, P/4, P/6, P/7, P/8, P/9, P/10, P/11
42M/5, M/12

Ministry of Natural Resources Maps
Scale 1:126,720: Armstrong 52I/SW
Whitewater Lake 52I/NW

Northern part of route not covered by MNR maps; use NTS 1:250,000 sheets 52P and 42M instead.

Ministry of Natural Resources Offices
Box 970, Nipigon, P0T 2J0
Box 309, Sioux Lookout, P0V 2T0

Misehkow River–Map 1

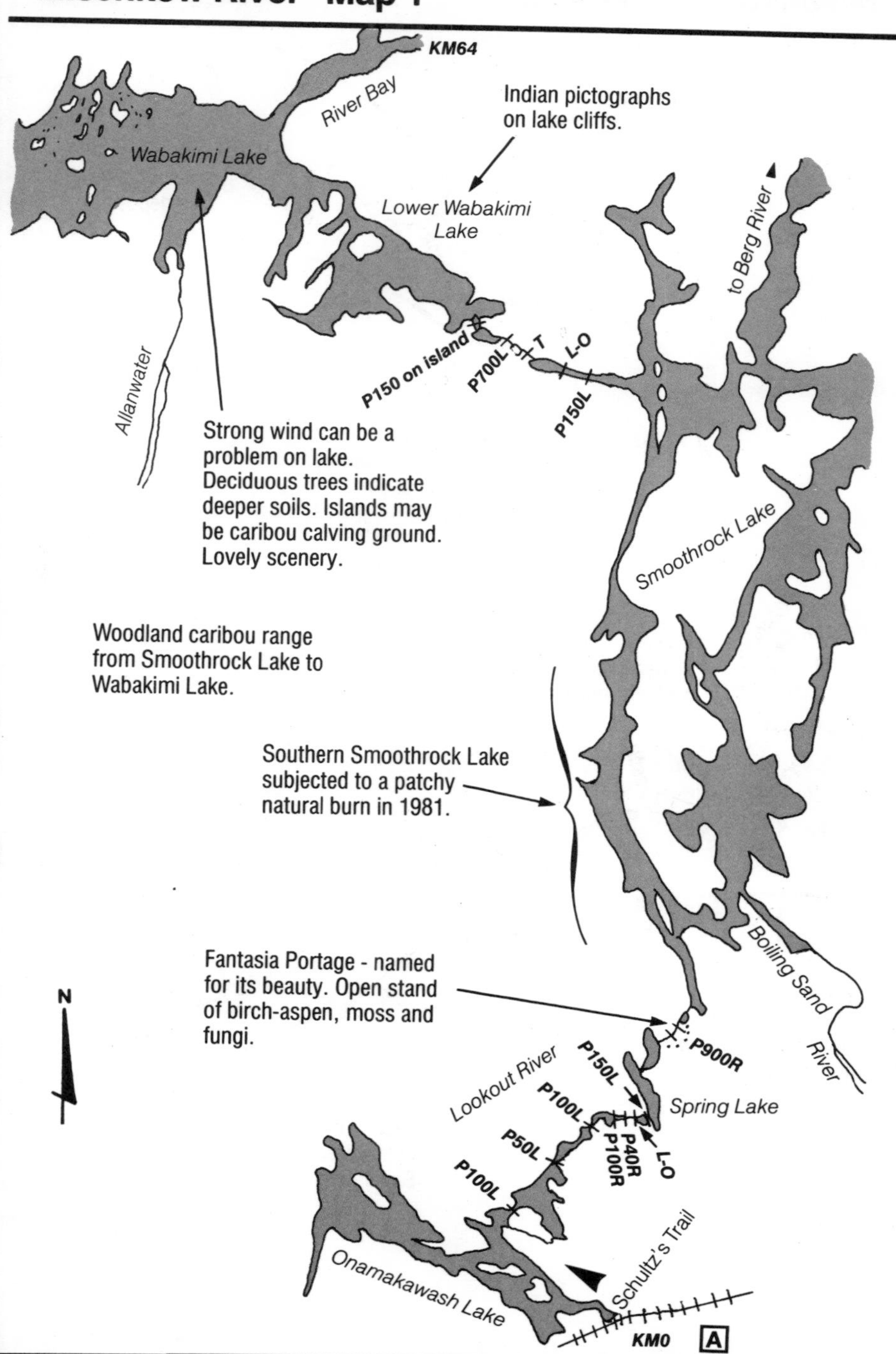

Ref: N.T.S. Map 52I, 1:250,000

Misehkow River–Map 2

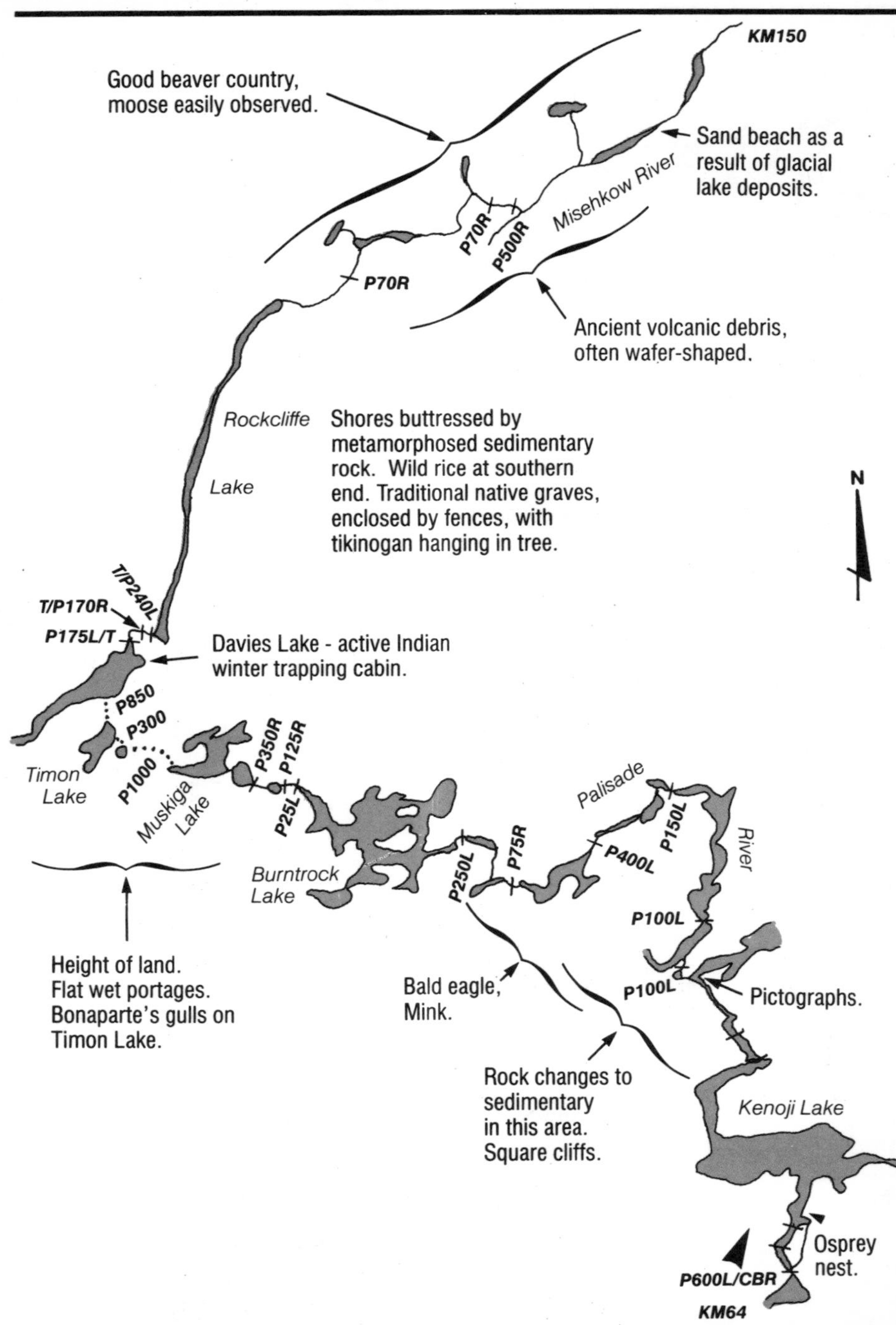

Ref: N.T.S. Map 52I, 52P, 1:250,000

Misehkow River–Map 3

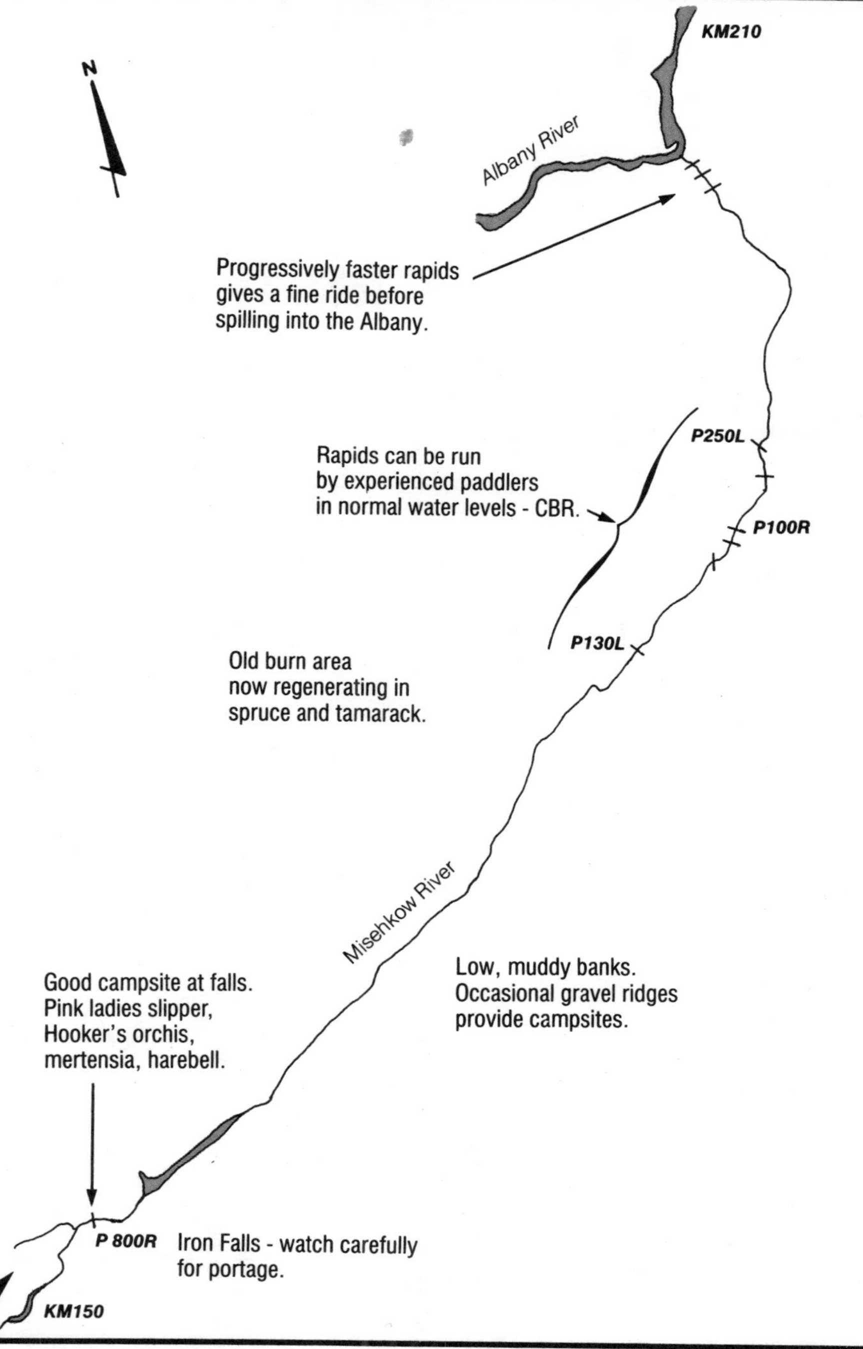

Ref: N.T.S. Map 52P, 1:250,000

Misehkow River – Map 4

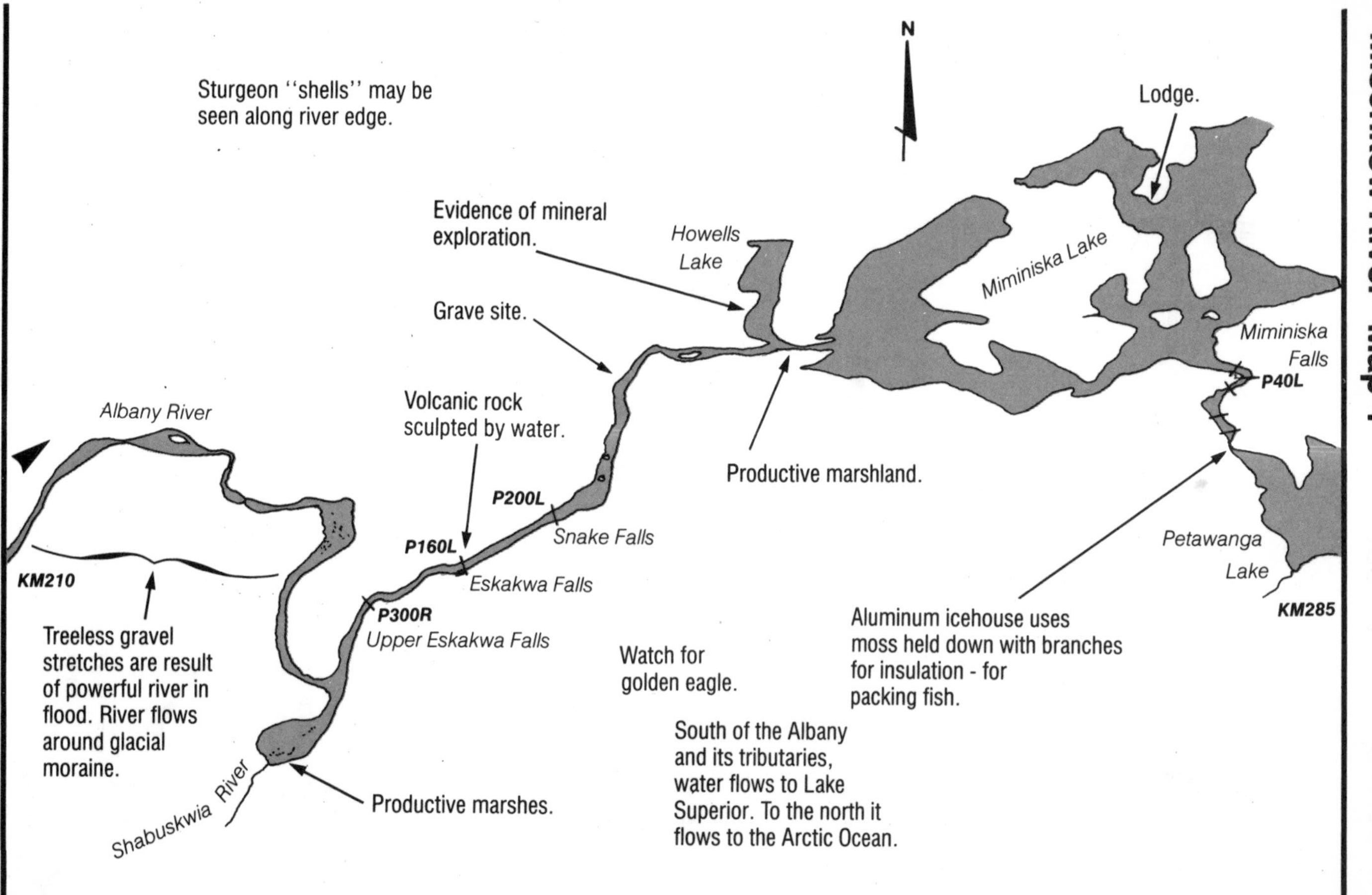

Ref: N.T.S. Map 52P, 1:250,000

Misehkow River – Map 5

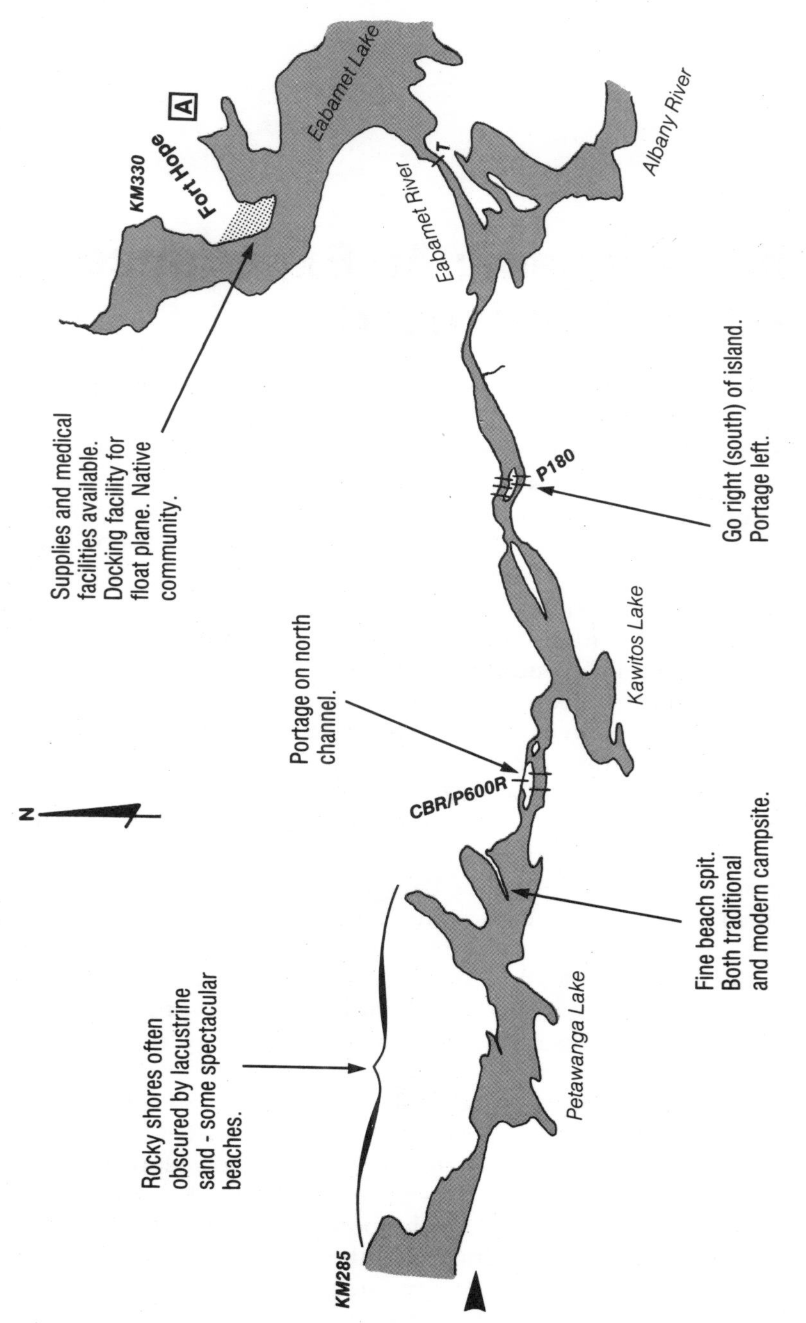

Ref: N.T.S. Map 52P, 42M, 1:250,000

The Kesagami: An Experience for the Experienced

"The Kesagami river is an exceedingly difficult river to navigate. On the coastal plain it is merely swift, but inside the old land area [Precambrian], fall after fall separates shallow stretches of boulder-filled rapids from each other." J.M. Bell, Provincial Geologist, reporting on his visit to the area in 1903.

At first it looks quite impossible. The Kesagami River, most easterly of the Ontario streams flowing north into James Bay, should be out of the question for recreational canoeing. Its headwaters, leading northwards from the Detour Lake Access Road, are choked with fallen trees. After leaving the wind-blown expanses of Lake Kesagami, the river plummets down towards the sea. In its central 35-km stretch, the river loses almost 220 m in altitude, a gradient that means virtually continuous rapids and falls. And at its end, the Kesagami empties into the desolate tidal flats of an uninhabited section of James Bay, an area where unpredictable weather can leave canoeists stranded for days.

But the Kesagami is canoeable. In the late 1960s Terry Damm and Xavier Bird made the only recorded journey down the river, and their account described a route with "rapids to prove a man's skill, portages to measure his endurance, and scenery to reward his perseverance."

In 1983 the Ministry of Natural Resources declared Kesagami one of its six new wilderness parks for the province. Our expedition the next year set out in the hope that its selection for such distinction, based on very scanty information, would be justified.

What we found was one of the best whitewater rivers in the province. In the 134 km from the southern tip of Newnham Bay to the river's junction with the salty estuary of the Harricanaw, the

Kesagami serves up an incredible assortment of swift-water hazards to thrill the most experienced whitewater enthusiast. It offers a slice of Canada's subarctic ecology that few have an opportunity to experience so intimately. And it does so in a setting so remote and unspoiled that the scattered signs of man's previous passage stand out as exceptions for comment.

The remoteness and whitewater attractions of the Kesagami have a double edge. Once you start down the river, there is no place to get off if you find the going too tough, nowhere to call for help if you need it. In places the river demands a high degree of whitewater skill, for there is no feasible alternative to running at least some serious rapids. It also demands a high degree of physical stamina and bush skills—we logged 26 portages, 25 linings and 14 lift-overs, most of them unmarked.

For these reasons the Kesagami can be recommended as a canoe route only with a host of qualifiers. If you have not already paddled some of the more strenuous northern Ontario rivers, you are not ready for the Kesagami. If you have not experienced the numbing chill of a wet northern wind for day after day, and learned how to cope with the diverse hazards that a difficult river can throw at you, the Kesagami is not for you. But if you can honestly rank your wilderness skills in the expert category, an intriguing river awaits you.

A Mosaic of Muskegs

The Kesagami flows through an area of discontinuous permafrost (some would say that also describes the weather). Flying in to the starting point on the lake, it is the mantle of muskeg on top of the frozen ground that gives the region its most striking characteristics. Mile upon mile of stunted and scattered black spruce poke out of the thick layer of insulating mosses. Where drainage is better, such as along river courses, the trees grow thicker and larger, and balsam fir and larch join the spruce.

Even in this flat and seemingly featureless landscape, a closer look reveals other variations as well. In colder areas of poor drainage, the bog mat supports only shrubs, with leatherleaf, sheep laurel and shrubby cinquefoil making up much of the vegetation. In areas of greater nutrient flow, the sedges and grasses of fens develop. The fen meadows along Newnham Bay are a good example of this habitat type. Back from the shore, there are several good examples of string bogs, where thin floating mats of bog moss alternate in a striking pattern with linear pools called flarks. Hidden beneath this mat of peatland, which is up to 4 m thick, is a shallow layer of glacial till and an underlying bedrock of granite and basalt. In a band below the centre of the lake, a belt of the possibly mineral-rich greenstone occurs.

Kesagami Lake is very shallow, a remnant of glacial action either through the eroding action of the ice, or perhaps through the grounding of a large block of stagnant ice. A few low kames, gravelly hills created by the glacial meltwater, provide the only topographic relief along its shores. The lake must always have been shallow, since a layer of clay, laid down from the deposit of fine sediments, lines its bottom. Along parts of its southern edge, peat cliffs have been created by the erosion of the organic soil mat, providing a very unusual spectacle.

As the river flows northwards from the lake, the countryside changes to a series of exposed granite ridges. The forest changes here too, for an extensive burn perhaps 20 years ago seeded a uniform stand of jack pine on this dry habitat. Even in areas not recently touched by fire, jack pine is the common tree on the rocks, with spruce and larch in the open bogs characteristic of lower ground.

For the last third of the Kesagami trip, the river leaves the Shield and drops onto the younger sedimentary rocks of the James Bay lowlands. These rocks are deeply covered by the marine clays left by the Tyrell Sea, so that poorly drained peatlands again become the standard riverside scene.

Wildlife in this remote corner of the province is poorly known, but certainly moose, bear and wolf are common. Woodland caribou are seen regularly around the lake and are thought to calve on Big Island. There is too little birch and poplar to support a large beaver population, but otter, marten and other northern furbearers can often be seen.

One of the more interesting "critters" commonly found in the bogs along this route is the Hudson Bay toad. Its vivid colours and sharply defined markings distinguish it from the garden-variety American toad, of which it is a subspecies. Toads will not give you warts, by the way, but if you handle one, wash off your hands afterwards to remove an irritating mucus secreted by the toad in self-defence.

The Kesagami is host to a run of speckled trout returning to the river from James Bay, and both pike and pickerel are found in the lake and river. However, we found fishing to be mediocre, as did

Terry Damm 15 years earlier. Perhaps the dark waters, stained by the tannins of boggy headwaters, contributed to our lack of success.

Pushing Back the Frontier

Canoeing the Kesagami is literally pushing back the frontier, for so few people have come this way before. The area lies within the hunting grounds of the Swampy Cree of Moosonee, and some Cree families still use the more accessible parts of the river near its mouth for hunting and trapping. Clearly the river was used occasionally by trappers, for Terry Damm reports evidence of old blazes on portages and old campsites in a few places. Just as clearly, that use was infrequent, for the traces of man's past are sparse indeed.

It is easy to understand why the Kesagami River was bypassed. The major fur trade routes in the heyday of northern river travel lay just to the west in the Moose and Abitibi. Even for access to Kesagami Lake, the frequent rapids and often-shallow waters of the Kesagami discouraged travel. The North French River, just to the west, provided an easier access route only a short portage away.

In the earliest days of exploration it appears that the lake did play a more important role. In July of 1774 a Hudson's Bay clerk named John Thomas visited the lake on a trip from Moose Factory to Lake Abitibi via the North French River. He reported meeting Indians who were fishing at the lake.

Three years later, a small post known as Mesackamee House was constructed on the north side of the lake by George Atkinson. In his journals Atkinson reported, "A vast maney Indian tents Hear we ar close to a Creek war the Indians Dam in all the Summer and get plenty of fish so I am in hopes thar will Not be aney want of Vittels when once Salted." Despite these encouraging signs, by 1780 the post had been abandoned because of lack of trade and the difficulties in supplying it.

Even though the "Mesackamy path" to Fort Abitibi was evidently well known to the Indian guides with John Thomas, the next expedition, under Philip Turnor in 1781, had difficulty finding the route. He was eventually successful, and his journals map out a route that crosses Kesagami Lake, goes down Newnham Bay and then takes a portage to link into the Burntbush River system.

It was the traditional Indian route that J.M. Bell followed in his visit to the lake in 1903. His report is full of enthusiastic detail

This unusual wood and moss winter lodge on the north shore of Kesagami Lake is used by the Cree while trapping. **Ron Reid**

about the peat cliffs but provides little else of insight about the watershed. He mentioned, however, that the lake served as a winter base for a large portion of the Moose Factory Indians on account of the fishing.

Today most traces of these past visits have vanished, awaiting discovery by an ambitious archaeologist. However, near the northeast corner of the lake, a Cree winter lodge, estimated at 30 to 40 years old, provides a fascinating look at the old ways. Constructed of logs with a moss covering, the teepee-shaped structure is of a type rarely found in this part of the province. The only other building on the lake is a modern fishing and hunting lodge near the entrance of Newnham Bay.

The origins of the name Kesagami, like so many northern names, is obscure. We were told by a young Cree from Moose Factory that the name meant "river of sticks," but others suggest that it is closer to the Cree words for "river of big water," perhaps in reference to the expanse of Kesagami Lake.

Exploring the River

Even though the total distance covered on this route is only 140 km, set aside at least 12 days for a reasonable trip. We spent two days exploring Kesagami Lake, but adverse winds could easily keep you there longer. In the midst of the rapids, an exhausting day might only cover 5 km, and the setting is so beautiful that you will want time to savour it. As well, be sure to carry enough extra food for several days wait at the coast if weather conditions are bad.

Late July and early August is the ideal time for the Kesagami, if water levels are normal. In a dry year parts of the river will be too shallow for passage, so check in advance with the Ministry of Natural Resources in Moosonee regarding water levels. Even at this time of year, you must plan on coping with numerous insects and periodic cold wet weather, so choose clothing accordingly. River wading is unavoidable on this trip, so good river shoes are especially important.

As paddling the Kesagami means flights in and out of Moosonee or Cochrane, it is a relatively expensive undertaking. A list of local aircraft outfitters is available from MNR, or you can consult *Lamont's Ontario Canoe Guide*. It may be possible to arrange freighter canoe transport from the mouth of the river at Hannah Bay back to Moosonee with an experienced Indian guide. Again, check on the availability of such local services with MNR. In any case, do not attempt the trip along James Bay in your canoe. Such a venture is not just foolhardy; given the history of the Bay in swamping open canoes, it is close to suicidal.

NEWNHAM BAY TO START OF RIVER

Although the most common landing place for float planes appears to be the entrance of Newnham Bay (Km 21), we have started our trip description from the southern end of the bay because of the many interesting features found there.

At the entrance of Newnham Creek, a broad grassy area is one of several extensive fen meadows, "likely without comparison in Ontario," according to a study by Dan Brunton. Watch for linear-leaved sundew, a small insectivorous plant very rare in Canada. Just up the bay, a similar fen meadow at the entrance of the Kesagami River supports a population of the uncommon bog lemming. At the entrance of the creek from Fen Lake, the fen meadows provide good summer caribou habitat. On the point across the bay on the east, a shrubby heath meadow shows a habitat typical of colder sites.

Near its entrance into the lake, Newnham Bay crosses between low sandy kames, mounds of gravel deposited in drainage holes within the retreating glacier. The remains of one of these kames forms a sand and boulder spit across the mouth of the bay, supporting a mixed birch-conifer forest with a southern flavour. Many interesting shrubs are found in this habitat—American mountain ash, highbush cranberry, dwarf raspberry. Wild sarsaparilla, starflower and oak fern also occur here.

Paddle west along the shore of the lake to see the peat cliffs, with their pillars and caves eroded into strange shapes by wave action. Note the pieces of wood exposed in the peat, some thought to be 6000 years old.

Kesagami Lodge stands on the east shore, blighted by the forest of dead birch trunks around its grounds. Opposite the lodge, Big Island serves as a calving ground for woodland caribou, protected from predators by the turbulent waters. Take a close look at the beach on its southeast shore, for the golden sand is actually a thin layer deposited on top of the peat.

You may have to choose your timing carefully to get across Kesagami Lake, for it can become very rough on windy days and there is little protection along the east shore. The Cree winter lodge, at the back of a small beach along the northeast coast, makes a useful target point, and a good campsite is located there as well.

START OF RIVER TO LAST PORTAGE

For the many falls and rapids in the central section of the river, this guide assumes that you are a competent whitewater paddler. Most of the portages are the bare minimum required, starting immediately above the lip of the falls. Different water conditions might produce a guide that would read quite differently for this section. Your own judgement must guide you in handling a particular obstacle. The names given for some of the rapids and falls, by the way, are our own creations and have no official sanction.

Two campsites can be found where the river leaves the lake, one on the south side at the exit, the other 200 m downstream on the north side. A trapper's camp at this second site is set among large white birch and balsam fir, with such northern specialties as checkered rattlesnake plaintain, one-flowered wintergreen and bunchberry among the underbrush.

An easy series of bouldery swifts now takes you into one of the most productive parts of the river. Swampy shores provide excellent areas for waterfowl, with Canada geese, goldeneye, common mergansers and black ducks everywhere. Along the shores clumps of blue flag and yellow pond lily provide spots of colour. Watch for moose along this stretch, especially in the quiet estuaries of tributary streams.

By the time you have covered the first 10 km of the river, the quiet waters are left behind as the gravelly swifts gradually build into the first major rapids. Be very careful here, for it is easy to be drawn into danger by this continuous fast water, and lining is necessary along part of this rapid.

A rough campsite is available on a high gravelly ridge by the rapids, but you should be careful to dig well below the organic mat for your fire. This area is part of an extensive burn about 20 years old, and the ground is a carpet of lichens, especially the British soldier lichen with its scarlet cap. Among the jack pine you might hear the sleepy calls of the boreal chickadee or the "quick-three-beers" that identifies an olive-sided flycatcher.

From here to Burn Creek the rapids are continuous but runnable. The banks are lined with an array of shrubby cinquefoil, sheep laurel, sweet gale and alders, thriving in the open conditions created by the burn. The mouth of the creek itself provides a possible campsite, and a small bog here yields bog goldenrod and rush aster along with the typical bog species.

A few hundred metres downstream, a 2-m ledge can be avoided by lining down the small channel on the left. Jack Pine Chutes, next in line, requires a short portage after the first stretch is lined or tracked down the right side. On this shallow rock ridge, notice the different plants—serviceberry, blueberry, pearly everlasting, common rattlesnake root and fireweed.

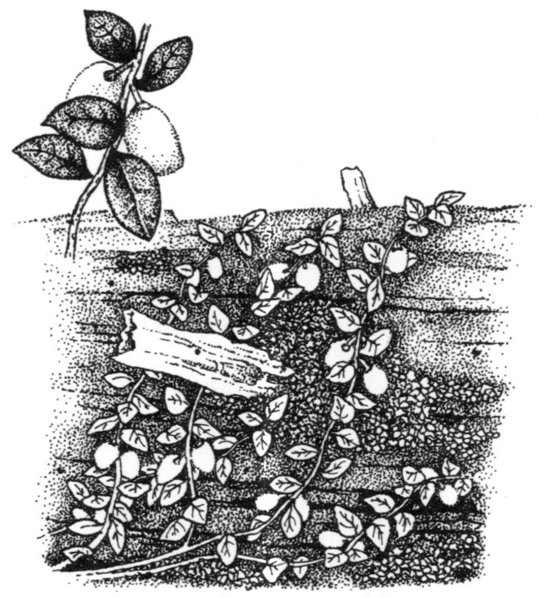

Almost buried in the moss among the miniature leaves of the snowberry, the tiny egg-shaped berries have a refreshing wintergreen flavour. **Hap Wilson**

Now the rapids come thick and fast, and our instructions begin to sound like some exotic dance—run two, line and portage the next, carry on the right over Snowberry portage, line twice more, run one, lift-over the next two, and line again. Have we lost you yet? The map makes the dance a little clearer, or you can obtain our more detailed trip notes from MNR in Moosonee, but remember that you will still have to establish your own pattern when you get there. Along the way, be sure to watch on Snowberry portage for these small vine-like plants creeping over the moss, for their edible white berries have a marvellous wintergreen flavour once used in alcohol to make liqueur d'anis.

The next major rapids, where the river splits around a long island, is one of the trickiest along the river. To get to the island portage at Twin Ridge Chutes, you have to carefully run the first part of the rapids and land on the head of the island, and God help you if you miss! The portage is easy, and the island would make a fine campsite, but at the lower end you still face a difficult rapid, which can't be avoided.

The next 4 km, from here to Rattlesnake Falls, are less turbulent, and a combination of lining, lift-overs and running will speed your progress a little. The falls are bypassed by a 75-m portage on the right. Watch for the triangular-shaped rattlesnake fern along the portage, among the red osier dogwood and Labrador tea. Cedar waxwings are common along this part of the river and you might see the woodpecker that feeds on the ground, the common flicker.

A lift-over past a small island and two more runnable rapids take you to Grand Falls, where the river pours through a slot in the rock barely 3 m wide. The 200-m portage on the right leads around the end of a barren rocky hill that drops 10 m into the water. Two more lesser rapids bring you to Reid Falls, this one bypassed by a portage on the left. Almost immediately, another 200-m portage on the right is necessary.

The pace slows in the next 4 km, but you will still have to line several times and to complete one short portage. A 125-m portage on the right begins a long series of step-like rapids, most of which can be lined. Along the edge of this dense spruce and fir forest you can find a variety of shrubs such as shaggy ninebark, mountain ash, wild rose and pin cherry. Just downstream, Bushwhack Falls requires yet another portage.

Once again the pattern of lining and lift-overs is resumed, until you reach a pretty falls 2 km downstream. This is easily avoided by portaging into a small channel on the right, which passes through a grove of massive white cedars. You are now finally past the effects of the old burn. We found sensitive fern and rose twisted-stalk among the cedars here.

Two more easy runs bring you to the Bog Walk, at 1500 m the longest portage of the trip. Fortunately this trail has been well blazed as it passes through open black spruce/Labrador tea bog. Watch for typical bog species such as cotton grass, round-leafed sundew and northern green orchis. This is a good area to pick up spruce grouse and sharp-shinned hawks. Just across from the end of the portage, which appears to be longer than necessary, there is a good campsite on Frank and Jill Point.

The next major obstacle, after several small rapids, is the 450-m portage around Whaleback Falls. Its end point is spectacular—a campsite on a granite island scoured smooth by the glaciers, with an unobstructed view of the roaring waterfall just upstream. In good weather this is the ideal spot for a rest day. You can try the fishing at the foot of the falls, beneath the first birch trees we had seen since Kesagami Lake. Or you can poke about the island, tracing the chatter marks left by rocks in the toe of the glacier

One of the best campsites on the river is just below Whaleback Falls, where the river plunges over a smooth hummock of granite.

Ron Reid

bouncing along, or figuring out such diverse wildflowers as brook lobelia, pink corydalis, harebell, flat-topped white aster, meadow rue, Canada hawkweed and grass-of-parnassus. Beside the campsite the river barrels through a smooth rock trough, just the place for floating through in life preservers or for a little solo canoeing.

The river here has widened to form a quiet stretch we dubbed Moondance Lake, in memory of a moonlight paddle. Along its sides a pair of parallel sandy ridges probably represent old marine beaches.

The first rapids below the lake can be lined, but the next set is bypassed by a 450-m blazed portage on the right. As you come onto the cobble beach at the end of this trail, take a close look at the limestone fragments around your feet, for many are full of fossils from the marine environment that once covered the area just to the north.

Sharprock Rapids, just downstream, can be handled by a combination of lift-over and lining. The granite here has been altered by a criss-cross pattern of harder rock intrusions, which now protrude several centimetres above the bedrock.

The next 3 km are broken often by short portages, six in all, and by three lift-overs. Some of the islands in the lower part of this section are not shown on the preliminary topographic maps, which can be confusing, but careful navigation will get you through. One compensation for the frequent portages is the fantastic crop of blueberries on these rocky knolls. Still, by the time you reach Tombstone Rapids, you will likely be ready for the campsite along the portage trail, reached by following the dry channel on the right.

About 500 m downstream the river splits around a large island. Take the left channel, where some lining, a lift-over and a short portage are necessary as well as several exciting runs through bouldery rapids. Below the island you must line, portage and lift-over again before reaching a blazed trail that marks Last Portage. At the end of this portage a cool spring bubbles out over the limestone rubble. The Precambrian rocks are now behind you, buried beneath a layer of gravelly till, and balsam poplar and white birch join the spruce and pine that have been your companions for so many days.

LAST PORTAGE TO HANNAH BAY

The character of the river now changes completely, with swift-flowing, often shallow waters speeding you towards the sea. Two days of steady paddling can now bring you to the river mouth, provided that water levels are high enough to float you over the shallows.

In many places along the Lowlands, the silty-clay banks have slumped into the river, sliding the ubiquitous black spruce into the current. In other areas the river is bounded by a wide grassy verge, with wildflowers such as the turtlehead, whose white blooms resemble their namesake. The swift waters are now bouldery and running the rapids is mostly a matter of finding the deepest channel.

The Bodell River adds its clear orange waters to the darker flow of the Kesagami, and just downstream several islands provide rough camping. The wildflower communities are now quite different from those on the granitic uplands, with grass-of-parnassus, yellow loosestrife, cow parsnip, Canada anemone, swamp thistle and silvery cinquefoil commonly found along the banks of the river. Even the bright orange bloom of the wood lily makes an appearance.

As the river nears sea level, different birds are also attracted to the brackish estuaries. Osprey take advantage of the rich fishing and Bonaparte's gulls flock over the muddy shallows. So do migrating shorebirds, which have already begun their flight southwards in August. In the shrubby edges, northern waterthrush are a local specialty.

You must now deal with the tides, which can be up to 2 m high. Tide tables are available from MNR, but be extra cautious in your choice of campsite, especially if an onshore wind might raise the tide levels. A small creek on the left about 2 km from the river mouth is the site of a McMaster University Field Camp, one of the few suitable camping spots in the area.

At the junction of the Kesagami with the Harricanaw River, you have an unobstructed view into James Bay to the north. With an incoming tide, watch for beluga whales along the Harricanaw. A popular spot for pickup is the Hannah Bay Goose Camp, 5 km back up the Harricanaw on the east shore. While the camp is abandoned in summer, its cabins can offer welcome shelter from the polar winds that sweep down the Bay.

National Topographic System Maps
Scale 1:50,000: 42I/1, I/8, I/9, I/16
32L/13, 32M/4

Ministry of Natural Resources Office
Box 190, Moosonee, P0L 1Y0

Kesagami River – Map 1

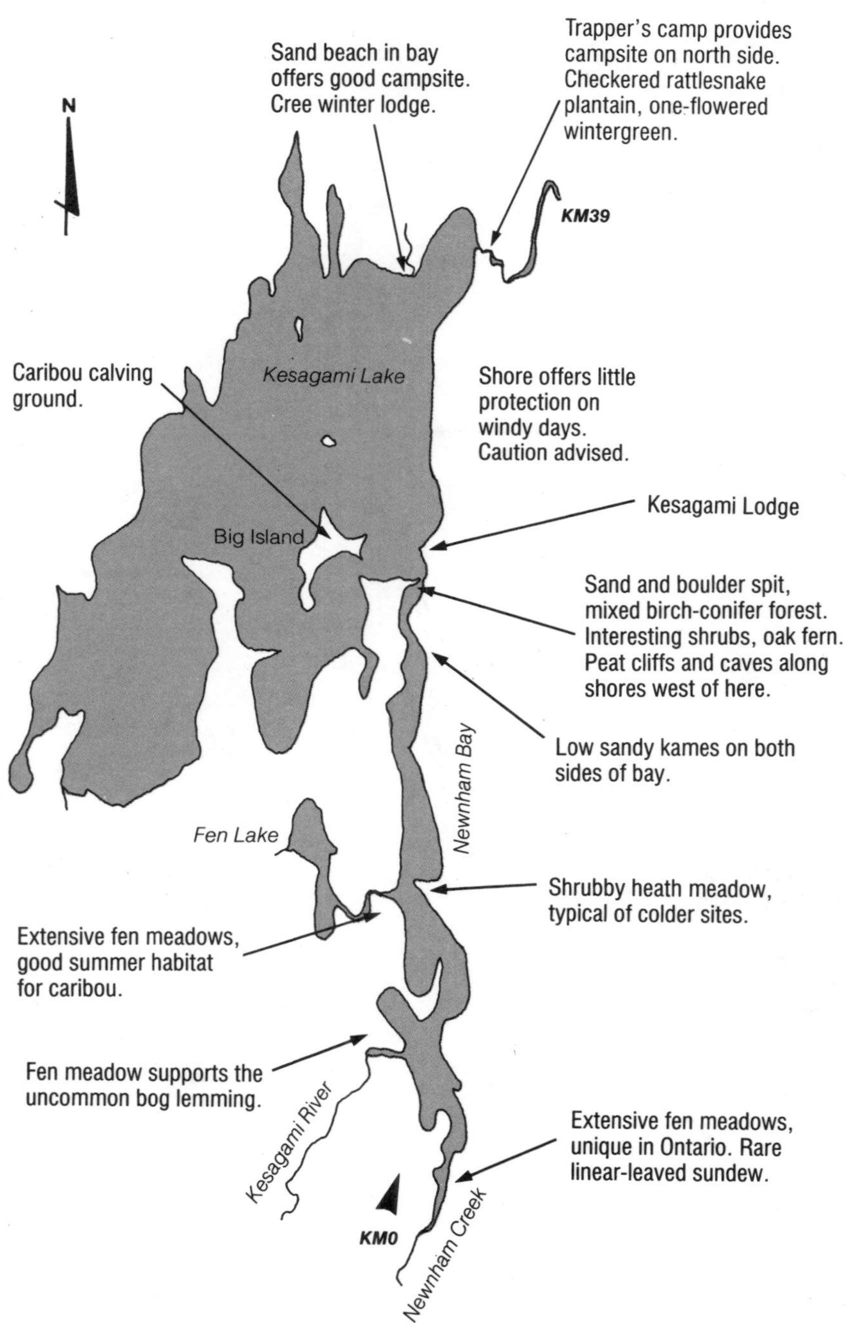

Ref: N.T.S. Map 42I, 1:250,000

Kesagami River – Map 2

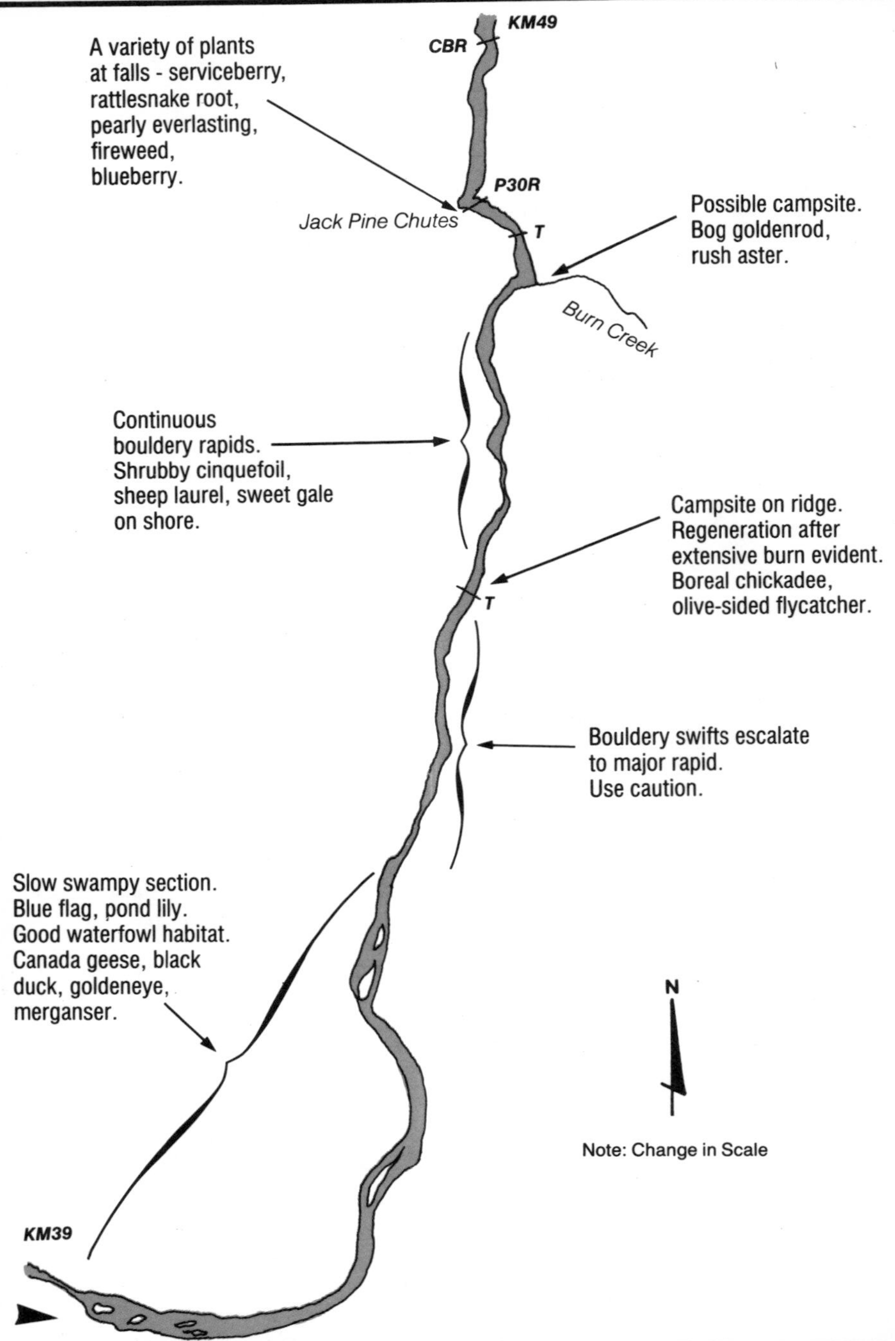

Ref: N.T.S. Map 42I/8, 42I/9, 1:50,000

Kesagami River – Map 3

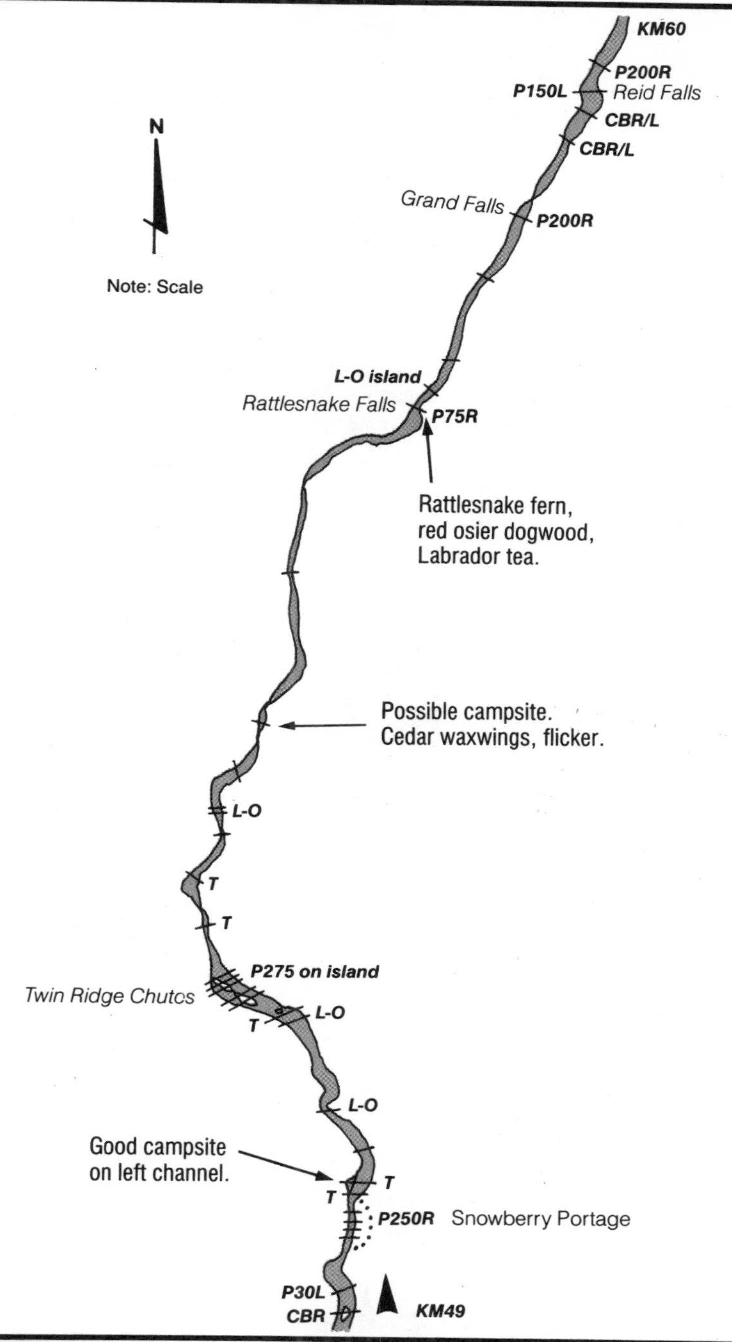

Ref: N.T.S. Map 42I/9, 1:50,000

Kesagami River–Map 4

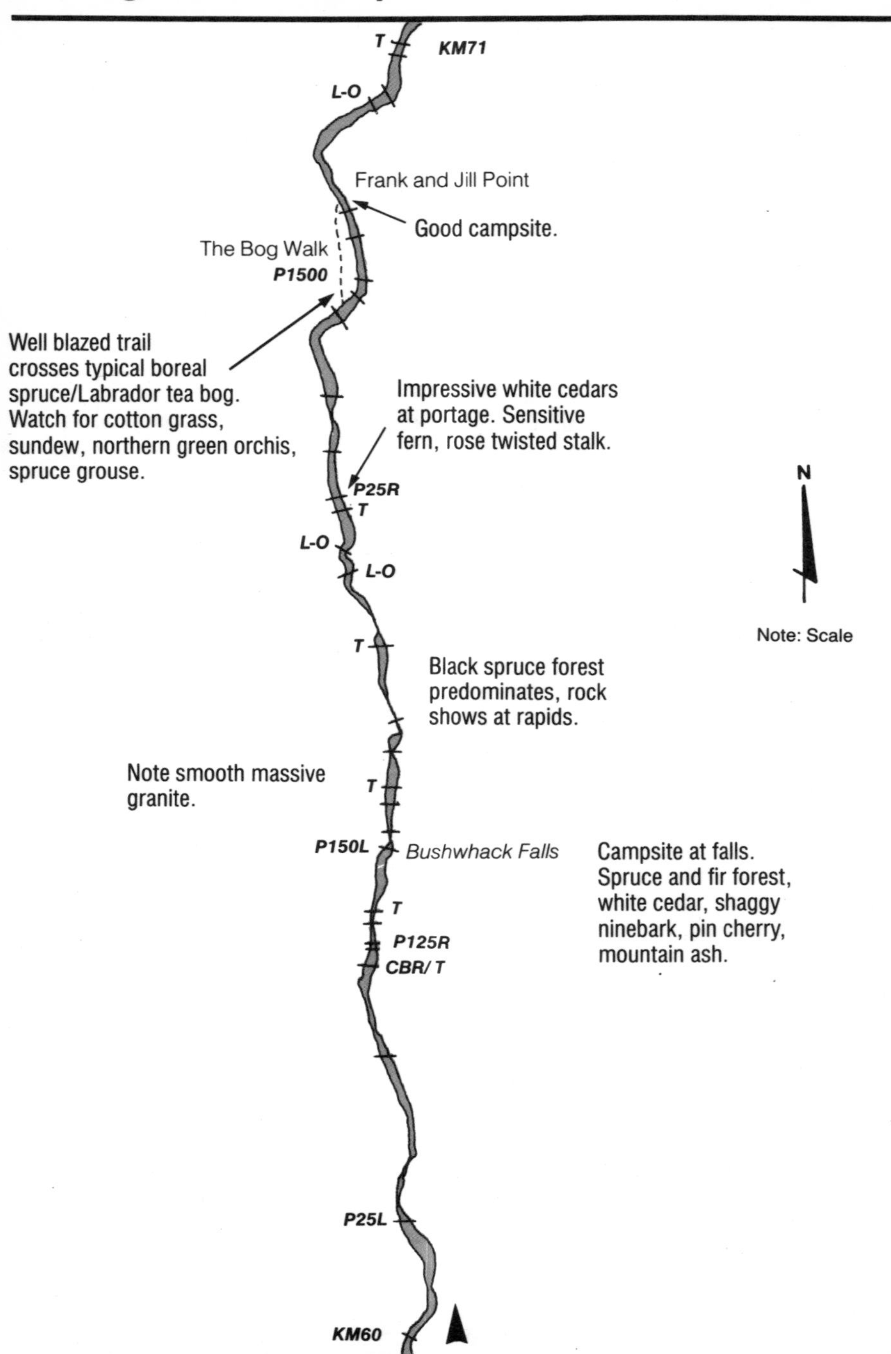

Ref: N.T.S. Map 42I/9, 1:50,000

Kesagami River–Map 5

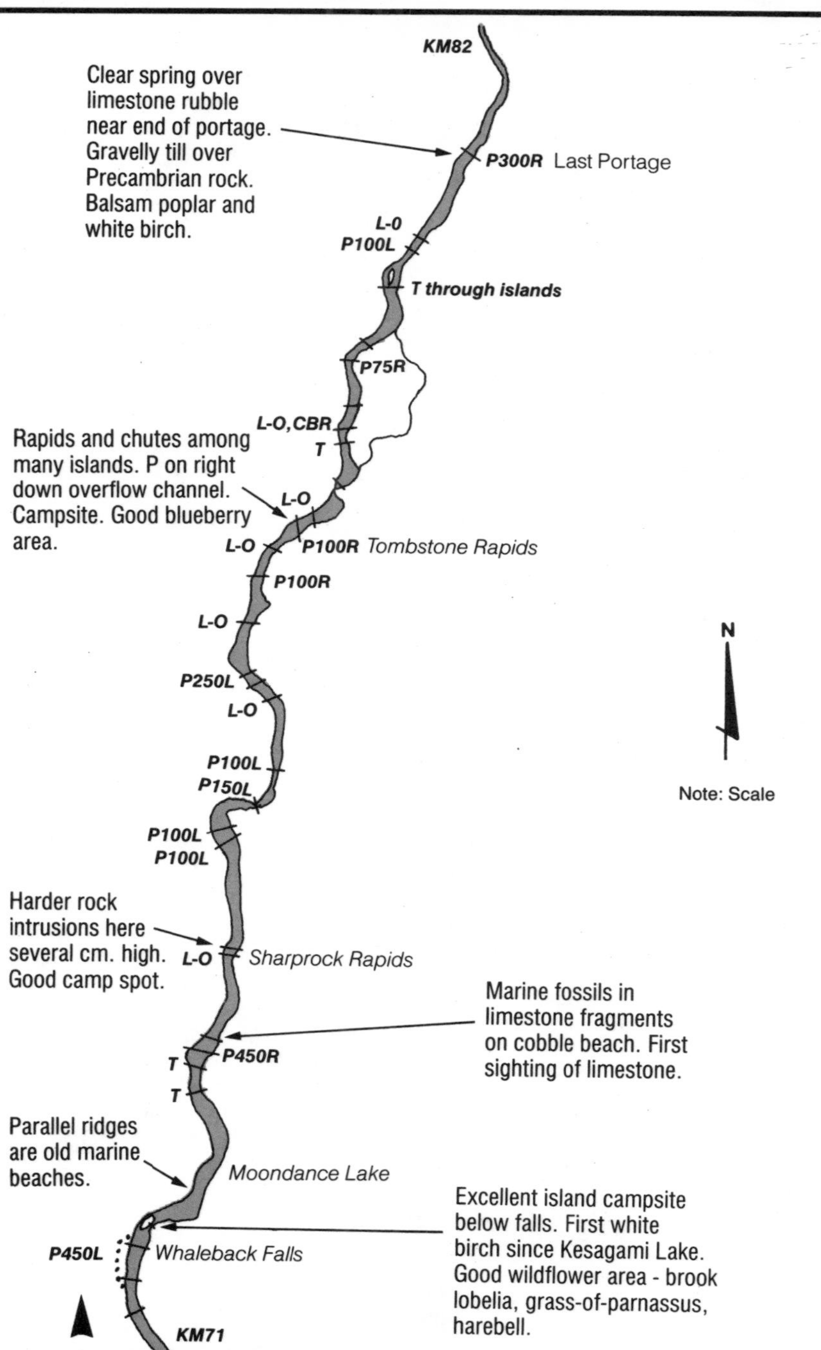

Ref: N.T.S. Map 42I/9, 42I/16, 1:50,000

Kesagami River – Map 6

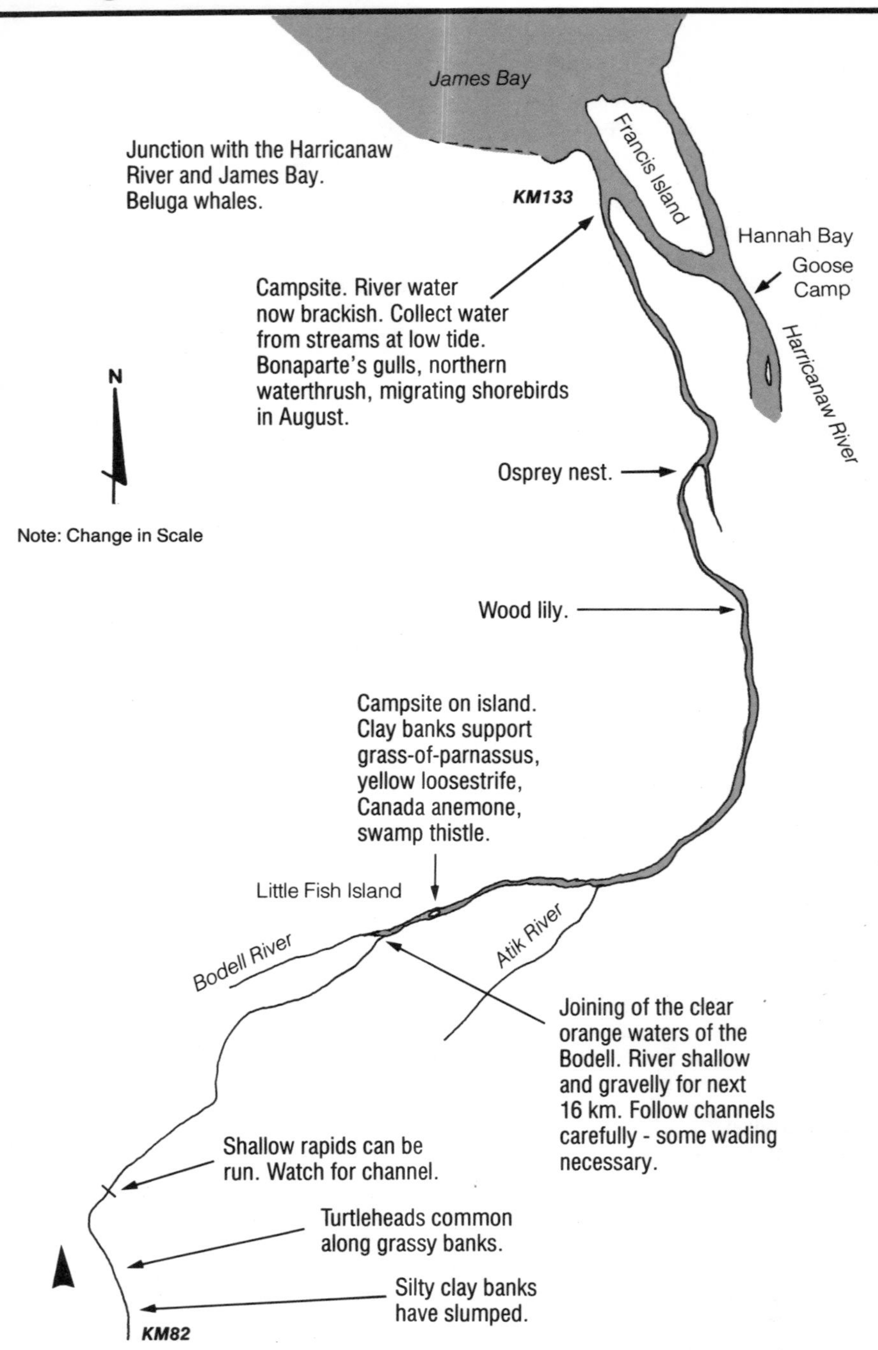

Ref: N.T.S. Map 42I, 32L, 32M, 1:250,000

Other Arctic Watershed Rivers

For those with the experience and the skills necessary to travel safely in remote country, there are few places that can match the opportunities for extended canoe trips in Ontario's Arctic waters. Unfortunately this remoteness has a price, for expensive air service is usually necessary at least from the end of your trip. The notable exception is the series of tributaries of the Moose, which have rail access to the south from Moosonee.

In the northwest a series of large rivers are so remote that guides are recommended. The most popular of these is the Winisk, now within a provincial waterway park. In its 434-km length, the river includes many stretches of fine whitewater and passes desolate reaches of muskeg. The Fawn and Severn rivers are of similar character, but even more remote, with remains of an old trading post and Indian grave sites to trace their history. To the east the Ekwan River begins near the massive Precambrian outcrops known as the Sutton Ridges and plunges swiftly to James Bay. Brochures on all three of these routes are available from the MNR office, Box 190, Moosonee, P0L 1Y0.

The lower Albany River, from Fort Hope eastwards, provides another challenging route, over 600 km in length. As it drops off the rocky Shield country, the Albany flows past high clay banks, and northern wildlife such as the sandhill crane becomes common. It is possible to link into the Albany from the Kenogami River, with road access to your starting point from Hwy. 11. This 400-km route features both abandoned and active trading posts, and no portages! Again, detailed information is available from MNR in Moosonee.

Sadly, many of the tributaries of the Moose have been dammed or polluted to a point where their use is severely restricted. On both the Abitibi and the Mattagami, for example, you must make arrangements for transportation around series of Hydro dams. The lower Kapuskasing is degraded by the effluent from a pulp mill. Still, the watershed of the Moose offers many fine routes, including the Missinaibi. Most of the headwater areas above Hwy. 11 are canoeable and relatively unspoiled, with rivers such as the Groundhog, upper Mattagami and Tatachikapika enjoying good reputations.

For those who seek their canoeing experience even further from the madding crowd, there are still rivers in the north that have rarely seen recreational canoeists. The Attawapiskat, for example, is a major water body little known to canoeists. Even in the Moose basin, tributaries such as the Little Abitibi and the North French are said to be fine canoeing in unknown country. Information on these routes will be difficult to find, but contact the MNR office in Moosonee and the Wilderness Canoe Association, Box 496, Station K, Toronto, M4P 2G9, to see what's in their files.

Recommended Reading for Further Information

GENERAL CANOE GUIDES

Jim Brown and Jim Sutherland. *Lamont's 1984 Annual Ontario Canoe Guide*. Lamont Press, 1984. An annual directory of equipment, outfitters, and clubs.

Canoe Routes of Ontario. Ministry of Natural Resources and McClelland and Stewart, 1981. Brief summaries of over 100 routes.

James West Davidson and John Rugge. *The Complete Wilderness Paddler*. Alfred A. Knopf, 1976.

William W. Forgey. *Wilderness Medicine*. Indiana Camp Supply Books, 1979.

C.E.S. Franks. *The Canoe and White Water*. University of Toronto Press, 1977.

Carol Hodgins. *Wilderness Cooking for Fun and Nutrition*. Highway Book Shop, Cobalt, 1982. Excellent recipes and packing tips for canoeists.

Cliff Jacobson. *Canoeing Wild Rivers*. ICS Books, Merillville, Indiana, 1984. Includes accounts of canoeing expeditions in northern Canada.

Joanne Kates. *Exploring Algonquin Park*. Douglas and McIntyre, 1983.

Bill Mason. *Path of the Paddle*. Van Nostrand Reinhold, 1980. A superlative guide to canoeing skills.

Nick Nickels. *Canoe Canada*. Van Nostrand Reinhold, 1976.

Hap Wilson. *Temagami Canoe Routes*. Smoothwater Outfitters, 1984.

NATURAL HISTORY GUIDES

A.W.F. Banfield. *The Mammals of Canada*. University of Toronto Press, 1974.

L.J. Chapman and D.F. Putnam. *The Physiography of Southern Ontario*. University of Toronto Press, 1973. Excellent summary of the development of Ontario's landforms.

Geological Highway Maps. Ministry of Natural Resources, undated.

W. Earl Godfrey. *The Birds of Canada*. Information Canada, 1966.

Clive E. Goodwin. *A Bird-Finding Guide to Ontario*. University of Toronto Press, 1982. Includes good summary of birds in regions of Ontario.

D.F. Hewitt. *Rocks and Minerals of Ontario*. Ontario Department of Mines and Northern Affairs, 1978.

R.C. Hosie. *Native Trees of Canada*. Information Canada, 1975.

W.W. Judd and J. Murray Speirs. *A Naturalist's Guide to Ontario*. University of Toronto Press, 1964. Dated but good summary of natural features.

Sheila McKay and Paul Catling. *Trees, Shrubs, and Flowers to Know in Ontario*. J.M. Dent & Sons, 1979. Our favourite plant guide to carry with us in the field.

James H. Soper and Margaret L. Heimburger. *Shrubs of Ontario*. Royal Ontario Museum, 1982.

Shan Walshe. *Plants of Quetico and the Ontario Shield*. University of Toronto Press, 1980. Photographic guide by habitat type of many common plants.

Zile Zichmanis and James Hodgins. *Flowers of the Wild: Ontario and the Great Lakes Region*. Oxford University Press, 1982.

CULTURAL HISTORY

A Topical Organization of Ontario History. Ministry of Natural Resources, 1974.

Matt Bray and Ernie Epp (ed.). *A Vast and Magnificent Land*. Ministry of Northern Affairs, 1984. Many historical photos and anecdotes.

Thor Conway. "Archaeology in Northeastern Ontario: Searching for our Past." Ministry of Culture and Recreation, 1981. Very interesting booklet on archaeology in the north.

Selwyn Dewdney and Kenneth E. Kidd. *Indian Rock Paintings of the Great Lakes*. University of Toronto Press, 1973.

R. Louis Gentilcore and C. Grant Head. *Ontario's History in Maps*. University of Toronto Press, 1984.

Richard S. Lambert with Paul Pross. *Renewing Nature's Wealth*. Department of Lands and Forests, 1967.

Donald MacKay. *The Lumberjacks*. McGraw-Hill Ryerson, 1978.

Eric Morse. *Fur Trade Canoe Routes of Canada: Then and Now*. Information Canada, 1969. The classic description of important rivers in the fur trade.

PIONEERS AND PASTURES

Credit

"Credit River Watershed Environmentally Significant Areas." Ecologistics Ltd, 1979.

Credit Valley Conservation Report. Department of Planning and Development, 1956.

Credit Valley Series. Boston Mills Press. Especially:

- # 9, "Meadowvale and Churchville"
- #11, "Saunder's History of Georgetown"
- #14, "The Barber Dynamo"
- #15, "At the Mouth of the Credit"
- #17, "Terra Cotta: A Capsule History"

"Environmentally Sensitive Areas Study." Regional Municipality of Halton, 1978.

John A. MacDonald. *Halton Sketches*. Boston Mills Press, 1975.

Donald B. Smith. "Peter Jones, the Mississaugas of the Credit, and the Indian Department of Upper Canada." Canadian Historical Society Annual Meeting, 1976.

Robert Turnbull. "Crisis on the Credit." *Globe and Mail*, April 15–18, 1963.

Saugeen

An Historical Album of Paisley. Paisley Centennial Book Committee, 1974.

Stewart G. Hilts and Martin Parker, (ed.). "Environmentally Significant Areas of Southern Bruce County. "Saugeen Field Naturalists, 1980.

Norman McLeod. *History of the County of Bruce 1907–1968*. Bruce County Historical Society, 1969.

Norman Robertson. *History of the County of Bruce*. Bruce County Historical Society, 1906.

Saugeen River Canoe Route. Ministry of Natural Resources, undated brochure.

Saugeen Valley Conservation Report. Department of Planning and Development, 1952.

Rankin

A Special Issue Celebrating the Bruce Peninsula. *Seasons*. Federation of Ontario Naturalists, Spring 1984.

Irene Bowman. "History of the Peninsula Portage and Canoe Route: Colpoy Bay to Lake Huron." Mimeo, 1975.

W. Sherwood Fox. *The Bruce Beckons*. University of Toronto Press, 1952. Anecdotal history of Bruce Peninsula; some inaccuracies.

"Rankin Resources Management Area: Draft Planning Study." Ministry of Natural Resources and Sauble Valley Conservation Authority, 1977.

Rankin River Canoe Route. Ministry of Natural Resources, undated brochure.

Sauble Valley Conservation Report. Department of Lands and Forests, 1962.

Moira

Gerald E. Boyce. "Historic Hastings." Hastings County Council, 1967.

John Macoun. "Our Forest Trees." *Directory of Hastings County*, 1864.

Moira River Watershed Plan. Moira River Conservation Authority, 1983.

Moira Valley Conservation Report. Department of Planning and Development, 1950.

Moira Watershed Canoe Routes. Moira River Conservation Authority, 1979. Brochure with detailed portage information.

U. Sibal, K. Goff, and A.V. Choo-Ying. "Water Resources of the Moira River Drainage Basin." Ministry of Environment, 1974.

"Unto These Hills." The Pioneer Club, Cloyne, 1978.

BIG PINE COUNTRY

Magnetawan

"A History of Parry Sound Forest District." Ontario Department of Lands and Forests, 1964.

James Barry. *Georgian Bay: The Sixth Great Lake*. Clarke Irwin, 1968.

Guide Book and Atlas of Muskoka and Parry Sound Districts. H.R. Page & Co., Toronto, 1879.

John Macfie. *Now and Then: Footnotes to Parry Sound History*. 1983. Anecdotes of logging days along the Magnetawan.

Magnetawan River Canoe Route. Ministry of Natural Resources, 1983. Brochure covering west half of route only.

"Parry Sound District Atlas." District of Parry Sound Local Government Study, 1976.

Black

Rachele E. Cooper. "The Coopers Came to Stay: A History." Mimeo, 1956.

Watson Kirkconnell. *County of Victoria Centennial History*. Victoria County Council, 1967.

Francis Vernon LeCraw. *The Land Between*. Laxton, Digby and Longford Council, 1967.

Frankie MacArthur. *Green and Sparkling: The Story of Washago*, 1975.

Florence B. Murray (ed.). *Muskoka and Haliburton 1615–1875*. The Champlain Society, 1963. Excellent collection of historical accounts.

Lady Evelyn

Edward F. Mantle. "A Montreal River Pioneer." *Your Forests*, Vol. 9, No. 2, 1976.

Terry Noble. Life Sciences Report, Site Region 4E. Ministry of Natural Resources, 1982.

S.A. Pain. *The Way North*. Ryerson Press, 1964.

"Preliminary Environmental Overview of the Maple Mountain–Lady Evelyn Wilderness Area." Canadian-British Consultants Ltd., 1977.

LAND OF GREY OWL

Spanish

A.N. Boissonneau. "Glacial History of Northeastern Ontario II: The Timiskaming-Algoma Area." *Canadian Journal of Earth Sciences*, 5, 97, 1968.

Vincent Crichton. *Pioneering in Northern Ontario*. Mika Publications, 1975.

"History of the Sudbury Forest District." Ontario Department of Lands and Forests, 1967.

Frank Longstaff. "The River Everyone Wants." *Seasons*, Autumn 1980.

Spanish River Canoe Route. Ministry of Natural Resources, undated brochure.

T.A. Thorpe. "A Review of Logging and Pulp Operations in Sudbury District 1901–1950." Ontario Department of Lands and Forests, undated.

Mississagi

"A History of Chapleau Forest District." Department of Lands and Forests, 1967.

Grey Owl. *Tales of an Empty Cabin*. Macmillan of Canada, 1936. Includes extensive description of canoeing the Mississagi.

HBC Post at Green Lake, Ontario. Enclosure to L.C. No. 17624. Hudson's Bay Company Archives, 1934.

Mississagi Canoe Route: Biscotasing to Aubrey Falls. Ministry of Natural Resources, 1983. Brochure.

Temagami

"Temagami, A Peerless Region for the Sportsman, Canoeist, and Camper." Grand Trunk Railway System, 1909.

Temagami Canoe Routes. Ministry of Natural Resources, 1983. Map and brief route descriptions.

"Our Northern Districts, Eastern Algoma, North Nipissing, Rainy River, and the Timiskaming Settlement." Commissioner of Crown Lands, 1894.

TRAILS OF EARLY TRADERS

French

Daniel F. Brunton. "Life Science and Interpretive Potentials of the French River Study Area: A Pilot Study for the Proposed Canadian Heritage Waterways System." 1979.

William A. Campbell. *Northeastern Georgian Bay and Its People*. 1984. Includes photos and accounts of Coponaning.

Penina Coopersmith. "Man-Made Heritage Component: Resource Identification and Evaluation." Canadian Heritage Waterway System Pilot Study: the French River. 1980.

French River Canoe Route. Ministry of Natural Resources, undated brochure.

Joe Mason. *My Sixteenth Year: An Account of Logging on the French River*. Cobalt Highway Book Shop, 1984.

Ian D. McKenzie. "Assessment of Earth Science Processes and Features of the French River, Ontario." French River Canadian Heritage Waterway Pilot Study, 1979.

Mattawa

M.D. Billings. "Survey of the Geology and Geomorphology of the Mattawa Wild River and Samuel de Champlain Provincial Parks." Ministry of Natural Resources, 1974.

D.G. Cuddy. "Preliminary Ecological Inventory of Mattawa Wild River and Samuel de Champlain Provincial Parks." Ministry of Natural Resources, 1974.

Murray Leatherdale. "Nipissing from Brulé to Booth." North Bay and District Chamber of Commerce, 1975.

Mattawa River Provincial Park. Ministry of Natural Resources, 1983. Brochure including portage information.

Allan Edwin Tyyska and James A. Burns. "Archaeology from North Bay to Mattawa." Ministry of Natural Resources, 1973.

Missinaibi

David Arthurs. "The Spirits of the Pictured Waters; The Archaeology of the Missinaibi River Valley." Ministry of Culture and Recreation, 1979.

Doug Baldwin. "The Fur Trade in the Moose-Missinaibi Valley, 1770–1917." Ministry of Culture and Recreation, 1975.

E.D. Frey. "Geology of the Missinaibi River Provincial Park Reserve." Ministry of Natural Resources, 1979.

Missinaibi River Canoe Route. Missinaibi Lake to Mattice; Mattice to Moosonee. Ministry of Natural Resources, 1983. Brochures.

C.S. Paddy Reid (ed.). "Northern Ontario Fur Trade Archaeology: Recent Research." Ministry of Culture and Recreation, 1980.

Gary A. Shea. "Life Science Survey of Missinaibi River Park Reserve." Ministry of Natural Resources, 1977.

R.G. Skinner. "Quaternary Stratigraphy of the Moose River Basin, Ontario." Geological Survey of Canada, 1973. Detailed account of glacial sediments.

NORTHWARD TO THE COAST

Chapleau-Nemegosenda

A.N. Boissonneau. "Glacial History of Northeastern Ontario I: The Cochrane-Hearst Area." *Canadian Journal of Earth Sciences*, Vol. 3, No. 5, 1966.

Chapleau-Nemegosenda Provincial Waterway Park. Ministry of Natural Resources, 1983. Brochure.

"Emerald Circle Canoe Cruise." Canadian Pacific Railway Company, Sport and Recreation Bulletin No. 212, 1954.

Misehkow

Canoe Routes: Nipigon District. Ministry of Natural Resources, undated maps.

Canoe Route: Sioux Lookout to Fort Hope on the Albany River. Ministry of Natural Resources, undated brochure.

Joel and Mary Crookham. "The Trappers of Wabakimi Lake." *Seasons*, Vol. 21, No. 2, Summer 1981.

Ron Reid. "Ogoki-Albany." *Seasons*, Vol. 21, No. 2, Summer 1981.

David K. Riddle. "Archaeological Survey of the Upper Albany River." Studies in West Patricia Archaeology, No. 1, 1978–79. Ministry of Culture and Recreation, 1980.

David K. Riddle. "Archaeological Survey of the Albany River, Year 2: Triangular Lake to Washi Lake." Studies in West Patricia Archaeology, No. 2, 1979–80. Ministry of Culture and Recreation, 1981.

"West Patricia Land Use Plan: Background Studies." Ministry of Natural Resources, 1978, 1979.

Kesagami

"An Assessment of Earth Science Processes and Features for Land Use Planning of Kesagami Wilderness Provincial Park." McKenzie McCulloch Associates, 1983.

J.M. Bell. "Kesagami Lake and Kesagami River." In: T.W. Gibson, *Report of the Ontario Bureau of Mines 13: Parts One and Two*. 1904.

Daniel F. Brunton. "A Reconnaissance Life Science Inventory of Kesagami Provincial Wilderness Park." 1984.

Terry Damm. "The Kesagami Experience." *Canadian Geographical Journal*, Vol. 83, No. 2, 1971.

Elaine Mitchell. *Fort Temiskaming and the Fur Trade*. University of Toronto Press, 1977.

"Notes on Mesackamee from Hudson's Bay Company Archives." Manitoba Department of Cultural Affairs and Historical Resources, Winnipeg.

J.B. Tyrrell. *The Journals of Hearne and Turnor*. The Champlain Society, Vol. XXI, 1934. Records earliest European visits to Kesagami Lake.

CONSERVATION GROUPS

The following groups are especially active in promoting the protection and appreciation of Ontario's rivers. They deserve your support if the rivers we love are to be preserved intact.

Federation of Ontario Naturalists,
355 Lesmill Rd., Don Mills, Ontario, M3B 2W8.

Sierra Club of Ontario,
6–191 College St., Toronto, Ontario, M5T 1P9.

Canoe Ontario,
1220 Shepherd Ave. East, Willowdale, Ontario, M2K 2X1.

Wilderness Canoe Association,
Box 496, Postal Station K, Toronto, Ontario, M4P 2G9.

Wildlands League,
Suite 313, 69 Sherbourne St., Toronto, Ontario, M5A 3X9.

Che-mun, The Newsletter of Canadian Wilderness Canoeing,
Box 548, Station O, Toronto, Ontario, M4A 2P1.

Index

Abitibi River, 221, 302
Acid Rain, 133
Actinolite, 88
Agnew Lake, 157
Agnew Lake Air Services, 153
Agutua moraine, 267
Ahmic Lake, 106, 110
Alligator tugs, 113, 134
Anahareo, 148, 177
Anticlines, 115
Archaeological sites, 14, 157, 176, 208, 211, 215, 225, 251, 268
Arctic Ocean, 248
Armstrong, 269
Armstrong Outfitters Assoc., 269
Arrowhead, 157, 255
Ash, black, 181, 231, 254
Askins, Charles, 37
Aspen, trembling, 256
Atkinson, George, 285
Attawapiskat River, 302
Aubinadong River, 161, 187
Aubrey Falls, 165, 168, 169

Baneberry, 214
Bannockburn railway, 89
Barber dynamo, 42, 45
Barnhart, John, 41
Bats, 92
Beach bar, glacial, 55
Bear, black, 19, 81, 127, 180
Bear Island, 177
Beaver, 19, 61, 148, 151, 252
Beaver River, 98
Beetles, whirligig, 128
Belaney, Archie, 148, 161, 167, 177
Bell, J.M., 282, 285
Belleville, 82
Bellwort, sessile, 84
Birch, 64
Birch, yellow, 109
Bird, Xavier, 282
Birds, field, 56
  mixed parties, 212
  prairie, 25
  winter, 26
  water, 70, 251
Biscotasing, 151, 153, 161, 165
Bison, American, 194
Bittern, American, 136, 137
Black fly larvae, 20
Black River Wilderness Park, 128
Black tern, 72
Bog Walk, 291
Boland River, 146
Boneset, 127
Bonfield Batholith, 213
Boundary Water Canoe Route, 245
Brebuf, Father, 195
Bressani, Francois Joseph, 71
Bridgewater, 88
Britt, 107
Brucite, 208, 213
Brule, Etienne, 29, 40, 195, 208
Brunswick Lake, 230
Brunton, Dan, 193, 288
Buck's Crossing, 57
Budworm, spruce, 166, 178
Bullfrog, 179, 180
Bunchberry, 111
Burk's Falls, 104, 106, 108
Burns, James, 211
Butterflies, 223
Butternut, 64
Byng Inlet, 107, 116

Caddisfly larvae, 20, 255
Canada Company, 52
Canada geese, 47
Canada Land & Immigration Co., 125

Canadian Nature Tours, 14
Canadian Shield, 21, 79
Canals, 105, 125, 196
Cannifton, 82, 93
Canoe, birchbark, 28, 190, 195, 217
Canoe Ontario, 43, 46
Cardinal flower, 124
Caribou moss, 266
Caribou, woodland, 133, 176, 178, 180, 223, 270, 271, 284
Cataraqui, 81
Cedar, eastern red, 91
Champlain, Samuel de, 29, 40, 195, 267
Champlain Sea, 193
Chantry Island, 65
Chapleau, 251, 252
Chapleau Game Preserve, 249, 251
Chatter marks, 192, 291
Chaudiere Falls, 196, 197
Check before running (CBR), 17
Cheltenham, 43
Chickadee, boreal, 289
Chisholm, 79, 91
Churchville, 41
Clark Island, 116
Clay, varved, 250
Climate, and vegetation, 44, 45
Clintonia, 111
Cochrane, A.C., 177
Collins, Deputy Surveyor-Gen'l, 192
Conjurer's House, 223, 232
Conkey and Murphy Lumber Co., 134
Continental Wood Products, 252
Conway, Thor, 149, 169, 197, 226
Coontail, 255
Cooper's Falls, 126, 128
Cooper, Thomas, 126
Coponaning, 191, 201
Corby, Henry, 93
Corbyville, 82, 92
Coulange River, 221
Coureurs de bois, 31, 195
Crane, sandhill, 168, 223
Credit Valley Cons. Auth., 48
Creeper, Virginia, 207

Damm, Terry, 282, 285
Deer, white-tailed, 19, 105, 110, 132, 176
Delta formation, 215
Denny, John, 64
Deserontyou, John, 82
Diabase, 163, 168
Dock, great water, 254
Dog Lake, 226
Dogwood, 83
Dokis Indian Reserve, 197
Dolomite, 70
Draper, William, 161, 167
Drumlin, 23, 53, 79
Duck, black, 257
Duke Lake, 150, 153
Dummer moraine, 79, 88
Dunes, 70, 140

Eagle, bald, 228, 254, 272
  golden, 234, 275
Eagle Rock, 157
Earle of Erne, 131
Ekwan River, 301
Eldorado Park, 46
Elk, 194, 223, 228
Elm, 55, 81, 232
Elsas, 251, 252, 255
English River, 221
Erindale, 39, 42, 49
Erosional forms, 62, 294
Espaniel, Jimmy, 149
Espanola, 149
Explorer's Park, 216, 217

Fairy Point, 227
Falcon, peregrine, 214
Fawn River, 301
Federation of Ontario Naturalists, 14, 264
Fern, long beech, 124
  polypody, 211
  rusty woodsia, 200
  sensitive, 124
  virginia chain, 193, 200
Fiddleheads, 45

Fish, game, 26, 75
Flint, Billa, 82, 85
Flinton, 82, 85
Flycatcher, least, 181
  olive-sided, 289
Forest, boreal, 25, 222, 248, 265
  carolinean, 25, 39
  deciduous, 25, 39
  fires, 163, 198, 253, 266
  Great Lakes-St. Lawrence, 25, 80
  mixed, 25
  regeneration, 258
  soils and, 126
Forks of the Credit, 43
Fort Hope, 276
Fort Mattawa, 216
Fox, Sherwood, 71
Foxboro, 82
French River, 199
Fur trade, 30, 31, 72, 190, 194, 196, 233

Gabbro, 140
Gentian, closed, 154
Geology, Ontario, 22
Georgetown, 42
Georgian Bay, canoeing, 197
German Company, 52
Gereaux Island, 116
Glaciation, 23, 53, 192, 207, 234
Glen Williams, 45
Gneiss, 23, 88, 104, 122
Gold fever, 89
Goulais River, 161
Goshawk, 270
Grand River, 99
Grand Trunk Railway, 174
Granite, 21, 53, 104, 150, 223
Great Lakes Forest Products, 264
Green Lake Post, 164
Greenock Swamp, 60, 63
Greenstone, 21, 267
Gregg, T.A., 177
Grenville Front, 175, 181
Grey Owl, 31, 148, 151, 161, 162, 167, 169, 174, 186
Greywacke, 23, 175, 180
Ground moraine, 122, 250
Groundhog River, 302
Gull River, 124
Gulls, Bonaparte's, 273
Gypsum, 234

Hanover, 57, 58
Hanna, D., 58
Hazel, beaked, 253
Henry, Alexander, 195
Hobblebush, 111
Honeysuckle, 115, 179
Hopkins, Francis, 195
Hudson Bay lowlands, 26
Hudson's Bay Company, 31, 176, 190, 196, 210, 216, 217, 225, 233, 248, 259, 269
Hurley, H.L., 116
Huttonville, 41, 46
Hyer, Bruce, 264, 265

Identification, wildlife, 15
Inco, 150
Indian Narrows, 114
Indian River, 99
Indians, Algonquin, 29, 133
  burial mounds, 56, 273
  Chippewa, 56
  copper, use of, 268
  Cree, 29, 223, 285
  history of, 29, 30
  Huron, 29, 124, 194, 195
  Iroquois, 29, 41, 56, 125, 176
  Mississauga, 37, 40, 41, 57, 81
  Neutral, 29
  Nipissing, 176, 225
  ochre mines, 210, 215
  Ojibway, 29, 56, 131, 133, 151, 194, 223, 224
  Ottawa, 71, 195
  Petun, 29
  pictographs, 154, 180, 211, 223, 225, 227, 254, 271, 272
  spirits, 215, 227
  Tobacco, 29
  trade among, 29, 269
  wars, 29, 56, 125
  winter lodge, 286, 287
Iris, wild blue, 255
Ishpatina Ridge, 132

James Bay, 287
James Bay lowlands, 222, 284
Joe-Pye-weed, 165
Jones, Augustus, 37

Kame moraine, 23, 284, 288
Kaministikwia River, 245
Ka-nah-nosing, 131
Kapuskasing Lake, 255
Kapuskasing River, 250, 302
Karst topography, 92
Kemp, Kenneth, 59
Kenogami River, 301
Kesagami Lodge, 288
Kestrel, 165
Kettle hole, 87, 182, 197, 231
Kettle Lake, 258
Kingfisher, belted, 61

Lady Evelyn Lake, 140
Lake Agissiz, 267
Lake Algonquin, 55, 104, 122, 193, 207
Lake, glacial, 55
Lake Iroquois shoreline, 39, 49
Lake Ojibway, 229
Lake Temagami, 131, 174
Lake Warren, 55, 62
Lalemont, 195
Lamprey, sea, 65
La Prairie des Francais, 191
Latchford, 134
Latta, 92
La Vase portage, 210
Lawrence, Louise de Kiriline, 214
Leatherwood, 74
Lift-over (L-O), 17
Limestone, 23, 25, 38, 79, 89, 92
Littlejohn, Bruce, 45
Little Abitibi River, 302
Logging, history of, 30, 32, 103, 107-8, 125, 177, 209
  river drives, 32, 82, 86, 107, 151
Longford Township, 122, 125
Loons, 140
Luste, George, 221, 228, 232

MacKenzie, Alexander, 192
MacPherson Lake, 137
Macoun, John, 80
Madawaska River, 146
Magnetawan, 106, 100
Magnetawan Indian Reserve, 116
Magnettawan, 107
Maitland River, 78
Maple, 85, 208
Maple Island, 104, 112
Maple Mountain, 132, 135, 140
Maps, use of, 15
Marble, 79, 88, 208, 213
Marlow, W.B., 125
Marten, 81, 88, 249
Matachewan, 146
Mattagami, 302
Mattawapika Falls, 134, 140
May-may-gway-shi, 227
McBeath Conservation Area, 62
McIntosh, Robert, 191
McNab, James, 41
Meadowsweet, 155
Meadowvale, 46, 47, 48
Meadowvale Conservation Area, 46
Mem-skhoo-nah-kuck, 165
Merganser, hooded, 109
Mesackamee House, 285
Mesackamy Path, 285
Mesquakie, 128
Messinnike, 37
Mica, Purdy Mine, 208, 217
Mice, white-footed, 20
Michipicoten River, 245
Mills, 33, 41, 42, 107
Minesing Swamp, 98
Mishipizhiw, 227
Missinabie Station, 226
Missinaibi Formation, 234
Missinaibi Lake House, 226, 227
Mississagi Forest Reserve, 164, 167, 186
Mississauga, 49
Mississippi River, 99
Moira Cave, 92
Moira River Conservation Auth., 82
Monzkananing, 131

Montreal River, 132, 134, 140
Mooneye, 223
Moose, 19, 105, 168, 176, 223, 228, 273
Moose Fort, 31, 225
Moose River Crossing, 234
Moosonee, 235
Morse, Eric, 206, 217
Mowat, Charlie, 141
Mowat's Landing, 134, 140
Muskeg, 283
Muskoka River, 145
Muskrat, 18, 212

National Topographic System, 16
Nemegos, 251
New Brunswick House, 226, 230
Niagara Escarpment, 38, 70
Nicolet, Jean, 195
North French River, 285, 302
North West Company, 31, 151, 166, 190, 196, 210, 225, 233
Norval, 41, 43, 45, 46
Nottawasaga River, 98

Oak, red, 127, 200
Ononront River, 37
Ontario Breeding Bird Atlas, 127
Oriole, northern, 108
Osnaburg House, 269
Osprey, 136, 194, 272
Ottawa River, 246
Otter, 19
Outfitters, 14
Ovenbird, 86
Owls, 19
  barred, 155, 270

Paisley, 57, 58, 62, 63
Paisley Brick and Tile, 62
Passenger pigeon, 71
Paul, Michael, 176
Peat cliffs, 284, 288
Peninsula portage, 71, 72
Permafrost, 283
Peterbell, 226, 228, 229
Petawawa River, 146
Physiography, Saugeen basin, 54
Pickerel River, 145
Pickerel, yellow, 194
Pine, jack, 198, 213, 265
  red, 110, 131, 175-6, 180, 208, 256, 257
  white, 55, 102, 131, 175-6, 208, 256, 257
Pinesap, 200
Pioneers, use of wood, 55
  rafts, 62
Plain, clay, 104
  limestone, 79
  sand, 55, 61, 88, 104
Plainfield, 79, 92
Pogomasing Lake, 153, 155
Pointer boats, 134
Pope, Alan, 135
Poplar, balsam, 256
Porcupine, 19
Portage (P), 17, 249
Porte de l'Enfer, 214, 215
Potholes, 214, 217
Price Conservation Area, 88
Provincial Parks,
  Algonquin, 145
  Chapleau-Nemegosenda, 252
  Driftwood, 246
  Grundy, 105
  Lady Evelyn-Smoothwater, 132
  Lake Superior, 246
  Michipicoten Historical, 245
  Quetico, 245
  Restoule, 197
  Samuel de Champlain, 217
  Sauble Falls, 75
  Tidewater, 235
  Wabakimi, 264, 270

Queen's Bush, 52

Radisson, Pierre, 195
Rama Indian Reserve, 128
Rankin, Charles, 52, 69
Rankin Wildlife Mgmt. Area, 74
Ransom, Israel, 41
Rapid River, 52
Rapids, 17
Recollet Falls, 199
Reed, Julian, 42
Reid Milling Co., 48

Revillion Freres, 226
Riddle, David, 268
River Valley, 182
Robichaud Lake, 212
Robinson Treaty, 106, 177
Rocks, classification, 21
  faulting, 23, 104, 132, 192, 207, 250, 254
  metamorphic, 23, 79, 104
  sedimentary, 21, 38, 70, 73, 104, 231
  volcanic, 84, 223, 231
Rose twisted-stalk, 258
Rutherglen moraine, 213
Ryerson, Egerton, 49

Sahging, 52
Sakatawi River, 186
Salmon, 43, 44, 75, 208
Salmonville, 43
Sand spits, 254
Sandpiper, solitary, 257
Sandstone, 132
Sang's Creek, 64
Sauble Falls, 70, 72
Sauble River, 75
Sauble Valley Conserv. Auth., 69
Saugeen Bluffs Conserv. Area, 64
Saugeen Field Naturalists, 61
Saugeen Indian Reserve, 65
Scuttle Holes, 92
Season, canoeing, 17, 18
Season, nesting, 18
Serviceberry, 83
Settlement, history of, 30, 32, 81, 106-108, 125-126
Severn River, 301
Shaggy ninebark, 61
Shale, 38, 44, 48
Sheahan, 155
Sheep laurel, 138
Sierra Club of Ontario, 226
Skink, five lined, 124
Skim-Sak-Djee-Ashing, 136
Skootamatta Lake, 82, 83
Smith, Lt., 125
Snake, ring necked, 49
  massasauga, 73, 194
Snowberry, 290
South Nahanni River, 221
Southampton, 57
Spanish Lake, 156
Spanish River Lumber Co., 153
Sparrow, boreal species, 234
  song, 138
Spillway, glacial, 44, 55, 79, 89, 155, 156, 169, 211
Sponge, freshwater, 255
Spruce, black, 265, 267
  white, 266
Spruce Falls Pulp & Paper, Co., 230
Squashberry, 267
Squirrel, flying, 123, 124
  red, 19
Starflower, 111
Stavebank Woods, 49
Steamboats, 106, 107
Stemless ladies slipper, 266, 267
Stoco Lake, 79, 82, 90
Street, Timothy, 41, 48
Streetsville, 41, 42, 48
Sturgeon, 65, 268, 275
Sturgeon River, 186
Swallows, 61
Sweet gale, 108
Sweetfern, 115, 155
Sucker Gut Lake, 135, 138
Sugar Island, 88
Syncline, 115

Tamarack, 81
Tatachikapika River, 302
Terra Cotta, 43
Teeswater River, 57, 63
Temagami Forest Reserve, 177
Temagami Lakes Association, 176
Temeagama, 176
Thirty Thousand Islands, 116
Thomas, John, 285
Thompson, David, 145, 200
Thompson and Dodge Co., 125
Thrush, 167, 179
Thunderhouse Falls, 232
Thurlow Wildlife Area, 92
Till, 23, 104, 223, 234
Till moraines, 53
Till plains, 53, 79

Toad, Hudson Bay, 284
Tombolo, 213
Toronto Suburban Railway, 46
Tote road, 114
Tracking and Lining (T), 17
Trailing arbutus, 83
Tree, pioneer species, 113
Trillium, nodding, 258
Trout, Aurora, 133
  lake, 207
  rainbow, 39, 75
  speckled, 251, 256
Trout Lake, 114, 208, 211
Troy, 82
Tundra, 26, 248
Turnbull, Robert, 37
Turnor, Philip, 285
Turtle, snapping, 124
Turtlehead, 294
Tweed, 82, 89
Tyrell Sea, 222, 284
Tyyska, Allen, 211

Upper Canada College, 39, 45

Valley train, 132
Vanderwater Cons. Area, 91
Vankoughnet, 122, 125
Veery, 272
Vegetation, prairie, 49
  regions, 24
Verendrye, la, 195
Victoria Falls, 126
Vireo, Philadelphia, 166
  red-eyed, 127, 253
  solitary, 166
Von Koerber, Elise, 107
Voyageurs, 191, 196, 199, 206, 210, 214

Wabakimi Lake, 271
Wahwashkesh Lake, 113
Wakami River, 186
Walker, Joseph, 57, 59
Walkerton, 53, 57, 59
Walkerton moraine, 60
Wanapitei River, 186
Wanigan, 177
Wapiscogamy House, 225, 233
Wapiti, 194
Warbler, black-throated blue, 136
  golden-winged, 84
  Nashville, 136
  pine, 194
  yellow, 136
  yellow-rump, 136
Washago, 122, 128
Wa-sha-quon-asin, 148
Waterthrush, northern, 136
Waterwitch, 58, 72
Wenebegon River, 186
Wetlands, 69, 70, 75, 86, 178, 229, 251, 252, 256, 257, 283, 288
Wetlands, and drainage, 72
Whale, beluga, 294
Whaleback Falls, 291, 292
Whippoorwill, 127
Wild calla, 108
Wild rice, 212, 269, 273
Wilderness Canoe Association, 150, 302
Wildlife, how to see, 18-20
Wildwater Outfitters, 265
Wilson, Hap, 131, 174
Winisk, 301
Winterberry, 18, 207, 211
Wolf, timber, 56, 163
Wolf River, 145
Wood duck, 73
Woodpecker, pileated, 91, 127

Yellowhead, 128
Yellowthroat, 127, 136
York boats, 228, 248

ABOUT THE AUTHORS

Ron Reid and Janet Grand are freelance writers and consultants living on the banks of the Black River in Washago, Ontario. Both have travelled extensively, but their favourite means of transport is their 16-foot ABS canoe, which has carried them over many of the waterways of their home province.

Ron is a wildlife biologist who spent five years on the staff of the Federation of Ontario Naturalists, where he fought for the establishment of many of Ontario's new parks. As well as becoming one of Ontario's best-known conservation writers, he has served in a volunteer capacity with several other environmental groups.

Janet used her training in natural history interpretation as National Program Director of the National and Provincial Parks Association of Canada. She also served as editor of the Sierra Club of Ontario newsletter, and as their representative to the Conservation Council of Ontario.

Both Ron Reid and Janet Grand have been frequent trip leaders for Canadian Nature Tours, teaching canoeing and natural history skills in the Ontario wilderness.